1.28.80

THE ROLE OF THE NUN
IN NINETEENTH CENTURY AMERICA

THE AMERICAN CATHOLIC TRADITION

See last pages of this volume
for a complete list of titles.

THE ROLE OF THE NUN
IN NINETEENTH CENTURY AMERICA

Mary Ewens

ARNO PRESS
A New York Times Company
New York ● 1978

Editorial Supervision: JOSEPH CELLINI

———•———

First publication 1978 by Arno Press Inc.

Copyright © 1971 by Mary Ewens, O.P.

THE AMERICAN CATHOLIC TRADITION
ISBN for complete set: 0-405-10810-9
See last pages of this volume for titles.

Manufactured in the United States of America

———•———

Library of Congress Cataloging in Publication Data

Ewens, Mary.
    The role of the nun in nineteenth century America.

    (The American Catholic tradition)
    Originally presented as the author's thesis,
University of Minnesota.
    Bibliography: p.
    1. Nuns—United States. 2. Monastic and religious
life of women. I. Title. II. Series.
BX4220.U6E93 1978   271'.9'073   77-11285
ISBN 0-405-10828-1

THE ROLE OF THE NUN IN NINETEENTH-CENTURY AMERICA:

VARIATIONS ON THE INTERNATIONAL THEME

A THESIS

SUBMITTED TO THE FACULTY OF THE GRADUATE SCHOOL

OF THE UNIVERSITY OF MINNESOTA

2082761

BY

MARY EWENS, O.P.

IN PARTIAL FULFILLMENT OF THE REQUIREMENTS

FOR THE DEGREE OF

DOCTOR OF PHILOSOPHY

March, 1971

ACKNOWLEDGEMENTS

I wish to acknowledge my indebtedness, first of all, to Miss Mary Turpie, chairman of the Program in American Studies at the University of Minnesota, for her patience, her encouragement, and her suggestions during the years in which this dissertation was being written. Thanks are also due to my family and to the Dominican Sisters of Sinsinawa, Wisconsin for the moral and financial support which enabled me to bring my doctoral studies to a successful conclusion.

I am grateful to the late Reverend Thomas T. McAvoy for granting me access to the riches housed in the archives of Notre Dame University; to Mr. Francis P. Clark of the Notre Dame University Library for his generosity in sharing documents and books from his personal collection; and to Sister John Francis, C.S.C., who made her broad knowledge of the history of battlefield nursing available to me. Mr. Paul Messbarger provided bibliographical aids, and Mrs. Betty Ann Perkins shared her unpublished master's thesis with me. I wish to thank the Reverends Finian McGinn, O.S.F., and Bertrand Mahoney, O.P. for their help in the translation and interpretation of Latin documents.

December 2, 1970   Mary Ewens, O.P.

Errata:

p. 46, line 1, "actuely" should be "acutely"
p. 60, line 7, 1st word should be "whom"
p. 77, line 8, "was" should be "has"
p. 94, footnote "29" should be "24"
p. 95, footnote "32" should be "27"
p. 117, Insert quotation marks before footnote 96.
p. 130, line 10, "that" should be "than"
p. 157, line 5, first word should be "escape"
p. 163, footnote "227" should be "277"
p. 174, bottom paragraph, Insert quotation marks after /sic/.
p. 225, paragraph 2, line 6, "Adam" should be "Adams"
p. 291, line 27, "fell" should be "felt"

TABLE OF CONTENTS

CHAPTER I

INTRODUCTION

In its decree on the renewal of religious life, Perfectae
Caritatis,[1] the Second Vatican Council of the Roman Catholic
Church called for the adjustment of religious communities to the
changed conditions of the times and the requirements of the culture
in which they live and work.[2] "Religious should be properly instructed," the document states, "in the prevailing manners of contemporary social life, and in its characteristic ways of feeling
and thinking . . . . Fresh forms of religious life . . . should take
into account the natural endowments and the manners of the people,
and also local customs and circumstances."[3]

Norms for the implementation of this decree were issued in
the Motu Proprio "Ecclesiae Sancta" on August 6, 1966. Since the
publication of these two documents, the more than 170,000 religious
sisters of the United States have been searching for the best means
of carrying out these directives and of making their Christian
witness relevant to twentieth-century American culture. Some, in
doing this, have discovered that their ideas were very different
from those of the churchmen who claimed jurisdiction over them.[4]
Numerous books, articles, and questionnaires have examined many
facets of the sister's role in the modern world, and have made
projections for the religious life of the future.

1

But adaptations of religious life to the needs of contemporary American culture must take into account the history of that culture, if they are to be successful. The future role of the American nun[5] cannot be adequately delineated and planned for without some consideration of what her role has been in the past. Valid traditions may be discarded and irrelevant ones retained if there is no understanding of the original reasons for their adoption, or of their relationship to the predominant strains of American culture.

Scope of the Study

With the exception of the histories of religious communities and individual biographies, few studies have been made of the changing relationship between American nuns and the society in which they have lived. When they have received any mention at all in scholarly studies, it has been in minor sections of works on the Catholic Church or on special aspects of American Catholicism. There is need for a more thorough study of the role which the nun has played in American life, not only to aid in the adaptation of religious communities to contemporary needs, but also because of the intrinsic value of such a study. This is the task which has been undertaken in the writing of this paper.

Foreign observers and scholars working in various disciplines have spent a great deal of time in trying to describe the American character, to define the ways in which its distinctive traits gradually evolved as the American experience modified the English culture brought to America by the first settlers of her Eastern seaboard.[6] A part of the European heritage which underwent

substantial change on the frontier was the attitude toward women.
In new settlements, where women were few and the need for them
great, they were held in high regard and carefully trained for
their role in the pioneer home.[7] Foreign observers commented
again and again on the differences between the European and
American attitudes towards women, none more perceptively than
Alexis de Tocqueville, who visited America in 1831. In Democracy
in America, he discusses the differences in the education and
treatment of European, English, and American women. In France, he
writes, "women commonly received a reserved, retired, and almost
conventual education, as they did in aristocratic times."[8] But in
America they are taught to be independent, to think for themselves,
to speak with freedom, and to act on their own impulses. They are
given a knowledge of evil of all kinds, that they may learn to
shun it.[9] Religion was also influential in determining attitudes
towards women, he found:

> Among almost all Protestant nations young women are
> far more the mistresses of their own actions than they
> are in Catholic countries. This independence is still
> greater in Protestant countries like England, which
> have retained or acquired the right of self-govern-
> ment; freedom is then infused into the domestic
> circle by political liberty and a most democratic
> state of society, and nowhere are young women sur-
> rendered so early or so completely to their own guidance.[10]

Tocqueville also contrasts the state of European women after
marriage, when they are free to manage their own affairs, with
that of their American counterparts, who are strictly confined to
their own homes.[11] These observations of Tocqueville provide the
setting for the dominant theme of this paper: that a study of the
role of the nun in nineteenth-century America reveals many conflicts that occur because of the different role definitions for

women of European and American culture, and particularly because of
the outmoded role definitions of canon law. A cultural clash inevitably occurs when nuns adhering to European expectations for
women begin to live and work in an American setting.

The Catholic nun in America has not only been a product of
European cultural attitudes; she has also represented the Church
to which she belongs in a unique way in America. Though institutions are often judged by their leaders, the nun has been connected
with the Catholic Church, through her highly conspicuous garb, even
more closely than her priests and bishops have been. To those
whose forebears came from post-Reformation England, where Catholic
Spain and France were hated enemies, all monasteries had been dissolved, and Catholics disenfranchised, she symbolized all that was
considered foreign, threatening, and evil in the Catholic Church
and in the civilization of the Continent.

Methods Used

This dissertation is an attempt to study the role of the
nun in America, using the insights provided by the methods and
materials of several different disciplines in order to gain a
clearer picture than would be delineated by the use of a single
discipline or method. The sociological concept of "role" will be
used to study historical and literary materials and the products
of popular culture. In recent years both historians and sociologists have been exploring ways in which they could gain richer
and broader insights through the use of one another's tools and
methods. As Cahnman and Boskoff point out in an article entitled
"Sociology and History: Reunion and Rapprochement," both

disciplines deal with interaction. The historian is interested in sequences of interaction, with the acting individual as his point of focus, while the sociologist studies the institutionalization and transformation of patterns of interaction. Sociologists extend the historian's knowledge of specific events to discover the extent to which explanations applicable in one situation may be extended to comparable situations from other times and places.[12] The sociologist sometimes uses sociological concepts to describe and analyze historical situations and problems on a higher level of generality than would be expected of the historian. He also uses historical data to illustrate and test the validity of sociological concepts and theories.[13]

Edward Saveth has studied, as have Cahnman and Boskoff, ways in which historians and sociologists can co-operate in their study of man. One of his most fruitful ideas is his suggestion that a concept, the "ultimate element . . . not further reducible which enters into larger units of abstraction called generalizations," can be "a nuclear factor in integration among the social sciences and history."[14] The concept is interdisciplinary and transdisciplinary, he points out, but theories in which it is embodied are often best tested and illustrated by concrete historical examples.[15] Such an interdisciplinary use of the sociological concept of "role" seems to offer a convenient method for using the available historical data on the nun, as well as that from fields such as literature and popular culture.

Shakespeare, in his comments on the many parts men play in their daily lives, made use of the role concept, which has been

the subject of a good deal of study by sociologists and others in
recent years. The importance of role definitions in influencing
behavior has been stressed especially by those social psychologists
called symbolic interactionists, who have continued the study of
social interaction begun by Charles H. Cooley and George Herbert
Mead[24] and also by those psychiatrists and psychologists who adhere
to the "interpersonal theory" of Harry Stack Sullivan.[17] Erving
Goffman used the insights of this school in studying total institutions such as convents, concentration camps, and mental
hospitals,[18] and Stanley Elkins found them helpful in explaining
what happens to the personality of the slave.[19]

Gross, Mason, and McEachern discuss the many differences in
definitions of the role concept used by various scholars, and the
reasons for them. They define it thus: "A role is a set of
evaluative standards applied to an incumbent of a particular
position." Roles are learned through interaction with others,
especially those "significant others" who are closest to a person,
both through formal instruction and indirectly, through observation,
listening, gestures, books, films, facial expressions, and other
means of communication, both verbal and non-verbal.[20]

Formal roles for a particular office or job are often
rigidly defined in constitutions, by-laws, job descriptions, etc.
(For the nun, they are found in the Church's canon law regulations
concerning religious women, and in the rule and constitutions of
the community to which she belongs.) Informal roles are developed
through daily interaction in a changing society. Effective role-
playing involves harmonizing both the formal and informal role

definitions into a working plan of action.

A lack of consensus on specific role definitions can lead
to role conflict, which Gross and his associates define as "any
situation in which the incumbent of a focal position perceives
that he is confronted with incompatible expectations."[21] When conflict exceeds certain boundaries, "efforts to bring about greater
harmony will generally be initiated by some of those involved.
Sanctions of one type or another may be imposed." Since roles are
constantly changing, and new definitions being developed, conflict may result when formal role definitions do not keep pace, or
when there is an uneven rate of change of definitions.[22] The
result is described thus by Bates:

> The occupant of a position containing conflicting
> roles will, over a period of time, tend either to
> redefine these roles so that they are consistent,
> thus reducing tension, or to "invent" or "employ"
> mechanisms which will allow him to reduce tension
> without a role redefinition.[23]

From society's point of view role conflict may prove useful. It
often gives a social system flexibility by providing an opening
wedge for desirable social change.[24]

Since canon law definitions for the role of nuns in the
nineteenth century were based on medieval European attitudes towards women, one would expect that role conflict would occur when
American women of the nineteenth century tried to live according to
them, and that various adjustments would have to be made to reduce
the conflict. This is exactly what happened. This paper will
study the types of role conflicts which occurred, and the various
mechanisms which were employed to reduce the ensuing tensions. It
is hoped that something can be learned from this study which will

make it possible to lessen or entirely abolish such conflicts and tensions in the future.

Because people act on their role expectations, whether they are correct or erroneous, students of public opinion and mass communications have long sought to analyze the connections between attitudes and behavior, and methods of changing both through the use of mass media. Their findings should be helpful in the analysis of the changes in the public image of the nun, because mass media have been powerful influences in spreading stereotypes of the nun in certain periods of American history, and people have often acted upon the role expectations acquired in this way. Little actual research has been done on the relationship between attitude change and behavior change, however; nor do we have much under-standing of the opinion-forming process.[25]

What research there is on the effects of mass communication supports every kind of view regarding its effectiveness. A few of the variables which seem to be important will be summarized here for what they can tell about possible reasons for the changes in role expectations for nuns which are discussed below. A single exposure produces little effect, but the result pyramids as the number of exposures is increased. The effect is also increased if there are no deep-seated resistances, if there is a clear field with no counter-propaganda, if the audience has no specific in-formation or critical ability with which to resist propaganda.[26] Ideological beliefs are changed by periods of solitary confinement, strong invalidating evidence, the failure of important expectations, the shock of evidence coming "close to home," and an emotionally

upsetting traumatic experience.[27] In changing attitudes, a change
in the object's properties is the surest way to change attitudes
toward it. Hostile attitudes toward a person remain until further
experience provides opportunities for attitude change. "Restricted
association almost inevitably results in restricted communication,
and when barriers to association are erected because of existing
hostility, they are likely to perpetuate or even to intensify
feelings of hostility," Newcomb and his associates find.[28] (This
is what happened, as we will see, when nuns were required by
their constitutions to remain secluded and separated, sometimes
even by physical barriers, from their fellow-citizens.) In addition
to all of the factors already mentioned, the influence of family,
church, and school on opinion formation is very important, but
difficult to measure and constantly changing.[29] People cling to
their pre-judgments even in the face of conflicting evidence, and
actual violence is often preceded by a long period of pre-judgment,
verbal complaint, and growing discrimination.[30] Several instances
of this type of pre-judgment and violent action will be noted
below.

Fiction writers reflect, reinforce, and perpetuate popular
stereotypes or role expectations, particularly the writers of
popular fiction. Therefore literature which features nun characters has been used in this study. Leo Lowenthal has written much
about the value of literature, both popular and serious, as a
bearer of the fundamental values and symbols of a culture, and a
unique way of getting at the climate of opinion of a period. By
studying the organization, content, and linguistic symbols of mass

media, he says, we learn about the typical forms of behavior, attitudes, commonly-held beliefs, prejudices, and aspirations of large numbers of people.[31]

Popular ideas about the nun were both reflected in and acquired through the written word. Billington states that the barrage of propaganda materials against the Catholic Church and its convents eventually reached every literate person in America.[32] A study of the books that had to do with the nun is thus an important part of this paper. Works of popular fiction and fictitious narratives which purported to be true have been studied in it as reflectors of popular ideas about nuns, while the works of major writers like Henry James and William Dean Howells have been analyzed for the deeper insights of the perceptive artist. Though it is not claimed that every work which pictures the nun published prior to 1900 has been used in this study, every effort has been made to discover as many of these as possible, through the use of various indexes, bibliographic aids, and library subject headings. Occasionally a newspaper or magazine that is typical of several others has been included for its reflection of the popular image.

Though no comprehensive study of the nun in America has yet been attempted, a growing body of material is available for such a study. Hundreds of histories of individual religious communities have been written, and dozens of histories of dioceses and archdioceses, most of which mention the nuns who served in them. Studies of special areas of American history such as nativism,[33] nuns in the Civil War,[34] and attitudes towards Catholicism[35] have also included material about sisters. Though the degree to which these studies make use of primary sources, historical method, and scholarly documentation varies widely, many of them do contain information useful for tracing the changing role of the nun in American history. Additional light is shed on the topic by the many documents contained either in original form or in microfilm in the Notre Dame University Archives, which house the largest American collection of documentary material on the Catholic Church in America; by canon law studies, histories of textbooks, etc. No doubt a search of the archives of individual communities would have yielded even more evidence. The use of such a procedure, when one is dealing with more than three hundred communities, is prohibitive. Therefore, with the exception of archival material available in the University of Notre Dame Archives and in a few other places, this was not attempted. Many of the histories used doubtless omit controversial material which would have been useful for this study, but in what they do include there is ample evidence from which to draw conclusions about prevailing patterns for de-fining the role of the nun.

There has, of course, been no attempt to recite the his-tories of the hundreds of religious communities in America, though the stories of a few have been given in some detail. Rather, the intention has been to catch those aspects of the histories of communities, the popular literature, and various kinds of public testimony which would indicate the role definitions and role ex-pectations for nuns which actually prevailed in a given period, and to ascertain the extent to which there was role conflict, the reasons for it, and the measures which were taken to resolve it.

In using materials of various kinds, the guiding questions have been: What evidence is there which reveals role definitions and expectations for nuns, and the attitudes towards them (both positive and negative) of the Catholic Church, nuns themselves, and their fellow Americans? What roles did sisters actually play in American society? How could one characterize their interaction with the milieu in which they lived and worked?

This paper attempts to establish the fact that many of the role conflicts which developed were actually the result of cultural clashes between European and American values, that the nun in America played a role that was a variation of the international theme used so often by Henry James. In contrast to the self-reliant young American girl whose boldness, honesty, and independence shocked the sensibilities of Europeans, was the submissive, secluded European _jeune fille_, whose aristocratic foreign culture, "wasted" life, and lack of freedom clashed with the active, democratic, freedom-loving temper of Protestant Americans. This is a paradigm that cannot be carried too far; there are certainly many exceptions which would rule out its application in every case, but there are many respects in which the analogy holds true.

This paper shows that both European and American attitudes were modified as a result of the interaction of the nun with her American milieu. The American view changed from one of hostility to one of acceptance and respect, and the Catholic Church became aware that some of its obsolete European role definitions for nuns had to be changed if they were to work effectively in a different cultural milieu.

It seems best to study the changing role of the nun and her interaction with American society in the nineteenth century by dividing the century into chronological periods. 1829, the year in which the debate over the Catholic Emancipation Act in England un-leashed a flood of anti-Catholic sentiment in both England and America, marks the end of the first period. The second period comprises the pre-Civil War decades; the third the decade of the war itself. The last three decades of the century will be studied in the final section of the paper. An introductory chapter will summarize the backgrounds on which the nineteenth century built, and the final one will make certain projections into the twentieth century. Before we proceed to the nineteenth century itself, let us consider the backgrounds in the period which ushered it in.

CHAPTER II

BACKGROUNDS

Formal Role Definitions of Canon Law

Since formal role definitions for nuns in the Roman
Catholic Church are set down in its canon law, it is necessary to
know something about it in order to understand what happened when
nuns tried to live according to its prescriptions in an American
setting. No official collection of church law was made from 1317
until 1917. In the six centuries which intervened, the laws of
1317 were added to through the decrees of ecumenical and national
councils, decisions of Roman congregations, and various kinds of
papal documents.[36] To clarify a point of law, one had to consult
an immense number of works and to deal with ordinances that were
contradictory, some of which had been repealed, and others which
had become obsolete through long disuse.[37] Longstanding custom
also had the force of law.[38] The situation was further complicated
by the fact that the United States was considered until 1908 to
be mission territory and hence under the jurisdiction of the Roman
congregation of the Propaganda rather than general church law.[39]

Before the Church's laws for religious women are detailed,
it must be understood that the major ones date back to 1298 and
1563, and reflect the cultural milieu of their times. Both Simone
de Beauvoir[40] and Mary Daly,[41] among others, have fully described
the misogynous view which prevailed in Europe for centuries and

14

has continued to dominate the Church. Woman was seen as an ir-
responsible, soft-brained, misbegotten male, incapable of logical
thought, a piece of property useful only for reproduction. Though,
as Mary Daly points out, the nun enjoyed a kind of liberation from
the traditional subjection to the male, and symbolized "the value
and dignity of the human person, which transcends sex roles and
functions,"[42] she was still hemmed in on every side by regulations
which stemmed from the traditional view. The attitudes expressed
by Tertullian (that woman is "the devil's doorway") and St. John
Chrysostom ("Among the savage beasts none is so harmful as woman")[43]
were still influential a thousand years after they were written,
and it is such attitudes, coupled with contemporary economic
practices, which largely determined the Church's prescriptions
for religious women.

In this background section the Church's legislation up to
1800 will be summarized. It must be remembered that these laws
remained in effect, however, until a new codification of canon
law superseded them in 1918, and thus they continued to bind the
religious women who served in America (at least theoretically) until that time. Small wonder that they clashed with the very
different expectations for women which had developed in America.
Tocqueville and others have commented on the differences between
American and European attitudes toward women in the nineteenth
century. How much greater would the disparity be if American
attitudes were compared with European attitudes of the thirteenth
or sixteenth centuries.

The prescriptions for nuns which prevailed after 1298 must be understood in the context of their times. From the early days of the Christian Church, women ministered to its needs. Over the centuries the monastic system, in which women dedicated their lives to the service of Christ and his church, had been worked out. Monasteries were centers of learning and sanctity, benign influences in contemporary society. In this as in any institution peopled by human beings, however, abuses set in, and there were periods of decay.

In medieval society the convent became the only alternative for an upper-class girl who did not marry. Since the dowry required was considerably less than that necessary for marriage to a man of equal station, girls were often consigned to monasteries when their parents were unwilling or unable to pay the marriage price. Illegitimate children, unfaithful wives, and the deformed also found their way within.[44] The number of unsuitable inmates increased when, after the Black Death, monasteries took in guests who, in return for a lump sum, would be supported until death, but had no rules to follow.[45] Because of large numbers of unwilling nuns, who had not chosen their life of consecrated virginity, many irregularities crept into monastic life.

Bishops tried in vain to curtail the comings and goings, the luxuries and immorality with which some of these upper-class women filled their days, often encouraged by families who wanted their daughters to be happy, though single. Finally the pope himself set about remedying the situation, and this was the beginning of the strict role definitions for nuns which prevailed

until the twentieth century. Pope Boniface VIII issued the bull
"Periculoso" in 1298, detailing the regulations that were to be
followed by all religious women. In enunciating the principle of
cloister or enclosure, designed to keep nuns forever within the
walls of their convents and others out, he struck at the manifestations of the problem, but did nothing about their cause -- the
social and economic arrangements which consigned unwilling women
to convents for life. Since this decree set the standard that
would be followed for seven centuries, it merits rather extensive
quotation:

> Desiring to provide for the perilous and detestable
> state of certain nuns, who, having slackened the
> reins of decency and have shamelessly cast aside
> the modesty of their order and of their sex, some-
> times gad about outside their monasteries in the
> dwellings of secular persons, and frequently admit
> suspected persons within the same monasteries, to the
> grave offence of Him to Whom they have, of their own
> will, vowed their innocence, to the opprobrium of
> religion and to the scandal of very many persons; we
> by the present constitution, which shall be ir-
> refragably valid, decree with healthful intent that
> all and sundry nuns, present and future, to whatever
> order they belong and in whatever part of the world,
> shall henceforth remain perpetually enclosed within
> their monasteries; so that no nun tacitly or ex-
> pressly professed in religion shall henceforth have
> or be able to have the power of going out of those
> monasteries for whatsoever reason or cause, unless per-
> chance any be found manifestly suffering from a disease
> so great and of such a nature that she cannot, without
> grave danger or scandal, live together with others;
> and to no dishonest or even honest person shall entry
> or access be given by them, unless for a reasonable
> and manifest cause and by a special license from the
> person to whom /̄ the granting of such a license_/
> pertains; that so, altogether withdrawn from public
> and mundane sights, they may serve God more freely
> and, all opportunity for wantonness being removed,
> they may more diligently preserve for Him in all
> holiness their souls and their bodies.[46]

The cloistral regulations indicated here, which were based on a mistrust of woman's frail nature, came to include minute rules regarding all aspects of a nun's cont acts with "the world." She must have a companion when for the specified reasons she went out or when conversing with outsiders, and all communications with others were supervised. The enclosure was enforced physically wherever possible by the construction of high walls around the convent grounds and the use of special blinds on windows over-looking public streets.

Because it did not strike at the root of the problem, "Periculoso" failed to solve it. The Council of Trent (1545-63), which aimed at massive reform of the abuses in the Church, re-iterated the cloistral regulations of the earlier bull. But it paved the way for true reform of the monasteries when it decreed that no one could force a woman to enter the convent, and provided for the examination of all candidates to make sure that none entered unwillingly. Thus, if Trent's decrees were obeyed, the cloistral prescriptions would be continued, but the chief condition which made them necessary--the presence of unwilling nuns in monasteries--would be eliminated. Reforms of this kind are not carried out overnight, however, and the unwilling nuns already professed would continue to live in the convents and to interfere, to a greater or lesser extent, with the correction of the abuses to which they had become accustomed. Three papal bulls were issued within the decade after the closing of Trent reiterating cloistral prescriptions for religious women, in an all-out attempt to reform the monasteries.[47]

The bull "Circa Pastoralis" of Pope Pius V, issued in 1566,
listed requirements for the approval of religious communities of
women which would be influential for three hundred years. They
must live together in community and take solemn vows of poverty,
chastity, and obedience. Though there are other technical distinctions between solemn and simple vows,[48] the important effects
of solemn vows were the imposition of strict cloister and the loss
of the ability to acquire or own property. "Circa Pastoralis"
imposed solemn vows on the groups of women who had banded together
for common prayer and works of charity among the sick and poor as
well as on nuns in monasteries. This was partly because woman's
nature was thought to be so frail that she could not act res-
ponsibly or virtuously outside cloister walls, partly because
parents and relatives wanted religious women firmly settled in
solemn vows. They were loathe to have them remain at home after
their parents' death with the disposition of an inheritance at
their command, nor did they want them returning from their communities to claim their share in inheritances.[49] For these same
reasons, two communities of women founded in the post-Reformation
period to perform active works of charity, the Ursulines and the
Visitandines, were forced to change their focus from active works
in the world to contemplation apart from it.[50]

Communities which did not have solemn vows and strict
cloister continued to exist, despite "Circa Pastoralis." They
were dependent on local bishops and tacitly tolerated by Rome because of the obvious good which they did. In 1667 Clement IX,
in the constitution "Alias Propositas," gave certain favors to a

group of Dominicans with simple vows, although he knew they were
not conforming to the official norms of the Church. In the following decades popes wavered between approval of groups who were
doing great good in the world, and adherence to the earlier cloistral prescriptions necessitated by the abuses of an age which had
filled convents with unwilling members. In his "Pretiosus" of 1727
Benedict XIII said he did not wish to suppress those with simple
vows and no cloister, but "Romanus Pontifex," issued in 1732,
again stressed strict separation from the world. "Quamvis Justo"
of 1749 showed toleration, but not formal approval, of groups
actively engaged in charitable works within the world.[51]

The latter document was written by Benedict XIV, who has
been called "the greatest canonist of all times."[52] He no doubt
saw the anomaly caused by the imposition of a reform measure like
cloister on groups whose good works within the world were a great
boon for the Church. For the first time he gave religious congregations without solemn vows and cloister legitimate and juri-
dical existence. No longer need they fear suppression or the
imposition of cloister, but they would not be considered true
religious until 1900, because they lacked the solemn vows that
were technically required. To avoid scandal and protect the women
from themselves, however, many of the minute details which regulated
the contact of cloistered women with outsiders were also imposed
on these congregations, whose constitutions would not be approved
by Rome if they lacked them.[53]

This then is the background and substance of the canon law
for religious which prevailed in the Church not only until 1790,

but until 1900. It dates from 1298 and is based on efforts to reform flagrant abuses caused by the profession of unwilling nuns, and by the economic arrangements of the upper classes, who wanted assurance that the nuns of their families would be permanently barred from possessing property. It embodied the traditional misogynous European view of woman as incompetent and inept, and strove to protect her from her frail, evil nature. These are the role definitions and expectations which had to be written into the constitutions of both American and European religious communities in order to gain Rome's approval. The following chapters of this paper will examine what happened when sisters attempted to live according to them in an American environment which possessed very different attitudes and expectations.

First Nuns in Continental United States

There were nuns living according to these canon law regulations, in territory that would later become a part of the United States, in the period prior to 1790. Though they were not living, strictly speaking, in an American environment during this period, their activities and interaction with their milieu will be considered here for the sake of completeness and because of their importance in a later period of American history.

Ursuline nuns from France first arrived in Canada in 1639 to teach Indian girls and the daughters of French settlers, and "Gray Nuns" accompanied girls who came from Paris to Mobile in 1704 to become the wives of settlers there, remaining until all their charges were provided for.[54] Another group of nuns, probably Daughters of Charity, accompanied eighty-one girls to Biloxi in

1721, and returned to France after having witnessed the marriages of all of the girls.[55]

But the first permanent establishment of nuns in what was to become the United States was in New Orleans, where nine French Ursulines arrived in 1727. It was stipulated in their treaty with the Company of the Indies that they would take charge of a hospital, which would be run at the company's expense, and that they would be given land for a plantation whose income could support them. Their passage over and an annual salary until their own income would be adequate were guaranteed to them. It was taken for granted from the beginning that they would have Negro slaves, since the treaty provided that they be given eight Negroes (pièces d'Inde -- belonging to the company and of good physical condition) a year in each of their first five years.[56] One of the members of the pioneer group explained to her father in a letter, "Be not scandalized at it, for it is the fashion of the country, we are taking a negro to wait on us."[57] Other letters from the same nun tell of their receiving eight Negroes from the company, most of whom have been sent to their plantation to work under the supervision of an overseer,[58] and of taking in nine slaves as boarders to give them religious training, two of whom would be kept as servants.[59] These sisters worked in the hospital and school, and were asked to take charge of women and girls of ill-repute. They also instructed Negroes and Indians and cared for orphans, and in general elevated the tone of society. Burns says they were probably the first professional elementary schoolteachers to arrive in America.[60] They ran a boarding school and academy for the upper classes and a day school for those of all races who could not pay.

There seems to have been no doubt about the esteem in which these nuns were held by those among whom they settled. Their reception in this French colony was in contrast to that accorded nuns in the English settlements. One of them, Madeleine Hachard, wrote of their arrival, "Les Pères et Mères, sont transportez de joye de nous voir, disant qu-ils ne se soucient plus de retourner en France puisqu'ils ont dequoi procurer l'instruction à leur filles . . ."[61] And a "Memoire concernant l'église de la Louisiane" dated November 21, 1728 comments of them, ". . . Elles commencerent à instruire de jeunes filles avec succez qui causa beaucoup de satisfaction à la colonie."[62]

The "Americans" too were happy to see them. When a delegation from the Illinois tribe saw the nuns with a group of orphan girls the chief said to them, "You are like the Black Robes, our fathers; you labor for others. Ah! if we had above there two or three of your number, our wives and daughters would have more wit, and would be better Christians."[63] Thus the first sisters in America were esteemed for their instruction and example in forming Christian women. They nursed in the military hospital in addition to their teaching. A note in the convent archives says, "In January, 1770, the religious resigned the care of the hospital, because of their small number and of the difficulty of procuring re-enforcements from France."[64] Their influence is said to have changed the hospital from a place which soldiers had to be forced to enter to one which they gladly sought before their condition became serious.[65]

These nuns were thus cordially received and greatly admired. They cared for orphans in addition to their teaching and nursing, and experienced no cultural clash with their environment in the New World, no doubt because the people among whom they worked were of the same French culture as themselves, and shared their ideas about the role of women and of the nun. There were apparently plans for a convent in English America, judging from a note in the Baltimore Archdiocesan archives dated June 22, 1786 from the Rev. Ferdinand Farmer to the Rev. John Carroll.[66] It says, "I spoke to Mr. FitzSimons concerning the nunnery; as far as I understand he approves of it but rather in the country. He said he would write himself to your Reverence . . ." There is no other record of this convent to be built near Philadelphia however. Even so, the English colonists did have some contact with nuns during this time

Early American Contacts with Nuns

Some of these contacts were with French Canadian nuns. Several New England girls captured in King William's War and other Indian wars became Catholics in Canada, and some became nuns. These preferred to remain in Canada, where they could practice their religion, rather than return to their families.[67] English colonists no doubt applauded when they learned of a letter from Lord Hillsborough to the governor of Quebec, dated July 9, 1786, which said in part:

> So little has been done with regard to the Colony under your government, that I know not whether what we thought absolutely right and necessary when I sat at the Board of Trade in 1763 and 1764, was ever carried into Execution, I mean the prohibiting the

Nunneries and Monasteries from receiving any Increase of Nuns and Friars. It is not my intention
at present to signify any Directions in this matter,
but merely to make an Enquiry; at the Time I cannot
but think this pernicious confinement of good subjects should for the present be discouraged as much
as possible, till His Majesty's final Resolution is
taken concerning those Societies . . .[68]

The attitude of the upper-class Englishman which is revealed here

is not the one which prevailed in the signing of the Articles of

Capitulation of Havana in 1762. They included provision:

That the Catholic Religion shall be permitted and
preserved . . . and all ecclesiastics, Convents,
Monasteries, Hospitals, Communities, Universities,
and Colleges, shall remain in free enjoyment of
their rights and privileges, rents, moveable goods,
and cattle, as they have hitherto done . . . .[69]

and required soldiers to guard the churches and convents till the

evacuation was completed.

During the Battle of Three Rivers, Canada, in the early

part of the Revolutionary War, the wounded of both sides were taken

to the Convent of the Ursulines, where they were treated with kind-

ness by the nuns.[70] General Francis Nichols, captured during

General Arnold's expedition against Quebec, had this to say in

his diary:

March 10, 1776, was removed to the Hotel Dieu, sick
of the scarlet fever, and placed under the care of
the Mother Abbess, where I had fresh provisions and
good attendance. For several nights the nuns sat up
with me, four at a time, every two hours. Here I
feigned myself sick after I had recovered, for fear
of being sent back to the Seminary to join my fellow-
officers, and was not discharged until I acknowledged
that I was well. When I think of my captivity I
shall never forget the time spent among the nuns who
treated me with so much humanity.[71]

Nichols' words would be echoed again and again in the succeeding

American wars, down to World War I.

The traditional English Protestant antipathy toward Catholic France was transformed when France came to the colonists' aid in the Revolution. Age-old fears, however, did not dissolve overnight. One of the most persistent rumors of the time concerned the reported conversion of Samuel Adams and his future ordination to the Catholic priesthood and the desecration of meeting houses by changing them into cathedrals and convents.[72] On August 10, 1782 Watson and Cassoul, a French-American firm doing business in France, presented General George Washington with a Masonic apron of satin wrought in silver and gold, which had been hand-made by the Ursuline Nuns of Nantes, France.[73]

Some Americans came into contact with nuns when visiting in Europe. Benjamin Franklin, in the first part of the autobiography which he began in 1771 tells of his encounter, during his first stay in London, with an Englishwoman who lived the life of a nun. She had gone abroad to join a convent, but then returned to England where, in the absence of convents, she led a nun-like life of seclusion and simplicity. Franklin found her cheerful and polite, but was most impressed by the fact that she lived on twelve pounds a year, her diet mostly water-gruel and her fire used only to boil this concoction. An article in an English magazine enlarges on Franklin's sketchy story. The woman had belonged to the court of James II but repented of her frivolous life after the Revolution of 1688 and entered a convent at Bruges. She returned to England when the climate disagreed with her and began a half century of days filled with prayer, religious exercises and work among the poor, widely revered as "The London Nun."[74]

Thomas Jefferson placed first one and then both of his daughters in a convent school during his stay in France in the 1880's. In 1784 Martha ("Patsy") entered the Abbaye Royale de Panthemont, "a convent much patronized by English people and considered the most genteel in Paris."

The necessary recommendation of a lady of rank is said to have come from a friend of Lafayette's.[75] Jefferson visited her there quite often, especially during her first days there. After having observed the convent's influence on his daughter for three years, he also placed Maria ("Polly") there. Jefferson wrote to his sister, Mary Jefferson Bolling in 1787:

> She is now in the same convent with her sister, and will come to see me once or twice a week. It is a house of education altogether the best in France, and at which the best masters attend. There are in it as many Protestants as Catholics, and not a word is ever spoken to them on the subject of religion.[76]

When Abigail Adams wrote from England regarding Polly "I hope she will not lose her fine spirits within the walls of a convent, to which I own I have many, perhaps false prejudices,"[77] Jefferson replied, "At this moment she is in the convent where she is perfectly happy."[78]

In a letter to her father Martha asked, "Tell me if you are still determined that I shall dine at the abbess's table. If you are I shall at the end of my quarter."[79] He answered, "You ask me if it is my desire you should dine at the abbess's table. It is. Propose it as such to Madame de Traubenheim with my respectful compliments and thank her for her care of you."[80]

Jefferson removed his daughters from the convent school in late April, 1789. Family tradition has it that this was occasioned

by a letter from the seventeen-year-old Martha, who announced that
she wished to become a nun, and it was an ambition of which she
spoke to her own children later in life.[81] The papal nuncio in
Paris wrote to John Carroll on July 5, 1789 that Jefferson was
bringing back to the United States two daughters who had been
educated in a French convent. "The eldest," he wrote, "seems to
have great tendencies toward the Catholic religion. She is only
sixteen. Her father, without absolutely opposing her vocation, has
tried to distract her." Jefferson hoped she would not make any
decision regarding religion until she was eighteen.[82] And in June,
1790 the nuncio wrote to Bishop-elect Carroll, "I am sure that you
will not neglect to profit from the favorable dispositions Miss
Jefferson showed here for the Catholic religion."[83]

In 1793 Jefferson wrote in response to news of what had
become of his charming friend Maria Cosway,

> And Madame Cosway in a convent! I knew that to much
> goodness of heart she joined enthusiasm and religion;
> but I thought that very enthusiasm would have pre-
> vented her from shutting up her adoration of the God
> of the universe within the walls of a cloister; that
> she would rather have sought the mountain-top. How
> happy should I be that it were mine that you, she, and
> Madame de Corny would seek.[84]

Thus we see that the few contacts that Americans had with
nuns prior to the nineteenth century were of a positive kind.
Jefferson's experience was with an aristocratic convent school
which was so pleasant that his daughter wished to remain there and
become a nun herself. American girls in Canadian convent schools
sometimes had the same reaction. Franklin was impressed with the
frugality of the London nun. There is no hint in any of these
experiences of the slightest breath of scandal. Let us now see

what image was conveyed in the writings of the period. One cannot understand the image of the nun in fictional and non-fictional works unless he turns to the European and particularly the English literary traditions which the first settlers of the colonies brought with them and perpetuated.

The Nun-Figure in the English Literary Tradition

The nun had been a part of the English literary tradition which the first settlers brought with them. Sister Mary of the Incarnation Byrne studies the nun-figure in pre-Reformation didactic and historiographical works, Arthurian romance, satire, and exempla in The Tradition of the Nun in Medieval England.[85] Two types of nun recur in much of this literature. The simple nun is aloof from the world, modestly retiring, childlike, docilely obedient, and studious. She loves the solitude of her cell, and occasionally breaks forth in sighs and sacred song, and weeps tears of sorrow for her sins.[86] The abbess appears as a virtuous, prudent administrator, of noble birth, who participates in ecclesiastical and national synods, and is consulted even by kings.[87] In the sixteenth century the secular romantic theme of regret that a lovely young girl should bury herself in a convent enters the literature, along with a new emphasis on the sumptuous banquet, splendid decorations, and rich garments which characterize her farewell party. This new attitude links the medieval tradition with modern literature and reflects the cultural changes which had taken place in the Renaissance world, in which the focus was no longer on the hereafter, but on the here and now. Erasmus and other satirists attacked convents for their immorality and greed,

and denounced relatives who urged girls to become nuns, even when
they preferred to marry.[88] The themes of the nun unwillingly professed, and the renegade who leaves the convent to join her lover
were far more common in Continental literature than in that of
England.[89]

The Nun-Figure in Early American Publications

With the suppression of the English monasteries in the sixteenth century, references to nuns became fairly rare in English
literature. Attacks on Catholicism in the sixteenth and seventeenth centuries criticize many aspects of that institution's
teaching and practice, but rarely mention convents.

These are the literary traditions that the first English
settlers brought with them to America. Sister Mary Augustina Ray,
in her study of the American Opinion of Roman Catholicism in the
Eighteenth Century, finds very little mention of nuns. Nor does
Father Charles Metzger give additional citations either in his book
on American reactions to the Quebec Act,[90] or his study of
Catholics and the American Revolution.[91] No doubt the fact that
monasteries had been suppressed in England, and did not appear in
the predominantly English section of the United States until 1790,
had a great deal to do with this.

Riley finds only one instance of a statement concerning
immorality among nuns in all New England publications of the
colonial period. This is in William Bradford's Dialogue: Or,
3d Conference.[92] Nor are there any titles suggesting that they
might be about nuns in the appendix in which he lists the Catholic
and anti-Catholic books in colonial libraries. The few references

to nuns which are found in American writings of this period perpetuate the figure of Erasmus and the satirists who followed him,
and can actually be called "American" only by a rather free use
of that term.

Anthony Gavin is described on the title page of his book
The Great Red Dragon; or the Master-Key to Popery as "formerly one
of the Roman Catholic priests of Saragossa, Spain."[93] This book
was first published in London in 1725 and republished there in
1735, then in Newport in 1773, Philadelphia in 1816, Boston in
1854 and again in Philadelphia in 1855. The nuns depicted in it
are attracted to the convent by the superficialities of the
religious life, a charge which is repeated from some of the satires
of Erasmus. They are constrained to remain after they learn the
"truth" about convents by the threats of the civil government,
which is of course under the control of the Church.

Mrs. Charlotte Ramsay Lennox, who was born in America in
1720 but went to London to live in 1735, creates a character in
her play The Sister who runs away from her bigoted Catholic aunt
because, having failed to convert the girl to Catholicism, she is
attempting to force her into a convent.[94] Thus in the literature,
the unsavory view of the convent which originated in the days when
girls did not always enter them willingly--an abuse that was corrected by the Council of Trent in 1563--continued to dominate two
hundred years later, and this when at least a few Americans had
had an opportunity to see the excellent work done in teaching,
nursing, and other works of Charity by nuns in Canada, New Orleans,
and Europe.

CHAPTER III

1790 - 1829

Introduction

In the period from 1790 to 1829 twelve communities of nuns
founded convents in America, and one already established group
came into the Union after the Louisiana Purchase. Five of these
twelve communities originated in America[1], and a sixth[2], though
founded from Belgium, counted three Americans among its first four
members. The rest of these convents were founded from European
motherhouses, with the exception of the Boston Ursuline convent,
which was started by Irish women trained in Canada. It is significant that all of the six communities founded by Americans survived and became flourishing institutions in the American Church.
Of the six founded by Europeans, only one achieved permanent stability.[3] Though there are many variables which determined whether
a community succeeded or not, the ability or inability to adapt
European customs and role definitions for nuns to the necessities
of the American environment was a very important factor.

Formal Role Definitions of Canon Law

All of these religious communities were governed by the
canon law regulations discussed above in Chapter I and II.
Apparently only one general decision given in Rome during the
years 1790 to 1828 altered these laws. This was a decree of

32

Cardinal Caprara of 1803 which applied to Benedictine, Carmelite, Cistercian, Dominican, and Franciscan nuns of France and Belgium. In the upheavals which followed the French Revolution, many of the monasteries were dissolved and their property appropriated by the government. It seemed wise therefore for women entering communities in these countries to retain the ownership of property in their own names rather than give it up as required by solemn vows. This decree stated that their vow of poverty would no longer be solemn but simple, though the vow of chastity remained solemn.[4] This gave rise to various problems when nuns of these communities came to America.

Questions concerning adaptation to new conditions which arose after the establishment of convents in America, were submitted to Rome by individual communities for solution. The Roman responses to these questions will be discussed in the context of the history of the community involved. Out of the experience of the pioneer communities came certain patterns of interaction with American society and adaptation to American needs which would recur as succeeding generations of nuns repeated the experiences of the early sisters.

One of the most serious problems faced by newly established communities was that of economic survival. In Europe convents were aristocratic institutions founded with an initial endowment designed to support a specified number of nuns for life. From the late sixteenth century on, dowries which would provide financial support also came into use.[5] Both endowment and dowry were necessary for the financial stability of cloistered communities,

which did not engage in remunerative work. The dowries required
by them were much larger than those for congregations supported by
such works as teaching or nursing.[6] Only the patronage of the
wealthy enabled the Daughters of Charity to work among the poor
gratis. This practice of achieving financial stability through
large endowments and dowries would require some modification in a
country where there were few wealthy Catholics and areas where
Catholic planters were land poor and held much of their fortune in
slaves.

Communities whose purpose was prayer and reparation for all
of mankind would find that the addition of teaching to a schedule
meant to govern a completely different type of life created serious
problems. Yet a scanty endowment forced them to find some means
of supporting themselves, and hard-pressed bishops often urged
them to open schools. European priests required time and experience
before they could balance ascetic practices with the needs of the
American sisters whom they directed. European motherhouses which
sent colonies of nuns to America would have to change their interpretations of enclosure if they were to succeed in settlements
where walls were unheard-of.

These and other problems faced the women who pioneered in
religious community life in America. Their skill in adapting what
was essentially a European institution to the needs of the American
environment often determined whether they would succeed or fail.
Since these early communities were important in the establishment
of patterns which would continue, the history of each will be
examined in some detail for the light it can shed on the emergence

of these patterns. This study will include types of work undertaken (roles played), problems faced, and solutions attempted by
these nuns. It will be followed by a discussion of their interaction with society and their image as portrayed in the fiction of
the period.

First American Communities

Carmelites

The first community to be established in the United States
had its roots in the English Carmelite convent at Hoogstraeten,
Belgium, which included among its members daughters of the Catholic
families of Maryland. After the suppression of the Carmelite
houses in the Low Countries in 1789, many of these nuns looked to
their own country as a place of refuge.

Others were also considering the establishment of a convent
in America. From Rome in 1788, Father John Thorpe advised John
Carroll, soon to become America's first Catholic bishop, that "A
house of Ursuline nuns, or of any other who by institute make a
profession of educating female youth, might be of singular advantage
in the provinces contiguous to your own residence."[7] "If means can
be procured for settling both Theresians and Ursulines, perhaps it
would be advisable to bring in the latter before the others on
account of their immediately visible utility," he wrote a little
later. Clearly he was aware of the active character of his countrymen, who looked for visible productivity as evidence of one's
worth.[8] If only Theresians came, he said, they would have to
become schoolmistresses. At the end of the American Revolution

the Jesuit Father Ignatius Matthews wrote to his Carmelite sister
at Hoogstraeten, Mother Bernadina Metthews, "Now is your time to
found in this country, for peace is declared and Religion is
free."[9]

In response to this letter three Carmelite members of the
Matthews family, and an Englishwoman, set out for America in 1790.
They were the first of a long procession of nuns who would wear
secular attire while traveling because they feared the violent
reaction that might be aroused by religious garb. They also used
the titles "Mrs. Matthews," "Miss Matthews," and "Miss Nellie" in
preference to their religious names. Mother Clare Joseph Dickinson
noted in her diary on June 3 that she looked extraordinarily fine
in her silk petticoat and chintz jacket, but there must have been
some indication that they were not ladies of fashion, for they
were openly ridiculed in the streets of Amsterdam.[10] And when
their ship stopped at Santa Cruz, the captain went ashore to report
that he had four escaped nuns on board.[11] They arrived on July 10,
1790, and soon took over the Brooke Farm near Port Tobacco,
Charles County, Maryland, and donned their traditional garb.

The Discalced Carmelite Order is a strictly contemplative
one which devotes its time to prayer and reparation for sin rather
than to active works like teaching. Its first American members
spent much time spinning to clothe themselves. They also printed
and bound prayer books, Mother Clare Joseph compiling The Pious
Guide, the first prayer book printed in the United States. They
raised sheep for wool and grew their own food.

John Carroll possessed the active American temper and
shared the convictions of his friend Thorpe quoted above. He
hoped that these sisters would contribute to the needs of the infant American Church by teaching as well as praying. He wrote to
Rome, "They are a salutary example to the people of the vicinity,
and their singular piety has moved even non-Catholics to admiration."[12] He added, "Their convent would be a far greater
benefit in the future if a school for the training of girls in
piety and learning were begun by them."[13] He no doubt considered
this a more useful occupation than book-binding. Carroll wrote to
the Carmelite superior reporting Rome's response:

> The Cardinal Prefect of the Propaganda . . . informs
> me that, . . . considering the great scarcity of
> laborers and the defects of education in these United
> States, you might sacrifice that part of your in-
> stitution to the promotion of a greater good and I am
> directed to encourage you to undertake it; and, now in
> obedience to this direction I recommend to your
> Reverence and your holy Community to take it into your
> consideration . . . .[14]

But Cardinal Antonelli had written, "While they are not to be urged
to undertake the care of young girls, against their Rule, they
should be exhorted not to refuse this work, which will be so
pleasing to God, and which is badly needed on account of the great
scarcity of workers and lack of educational facilities."[15] Thus
it was left to the sisters to decide whether they wanted to open a
school, and they chose not to use this dispensation. Carroll reported to his friend Father Charles Plowden,

> They have multiplied themselves considerably, and give
> much edification by their retirement, and total seclusion
> from the world, and I doubt not the efficacy of their
> prayers in drawing down blessings on us all; but they
> will not concern themselves in the business of female

education, though the late Pope, soon after their
arrival, recommended it earnestly to them by a letter
sent to me by Cardinal Antonelli . . . .[16]

As time went on daughters of Southern families entered
this community and relieved its poverty through dowries which often
included Negro slaves. These slaves, who numbered thirty by 1829,
lived outside the enclosure and did the farm work, thus taking the
place of the servants who often did this work in European monasteries. This adaptation of the European custom of endowment and
dowry to American economic practice, and the fact that the Southern
aristocracy produced conditions similar to those under which its
convents had flourished in Europe, help to explain this community's
ability to survive. Other contemplative groups which came to
America in this period were less fortunate.

Poor Clares

Such, for example, were three Poor Clare nuns who, driven
from their French convent in 1792, landed in Baltimore in 1793.
They amended their original rule in order to teach and take in
boarders, but continued many practices of the contemplative life.
The austere life of these barefooted nuns, their poverty, and their
scant knowledge of English doomed them to failure.[17] The school
apparently closed in 1801 and the few remaining nuns returned to
Europe in 1806.[18] An advertisement for their Georgetown school
gives some indication, in its final paragraphs, of the ways in
which financial stability was sought. It reads as follows:

MADAME DE LA MARCHE also informs the public that she
has Excellent Waters for the cure of almost all kinds
of Sore Eyes. There are bottles at half a dollar; and
others at three quarters of a dollar according to the

kinds of sores they are to be applied to,
--Directions will be given with bottles. She has
also Salves for the cure of different sorts of Sores,
hurts, wounds, etc.
It is more the good of humanity, than her own
interest that induces her to advertise the above mentioned things. Georgetown, March 8, 1799[19]

These nuns were the first of many who would learn through ex-

perience that the addition of active works like teaching to a

strictly contemplative schedule places insupportable burdens on

all concerned. Amid circumstances which made it difficult for

them to procure any kind of financial support, they failed in

their attempt to carry on a type of life based on endowment. Three

women who had assisted in this school, when they later became

nuns, chose to be Visitandines rather than Poor Clares because

of their dissatisfaction with a rule that could not be adapted to

contemporary needs.[20]

Visitandines

These women banded together in 1795 to live a religious

life according to rules devised by Father Leonard Neale. As time

went on, and they felt the need of more complete constitutions,

they sought those of the Visitandines, a cloistered community

which conducted schools within its monasteries. They had a diffi-

cult time obtaining a copy of the Visitandine rule. When they

finally procured one, they found that it would have to be adapted

before it could be followed in America, where the sisters had to

go out of their enclosure to do their marketing, attend church,

and accompany their pupils on walks through the woods.[21] Like

the other American communities of this period they grew their own food and lived in great poverty in their early years, but were relieved of some of this work by the acquisition of Negro slaves.[22] Pope Pius VII gave them permission to take solemn vows in 1816, and in 1826 three French sisters were imported to teach them the customs of the Visitandine Order.

Because of their inability to obtain the kind of endowment traditional in Europe, and the inability of young women who joined them to bring substantial dowries with them, these nuns supported themselves with the income from their school. To make up for this departure from their rules, they also opened a free school.[23] Pope Pius VIII gave them permission in 1829 to educate poor girls outside the cloister and to make other adaptations in their rule which were required by the times, since differences in climate and customs, and the necessities of their two schools, made it impossible to follow all of the details of the Visitandine rule. The admission of day pupils, for example, required some relaxation of the rigid rules for enclosure. The pope stressed, in his rescript of May 10, 1829, that these changes should not interfere with their being considered true Visitandine nuns.[24] Many of the important families of Washington and of the South sent their daughters to the "Young Ladies' Academy" which these nuns opened in 1799, a school which has attracted the daughters of prominent families ever since.

Thus, though this community followed traditional rules which had grown out of a European milieu, and even brought over French nuns to teach them unfamiliar customs, it was able to survive and flourish because of its willingness to make adaptations called for by the American milieu. French culture was undoubtedly one of the strong attractions of its school, but one which would also have repelled had it not been adapted. Its Irish foundresses had lived and taught in America for almost twenty years before adopting the Visitandine rule, and thus knew from wide experience just which provisions would have to be changed. Had they begun to follow it immediately upon their arrival, their history would no doubt have been different and their success much less certain.

A French Sister of Mercy and two Belgian Poor Clares came to Cincinnati in 1824 and 1825 to do educational work there. Bishop Fenwick dispensed the Poor Clares from parts of their rule, much to the disgust of their fellow Clarists of Bruges and Lyons, who correctly predicted their eventual failure. Since it belongs to the history of a later period, it will not be discussed here.[25]

The same fate befell a group of Irish Ursulines who came to New York in 1812. They had stipulated that they would not remain unless a certain number of American girls had joined them within three years. The sisters lived in the famous Jumel house and hoped to acquire, through the dowries of American girls who would enter, the $2000 which it cost them. Since no interested New Yorker of the day could afford the dowry, none entered, and the sisters returned to Ireland in 1815.[26]

A French Trappistine, who with a group of Trappist brothers and priests hoped to found a house of her Order in America, arrived in Boston in 1812. Though the foundation which was made in New York flourished for a time and received several American recruits, "unexpected opposition arose, money was lacking,

and the monks were eager to return to Europe."[27] Americans who
had entered the community were given the option of remaining in
America, and four chose to join the Sisters of Charity at Emmitsburg. Though there is some question about whether it was the
sisters, priests, or brothers who cared for orphans, the evidence
seems to indicate that it was not the sisters. They apparently
led the strictly contemplative life characteristic of Trappistine
nuns. Since the type of opposition they met has not been described,
one cannot definitely define the reason for their failure. It probably had to do with financial arrangements, and could also have
had some connection with the American custom of judging worth by
external productivity, a standard according to which contemplative
communities were worthless.

Ursulines

In 1803, when Jefferson purchased Louisiana from France,
the New Orleans Ursulines who had been educating the daughters of
the South since 1727 came under the jurisdiction of the United
States. William Duane, in a description of Louisiana published in
1803 says of them:

> They have always acted with great propriety and are
> generally respected and beloved throughout the pro-
> vince. With the assistance of an annual allowance
> of $600 from the treasury they always support and
> educate twelve female orphans.[28]

Sixteen sisters had left the New Orleans convent for one in
Havana when it became known in 1803 that Spain had ceded the
territory to France, whose persecution of religious they feared.[29]
The remaining sisters sought from President Jefferson a guarantee

that their property would remain in their hands after the United

States had bought the territory. This was not, they pointed out,

because they coveted earthly goods, but because of a solemn vow

to use their income for charity. In describing their role they

wrote:

> It is then less their own cause which they plead
> than that of the public. It is, in fact, the cause
> of the orphan and of the destitute child. It is,
> moreover, the cause of a multitude of wretched beings
> snatched from the horrors of vice and infamy, in
> order to be, by the petitioners, brought up in the
> path of religion and virtue, and formed to become
> happy and useful citizens.[30]

The "wretched beings" referred to here were the Negro girls and

women whom the Ursulines taught for several generations.

Jefferson replied on May 15, 1804 assuring them of perfect

liberty under the Constitution and saying,

> The charitable objects of your institution cannot be
> indifferent to any; and its furtherance of the whole-
> some purposes of society, by training up its younger
> members in the way they should go, cannot fail to ensure
> it the patronage of the government . . . .[31]

These letters were published in the Moniteur, the only paper of

New Orleans, to quell the disturbing rumors rampant in this city

which had belonged to three different countries within a month.

It has been noted above that Ursuline sisters nursed

American soldiers wounded in the Revolutionary War. These New

Orleans Ursulines showed their loyalty to America when they per-

formed a similar service in the War of 1812, the first of hundreds

of American nuns who would help to dispel bigotry by their selfless

care of the wounded in time of war. After the Battle of New

Orleans the convent received the wounded of both armies, who were

nursed there for three months. For many years afterwards men of
Kentucky and Tennessee continued to send the convent baskets of
bacon, fruit, etc. to show their gratitude to their former
nurses.[32] General Jackson himself, with his staff, visited the
convent to thank the nuns for the prayers offered for his success
in the battle for the city, and later, as president, was given
the rare privilege of entering the convent cloister.[33]

Another Ursuline convent, one established in Boston in 1820
by two Irish girls trained in Canada, caused a stir among the
descendants of the Puritans. Its school's reputation soon drew
the daughters of the aristocracy, not only of Boston but of Canada,
the West Indies, and the South as well. Because the unhealthy
surroundings caused the premature deaths of some of the sisters, a
new school, the ill-fated Mount St. Benedict's, was built at
Charlestown in 1826. This was the school destroyed by a mob in
1834 which is discussed below in Chapter IV. Though the convent
and school were successful, the community was forced by the antagonism of nativists to disband, and is thus numbered among the
institutions which did not last.

Emmitsburg Sisters of Charity

The first native American sisterhood was founded in 1809
by Mrs. Elizabeth Bayley Seton, prominent New York widow who had
become a Catholic in 1805. Its history dramatizes the European-
American conflicts which were bound to occur as long as American
nuns attempted to conform to European role expectations, and thus
typifies the experiences of many subsequent American sisterhoods.

In this case as in several others, the European priests who directed the sisters felt that one could learn the correct role definitions for nuns only from experienced Europeans. Many of these priests, exiles from the French Revolution, learned gradually through their experience in living in America that American sisters could best formulate their own rules and their own solutions to American problems.

Mrs. Seton's advisers, most of them French, thought that her community should be modeled on that of the French Daughters of Charity, the group founded by Vincent de Paul to work among the sick and poor. Vincent had been very much aware of the Church's official role definitions for nuns, and warned his followers not to allow anyone to call them "religious," because "Who say 'religious' say cloistered and the Daughters of Charity must go everywhere."[34] Nor did they wear the veil, which also denoted cloistered religious.[35] Similarly, Mother Seton's sisters wore a simple white (later black) cap, with black cape, and a dress similar to those worn by widows of the time and modeled after that worn by religious Mother Seton had seen in Italy.

Bishop Benedict Flaget was commissioned, apparently by Father David, to bring back a copy of the rule and constitutions of the Daughters of Charity from a trip to France in 1810. He also arranged for three of the Daughters to come to Emmitsburg to initiate the women there in the customs of their community. As it turned out, however, these French women never arrived, and the Americans were thus enabled to develop in a distinctively American mode which would not otherwise have been possible.

Archbishop John Carroll was actuely aware of the minority
status of American Catholics, the deep-seated suspicions harbored
by the majority of Americans, and the unique characteristics and
needs of his Church in America. His many years of European training and travel had made him cognizant of the cultural differences
between the two continents, and he doubted that emulation of a
community founded to serve the needs of the French Church would be
the wisest course for an American group. Writing later about the
question of French affiliation for Emmitsburg he said,

> At the very institution of Emmitsburg, though it was
> strongly contended for its being entirely conformable
> to and the same with the Institute of St. Vincent de
> Paul, yet this proposal was soon and wisely abandoned
> for causes, which arose out of distance, different
> manners, and habits of the two countries, France and
> the United States.[37]

That Mother Seton also had doubts about the usefulness of
the French rule and the French sisters she revealed in a letter to
Carroll of May 13, 1811 in which she asked,

> What authority would the Mother they bring over have
> over our Sisters while I am present? . . . How could
> it be known that they would consent to the different
> modifications of their rules which are indispensable
> if adopted by us? What support can we procure to
> this house but from our Boarders, and how can the
> reception of Boarders sufficient to maintain it accord
> with their statutes? How can they allow me the un-
> controlled privileges of a Mother to my five
> darlings?[38]

She referred here to the fact that the French Daughters of
Charity worked primarily among the sick poor and were well enough
endowed so that they did not have to support themselves from their
work. When they did teach, it was only children who could not
afford to pay, since those with means were already provided for in

other ways. Once again the economics of the American situation
called for change, since Mrs. Seton and her community had no endowment on which to draw. They would have to accept paying pupils if
they were to do anything at all for the poor, and during their
first winter they had to augment their income by sewing for the men
and boys of near-by Mount St. Mary's College.[39] Carroll saw education of all classes as the great need of the American Church.
Though he was not correct in his predictions, he did make a point
when he wrote in 1811:

> A century will pass before the exigencies and habits
> of the country will require and hardly admit of the
> charitable exercises toward the sick, sufficient to
> employ any number of sisters out of our large cities;
> and therefore they must consider the business of
> education as a laborious, charitable, and permanent
> object of their religious duties.[40]

A teaching community in America could not educate the poor only,
and neglect the needs of the other classes. Therefore it seemed
that the rules of the French group, if they were to be used at all,
would have to be adapted to allow for this great need of America.

Even Flaget, who had arranged for the coming of French
sisters which was then halted by Napoleon's government, began to
have second thoughts and wrote to Bruté:

> I dread the arrival of the religious women who are to
> come from Bordeaux . . . . Their hopes will be frus-
> trated, they will be unhappy . . . . If there were
> yet time to turn them back, I would be of the opinion
> it should be done. I would wish at least that they
> be informed in detail of the spirit which reigns in the
> house at Emmitsburg, of the slight hope of serving
> in hospitals, and if they wish to come after that
> we would not have to reproach ourselves.[41]

The constitutions of the Emmitsburg sisters as finally
adopted stated that their institute was the same as the French one

except for its educational policies and "such modifications in the
Rules as the difference of country, habits, customs, and manners
may require."[42] This emphasis on the requirements of the American
situation was stressed again in an article in the Laity's Directory
for 1822 which described the society as one which was to be
"congenial to the habits, and in some measure to the prejudices of
the country."[43] And Archbishop Maréchal could write of the sisters
in 1818 in a report to Rome as:

> Sisters who live holy lives according to the rules
> of their holy founder with the exception of the
> modifications demanded by American customs and dis-
> positions. They do not take care of hospitals
> nor could they since the administration of these
> hospitals is Protestant.[44]

There evidently was no doubt in the minds of those connected with
the community that adaptations of the French rule were necessary if
it was to be used successfully in America.

The school at Emmitsburg became very popular with important
upperclass families, both Catholic and Protestant, though it always
had orphans and others who could pay little or nothing among its
pupils. These latter were soon put into a class separate from
that of the boarders, where they no doubt learned skills which
would prepare them for their future jobs.[45] Thus, though America
boasted of its democracy, the existence of social classes made
certain adaptations of the democratic principle necessary in its
schools.

Though Bishop Carroll was most aware of the need for
Christian schools, other needs of the Church in America were almost
as pressing, and the American Sisters of Charity soon turned their

attention to them. In 1814 the sisters took over an orphanage in Philadelphia,[46] and in 1823 they began hospital work in the Baltimore Infirmary. It was so successful that they were invited to nurse at the local Marine Hospital in 1827 and to run the Mullanphy Hospital in St. Louis in 1828.[47]

Thus the first native American sisterhood resisted the impulse to become affiliated with the French Daughters of Charity and while using their rule and constitutions, adapted them to the needs of the American Church. That they were not able to permanently resist this tendency toward Europeanization will become evident from the discussion of their fate in Chapter IV.

Three different communities of religious women were founded in Kentucky in the early years of the nineteenth century, two in 1812 and one in 1822. Each reflects in a different way the interaction between European and American values in its role definitions for sisters.

Sisters of Loretto

Father Charles Nerinckx began to gather a group of women together to lead Christian lives in common shortly after his arrival in Kentucky in 1805.[48] Though this first project failed, he was ultimately successful, his first sisters pronouncing their vows in 1812. A young school teacher who had sold her Negro slave for $450 in order to buy land for the group's school and home was elected superior, and thus America's economic and political practices played their part from the very beginning. (Election of superiors was not, however, a distinctively American practice.)

The first sisters, because of their poverty, wore whatever clothes they had, but tried to dye them black. In his first rules Father Nerinckx wrote, "The dress must be black and full every way, having nothing of a novel or fashionable appearance. The head-dress will be a black veil, sufficiently large to hide the shape; a simple bonnet is allowed when abroad or in the rain . . . ."[49]

The Belgian Father Nerinckx, who had hidden in a Catholic hospital for six years during the French Revolution, had some experience of the religious life as it was lived by the sisters in the hospital. He had been trained for the priesthood during the time when the Austrian Emperor Joseph II was trying to impose the very strict doctrines of the Jansenist heresy on the Church in Belgium. Though Nerinckx realized that these were heretical, he could not help but be tainted by them, and he himself was a very austere man who rarely smiled.[50]

Nerinckx first proposed that nuns be imported from Europe to teach the young women the rudiments of religious life, but they protested that he could do it better himself. He consulted Bishop Flaget who, as has been seen above, had had second thoughts regarding his invitation to the French Daughters of Charity to come and form Mrs. Seton's sisters. Having observed the evolution at Emmitsburg, he now insisted that Nerinckx form the new foundation without any foreign element. Therefore, at the urging of the sisters themselves and of his bishop, Father Nerinckx formulated rules for them.[51] That he was aware of the definitions for nuns which were set down in the canon law of his Church is apparent from his remark in a letter to Bishop Dubourg in 1823: "Their vows

are simplicia, sed perpetua. I wrote to have them solemnia,
because requested to do so. Rome, I think, will not agree,
unless they be sub stricta clausura."[52]

His own European background, tinged as it was by the Cal-
vanistic tendencies of Jansenism, would inevitably enter into his
ideas of religious life, and this was evident in the austerity of
the rules he wrote, and their unsuitability to American frontier
conditions. Silence was to be observed all day except during the
hour of recreation, and even that hour was omitted on certain days.
It is said that the sisters themselves asked to go barefoot except
between November 1 and March 25, in imitation of the anchorites of
old, and this they did.[53] (Some of these Catholics of Kentucky
had imbibed Calvinistic traits from their neighbors which accorded
well with the austere ideas of their French and Belgian priests.[54])
The descriptions of two bishops give an indication of the kind of
lives these sisters led. Bishop Rosati wrote to Bishop Dubourg
on August 16, 1823:

> Although not cloistered, they are entirely secluded,
> and our good people respect them so much that they
> never dare to intrude upon their silence. They go
> barefooted, have no other dresses but what they make
> themselves, of dyed linen in Summer and of wool in
> Winter, and they sleep upon a straw tick, spread on the
> bare floor. Their fare is no more delicate: no coffee,
> tea, or sugar. It is a true pleasure to witness their
> fervor, which equals that of the strictest communi-
> ties of Europe in the palmiest days of their first
> establishment . . . .[55]

He was anxious to point out that, though they were not cloistered,
their fervor rivaled that of the strictest European community.
And Bishop Dubourg wrote of them to his brother the following year:

> The great advantage with these good sisters is that
> to establish them, it is enough to give them a piece
> of land, a hut, some farming implements, kitchen
> utensils, and looms; with these they themselves provide
> for all their wants, and find the means of giving a
> solid education to the children, in return for a few
> provisions furnished by the parents. They even take
> upon themselves the gratuitous care of destitute
> orphans.[56]

A French sister wrote of some of their members,

> These sisters live in a very austere manner. They
> are completely veiled, having neither shoes nor
> stockings on their feet, and do every kind of hard
> work, ploughing, sewing, reaping, etc. I
> foresee that they will take the lead in many good
> works that we love but cannot carry out. Their
> rules are better adapted than ours to the poverty
> and habits in this country.[57]

Thus to the austerities typical of cloistered communities
and the spinning and weaving by which they helped to support
themselves, these sisters added the heavy work of the field and
farm, inadequate clothing, and a Spartan diet. And all of this
was secondary to their work of teaching and caring for orphans.
Small wonder that when Father Nerinckx submitted the rules to
Rome for approval in 1816 some modifications were suggested.
Various documents in the archives of the Congregation of Propaganda
Fide reveal that there was further discussion of the Loretto constitutions in 1818-20, and changes such as having the sisters wear
sandals when walking outside were suggested. Nerinckx wrote to
the community from Europe November 2, 1820, "I received letters
from Rome concerning your Society, that tell me that the R. Rev.
Bishop of Kentucky has received an ample instruction upon the rules
of which some they wish to be altered; I wrote to the bishop
about it . . . ."[58]

That the rule was too austere became apparent in America too, as hardship began to take its toll. Father Chabrat, confessor of the sisters at a mission in Bethania, where eleven sisters died in the first seven years, complained of it to Bishop Flaget. He listened and tried to reason with Nerinckx, who left Kentucky when his rules were questioned and died shortly afterward while visiting a convent in Missouri. The founder's reactions to the complaints against his rule are revealed in a letter to Bishop Rosati written January 24, 1824:

> I understand that shortly some remarkable alterations
> are to take place in our schools, and I doubt not in
> the rules, in the spirit of innovation and for the
> making common (or popular) not for bettering the
> religious rules and principles. Such is the spirit
> of the age. I will not oppose it to avoid dissensions,
> but I wish not to share in it . . . .[59]

After the founder's death Bishop Flaget prudently consulted other priests and bishops before adapting the rules. A letter to Bishop Joseph Rosati dated September 11, 1824 reveals much about the problems of the Lorettines. " . . . . There are certain rules that are revolting to everybody," he wrote, "and it seems to me that it is our duty to modify them." Then he spelled out two which doctors found extremely unhealthy: going barefoot, and sleeping with their clothes on and then praying in oratories open to the wind, all of which made the sisters prone to contract tuberculosis, which in fact many of them did:

> This observation is so just that it is confirmed by
> the most doubtless experience. Indeed, in the space
> of eleven years we have lost twenty-four religious,
> and not one of them had yet reached the age of thirty
> years. Besides, of the eighty religious of the same
> family, that we have in Kentucky, there are at present
> thirty-eight who have bad health and who are perhaps

not yet four years in vows. I learn that in your
convent you have five or six whose health is almost
ruined. All these deaths and other illnesses so
multiplied, do they not prove . . . that the rules
are too austere . . . ?[60]

Flaget also recounted Nerinckx's anger when he provided instruction

in grammar for some of the sisters in order to win the esteem of

the parents and attract pupils and revenue. Nerinckx considered

it vanity and worldliness, with the result that there were few

students in the schools in which grammar was prohibited, and a

large revenue from those in which he grudgingly allowed it to be

taught. Flaget turned to the financial aspects of the question and

showed his grasp of the unique economic problems of American sister-

hoods when he said:

> The principal reason of Mr. Nerinckx for the elimina-
> tion of grammar was that the community was not des-
> tined, except to train orphans and poor girls. If
> Mr. Nerinckx had added that he had some great revenue
> to carry on these good works, I should have been of
> his opinion, but as his daughters have no other re-
> sources, except that resulting from their industry,
> and their industry, active as it is, can scarcely
> suffice for their nutrition, I do not see how they
> could take charge of orphans. These would only in-
> crease their expenses and would not increase their
> income.

Nor did he agree with Nerinckx's old-world ideas of a static class

society:

> To say that the poor have no need of grammar demands
> an explanation, for in the United States, the poor
> classes have as many pretensions as those of the rich,
> and every day we see the daughter of a tailor or
> cobbler married to a doctor or a lawyer. The beauti-
> ful figure and education are entirely, in our republic,
> the reasons why all the girls everywhere will have
> instructions and be gracious so that they will have a
> good chance in society.[61]

Rigid as he was in his adherence to European values, Nerinckx showed his sensitivity to American needs in his plan to start a branch of his community for Negro sisters, who could work among their own people. In May, 1824 he wrote, "Two days ago twelve young ladies offered themselves at Loretto for the little veil, among them our three blacks who received nearly all the votes."[62] Two other Negro postulants entered the community a little later. They were all sent back to their homes when Chabrat became the ecclesiastical superior of the community.[63]

Father Guy Chabrat, who had complained about the austerities of the Loretto rule, was appointed ecclesiastical superior after the death of Nerinckx and set about revising the rule, requiring the sisters to bring him any Nerinckx writings in their possession. These he consigned to flames in an effort to rid the sisters of the austere spirit bequeathed to them by their founder. In the revised constitutions he gave less voice to the sisters in decisions affecting their lives, and more to the ecclesiastical superior, thus paving the way for future tensions between the community and its ecclesiastical superiors and changing its democratic character.[64] Apparently the changes in the rule suggested in Rome were also incorporated, for Cardinal Fesch wrote to Rosati in July 6, 1825 acknowledging the fact and saying, "Would to heaven it had been in your power to do so more speedily; perhaps the health and life of many sisters who died prematurely would have been preserved . . . ."[65]

Thus the Sisters of Loretto began with an austere rule which was ill-suited for American conditions but which gave them a

large share of self-government, and then exchanged it for one
which was more suitable for frontier conditions but deprived them
of their autonomy and self-government, defects which would not be
rectified until eighty years later.

Nazareth Sisters of Charity

In the same year in which the Loretto Sisters were founded
Father John David, who had been superior of Mother Seton's sisters
at Emmitsburg until 1811, founded a community of sisters at
Nazareth, Kentucky. It was Father David who had originally wanted
Mother Seton to import French sisters to give her community the
proper foundation and who wanted the sisters to follow every provision of the French rule.[66] He learned a great deal about the
needs of American communities through his experiences at Emmitsburg,
if one is to judge from his practice when he came to found another
American sisterhood. Almost as soon as he arrived in Kentucky he
wrote to Simon Bruté in Baltimore:

> We are determined to form a society of virtuous women
> for the education of young people of their sex. I
> believed, when I was in Baltimore, that the Sisters of
> Charity would not be suitable to this work, rather the
> Ursulines. But since we are on the spot it is evident
> that cloistered Sisters would not suit as well as
> Sisters of Charity as regards small pupils.[67]

In the same letter he asked for a copy of the rules of St. Vincent
de Paul which Flaget had brought to Mother Seton's sisters. Later
he asked that Emmitsburg send him some sisters to guide his young
community, and that his group be affiliated with that of Emmitsburg, though he proposed further changes in the rule. The superior,
he said, should not be called "Sister Servant," a title which might

lower her position in the eyes of the boarders, in this country
where "servant" was synonymous with "slave."[68]

In the controversy which ensued with Father Dubois, the
superior at Emmitsburg, over the question of affiliation, both
sides wrote to Bishop Carroll, Dubois citing French custom as the
absolute standard to be followed. In Carroll's answer to David he
recalled the decision that Emmitsburg's rules would differ from
the French model "in many points, even in that, which is the soul
and life of Saint Vincent's Institution, attendance on hospitals
and the sick, without which they would not be known in France to
exist."[69]

In the end David had to be content with founding his community as a separate autonomous group which based its constitutions
on those of the French Daughters of Charity but modified them.
Like the Emmitsburg sisters they had to spend much of their time in
schools which served the wealthy as well as the poor, and had to
charge tuition in order to maintain themselves financially.[70]
Their boarding school was especially popular with Southern families.
The sisters wore their own clothing at first and then adopted a
simple black cap, later changed to white, a black dress, cape and
apron which "seemed more suitable than the cornette worn by the
Sisters of Charity in France."[71] These sisters were also like
those of Emmitsburg in that they would be forced to consider the
matter of affiliation with the French community again at a later
time, but for the present they were allowed to develop as an indigenous American group. At first they supported themselves by
spinning, weaving, and sewing for college boys and other

neighbors, and later they acquired Negro slaves, who did the harder work in the fields.[72] The Sisters of Charity of Nazareth, as they were called, opened several schools in Kentucky and also cared for orphans.

Kentucky Dominicans

The third sisterhood to be founded in Kentucky during this period was that of the Dominican Sisters, founded in 1822 by Father Samuel T. Wilson, a Dominican. Though Bishop Edward Fenwick wanted to send for English sisters, Father Wilson's plans for an indigenous American group carried the day.[73] He was determined to found a "Third Order" group of Dominican Sisters, which differed from "Second Order" Dominican nuns in that they did not have cloister or solemn vows. The letter from the Vicar General confirming the election of the first superior specifically calls her a "professed religious of our college of Saint Mary Magdalen, Third Order of Saint Dominic,"[74] and a rescript from Pope Pius VII authorizing the foundation of the group also refers to them as sisters of the Third Order.[75] In a letter to the Superior General of the Order Bishop Fenwick too alludes to their Third Order status.[76]

In spite of this emphasis on their status as members of the Third Order, however, they were given a rule and constitutions taken from the Second Order, the cloistered nuns whose norms were those established in the Bull "Periculoso" of 1298. One of their historians remarks of them, "They immediately entered upon their regular conventional life, and the same exercises and rules observed by their unknown sisters in the stately convents of Europe, were followed in the rude cabin on the frontier,"[77] and here lies the crux of the problem which was to plague them for many decades. Though they were supposed to be an uncloistered group suited to active works of charity, they lived according to rules planned for a contemplative community whose chief work of charity was prayer. Like the Sisters of Loretto, they tried to follow European practices in an American milieu, and found that it did not work.

These sisters had regular hours of prayer throughout the day and also rose at midnight to pray. They had simple vows, but took them with the explicit intention of making solemn ones as soon as enclosure would be possible.[78] Though Bishop Fenwick felt that black clothing would be more practical, they prevailed upon him to allow them to wear the traditional white habit of the Dominicans.[79] In addition to all of their monastic observances, they studied and taught, cared for the house and fields, and sold linen and wool of their own spinning in order to support themselves.[80] Needless to say, they soon found it necessary to lighten their burdens.[81]

The Dominican Fathers who came to Kentucky in the early nineteenth century and guided this community of sisters exhibit curious paradoxes when one examines their interaction with American society. They were of English parentage, having fled from the English convent at Bruges to escape the persecutions of the French Revolution. Finding little success in England, they came to Kentucky where the people who had chafed under the austerities of the French and Belgian priests rejoiced to receive the far milder ministrations of these Englishmen who shared their culture.[82] They were able to adapt to the American milieu in many ways, yet when dealing with the sisters they imposed the traditional European functions on them even while they added new burdens required by American needs. Father John Hill could write to Fenwick, in London recruiting missionaries for Ohio, "The nuns you speak of will be of no use, as I suppose they are of the Second Order with solemn vows, which will not do in this country."[83] Yet the Third Order sisters who he recommended in their stead were expected to live lives very similar to those of nuns of the Second Order. The definitions of canon law and their own European ideas of nuns apparently prevented them from seeing the type of creative adaptation required by the American milieu. In time it became clear, however, that American conditions required a type of feminine religious life different from that of Europe. In 1829 Fenwick's advice to Father Samuel Smith, who apparently had proposed a rule for a religious community, reflected that which Father Hill had given him five years earlier. He approved of sisters and a female school, but objected to references to a "monastery" and to solemn vows, both of which connoted the cloistered religious who were the only ones officially recognized by canon law.[84]

These sisters had actually added to the work of cloistered Second Order nuns the active works of Third Order members, and did their own farming, weaving, spinning, etc. under primitive frontier conditions. The anomalies of the situation were increased when Father Raphael Munos, a Spanish Dominican who had been confessor to the royal family, became their chaplain and director. He brought a strictly European attitude toward women and the Church's views on the proper decorum for religious to his scrutiny of their lives,

and was horrified. In his view they were not truly "religious,"
since they were not cloistered, and were engaging in pursuits entirely unsuited to the delicate nature of woman when they did their
own farming, carpenter work, etc. Since there was no need for
schools like theirs in Spain, he could not see any reason for them
in America. Nor was he pleased with the $2000 debt they had con-
tracted in the name of his predecessor--a debt not at all exorbi-
tant for a growing institution in those times, but of staggering
proportions to the Spanish mentality.

In this clear-cut confrontation between Spanish and
American culture, it seemed that the European would dominate.
Father Munos ordered the sisters to sell their farm, pay their
debts, and disband, and refused to minister any longer to their
spiritual needs. They held on, however, insisting that they had
been approved by Rome, until their position was changed by the
appointment of an American superior who understood their situation.[85] Gradually, as new members brought slaves as part of their
dowry, the most strenuous farm work was done by them and the sisters were freed to spend more time on study and teaching.[86]

Religious of the Sacred Heart

A different pattern, which is typical of that followed by
many European communities in their establishment of American houses,
is seen in the development of the convents of the Religious of the
Sacred Heart in the United States. This community was founded in
France in 1800 to educate young women of the upper classes, though
it often taught the poor as well. In 1818 Philippine Duchesne led

the first group of these French sisters to America, where they

soon opened several schools on both the upper and the lower Missi-

ssippi. The development of these missions and the problems en-

countered were typical of those faced by groups whose headquarters

remained based in Europe. Many of these eventually formed auto-

nomous American groups when tensions became unbearable, but this

did not happen to the Religious of the Sacred Heart. They are re-

presentative of those communities whose European superiors fostered

unity among all of their members but wisely allowed adaptations to

be made so long as they did not jeopardize the principal aims of

the institute.

Mother Duchesne reported the first adaptation to the

American climate to her French superior from New Orleans on July 9,

1818:

> The doctor insisted on our buying dresses of light-
> weight material. They are black cotton with a single
> thread of white; the [lay] sisters have dark purple
> dresses, nearly black. We wore our religious habit
> on the ocean and no one thought it extraordinary.
> The Ursulines, even those who have come out during
> the last thirty years, wore secular dress, and we may
> have to make some changes in our costume during the
> journey up the river . . . .[87]

When these nuns arrived in St. Louis they found the populace eager

to catch a glimpse of their garb. From the moment of her arrival

in America Mother Duchesne wondered about how they would adapt

their French customs to American needs, and the extent to which it

would be advisable to do so.[88] They found it impossible to adhere

to the rule of cloister which canon law imposed on all religious.

Mother Duchesne wrote from St. Charles in 1818, "As to enclosure,

there is not a wall within a thousand miles of here; and wooden fences keep out animals, but not men. Our enclosure consists in remaining at home . . . ."[89] When one of the nuns complained about the inability to follow every point of the rule as was customary in France, the French foundress of the Order, Mother Barat, assured her that this was to be expected.[90] As foundress, she had a clearer vision of what was essential to the spirit of her community than others to whom the letter of the law had become more important than the spirit which it sought to perpetuate.

Bishop Dubourg, having read their rule, tried to get them to change certain parts of it, but Mother Duchesne and her nuns refused to do so without the permission of their French superiors, thus setting a precedent which would ensure continued unity with the motherhouse.[91] This stress on unity with the European motherhouse sometimes caused a certain rigidity and conservatism where necessary adaptations to the American apostolate were concerned.

Both parents and students rebelled against the European structure that these French sisters imposed on their schools. The more democratic American temper militated against class distinctions in types of education, though the upper classes helped to perpetuate them, and affectionate American families saw no reason for restrictions on visits with their daughters who were in boarding school.[92]

Adjustment to these American expectations was not easy. There was much discussion between the American and European superiors regarding the amount and type of education to be given to children whose paretns were not wealthy. The necessity of accompanying pupils on walks through the woods and to church wrought

havoc with traditional cloistral regulations.[93] Finally the French
superiors agreed that necessary adaptations should be presented to
the motherhouse for approval. Permission was subsequently given to
use English rather than Latin in the children's prayers, take walks
without cloistral restrictions, change the daily schedule of classes,
etc.[94] Other adaptations to American practice occurred when the
nuns who went to Grand Coteau, Louisiana in 1821 used slaves to
cultivate their large plantation. (Some were purchased, some acquired through dowries, and others received through inheritance.[95])
Their willingness to make the adjustments that were required and
the flexibility of the French foundress were important factors in
the success of this community, which was the only strictly European
one of this period to make a permanent foundation in America.

These are the relevant facts regarding the religious communities of women which established convents in America from 1790
until 1829 and the previously established Ursuline convent of New
Orleans, which came within the American orbit in 1803. Certain
patterns of works undertaken, role definitions held, and interaction with the American milieu emerge which are more or less typical not only of this era but of succeeding periods. The same problems, clashes, and attempted solutions will continue to recur as
long as role definitions for nuns continue to be dictated by
European attitudes toward women and necessities that arose in the
earlier medieval cultural milieu.

Roles Sisters Played

The works which these sisters performed, the roles that
they played, were overwhelmingly those required by active works of
charity. Only the Carmelites and the Trappistines led strictly
contemplative lives of prayer and reparation. All of the others
took up teaching which, in the case of several communities, was
added to a schedule originally planned for nuns who were cloistered
rather than active. Many also cared for orphans, and the Emmitsburg sisters took up hospital work as well.

Several aspects of the early American convent schools
deserve further comment because they reflect facets of the inter-
play between the nuns and eir society, between European and
American culture, which are important for the purposes of this
paper. Tensions were aroused in these schools when class consciousness clashed with democratic aspirations. The sisters
opened them to the wealthy because of a lack of educational facilities for them and also because they provided the means for conducting free schools for the poor. Though all students were
taught together at first, the two types of students were separated
as soon as this was feasible, according to French custom, except
in the schools of the Loretto sisters.[96] However, they did provide
in varying degrees for the education of orphans and the poor, and
several had classes for Negroes.[97]

Boarding and day schools modeled their curriculum on that
of Franklin's Academy, offering terminal education in which both
the Classics and the domestic arts were taught.[98] The French nuns

brought with them definitely formulated plans of study, the
Règlemens of the Ursulines, the Règlement des Pensionnats et Plan
d'Études of the Religious of the Sacred Heart, and the Method
D'Enseignement pour les Classes de Soeurs de St. Joseph. Thus they
spread in the wilderness of America the culture of the Old World.[99]
Many of the schools were located near colleges run by educated
professors from Europe who could help to broaden their curricula.[100]
In the convent schools of the Ursulines and the Religious of the
Sacred Heart in New Orleans, Grand Coteau, and north to St. Louis
the French tradition of the boarding school for the wealthy, where
ladylike accomplishments and elegant manners were inculcated, was
perpetuated among both Protestants and Catholics. The files of
these academies show that the daughters of the best families
attended them.[101] Many Protestants of this period, including
Harriet Beecher Stowe and Sarah Josepha Hale, thought of Catholicism
as the quiet, aristocratic religion of the Calverts and the Carrolls
which stood for tolerance, reason, and moderation.[102] Since a
large number of the students were often Protestant, pains were
taken to assure parents that freedom of conscience would not be
interfered with.[103]

Illustrious visitors often attended the commencements of
these schools, thus showing the esteem in which they held them.
This is especially true of the Georgetown Visitation Academy, which
has always been a favorite of those connected with the Federal
government. President James Madison presided over commencement
exercises there,[104] and John Quincy Adams noted, during the
exercises at which he presided in 1828, the presence of the daughter

of Commodore Jacob Jones "in the sable weeds of the order."[105]

Among those receiving awards at this commencement attended by

Adams, his wife, and his son were three daughters of Yturbide,

former emperor of Mexico, whose widow lived as a nun in the convent

for many years.[106] Henry Clay gave out the diplomas at the first

commencement of the Nazareth Academy in Kentucky in 1825.[107]

Sister Murphy, in her study of early convent schools, found very

little adverse criticism of them[108] and no record of attacks

against nuns in their annals.[109] Thus those who came in contact

with sisters through their works in these years held them in high

esteem.

The economic necessities of a religious community newly

begun in America placed burdens on the pioneer sisters that were

unknown in European convents established through royal grants or

endowments from wealthy patrons. The Ursuline foundation in New

Orleans had been financed by the Company of the Indies, but the

other communities had to rely for financial stability on the far

less affluent generosity of friends and their own efforts. The

communities founded from France after the French Revolution had

very little financial support from their homeland, and had to rely

chiefly on their own resources and the generosity of American

Catholics. The groups begun in Kentucky had to find ways of adding

to the often meagre dowries that new members could afford.

To support themselves these early nuns used the avenues

open to American women of the time. Some turned to spinning and

sewing for neighbors, college boys, and themselves.[110] Others

raised their own food, doing all of the farm work themselves until

other means were available.[111] The fact that they were accustomed
to such work in their own homes no doubt made it easier for them
to take it up when necessity forced them to. The French nuns'
admiration for the Americans' greater ability to perform the rough
manual work of the frontier has been noted above. The Carmelites
printed and bound prayer books for added revenue.

The effort required by these works, when added to those of
teaching and of following religious exercises actually intended
for a less strenuous form of life, imposed a great burden on the
early nuns, and many of them ruined their health in trying to carry
them out. Tuberculosis was the scourge of the early sisterhoods.
Seven of the eight communities of this period which survived acquired slaves through dowry, inheritance, gift or purchase. They
performed the heavier manual labor so that the sisters might be
free for contemplative or charitable works. This adaptation to
American economic practice, which was comparable to the European
custom of having peasants, servants, or lay sisters perform the
menial work, seems to have been a factor in the survival of these
communities.[112] None of the groups that did not succeed in establishing permanent foundations in America seems to have had slaves.

Problems Posed by the American Milieu

The constitutions of these communities, which enumerated
the formal role expectations for members, were almost entirely of
European origin. Only the Loretto sisters followed constitutions
which originated in America, and these were so redolent of the
European backgrounds of their Belgian founder that, as has been

noted above, even Rome objected to them. Many of these over-
burdened women found that the austerities of European rules for
religious women, most of which were intended for strictly contemplative communities, were unsuited to American conditions and
had to be changed if their apostolic work was to succeed. When
adaptations were made, there were always fears that changes in
details of the rules would lead to general dissipation and a fall-
ing away from the original fervor and ideals of the community. It
was difficult to distinguish between those things which were essential to the life and spirit of a community and those which were
merely a part of an earlier culture whose usefulness had disappeared
when the culture itself changed. Thus when the Poor Clares, whose
aim was a strictly contemplative life, took on the work of teaching,
they completely altered the character of their community and doomed
it to failure. But when the Visitandines and Religious of the
Sacred Heart changed the schedules of classes found in their
European rules to fit American needs, they were only facilitating
the success of the work to which they had always been devoted.

The degree to which the constitutions of European communities could safely be adapted to American needs without dissipating
a community's original spirit was a matter of dispute among
European sisters who founded convents in America. The problems
arising from this question caused tensions throughout the nineteenth century, not only in convents with European roots, but also
in American ones in which the Church's European role definitions
for sisters were followed. In this period Europeans seem to have
found adaptation an all but insurmountable difficulty, while those

who were American by birth or had lived in America for many years
were able to succeed at it. Of the six foundations begun between
1790 and 1829 by Europeans directly from Europe, only one, that of
the Religious of the Sacred Heart, succeeded. All of the six begun
by women who were American by birth or by adoption prospered and
are still carrying on their work in the 1970's. Five of these groups
grew indigenously, "from scratch," on American soil, while all but
one of the communities which failed (the Boston Ursulines) were founded by mature experienced religious. This seems to indicate that it
was far easier to begin religious life in America, away from the influence of outmoded European cultural impediments, than to try to
adapt these to a new environment.

Even those communities which were American in origin had the
European backgrounds of their priest-directors to contend with in
formulating their rules, and the ever-present attitude that Europeans
had perfected the forms of religous life and Americans needed only to
imitate them to succeed. Bishop John Carroll, who was aware of the
Anglo-Saxon temper and prejudices of his fellow countrymen, and of
the unique needs of his American church, opposed this idea from the
first, and French priests like David and Flaget gradually learned
through experience the wisdom of his position.

Solutions

The sisters learned to seek dispensations from their rules
and constitutions when their prescriptions were hindrances rather
than helps in the living of religious life in America. The Visitandines received a dispensation to accept paying students, to change

their daily schedule, and to go outside their cloister. The Poor
Clares took up teaching to solve their financial problems but were
unsuccessful because they were unprepared for it and their rules
were not suitable. The Emmitsburg Sisters of Charity modified the
French rule of St. Vincent de Paul to enable them to teach the
wealthy, and the Nazareth Sisters of Charity modified it even more
to eliminate the title "Sister Servant" and make other provisions
for the Kentucky frontier. The Religious of the Sacred Heart ad-
justed their educational policies and the cloistral practices of
their rule to the needs of the times. The Kentucky Dominicans refused to accede to their Spanish director's demand that they disband
because they could not live a European type of religious life. When
bigotry seemed to threaten, the Carmelites and Ursulines donned
secular dress for travel, and doffed their religious names -- practices which were carried over from European custom during periods of
persecution.

It was not only the sisters, but their bishops, cognizant of
the special needs of their dioceses, who urged the sisters to adapt
their constitutions. Both Roman and local ecclesiastics insisted on
a lessening of the austerities of the Loretto rule, and Bishop
Carroll urged the Carmelites to take up teaching. Bishop Dubourg
asked the Religious of the Sacred Heart to change their rules.

Interaction With Society

European clergymen and nuns noticed the contrast between
American and European culture and were often unfavorably impressed
by the independence of the Americans among whom they worked. The

Irish Ursulines who came to New York in 1812 noticed a strong
contrast between their former Irish pupils and "the assumption,
pride, and petulance, which the name, and perhaps, the reality, of
political independence were developing in the youthful character of
America, and which in almost every instance interfered with the
efficiency of their teaching."[113] Mother Duchesne in a letter to
her French superior noted the American attitude toward the for-
eigner: "Their national pride seems to make them scorn those who
do not speak their language, so English is a real necessity."[114]
She repeated the same refrain later: "The most marked characteristic
of the Americans is scorn for anyone and anything that is not American,"[115] indicating an attitude which would lead to much dissen-
sion in future years for nuns and all Catholics. Archbishop
Dubourg, writing to Peter Caprano of the Congretagion of the Propaganda in 1826, expressed the idea that religious communities could
best cope with American independence:

> It is scarcely possible to realize how contagious
> even to the clergy and to men otherwise well dis-
> posed, are the principles of freedom and indepen-
> dence imbibed by all the pores in these United
> States. Hence I have always been convinced that
> practically all the good to be hoped for must come
> from the Congregations or religious Orders among
> which flourish strict discipline . . . .[116]

Positive

In the interaction between these first American sisters and
the predominantly Protestant and Anglo-Saxon culture in which they
lived, a culture which had a history of hostility towards Catholics,
there were reactions of all kinds but surprisingly few negative
ones.

The works of the nuns evoked favorable reactions among those who observed them, whatever their faith. Thus Sister Rose White wrote to Mother Seton from her Philadelphia orphanage in 1817: "You have no idea how the lovers of money admire the disinterestedness of those who serve God, and how eagle-eyed they are to all the actions of the sisters . . . ."[117] Bishop Carroll attested to the esteem in which Catholics and non-Catholics held the Carmelites in the letter to Rome quoted on the page above. The people of New Orleans, the soldiers who were nursed by them, Madison and Jefferson, all praised the work done by the New Orleans Ursulines. Even the descendants of staunch New England Puritans flocked to the Ursuline school in Boston. The convent schools, which were the chief work of all but the contemplative communities, were patronized by the leading families and praised by important dignitaries, as has been shown above.

The schools and convents were given legal existence, and some recognition for excellence, when they obtained state charters. The short-lived Ursuline convent in New York was incorporated by the state legislature on March 25, 1814. The collector of the laws subjoined a note to the articles of incorporation which is interesting for what it reveals of the attitudes of the time:

> This is perhaps the first incorporation of a Convent in a country decidedly Protestant and evinces the liberality of the legislature. . . . This act from its title would seem to warrant something more than the mere establishment of a seminary for education. It is presumable that it will furnish an asylum to such distressed females as may enter its walls, and become subject to its ecclesiastical discipline.[118]

Negative

That there were some negative reactions to the first nuns
to become established in the United States was to be expected. It
was in fact the Catholics who opposed the foundation of the Georgetown Visitandine convent, for the very reason that it might arouse
hostility among their fellow citizens.[119] Neighbors who witnessed
the beginnings of Father Nerinckx's Loretto community sarcastically
praised him at first for ridding the country of its old maids, but
then turned on him in 1814 for the hypnotic power which they felt
he had over young girls. They complained that he removed marriage-
able girls in the bloom of their youth from their places in society.
This murmuring seems to have been silenced by a sermon of Bishop
Flaget's in which the significance of religious life was explained.[120]
When Boston newspapers carried unfriendly notices of the establishment of an Ursuline convent there, Bishop Cheverus tactfully calmed
the public mind by publishing an explanation of the significance of
the institution.[121]

Opponents seem to have been silenced by reasoned explanations. Those who came into contact with nuns reacted very favorably
to them despite the hostile attitudes prevalent at the time. Thus,
the actual attitudes of American townspeople seem to corroborate
some of the theories of students of public opinion mentioned in
Chapter I. Pre-conceptions about nuns changed in the face of
strong invalidating evidence, the failure of negative expectations,
and the rational presentation of a positive viewpoint. That this
was so is the more remarkable when the image of the nun which came
to Americans through the fiction of the time is considered.

Roles Seen In The Literature

Much of the American fiction of the period from 1790 to 1829 was patterned after the Gothic novels of England. This genre, begun by Horace Walpole in The Castle of Otranto (1764), uses a medieval setting and usually employs elements of mystery, magic, and the supernatural to convey an atmosphere of horror and terror. Since the emphasis in these works is on setting and story, the characters tend to become stereotyped.[122] Anything characteristic of the Middle Ages was called "Gothic," including Catholicism and its convents. The gloomy recesses of a cloister, with a crafty priest, penitent nun, pious abbess, and trembling novice were often used in English Gothic novels.[123] Elements of immorality from the satirical tradition and exempla were combined with the terrors of the Inquisition and the Continental theme of the nun unwillingly professed to create sensational horror stories of seduction, imprisonment, torture and murder which were violently anti-Catholic.[124]

Sister Reddin, who studied representative American Gothic novelists, found that they did not follow the English practice of using monasteries and convents as places of evil and duress, nor did they make much use of the character of the friar.[125] She did find some use of the conventual setting, however, in American magazines from 1765 to 1800, and the following summaries are based on her findings.

"The Friar's Tale," which appeared in the Philadelphia Columbian Magazine in 1789[126] tells of a girl, immured in a convent by her father, who continues to see the lover he disapproves of.

She escapes but is immured again by a nephew greedy for her inheritance, who tells the abbess to treat her cruelly, which she does. When her lover finally arrives at the convent he discovers that she has long since escaped.[127]

A variation of the Abelard and Eloise theme is "Constantia and Theodosius," in which the girl enters the convent and her lover becomes an exemplary priest.[128] He gives her good advice when she confesses to him, not knowing it is he. Both die on the same day, and are buried in the same grave. "The Nuns," from the New York Magazine of 1794 is more eventful. In it a recently married escaped nun dances with a monk who recognizes her as his daughter. Since the abbess' letter telling him of her escape has been intercepted, he wonders about her presence at the party.[129]

Boston's Massachusetts Magazine published "The Nun, Related by a traveler through Normandy" in 1796.[130] The traveler comes upon a monk weeping at the tomb of his daughter whose memoirs he shows to the traveler. They tell of her unwilling enclosure in a convent for life and the ensign for whom she sighs. In "A Dialogue on Avarice and Covetousness, The History of Two Genoese Merchants,"[131] a girl is put into the convent so that others can enjoy her inheritance, but she finally escapes and marries her lover.

"The Horrors of a Monastery, A Tale," lives up to its title.[132] It depicts a girl mourning her father's death in a convent, who is put in a dungeon by a monk whom she has repulsed. He announces that she has burned to death and uses a closed coffin at her "funeral." The man she was to marry after a year of mourning enters the same monastery to live out his life in the place where she died.

Needless to say he discovers and releases her, and they live happily ever after. Monimia of "Marcus and Monimia,"[133] is put in a convent by an aristocratic father, who opposed a marriage to lower-class Marcus. At the reception ceremony, when the Bishop asks her if she will devote her life to religion, she chooses Marcus instead and vows herself to him for life, much to the disgust of her father. Laura of "The Serenade, or Laura and Alonzo"[134] sees her brother kill her husband, who was serenaded nightly outside her convent window. She escapes but is a lunatic for the rest of her life.

These are the images of the nun found in some of the magazines of this period. Though the stories in which they occur constitute only a small part of the seventy-five compositions studied by Reddin, they were printed again and again in magazines all over the country in that day of no copyright laws and hence were more influential than it might seem.[135] An analysis of nativism in the textbooks of the time reveals only one reference to nuns, that in Nathaniel Heaton's The Pleasing Library, a reader of 1801. It is found in "The Friar's Tale," and is similar to the story of that name published in the Columbian Magazine in 1789. It features an unscrupulous prioress who connives with a man who wants her to keep his cousin in the convent.[136]

In Julia and the Illuminated Baron, a novel about the evils of rationalism and atheism in post-Revolutionary France published in 1800, Mrs. Sara Wood depicted the convent as a good place rather than a house of detention or correction. Mrs. Leonora Sansay, "a Lady of Philadelphia," uses a gloomy convent atmosphere in her novel Laura, published in 1809.[137] Its first sentence sets the scene for what follows: "Rosina, a destined victim to monastic gloom, leaned weeping against the grated window that terminates one of the vast corridors of the convent of Santa Clara."[138] The abbess' sermon on the advantages of convent life does not impress her nearly as much as a letter from a friend describing the gay life she has led since leaving the convent (p. 2). The friend argues that one who obeys because she has no choice gains no merit, and virtue that has not been tested is not true virtue. "We are good because all occasion of doing ill is kept from us," she writes (p. 2). Though Rosina's family has decided that she will take the veil in the Lisbon convent, she dreams of being rescued by her friend's brother. Mrs. Sansay acknowledges the literary tradition when she notes that Rosina had read some novels and "had gathered from them enough to know that such occurrences were not infrequent . . . ." (p. 6). "But the iron bars, the gloomy windows, the impenetrable walls that surrounded her, dispelled the charming vision" (p. 7). Her dream of rescue is eventually fulfilled, and the happy couple travels to America. Her husband later dies and she remarries but urges Laura, the child of her first marriage, to enter Santa Clara convent and devote herself "to that religious solitude from which she had herself so thoughtlessly fled" (p. 9). Laura falls in love, however, and marries.

The imagery of grated windows, vast corridors, iron bars, and impenetrable walls which is used here to describe the convent of Santa Clara conveys the dominant impression that the convent is a prison. In the context of the story and the theme of the unwilling nun the imagery is apt. It will be used so often in stories about nuns that it becomes stereotyped. The novel is ambiguous in that with all of this use of prison imagery the heroine is made to regret that she ever left her prison, and urges her daughter to incarcerate herself, reversing the image so that there are reverberations of "Stone walls do not a prison make, nor iron bars a cage . . . ." The name "Santa Clara" was used in many Gothic novels, notably in Matthew Lewis' The Monk (1795), to denote a convent.

A tale told in couplets by poet Sumner L. Fairfield is worthy of note as a portent of things to come. The Sisters of St. Clara, A Portuguese Tale, which was published in Portland in 1825, makes use of the same setting and imagery. Fairfield writes of "Blackened prison walls," and a cloister that is "a living grave" in which "to be entombed" (p. 8). Though he depicts the usual unwilling young nuns longing to be freed by their lovers, he goes further than have other American writers in his references to lurid crime. "Deeds unweened by him of hell / Are done in murder's fatal cell" (p. 8). During an escape attempt one of the two nuns faints just as she reaches the top of the wall, falls, and dies. The "cloister horde" with "venom hate" rush "like hyena troops" upon the body. The tone of biting hatred which pervades certain sections of this tale links it to the works of the succeeding period, discussed in Chapter IV below. It is certainly the most negative work on convents to be written by an American up to this time, and its appearance heralds the floods of defamatory materials soon to inundate the country.

A novel by an English writer that was influential in America after its publication in New York was Grace Kennedy's

Father Clement, a Roman Catholic Story.[139] A subplot concerns a
girl who is "going to be shut up forever in a nunnery!" (p. 15).
She treats her Protestant friends rudely and spends her last year
before entering the convent in rigid mortification (p. 39). A
priest urges her to use her wealth to found a convent in England
so that Catholics will not have to attend Protestant schools
(p. 161ff). She does this, and of course becomes the lady abbess
of the convent she endows (p. 243).

The typical image of the nun which appeared in the American
fiction of this period is thus one of a European girl who has been
forced into the convent despite the fact that she is in love and
would like to marry. This theme appears in ten of the thirteen
stories. In seven of them the girl is able to escape and join her
lover. Thus the emphasis is primarily on unwilling nuns and the
action inevitably takes place in Italy, Portugal, or some other
Catholic country. The foreign setting adds to the aura of mystery
and romance and carries with it the implication that "it couldn't
happen here."

In three stories it is explicitly stated that others are
seeking the inheritance the girl would be entitled to were she not
a nun. Immorality forms only a minor part of the image depicted
in them. In two cases a nun is a priest's daughter, in one a monk
tries to seduce a nun. There is one reference to unspecified
cruelties, one to murder, and one to a dungeon.

Thus the theme of the nun unwillingly professed which was
common in the lyrics of the Continent enters the English literary
tradition in the Gothic novel and is then transmitted to American

writers, who use it as a major theme when they are depicting nuns.
It is a theme which will capture the imagination of freedom-loving
Americans and impel them to action in a later period, as will be
shown below. Though these stories are less melodramatic than those
of the English Gothic writers, they share the same ingredients of
sentiment, adventure, and history. The conventual life appeared
to the eighteenth-century intellectual as an unnatural and ir-
rational one full of supersitition, but it appealed at the same
time to the sentimentality of the age, which reveled in the emotions
of melancholy despair, gloomy solitude, mystery, and suspense that
it evoked.[140]

The moderation which marked the treatment of the nun in
American Gothic fiction is also evident in a description of Italy
which was published in America during this period. The Political
State of Italy was written by Theodore Lyman of Boston after a
journey there in 1819.[141] His chapter on convents (p. 110ff) describes the situation as he found it in Italy. He stresses, as do
the fiction writers, the social custom which filled convents with
unwilling nuns, but attacks as untrue the implication of immorality
which was so prevalent in English novels and would soon invade the
American market.

Most noble families cannot afford to marry their daughters
to men of equal rank, and so consign them to convents, he notes.
The cost of banquets on reception and profession days is between
$3000 and $3500 for daughters of the nobility and from $500 to
$600 for a citizen's daughter (p. 120). Lyman describes various
communities, the monastic cell, reception ceremonies, etc. Women

are no more secluded in convents than they would be in their own
homes, he points out, and their life is no more boring than that
of the upper classes in general (p. 126). The convents are free
from the vices with which they were formerly reproached (p. 127).
At a "Vive Sepolte" convent he has a delightful conversation with
the abbess, through the grille (p. 141). In his conclusion he explicitly refers to the great difference between the image of the
nun which exists in the popular mind and the reality which he has
observed in Italy:

> Having seen and heard much of the convents at Rome,
> I am satisfied that the inhabitants of them do not
> condemn themselves to many deprivations and mortifica-
> tions, which they would not have suffered in the ordinary
> chances of a different life, that the passions, which
> exist there, are less active, violent and frequent, and
> that the carelessness of mind, health of body, and
> absence from all gloom and severity, utterly contradict
> and put to shame the theories and creeds of the world
> . . . . A foreign gentleman, who had lived twenty years
> in Rome, told me that he had never heard of any
> scandalous conduct in any nunnery during all that time.[142]

These observations are all the more interesting in view of the fact
that it is Lyman who will be mayor of Boston at the time of the
burning of the Charlestown convent. (See page *149* below.)

Though the picture Lyman gives contradicts that of the
English and American novelists in some respects, it does reinforce
the dominant image of the nun who is in the convent merely because
of social and economic custom. He is careful to point out that the
abuses of an earlier period have been corrected. Much of what he
says would repel his New England readers nonetheless. The extra-
vagance of the banquets mentioned, and the indications that this
was a decadent aristocratic institution in which nuns lived out

their lives in cheerful indolence and boredom would offend the Yankee instincts for industry, thrift, and democracy.

Lyman was not the only observer of the European system to speak out against it. Joel Barlow struck at the root of the problem in his Advice to the Privileged Orders, in which he pointed out the evils of the institution of primogeniture, which consigned daughters to forced marriages or the convent and younger sons to the priesthood in order to preserve the inheritance for the first-born.[143] And Crevecoeur states in his Letters to an American Farmer (the French edition of which was dedicated to Mother Seton's father-in-law[144]):

> I had rather record the progressive steps of [an]
> industrious farmer, throughout all the stages of his
> labours and other operations, than examine how modern
> Italian convents can be supported without doing any
> thing but singing and prayer.[145]

When one examines the literary record of the nun image in this period one is struck by the almost total absence of bitter invective and lurid descriptions of crime and immorality in descriptions of convents. These abounded in the English Gothic novels and in the sermons, speeches, newspaper articles, pamphlets and other media through which tirades against the Catholic Church flooded the American consciousness at this time.[146] Their omission in descriptions of convents is thus significant. The chief theme is that of the nun unwillingly professed who escapes with the man for whom she has been sighing. The social and economic customs which were the cause of so many abuses during the centuries before the Reformation continue to color popular thinking about the nun even though the Council of Trent had moved to correct these abuses over two hundred years before. Though many monasteries were either reformed or closed during the ensuing centuries, social custom changes slowly, and Lyman reports the continuance of the old customs in Italian convents into the nineteenth century.

The dominant image used in connection with the convent in the works examined is that of a prison with high thick walls and long dark corridors. In view of the canon law regulations which stressed an enclosure of nuns that was expressed physically by means of walls, grates, etc. this use of the wall is apt. The "prison" connotations would be appropriate for those monasteries which continued to receive members who had not freely chosen the religious life but had been assigned to it by their families. The walls of convents in which unwilling nuns were enclosed kept nuns within and potential lovers without. The stereotyped image does not refer at all to another purpose of cloister walls: protection, particularly in turbulent times, against those who would despoil the monastery.

Conclusions

In comparing the actual role definitions of the American nuns of this period with the roles for nuns depicted in the writings of the time, one notes a wide discrepancy between the image and the reality. The stereotyped image of nuns as unwilling members of cloistered European contemplative communities has very little connection with American actualities. There is no evidence to indicate that anyone was ever forced against her will to become a member of an American convent, nor did the sisters within them sigh for lovers left behind. In most instances there was no cloister wall, though the other practices which flowed from enclosure were carried out to the extent that this was possible.

One of the greatest differences between the image conveyed and the actual reality is in the roles played by nuns. In the literature they are contemplatives who are at worst fiendish murderers (and this is portrayed only by Fairfield) and at best indolent aristocrats living in cheerful boredom (Lyman's depiction). All but two of the thirteen communities in America at this time performed active works of charity: teaching, nursing, and caring for orphans. In addition they engaged in farming, weaving, spinning, book-binding, and other strenuous occupations.

Those whose role expectations for nuns were reflected by or learned from popular literature of the period 1790 to 1829 would find them contradicted if they actually came into contact with American sisters. The small number of negative reactions to the sisters on the part of their fellow citizens may very well have been the result of attitude changes caused by confrontation with a reality drastically different from the expected one. When Mother Duchesne reported that her sisters could not establish a proper enclosure in a country where there was no wall within a thousand miles, she may have pin-pointed the very factor, both literally and figuratively, which would differentiate American nuns from their European counterparts and lead to their acceptance by people whose early prejudices derived from the inaccurate stereotypes perpetuated in the popular literature.

CHAPTER IV

1830 - 1859

In the years from 1829 to 1859 there was a great increase
in the number of Catholics in America, as immigrants from Ireland,
Germany, and other countries poured in. Bishops were hard-pressed
to provide the schools, hospitals, orphanages, and other charitable
institutions necessary to care for their needs. Many American bishops were obliged to undertake journeys to Europe in search of
funds and personnel. Thirty-nine new foundations of religious
women were established during this period to meet the needs of the
growing Catholic population. Eleven of these were founded in
America; twenty-eight were instituted from well-established
European motherhouses.[1]

As the numbers of European missionaries to America multiplied, clashes between European and American cultures became more
numerous. This is the period when the heavy influx of immigrants
gave rise to nativist attacks on the foreign born, and the Catholic
Church took on the image of a foreign church. Patterns of adaptation to American needs were examined in some detail in Chapter II.
In this chapter the continuation of these patterns and the development of new ones will be discussed. Individual communities cannot
be studied in detail, but relevant information will be included in
the general study of the roles played by nuns, the problems caused

86

by the American situation, and the interaction of the nuns with contemporary American society.

Formal Role Definitions of Canon Law

During the period from 1829 to 1859, the Church's formal role definitions continued to be based on the papal bulls and decrees discussed above. The decree of 1803, which stipulated that the vow of poverty of French and Belgian nuns would be simple rather than solemn, remained in effect and caused various problems. A decree of December 23, 1835 stated that convents of French and Belgian nuns would henceforth be classified as "communities of pious women."[2] The emphasis on cloistral practices in canon law prescriptions and definitions for religious women was reflected in the constitutions or formal role definitions of communities established in America between 1829 and 1859. Two types of cloistral practice greatly affected the daily lives of sisters.

Prayer

The first had to do with the custom, common in houses of contemplative nuns, of rising at midnight to chant matins and lauds, the official night prayers of the Divine Office of the Church. A variation on this was the practice of taking turns spending hours of the night in the chapel praying, either every night or one night a week. These customs, though suitable perhaps in convents in which prayer was the chief work of charity, caused great hardship when pursued by sisters engaged in active works like teaching or nursing. A concomitant of this strong emphasis on prayer was the provision for silence during most of the day. Among the communities whose constitutions imposed obligations of this kind were the Columbus Dominicans, the Oldenburg Franciscans, the Sisters of Loretto, Amityville Dominicans, School Sisters of Notre Dame, Benedictines, and Sisters of the Precious Blood.[3]

Enclosure

The second type of cloistral regulation which affected the lives of most religious women was the rule of enclosure, which provided that no sister could go out of her convent without permission of the bishop (if she was under simple vows) or the pope (if her vows were solemn), nor could strangers be admitted. A whole system of observances grew out of this emphasis on separation from the world. A grille separated the convent proper from the parlor in which visitors might sit, and divided the sisters' chapel from the public church. Sometimes a separate side choir for the sisters would be added to the church.[4] The convent, church, and school had to be built in such close proximity that the sisters could teach and fulfill their religious obligations without ever leaving their enclosure.[5]

Sisters without a private chaplain could go to the parish church for Sunday Mass only if they had the express permission of the bishop. The sisters could not speak to their students outside the classroom, nor could they accompany them to the parish church for religious exercises, or have anything to do with their playground activities. Surveillance during recess periods was carried on from the windows of school or convent.[6] In some communities school affairs could not be discussed with other teachers within the convent precincts.[7] Several communities were forbidden until the 1960's to enter stores.[8] Others forbade members to visit their

own homes.[9]

Communities like those of the Sisters of Charity of

Nazareth and of Emmitsburg, whose constitutions were based on those

of St. Vincent de Paul, were not ordinarily hampered by cloistral

prescriptions. St. Vincent, aware that the active works of charity

which he envisioned for his sisters were incompatible with the

cloistral prescriptions of the Church, had specifically stated that

his "Daughters of Charity" were not "religious," in the strict

meaning of that term, and contrasted their lives with those of women

who were. Ordinarily, he wrote, his sisters have

> no monastery but the houses of the sick, no cell but a
> hired room, no cloister but the streets of the city or
> the wards of hospitals, no enclosure but obedience,
> no grate but the fear of God, no veil but holy
> modesty . . . .[10]

The Countess de la Rochejacquelin, noble patroness of the Sisters

of St. Joseph in France, in urging Bishop Rosati to bring these

sisters into the diocese of St. Louis, stressed their lack of

cloister as a characteristic which particularly qualified them for

the American frontier.[11]

Other

In addition to the regulation of prayer life and of

cloistral practices, a community's constitutions also specified how

it would be governed. Many groups were under the jurisdiction of

an ecclesiastical superior, who was appointed by and responsible

to the bishop. Among them were the Nazareth Sisters of Charity,

the Loretto Sisters, and the Emmitsburg Sisters of Charity prior to

their affiliation with France. Some, like the Mercy Sisters and
the Josephites, were directly under the local bishop. Foundations
which had been established from Europe such as the School Sisters
of Notre Dame, the Sisters of Notre Dame de Namur, the Sisters of
Providence, and the Religious of the Sacred Heart, continued, at
least for a time, to be governed from the European motherhouse.
Members of orders which also had men's branches often looked to
them for leadership, among them the Dominican, Benedictine,
Precious Blood and Holy Cross Sisters.

A community's constitutions also limited the type of work
which its members could engage in. The Sisters of Mercy were to
work among the poor, as were the Sisters of Notre Dame de Namur.[12]
The Sisters of Charity, after their affiliation with France, leaned
more towards hospitals and orphan asylums than towards schools.[13]
The Sisters of Notre Dame de Namur, Ursulines, and many others did
not teach older boys.[14] Other aspects of a community's life which
were regulated by its constitutions were the formula for the profession of vows and prescriptions regarding them, ascetical practices, and the daily schedule.

The wearing of a religious habit or some type of uniform
dress was another one of the Church's requirements for nuns which
was reflected in the constitutions of individual communities. These
habits often originated in European countries as the simple dress
of the poor, or that worn by widows of the upper classes. What was
worn by the foundress usually became standard for women who joined
her community decades or even centuries later. The veil, which had
originally signified a woman's unavailability for marriage, was

sometimes perpetuated in the garb of the sister long after a changing culture had forgotten its earlier significance. That the veil was reserved for enclosed nuns, not those engaged in active works, is implied in the statement of St. Vincent de Paul quoted above. That this was actually the custom in France at the time is indicated in the memoirs of an Irish Mercy Sister who nursed with Florence Nightingale in the Crimean War. She tells of the reactions when her party stopped at a hotel in Boulogne, France for lunch on their way to the Crimea: "The host and hostess got quite beside themselves at having fifteen veiled Nuns in their house. It appears that all of the French veiled Nuns are cloistered."[15]

Since the veil did not have the significance in nineteenth-century America that it had in some countries of Europe, it was appropriate that American communities should choose not to wear it. Most wore a simple garb not unlike that of their contemporaries, save for its plainness. A cap or bonnet superseded the veil. Among the groups which followed this practice were these: Mercy Sisters of Charleston, Franciscans, Holy Cross Sisters, Sisters of Charity of Emmitsburg, Nazareth and Leavenworth and Precious Blood Sisters.[16]

Many aspects of these constitutional provisions, which had their basis in the norms of canon law, were bound to cause difficulties when sisters tried to live them in a new environment very different from that for which they had been intended. We have discussed the formal role definitions set down for sisters in canon law and in their constitutions. Now let us examine the roles which the sisters actually played in American society in the decades before the Civil War.

Roles Sisters Played

European Attitudes and Manners

It is to be expected that the twenty-eight communities which were established in America from European motherhouses would be characterized by strongly European customs and manners. The same would be true, though to a lesser extent, of the communities which originated in America, but whose membership contained a high percentage of immigrants. French, German, or Irish backgrounds conferred many advantages upon groups working among immigrants from those countries, but increased the difficulties when interaction with native Americans or immigrants from other countries was attempted.

Aside from their language, the most notable European trait of these sisters was their class consciousness--a trait which often aroused hostile reactions from Americans who stressed equality (of white men, at least) in the pre-Civil War decades. It was so pervasive that it must be considered an important aspect of the role which sisters played in America during this period.

This class-consciousness was built into the structure of communities which had two classes of members, choir sisters (who possessed some degree of education and chanted the office prayers of the Church, often in Latin) and lay sisters (who had less education, were often from the lower class, and performed the menial work). The "Frau" often wore a habit different in some details from that of the "Schwester." (Among the Mercy Sisters, for example, those of the lower class did not wear trains on their habits.)[17]

The communities themselves were often ranked as upper-class or lower-class according to the social stratum from which the majority of their members came, and the status of the people among whom they worked. The Visitandines, Ursulines, Religious of the Sacred Heart, and Irish Mercy Sisters were connected in the popular and ecclesiastical minds with the upper classes, while the Sisters of Charity were thought to be daughters of "the people," as were the members of most other indigenous American communities.[18] However, many of the communities which were associated with the upper classes also provided schools and other works of charity for the poor. Thus an American writer could say of nuns of the pre-Civil War era:

> [The Religious of the Sacred Heart] educate the daughters of the rich in the most elegant and fashionable manner; but they also keep free schools for the poor, which is the rule with most of the religious orders. In the suburbs of Mobile there is a beautifully situated Convent of the Visitation, in which the belles of Alabama are educated in a quiet retreat . . . .[19]

Bishop Hughes wrote on November 22, 1847 to Mother Hardey of the Religious of the Sacred Heart regarding the school her sisters planned to open in New York, "When Madame Gelitzin arrived here it was deemed most expedient to commence in the city, and the price of tuition was put at rather a high rate, with a view at once to secure the attendance of what are called the better classes, and at the same time not to injure the other schools."[20]

The Mercy Sisters did not accept candidates from the ranks of the very poor, because it was thought they could not possess the requisite qualities. Bishop Michael O'Connor of Pittsburgh recognized the fact that education confers a certain superiority,

and cautioned Bishop Purcell in 1845:

> You are aware that the duties of the Sisterhood of
> Mercy require them to be fit to teach adults and
> assume in their regard a very responsible position,
> one where they need not only the respect which virtue
> alone can win, but one also which cannot be acquired
> when a certain degree of education and dignity of
> manner are not possessed.[21]

When Bishop England brought the Ursulines to Charleston,

it was for the specific purpose of educating the higher classes of

society, but "his measures and the high order of Catholic civili-

zation introduced, were in advance of the backward state of socie-

ty."[22] In contrast, the community of Mercy Sisters which England

founded for Charleston was to "provide for the solid and plain

education of those young females whose means do not permit, and

whose prospects do not require attention to the higher accomplish-

ments of their sex."[23]

Bishop James Roosevelt Bayley, a nephew of Mother Seton,

wrote to Archbishop Purcell in 1858, "Most of the people in this

Diocese [Newark] , are plain simple people, and we have no need as

yet of such religious communities as the Ursulines or Visitation

nuns. The Sisters of Charity would suit our purpose best . . . .

What I want is the plain, old-fashioned Mother Seton Sisters

. . . ."[29] Bishop Chanche, however, wrote to Purcell regarding th

union of the Emmitsburg Sisters with the French Daughters of

Charity, "It will give them a more elevated standing in the

Church."[25]

Aristocratic manners, attitudes, and expectations were re-

vealed by European sisters in various ways. When the School Sisters of Notre Dame arrived at St. Mary's, Pennsylvania in 1847, they were dismayed to find that the pupils they were to teach were poor children in tattered garments, not at all like those from refined families whom they had taught in Bavaria.[26] French Sisters of Providence hesitated to lie down on the straw ticks which had been spread on the floor to accommodate women on their Cincinnati-bound steamboat. Finally the superior, having prayed for the grace to bear this humiliation, settled herself for the night on one of the mats, and bade her sisters join her. The whole procedure aroused the mockery of amused American passengers.[32]

French sisters also found it difficult to accustom themselves to the simple manners of American priests. One who traveled in the same carriage with some Ursulines on their way to Ohio in 1845, was amazed to learn that they had accused him of advances meant to dissuade them from their vocations. His saying that he would visit one of them on her vow day was apparently the basis for the charge. He wrote to Bishop Purcell complaining of "this rather hasty condemnation of the good Ursulines fresh from France with all their ideas of French ecclesiastical manners strong in their minds," and attributed the whole affair to "their own notions of manners and their own interpretations of a look--a very doubtful sort of testimony."[28]

The extreme sensitivity of the French sisters of the time is exemplified in an incident recorded of Sisters of Notre Dame de Namur. When the ship taking them to America was delayed for a month, the sailors broke forth in violent language. One Fleming so shocked the only sister who could understand him that she fell into a melancholy and cast a gloom over the whole group. Because her mental collapse seemed imminent, she was sent home before the ship embarked for America.[29] (An interesting explanation of the peculiar mentality of nineteenth-century French Catholics is given by Ida Gorres in The Hidden Face.)[30]

The Sisters of Providence were shocked when their chaplain proposed hearing their confessions in the parlor of their backwoods convent, without benefit of confessional or surplice.[31] They were even more surprised when the bishop, who had been faultlessly attired for his visit to their motherhouse, appeared dressed like any other man of the Indiana woods, sunburnt, dusty, and with dry mud on his clothes.[32] Several other priests whom they had known in France pained them when they appeared in the flat lie-down collar and black string tie of the laity, which was worn by all American priests before 1884. The sisters noted sadly that the priests had exchanged the "joyous grace of France" for the "chilly manner of the Americans."[33]

Class consciousness also revealed itself in the sisters' dealings with students and domestic help, and evoked an immediate reaction from American girls who had entered the community. Later generations of European nuns reacted to Americans in much the same way that the Religious of the Sacred Heart had in an earlier period. "I am not sure whether I told you of the insupportable pride of the Americans," wrote Mother Theodore Guerin to her French superior.

> When dinner time came, there was my washerwoman sitting down at table with us. I was so indiscreet as to say it would be better for her not to take her dinner with the Community. I wish you could have seen the change in the countenances of our American postulants! . . .

> The mere name of "servant" makes them revolt, and
> they throw down whatever they have in their hands and
> start off at once.[34]

The American emphasis on the independence, dignity, and

importance of each individual and his ability to determine the

direction of his own life was incompatible with the European idea

of the superior as a monarch, to whom all should submit the total

control of their lives. Mother Guerin noted the basic incompati-

bility between the values of European religious life and those which

Americans imbibed from their earliest years. She assumed that the

American values would have to be given up by those who wished to

become religious, and did her best to see that they were. The

reactions she wrote to her French superiors reflect those of many

other European sisters as well:

> Nothing is more odious in America than the office of
> superior, for from it flow dependence and submission,
> virtues which the Americans do not recognize. To
> bear the name of superior in the United States of
> America is to acquire the inalienable right to the
> public hatred, contempt, and so forth. This pre-
> vailing attitude is due to the republican education
> given to the children. All our postulants have it
> on coming to us . . . .[35]

Later she reported, "The postulants are becoming gentle, confiding,

humble, and submissive," but she had to add, "as far as could be

expected of Americans."[36]

Perceptive European sisters like Mother Guerin noticed

some of the same differences in attitudes towards women that

Tocqueville commented on in Democracy in America. "A woman in this

country is never seen transacting the least business, religious no

more than others," she wrote in 1842. "Eyes are opened wide at

Terre Haute and everywhere when I appear to pay bills or to make

purchases. Everyone is astonished."[37] By 1851 there were hints
of a change in this attitude, as she noted in a letter to a French
bishop: "Women are not employed in any kind of business in America.
It is said that in the East they are beginning to take up the French
way, but as yet, we are strangers to this movement in our Woods.[38]

Teaching

Other important roles in which sisters interacted with
society flowed from the works of charity which they performed. Most
communities established in America in the pre-Civil War period,
whatever the works prescribed for them by their constitutions,
opened schools to meet the needs of the Church and their own financial need.[39] The free school for the poor was carried on side by
side with the select school, often called an academy, in which the
more well-to-do paid tuition. The boarding school provided education for those whose homes were at a distance from other educational facilities.

These schools, even those run by American sisters, were influenced by European customs. The administrative structure of the
academies was largely French.[40] Almost every one of them was near
a college staffed by European teachers, and was under the direction
of a priest who had fled the French Revolution.[41] The first immigrant sisters brought the spirit of European humanism with its love
for art and scholarship into the frontier schools of America, and
passed it on to the teachers who would come after them.[42] The
weekly awarding of points, oral examinations at the end of each
session, and the solemn distribution of prizes at the end of the

year were taken over from the French system.[43] Often European

sisters brought with them knowledge and experience of the latest

European educational trends. Sister Antonia of the Oldenburg

Franciscans, for example, was familiar with the best Swiss schools.

Coming to America only twenty-five years after the death of

Pestalozzi, she must have brought extensive knowledge of his ideas

and methods and those of his disciples.[44]

One advantage of the sisters' academies was the opportunity

they offered to learn foreign languages, particularly French, from

native speakers. A comment about the Georgetown Visitation Academy

reveals a typical attitude: "The languages are taught here with

great accuracy, and with a pure, lady-like, and natural accent,

the charm of polished society."[45] This is echoed in a letter from

Mr. F.J. Flanagan of New York to the Directress of Studies at St.

Mary's, Bertrand, written in 1853:

> In her studys [sic] as named on the list, I desire
> no alteration except as regards the study of French,
> which I consider very necessary and useful, to be
> familiar and thoroughly acquainted with, in our con-
> nection with the world, independent of my liking the
> language itself for its beauty of softness . . . .
> I have always thought that the earlier the conveniences
> to learn to speak French, the better, provided the
> teacher is French by birth and education.[46]

Sometimes adherence to European methods in American schools

was considered an important aspect of the sisters' unity with the

motherhouse from which they had come. Thus Mother Ignatius, SND,

wrote from Namur to her sisters in Cincinnati, "I hope that you

are very careful . . . to introduce in your classes our method of

teaching."[47]

Though the Old World influence was strong in the sisters'
schools, there were also distinctly American ideas about education
to which the sisters had to conform if their schools were to
succeed. Newcomers to America were often amazed at the broad curriculum which was demanded by the Americans, particularly the emphasis
on music. Mother Guerin reported of the Sisters of Charity at
Frederick,

> They teach the various sciences scarcely known in our
> French schools, but they excel in music, which is an
> indispensible thing in this country, even for the poor.
> No piano, no pupils! Such is the spirit of this
> country--Music and Steam! At Frederick, of the five
> Sisters, three teach piano and guitar.[48]

Another observer wrote from Notre Dame in 1848, "I understand why
Father Sorin asked with such entreaty for a musician. In America
one hears everywhere of nothing but music. Whoever has ever so
little a fortune cannot do without a piano or some other instru-
ment."[49] Irish priests were amazed to find a sister teaching advanced subjects to women in Madison, Indiana, but she pointed out
to them that this was part of the American system, to which the
sisters had conformed.[50]

The sisters' academies offered terminal education in which
both the Classics and practical training (chiefly domestic arts)
were important.[51] What Sister Maria Concepta found in her study
of the Bertrand Academy was probably true of many of these schools
of the pre-Civil War era:

> From the prospectus of 1851 it is clear that the
> curriculum included those subjects most frequently
> taught in established schools of the East. Bertrand
> had a course of study comparable to that which
> Elsbree describes as used in the common schools of
> Cincinnati in 1848 . . . . In the first curriculum

of the academy there were included the fifteen
highest scored subjects which Woody found offered
in female seminaries (162 institutions) from 1742
to 1871.[52]

Courtesy, refinement, and good manners were also stressed
in many of these schools. As a description of the Georgetown
Visitation Academy published in 1830 states,

[The sisters] care and watchfulness are so sisterly
and maternal, that the pupil is naturally moulded, not
drilled, to good manners. Discipline is constantly
going on even in those hours of relaxation in which
girls left to themselves often acquire an awkwardness
of manners that cleaves to them for the whole course
of their lives. Such schools are rare. The Ursulines
have just opened one on the same plan, near Boston.[53]

In addition to the Classics and the arts, the sisters' schools also
taught what one admirer called "the profound ethics and the sublime
doctrines of the Christian religion."[54]

A few communities, the Josephites of St. Louis and the
Charleston Ursulines for example, taught Negroes in a separate
school or after regular school hours. Most of these classes were
short-lived because violence was threatened by mobs who preferred,
in an era of abundant abolitionist literature, to keep the slaves
illiterate. The Ursulines of Charleston had to stop their instruction of Negro children because it was against state law.[55] The
Oblate Sisters of Providence and the Sisters of the Holy Family,
two Negro communities founded during this period, engaged in various
charitable works in the Black community.

In some states, Indiana for example, the legislature provided that a township might recognize a private school as the public
school of the town. When the private school was one staffed by
sisters, they were then certified and reimbursed by the school

authorities as public school teachers. This was true in the case
of the Oldenburg Franciscans and the Sisters of Providence in
Indiana.[56] The Lowell Plan provided public funds for the salaries
of lay teachers in Catholic schools in Boston, and the Columbus
Dominicans taught in the district school of Somerset, Ohio.[57]

In addition to their teaching, sisters played an important
role in staffing orphanages during this period. Epidemics, deaths
in childbirth, and the various misfortunes which befell immigrants
left many children homeless. Bishops were hard-pressed to provide
for these needy members of their flocks, but they feared the proselytizing that was common in orphanages not under Catholic auspices. Sisters of many communities were called upon to staff
orphanages and they responded with alacrity to this need of the
Church.

Nursing

Another role played by sisters in the pre-Civil War generation was that of nursing, in private homes, almshouses, and hospitals. Most groups, and particularly the Sisters of Mercy, included visits to the sick among their regular works of charity.
Crises like the cholera and yellow fever epidemics which ravaged
the country in 1832-34, 1849-50, and 1855 involved all but the most
strictly cloistered communities in the nursing of the suffering.
During the first of these epidemics the Sisters of Charity nursed
in hospitals, private homes, and almshouses in St. Louis, New
Orleans, Philadelphia, Baltimore, Boston, New York, and Washington,
D.C. They served as nurses to all, regardless of creed, again in

1849-50, offering the city the use of their hospital in Buffalo and valiantly responding when the mayor of Milwaukee asked them to nurse a boatload of Norwegians and Swedes stricken with typhoid.[59] The Charleston Sisters of Mercy went from street to street and alley to alley to nurse during the epidemics of the 1850's. Often people called them to the sickbed even before consulting a doctor, so highly was their skill esteemed.[60] The Sisters battled yellow fever in the South for fifty years and assisted in the especially virulent outbreak of 1855 at Norfolk and Portsmouth. During this epidemic the sisters did not limit themselves to work in emergency hospitals and patients' homes, but also nursed on shipboard when that became necessary.[61] The Mercy Sisters who arrived in California from Ireland in 1854 were the only people on the West coast who had experience in nursing cholera when it broke out there the following year. Thanks to their knowledge of the proper remedies, they were able to save hundreds of lives.[62] The Josephite Sisters in St. Paul nursed victims up and down the Mississippi during the summer cholera seige of 1854.[63]

Sisters were often asked to take over the administration of public hospitals, infirmaries, and almshouses during periods of great need. They also continued the practice begun in 1823 of opening hospitals of their own. Approximately twenty-five Catholic hospitals were opened between 1829 and 1860, the Sisters of Charity being responsible for eighteen of them.[64]

Other Works

Various other works occupied members of particular communities during this period. The Sisters of Mercy opened a House of Protection for girls of good character in New York in the 1850's. The Sisters of the Good Shepherd worked to reform delinquent girls. They established houses at Louisville, Philadelphia, St. Louis, New York, Chicago, Cincinnati, and New Orleans. When they began their New York house, Archbishop Hughes did not encourage, but only tolerated them. Like many other Irishmen, he thought it impossible to reform a woman who had lost "the glory of her womanhood." The Sisters of Our Lady of Charity of the Refuge did work of the same kind, opening a house at Buffalo in 1855.[65] Homes for the aged were opened by sisters in New Orleans in 1842, Philadelphia in 1849, and Buffalo in 1855.[66]

Some groups of sisters did the domestic work in seminaries and colleges run by priests. The Holy Cross Sisters worked in the laundry and infirmary at Notre Dame, while the Milwaukee Franciscans did the cooking, farmwork, etc. for St. Francis Seminary and were often called "seminary maids" by those who observed them.[67] This practice is another which seems to have stemmed from European origins. Bishop James Roosevelt Bayley wrote, in 1856, to the head of a community, "I propose opening a College at Madison [New Jersey] . . . and am very anxious to obtain some Religious to take charge of the Infirmary and domestic arrangements, as is the custom in France."[68] (New York Sisters of Charity answered his call.)

Problems Posed by the American Milieu

Restrictive Constitutions

As has been noted above, the constitutions of each community prescribed in detail the manner in which canon law prescriptions would be implemented in the daily lives of its members. Many prescriptions reflected the cultural milieu in which the founder had lived. Others embodied attitudes of the even earlier period when the various Roman decrees, forerunners of the Tridentine ones, were first enacted. When the sisters who had promised to live according to such constitutions or formal role definitions attempted to do so in pre-Civil War America, they experienced a cultural clash which engendered severe tensions and seemed, at times, to threaten the very existence of the religious community. Solutions had to be found before the traditional forms of Roman Catholic religious life in community would be feasible in America.

Since all phases of religious life--prayer, the vows, enclosure, works of charity, clothing, and finances--were regulated by constitutions, constant problems arose regarding them. Bishops and pastors were acutely aware of the needs of the Church and the lack of personnel. To them, it seemed more important to serve the needy through education, nursing, care of orphans, etc. than to follow the minute details of a rule compiled for another country and another age. Therefore the bishops were constantly urging the sisters to adapt their constitutions, expand their works, and step outside their cloisters to aid the people who needed them.

In the constitutions of some communities there was provision for adaptation on the local level. Angela Merici, foundress
of the Ursulines, had cautioned her sisters to remain flexible in
order to serve the changing needs of the Church. Those of her
daughters who took this advice seriously had no trouble in adapting
to American ways. But any permanent change in constitutional prescriptions requires the permission of higher authorities, of the
bishop and sometimes of Rome. This is a safeguard to insure uni-
formity and preservation of a common spirit among houses that might
be widely scattered geographically. When bishops, pastors, and
the sisters themselves realized that adaptations had to be made to
meet American conditions, tensions ensued, and relations among
bishops, pastors, sisters, and motherhouse officials were strained.
While there was no doubt that bishops had jurisdiction over the
Church's works of charity within their dioceses, the extent of their
jurisdiction was not spelled out. They resented it when motherhouse
superiors, either in Europe or in other American dioceses, regulated
the sisters under them in a way that was detrimental to the work
of the Church in their dioceses. Mother Seton's last counsel to
her sisters, "Be children of the Church," embodied an essential
definition of what a sister should be. There were communities, however, among whom the aim seemed instead to be the exact imitation
of St. Vincent de Paul or of some other founder or foundress.

Bishops sometimes insisted on governing communities according to their own ideas, even though they had read and agreed to
uphold the constitutions which strictly limited the areas in which
bishops could validly interfere in the lives of the sisters. The

sisters were placed in a difficult position between bishops who
insisted on adaptation, and community superiors who maintained
that salvation depended on adherence to the constitutions according
to which sisters had made their vows. When superiors refused to
allow adaptation to American conditions, or when it became obvious
that the great distance made government by European motherhouses
extremely impractical, American houses often responded by breaking
completely with the motherhouse and becoming autonomous. Sometimes
European superiors themselves saw the wisdom of making American
houses independent, and insisted that this be done. Among some
communities it was the practice for daughter houses to become autonomous as soon as they were financially independent. Where there
was great emphasis on loyalty to the European motherhouse, and at
least a minimum of adaptation to new conditions, ties with Europe
were kept. This was the case with the Religious of the Sacred
Heart, as was indicated above in Chapter III. In communities of
this kind, American sisters often chafed under the yoke of in-
sufficient adaptation, and many Americans who entered the communities left because they did not care to live a form of religious life
that was unsuited to their temperaments.[69]

Ironically, while European forms of religious life were
being adapted to meet American conditions, the reverse trend,
which was evident among indigenous American communities from the
beginning, continued to make itself felt in succeeding decades.
The practice of looking to Europe for models of excellence while
despising native creations, against which Emerson spoke so strongly,
was as prevalent within cloister walls as it was without. The

priests who directed the American communities continued, during this period, the effort to make them like the "real" religious houses of Europe, an effort which would plague American communities through the 1960's. These attempts often evoked strong resistance from the sisters themselves. Sometimes they were successful in keeping their communities' distinctly American approach to the needs of the local church; sometimes they failed.

In order to understand the many ways in which constitutions had to be adapted before communities could provide useful servants for the American Church, it is necessary to examine in some detail the cultural clashes which arose over the vows, prayer life, cloistral practices, habit, works of charity, government, finances, and other aspects of the sisters' lives.

The Vows

The status of the vows of American sisters was in question for several decades because of the decree of 1803 which stipulated that the vow of poverty of French and Belgian nuns was simple rather than solemn. What was the status of the vows of members of these communities who had come to America, and of those who had joined the American branches of these communities? If their vows were solemn, they would be subject to strict papal enclosure, which could be dispensed only by the pope. Violation of the cloister would result in automatic excommunication. A woman under solemn vows could not validly possess private property or contract marriage.[70] A girl who changed her mind after taking solemn vows, and wished to be released from them, would have great difficulty in obtaining an

official dispensation from the pope. Various American bishops
submitted queries to Rome as problems arose which they felt themselves incapable of solving. Many years passed before Rome gave a
final decision on this question, which held serious implications for
the daily lives of nuns.

In 1843 Bishop Rosati of St. Louis sought a decision from
Rome regarding the vows of the Religious of the Sacred Heart and
the Visitandines. He proposed three reasons for questioning their
profession of solemn vows: cloister could not be completely observed because of the admittance into the enclosure of little girls
and others; civil laws did not recognize the effects of the vow of
poverty; there was no coercive force recognized by American civil
law which could prevent nuns from leaving the convent after their
profession.[71] In its reply to Rosati's query, Rome ruled that the
vows of the Religious of the Sacred Heart were simple and their
enclosure episcopal.[72] As for the Visitandines, they posed a problem which did not admit of a simple solution. Propaganda requested
that the American bishops be polled regarding their vows. Rosati's
death in Rome on September 25, 1843 postponed the resolution of the
question.

In 1854 the uncertainty regarding the vows of nuns in
America was again brought to the attention of the Propaganda by
Archbishop F.P. Kenrick. He wrote asking about the vows of the
Visitandines, and requesting faculties for dispensing from these
vows and those of the Carmelites.[73] When the Rev. T.J. O'Toole
wrote a year later requesting a dispensation for a Visitandine, the
reply was sent to Archbishop Kenrick. He responded with a further

discussion of the vows.[74] In 1856 all the Visitandine superiors in
the country presented a joint petition to Rome, and a former Visitandine who wished to marry brought the question to the fore again
in 1857. Rome considered it "rei gravitate perspecta," and sought
the opinions of the Provincial Synods of the Cincinnati and
Baltimore archdioceses.[75]

On October 26, 1857, Archbishop John Purcell of Cincinnati
received a letter from Cardinal Barnabo, Prefect of Propaganda Fide,
"asking the advice of all our Prelates as to the nature of the vows
made by visitation nuns--are they solemn or simple?" Purcell wrote
to his fellow bishops requesting their opinions and noted, "The
greatest uncertainty exists as to the binding force of vows not
only of visitation nuns, but of all the religious communities in
the country."[76] Because this question of formal role definitions
for American nuns touched upon important aspects of their lives and
works, it is of more than merely academic interest for the purposes
of this dissertation.

The bishops' replies reflect the confusion that existed and
reveal contradictory opinions about the compatability between traditional religious practices and the American form of government.

Bishop Frederic Baraga of Sault Ste. Marie noted this in-
compatability, as Mother Guerin had earlier:

> I always considered the vows of the Nuns of the
> Visitation as solemn vows, which no power on earth,
> not even that of the Sovereign Pontiff can dissolve,
> according to some Theologians; others say that he
> can, but he alone. In this respect, according to
> my belief, the Church of God makes no difference
> between Europe, America, etc. Wherever this order
> exists, its vows are solemn and indissoluble. The
> only difference is that in this country almost

> every mind even of religious persons is
> imbibed [sic] with such a spirit of liberty,
> that they are induced to think that these
> religious obligations might not be so stringent
> in America as in Europe.[77]

To Baraga, the values of European religious life were absolutes

which must be adhered to by all who wished to join a religious

community.

From Vincennes Bishop Maurice de St. Palais wrote that the

vows were solemn, and nothing in the civil laws of the United States

interfered with the conditions required for their accomplishment.[78]

Bishop Martin J. Spalding, on the other hand, felt that Rome should

be asked to restrict solemn vows as much as possible in America,

because of civil conditions.[79] Archbishop Kenrick of Baltimore

wrote, "As the Holy See granted the Sisters of the Visitation leave

to make solemn vows at Georgetown, and subsequently in the other

convents, I regard them as such. The concessions are on record."[80]

Bishop Louis A. Rappe of Cleveland was uncertain and sugges-

ted that the matter be sent to Rome for an opinion. "In this

country," he remarked, "where government is entirely a stranger to

the matter, religious can make such engagements as they please."[81]

The bishop of New Orleans, Anthony Blanc, felt that the Visitandines

did not fulfill the requirements for solemn vows, and therefore

their vows were not solemn.[82]

From Detroit Bishop Peter Paul Lefevere wrote, "There are

no religious either male or female of any order established in the

United States, the nature of whose vows can be properly called

solemn according to the strict sense of the word." He suggested

that the question be discussed at the next provincial council.[83]

In a formal note he listed four reasons why Visitandine vows could not be solemn.[84]

The matter was discussed at the Ninth Provincial Council of Baltimore, which opened on May 2, 1858. Archbishop Francis Kenrick reported the result to Purcell, who was not present: "The vows of the Visitation Nuns were deemed solemn, but there was no decided or unanimous action as to the expedience of continuing to take solemn vows, although the matter is submitted to the Holy See."[85]

On May 9, 1858 a letter from the Provincial Council reported the results of the discussion to the pope and asked whether solemn vows should be taken in the future in America. The bishops saw no reason why they should not be.[86] However, a rescript of Propaganda Fide of August 5, 1858, which was apparently in response to the letter from the provincial council, echoed Mother Guerin and Bishop Baraga in its recognition of the incompatibility of American values and European practice:

> The character of the [American] people and their laws
> and customs favor liberty; therefore it hardly seems
> expedient that solemn vows should be taken, because it
> often happens that girls change their minds and wish
> to leave and cannot be detained for fear of the people;
> citizens, in fact, storm the convents and demand the
> girls' freedom.[87]

It was perhaps after receiving this rescript that Archbishop Kenrick, who had been chairman of the provincial council, wrote another letter to Rome, reporting that many prelates and priests felt that solemn vows should be taken in the future by American nuns.[88] Pope Pius IX then appointed a special commission to study the question of solemn vows in America. The members differed among themselves in their opinions and the reasons for them. The final decision was not given

until 1864; hence it will be discussed in the next chapter. This
is only an outline of the phases through which the inquiry passed
before the question regarding Visitandine vows was finally answered.
With such confusion as to the roles of nuns among the highest Church
authorities, and a prevailing opinion that American values were
detrimental to the full living of the religious life, it is no wonder that tensions and disagreements marked the sisters' attempts
to live out their roles in America.

Prayer Life

The confusion over the type of vows which could be taken in
America, and hence the type of enclosure which bound sisters there,
extended into all areas of their lives. Were they primarily contemplatives, who devoted much of their time to prayer, or was there
to be a greater emphasis on works of charity? The combination of
long hours of prayer with strenuous activities for the neighbor
had caused severe tension in the first American religious houses
for women; it continued to plague them in this second period. Many
communities, finding adherence to their constitutions extremely
difficult, and even detrimental to health, were forced to re-examine
their goals in view of American needs, and decided that their constitutions had to be modified if they were to successfully cope with
the new situations they faced. Like the first American sisters,
those of this period sought permission from Rome to alter their
constitutions, thus bringing their formal role definitions into
line with the informal ones which they had of necessity taken on.
Dispensations were sought from the extended hours of prayer and the

cloistral practices which flowed from the strict observance of cloister.

The Dominican Sisters of Ohio, Kentucky, and Tennessee, finding it extremely difficult to adhere to their regime of midnight prayer, teaching, and housework, sent a letter to Pope Pius IX asking to be relieved of the burden of the midnight prayers of the Divine Office and to give up once and for all the idea of enclosure behind a grille, which had continued to be an ideal for some. The sisters could see that solemn enclosure, were it ever carried out, would mean giving up many of the pupils who were benefitting from their care. It was several years before they actually obtained the adaptations which they sought.[89] The California Dominican Sisters substituted the little office for the Divine Office in 1852, because of the small number of sisters and the demands on their time.[90]

The School Sisters of Notre Dame also found midnight prayer, coupled with the arduous work of the classroom, a burden which sapped their strength. When three of the Milwaukee sisters died in 1857, a physician was consulted, and it was decided that the constitutions should be modified.[91] The Benedictine Sisters petitioned, in 1858, to substitute the Office of the Blessed Virgin, which did not require rising at midnight, for the Divine Office, as the Dominicans also had.[92] The first petition to Rome was ignored, but a later one was granted. The Sisters of the Precious Blood attempted to do farm work in addition to teaching and nocturnal adoration, and soon discovered that their health could not withstand the strain.

Cloistral Practices

Rules aimed at keeping sisters from crossing the threshold
of their convents were not only inconvenient; they were detrimental
to the best interests of the Church in America. The practices
described above (p. 82ff) which flowed from canon law legislation
regarding enclosure caused particularly serious difficulties for
American nuns. They had been devised as a means of keeping contemplative nuns, some of whom had been placed in convents against
their will, from leaving the precincts of their convents, and pre-
venting outsiders from entering. They were entirely unsuited to
sisters who had freely chosen to embrace the religious life and
who engaged in active works of charity outside their convents. In
a new country in which there were vast distances to cover, and few
priests, it was not always possible to assign a priest to say Mass
at a convent daily or even weekly. In the sale of city lots, it
was not always easy to acquire sufficient land to build a convent
next to church and school. Often there were no funds for buildings
of the type envisioned in canon law. A simple house in the neighborhood of the church might be the only convent available. Sisters
living in a particular convent might be asked to staff schools in
other sections of the city while continuing to live in the original
location. Heavily burdened bishops who saw urgent needs going un-
fulfilled because of outmoded customs and rules were understandably
angered. Many disputes with bishops and other members of the clergy
centered around cloistral prescriptions which were unsuited to
American conditions. The sisters were often torn between their
desire to serve the obvious needs of the local church and their

loyalty to the rules and superiors of a distant motherhouse.

Sisters who could not go beyond their convent precincts without the permission of the bishop--or perhaps the pope--were in a difficult position when a private chaplain was denied them. When the Religious of the Sacred Heart carried out the regulations from their French motherhouse which required the exclusion of day students from their boarding school, Bishop Lefevere refused to provide a chaplain, forcing them to go outside of their enclosure--and incur excommunication--if they wished to attend Mass. Mother Barat, the French foundress, protested vigorously, writing to him in 1853:

> Our constitutions . . . do not permit us to leave our enclosure either for Church services or for works of zeal . . . . I beg you to consider that it is not in my power to permit them to infringe their rules of enclosure, so that if you will not restore to them the spiritual help which is ordinarily granted, they will be placed under the necessity of giving up their mission in your diocese . . . . Your Lordship knows well that these rules have been wisely ordained, and that they are the safeguards of the religious spirit.[93]

The Visitandines had a similar experience in Ottumwa. When they refused to teach in the newly built parish school because they were "unwilling to compromise their constitution," the pastor refused to give them a chaplain, thus forcing them to leave their cloister to attend Mass.[94] Abbot Boniface Wimmer placed the pioneer Benedictines of Minnesota in the same position.[95] Thus cloister regulations gave ecclesiastical superiors a weapon which they could use in their attempts to force sisters to adapt their constitutions to American needs.

We see here the paradoxes which characterized the attitudes of sisters, ecclesiastical superiors, and bishops where adaptations

to the American milieu were concerned. Some sisters saw the need
for changes in their constitutions and worked to implement them.
Others felt that adherence to constitutions was more important
than adaptation to the American culture, and hence there were
differences of opinion among sisters over adaptation. Bishops were
often more concerned with the needs of the Church in their dioceses
than with the traditional practices of a particular community.
When they urged sisters to adapt, they found them unwilling to alter
their constitutions without the proper authorization.

Pastors learned to inquire about the rules followed by a
particular community before engaging them for their parish schools.
Thus Father John McElroy, S.J. wrote to Bishop Purcell from St.
Mary's, Boston in 1849, "I did not advert to it in my last but take
it for granted that the Sisters of Notre Dame can attend the Divine
Service in the Church, with their pupils, hear Mass in like manner
in the Church, as to do otherwise, or to have a private chapel in
their house would be attended with great difficulties with our
limited number of Priests.[96]

The uncertainty about whether their vows were simple or
solemn, their cloister episcopal or papal, is apparently what kept
Bishop Purcell from inviting the Ursulines in his diocese to staff
parish grade schools. If their vows were solemn, they would only
be allowed to teach within their cloister walls.[97] When Bishop
Rappe discovered that their constitutions would not allow the
Ursulines in his diocese to teach in schools outside their cloister,
he got Rome to dispense them from that part of their rules. Thereafter they traveled back and forth in a closed carriage to schools

in various parts of Cleveland.[98]

The question about the vows, and the fact that only those who professed solemn ones had strict enclosure and were true religious in the eyes of the Church, caused problems for individual sisters who wanted to be genuine religious rather than members of a half-caste group which was neither religious nor lay. Thus Immaculate Heart Sister Mary Whipple wrote a series of letters to Bishop Lefevere of Detroit in 1859 telling of her desire to belong to a "real" religious community, her fear for her salvation since she was neither a religious nor a secular.[99]

Religious superiors to whom the letter of the law was more important than its spirit were willing to forego the founding of new schools rather than modify their constitutions.[100] Others tried various expedients which allowed their sisters to adhere to the letter of the law while adapting to the needs of their apostolate. When the Sisters of the Incarnate Word and Blessed Sacrament decided to open a school for boys under twelve years of age, they bought a lot across the street from their convent, built a school on it, and then constructed a bridge from their convent to the school so that they could cross over the street without going out of their enclosure.[101] The sister-organist might accompany hymns from the sisters' side of the grille which separated convent from church, while the church choir sang from the parish side.[102]

Strict adherence to the letter of the law sometimes placed the sisters in ridiculous situations. A frontier convent which lacked a fence around its house and property, and hence had a cloister which extended only to the door sill, had a serious

problem when the woodpile at the door and window receded beyond
the reach of the nun with the longest arms. The sisters went without heat for a day and a night before aid came. Automatic excommunication would have been incurred by a sister who stepped outside to replenish the supply of wood.[103]

Perhaps the wisest expedient regarding enclosure was that
followed by Archbishop Murray of Ireland with the Sisters of Mercy
who had recently been founded there. Mother McAuley, in her manu-
script copy of the constitutions which would eventually be followed
by thousands of Mercy Sisters in America, had included a chapter
entitled "Enclosure." The archbishop, knowing that the active works
of mercy envisioned for the community were incompatible with traditional cloistral practices, struck out the entire chapter when
the rules were submitted for his approval.[104]

The Habit

Another regulation found in the constitutions of most
communities so endangered the lives of sisters in America that
there seems to have been little questioning, or referring to Rome
or to a European motherhouse, before deciding to disregard it. In
what concerned the religious habit, the distinctive uniform which
marked a sister as a member of a particular community, American
social and political conditions compelled the sisters to adapt, if
they wished to survive. And they did so with alacrity. (It is
interesting to note that, with some exceptions, the possibility of
being insulted was sufficient reason for adapting constitutions,
but the need of the local Church was not.)

In the period when nativism was strong, it became customary to reserve the religious habit for use within the convent precincts, and either disguise it or exchange if for ordinary clothing when traveling or walking the public streets.[105] Many sisters also wore lay dress on shipboard during their Atlantic crossing. These measures were considered necessary in order to avoid being spat upon, pelted with mud, or otherwise insulted and ridiculed, in an age when Catholicism and "nunneries" were looked upon with suspicion and sometimes loathing. The practice of donning secular dress, it will be recalled, had been introduced by the first American nuns, the Carmelites who arrived in 1790. They had no doubt learned its necessity during the French Revolution.

In New Orleans, the Ursulines advised all who stopped there to don a cap and the heavy veil of widows before proceeding up the Mississippi, so as to avoid being taken for escaped nuns.[106] The Sisters of St. Joseph added a black bonnet and cloak (later superseded by a shawl) to their regular habit for street wear.[107] Some of the Mercy Sisters wore long black cloaks and straw bonnets.[108] School Sisters of Notre Dame were not even allowed to wear the religious habit to cross the street from convent to school in Milwaukee. They found it expedient to curtain off a corner of the classroom for use as a dressing-room, where the sister-teacher could change from secular dress to habit and back again.[109] The lay dress chosen by the nuns was sometimes so outlandish that it caused more comment than the religious habit would have. Such was the case with the sisters of Notre Dame de Namur, who wore their night robes--loose "mother hubbards" of violet calico--topped by huge white sunbonnets, on a journey to California in 1851.[110]

Apparently the danger of injury was not always present.
The Sisters of Providence were recognized as nuns at each stage of
their journey from New York to Indiana, despite their secular
dress, but were treated with civility in every instance save one.[111]
A small number of sisters wore the religious habit on shipboard
during their voyage to America with no harmful consequences. The
Sisters of Providence disembarked in their habits in New York and
aroused only curiosity. "Every one who saw us seemed thunderstruck
or changed into a statue of salt like Lot's wife and stood staring
at us as if we were extraordinary beings," reported one of them.[112]

Three Ursulines who traveled from Cincinnati to a Brown
County (Ohio) convent in 1852 were the first of their community to
travel in religious garb. The annalist records, "No accident
happened to them."[113] The Visitandines who journeyed from Montluel,
France to Keokuk, Iowa in 1853 decided, despite warnings of bigotry,
to wear their habits during the entire trip. They were treated
courteously while on board ship, and attracted attention on the
streets when they went to Mass in New York. The newspapers applauded
them for their courage in wearing their unusual apparel. Later they
were told that they were the first nuns to wear religious garb
during the entire trip from Europe to their destination in America.[114]

In some instances American bishops wished to change the
style of the religious habit the sisters brought with them from
Europe, or replace it with lay dress in the convent as well as on
the street. To many of the sisters--and their superiors--this
meant tampering with one of the essentials of the religious life,

and they were adamant in their refusal to change.[115] Thus

Mother Guerin wrote from Indiana to her French superior in 1840:

> This holy habit, which we had given up, we resumed at
> Philadelphia to quit again. But at Vincennes we put
> it on again never to give it up, I hope . . . . This
> circumstance had caused trouble. Monseigneur wishes to
> make one change today, another tomorrow, but we have
> held firm, and nothing, absolutely nothing has been
> changed. In order that this may continue, we must have
> from France goods for habits and veils, our small
> crucifixes for the neck, and our chaplets.[116]

When the chaplain of the Oldenburg Franciscans suggested

that they wear simple secular dress for work and study, and reserve

the religious habit for prayer times, the foundress refused, saying

that giving up the religious habit meant relaxing religious dis-

cipline.[117] Mother Catherine Spalding's reply when Bishop Flaget

suggested that the Sisters of Charity of Nazareth change the color

of their cap from white to black, indicated the habit's symbolic

importance for the community's image:

> We attach little importance to the article of dress
> in itself, yet we think changes so striking as that
> which you propose in our cap, would be hazardous and
> calculated to arouse public observation, to elicit
> surmises and occasion prejudices which may be highly
> detrimental to Nazareth and perhaps to Religion in
> Kentucky. Had we worn the black cap for twenty-five
> years, as we have done the white one, we should feel
> equally reluctant to [make] so remarkable a change as
> that of the color; which undoubtedly would subject
> the community to animadversion and ridicule, and thus
> might tend to diminish public respect and confidence,
> which St. Vincent de Paul considered as most essential
> to the success of the Sisters' labors.[118]

A simple expedient of economy sometimes made the sisters set aside

the expensive medieval habit. In the early days of most of the

American communities the sisters or postulants wore whatever they

had brought with them, since money for uniform clothing was lacking.

During the depression of 1857, poverty forced the Benedictines to save their woolen habits for morning chapel services and wear calico dresses the rest of the day.[119]

Works of Charity

The particular works of charity set down in the constitutions of religious communities provided another source of tension and conflict. The Carmelites, a strictly contemplative community, had obtained a dispensation, during a period of great need, in order to open a school. When Archbishop Kenrick visited them twenty years later, he insisted that they give up the school and return to the works enjoined by their rules.[120]

When social needs called for adaptation, it was usually the bishop who urged that sisters expand their works beyond those envisioned by their foundresses, and the local superiors who resisted. When the first Mercy Sisters arrived in Pittsburgh from Ireland in 1843, and Bishop O'Connor asked them to open a boarding school for girls, Mother Warde hesitated. A work of this kind was not in accord with their constitutions, and might take too much of their time and energy from the poorer students whom they had come to serve. The bishop, convinced that the needs of the Church in his diocese superseded individual prescriptions of a rule drawn up to serve the needs of another country, wrote to Cardinal Barnabo in Rome. The cardinal agreed with him, pointing out that it was a work of mercy to instruct the ignorant, whether poor or rich.[121]

When Bishop Purcell offered the first Notre Dame sisters from Namur some property in an area that was inaccessible to the poor, the superior insisted that they must be assured of facilities for poor children, or return to Belgium. A narrator comments, "This was Sister Louis de Gonzague: rather leave the undertaking than fail in a point of the rule."[122] In Chicopee, Massachusetts, sisters of the same community opened a school, but closed it when a new pastor asked them to perform services not in accord with their established customs.[123]

Often when there were disputes over the type of work that was needed and the restrictions imposed by rules, a compromise was possible. Sometimes the dissenting community withdrew, and one with more reasonable or more flexible rules took its place. There were instances, however, when the sisters themselves were more moved by the needs of the American Church than by loyalty to outdated rules. Bishops resented the fact that motherhouse superiors in another diocese might have the power to limit the works of charity which sisters could staff within their dioceses. They took offense when capable sisters on whom they relied were removed from their positions and replaced by less competent personnel. Serious crises, in which both sides remained adamant, sometimes resulted in a permanent split within a community. Examples will be discussed below.

A point of dispute which became a central issue was the custom which decreed that sisters should have little to do with boys. Some communities clung to the letter of their constitutions, which described their work as the education of girls;[124] others would accept boys only up to a certain age. Very few communities taught boys beyond the age of ten or twelve.[125] The Sisters of the Incarnate Word took them up to age twelve.[126] Mercy Sisters of

Rhode Island did not teach boys in the upper grades until 1871.[127]

The Sisters of Notre Dame de Namur did not accept them above the

fourth grade until 1922.[128] When the Sisters of Charity took over

St. Mary's School in Philadelphia in 1833, one of the stipulations

was that no boy would be admitted after his ninth birthday.[129]

The "boy question" became a problem in the orphanages as

well as the schools, particularly among the Sisters of Charity of

Emmitsburg, who staffed most of them. From the time that they took

charge of their first orphanage in 1814, these sisters had cared

for both boys and girls. They preferred to limit their ministra-

tions to members of their own sex, but accepted boys when it was

impossible to support separate institutions for their care.[130] In

the New York asylum begun in 1817, in which one third of the orphans

were boys, outsiders were hired to teach them at first, but this

work was later taken over by the sisters.[131] In 1832, when Sister

Elizabeth Boyle had hesitated to accept another orphanage in which

there would be boys, Bishop Dubois, who had been one of the ad-

visors of the community in its earliest beginnings, wrote,

> There must be boys as well as girls, but I do not see
> on what ground this is an objection to our Sisters--
> in France and throughout Europe our good Sisters have the
> charge of foundling hospitals where boys as well as
> girls are admitted . . . . It is true that they must
> be placed in different dormitorys [sic] and made to play
> separately, but I found no great difficulty in that
> and the immense good which our Sisters produce among
> those boys compensates abundantly for the additional
> trouble.[132]

The reluctance to associate with boys seems to have stemmed

from the Jansenism which infected many French communities and the traditional attitude of the Church toward what it called "the weaker sex." Contact with young boys was thought to endanger the virtue of the sisters. (French Daughters of Charity were not even allowed to change the diapers of male infants.[133]) Sister Rose White wrote from Emmitsburg to Bishop Blanc that the administration could see the good that would come from placing male orphans under the direction of sisters, but also said, "It would be some old sisters who would take charge of that asylum if they could be had . . . . I see difficulties, yet leave all to our common Father, who can give mothers heads on virgin shoulders to these dear orphans," she wrote.[134] Joseph Code, in describing the situation at the New York orphanage where boys and girls lived under the same roof, writes, "To remove the beginning of such a moral menace the Emmitsburg authorities took immediate steps . . . ."[135]

Until 1845, then, it was common for American sisters to staff orphanages for children of both sexes. In that year, however, the Sisters of Charity of Emmitsburg, who ran most of the country's Catholic orphanages, began to take steps which would make possible their affiliation with the French Daughters of Charity. Those adaptations in the rule of St. Vincent de Paul which had been necessitated by American conditions and insisted on by Bishop Carroll, were no longer considered necessary. The stage was being prepared for the profession of the French rule in its entirety. Among many other European customs and tenets was one which forbade the sisters to care for male orphans over five years of age.[136] In 1845 the bishops were notified that Sisters of Charity would be withdrawn from the care of boys in the following year.[137] The

bishops were hard-pressed to staff the orphanages and schools
from which these sisters were being withdrawn. Many eventually
obtained Mercy Sisters, Josephites, or Christian Brothers to replace them.

Some found it difficult to understand how young boys could
be a moral menace to one community of sisters but not to another.
Bishop Michael O'Connor questioned this in a letter of Bishop
Purcell, but accepted the assumptions of the Emmitsburg superiors:

> Surely you were but joking when you spoke of the Sisters
> of Mercy taking charge of what the Sisters of Charity
> abandon on full deliberation . . . . I certainly must
> entertain the greatest respect for the opinions of
> those who govern their movements, and though I may have
> some reason to complain of their acts I must look upon
> their withdrawing the sisters from the Boys Asylums as
> having arisen only from the conviction which experience
> forced on them that such institutions were not suited
> for religious females.[138]

For Bishop Hughes of New York, who was campaigning for funds
for a new boys' orphanage to be staffed by these sisters, the
decision created serious difficulties. There was no doubt of the
need for a boys' orphanage. People would not contribute to the
building fund if it were known that the Sisters of Charity were
withdrawing. He protested to the authorities at Emmitsburg, but
to no avail. They were adamant in their insistence that French
customs be followed in American orphanages run by their sisters.
Father Deluol, the ecclesiastical superior at Emmitsburg, wrote
to Hughes on June 17, 1846:

> The male orphans could be taken care of by the Sisters
> of Charity here as they are in France, but not other-
> wise. In France the duty of the Sisters of Charity
> is to see that the orphans are properly taken care of,
> vis., that they are comfortably nursed, fed, clothed,
> etc. But they do not live in the same part of the

house; their apartments are distinct from each other.
A matron dresses and undresses them, cleans them, feeds
them, warms them, puts them to bed, and sees that
during the night they are comfortable and behave themselves, etc. The Sisters of Charity have nothing to
do with these details; moreover it is only foundlings
(and not boys 7, 8, 9, 10, 11 years old) who come
under their charge, and who whilst suckling have wet
nurses, and when weaned have matrons. We are willing
to adopt the same system where the persons concerned
are willing to cooperate.[139]

Hughes was not willing. Even if he had been, he did not

have the funds to pay the salaries of the matrons who were paid in

Europe from endowments. Nor were the sisters willing to give up

works of charity which could not easily be continued if they with-

drew. After a long correspondence, it was decided that those who

wished to, would remain in New York and form a new community which

would continue to follow the rules and customs of Mother Seton.[140]

About thirty-three sisters remained in New York, while twenty-nine

returned to Emmitsburg.[141] The new community prospered and aroused

the envy of other bishops, who also wished to have diocesan communi-

ties under their own control for their charitable institutions.

When the Emmitsburg motherhouse became officially affiliated

with the French Daughters of Charity in 1850, abrogating the rules,

customs, and habit of Mother Seton in favor of the French rules and

the cornette, there was another split. Seven sisters in Cincinnati,

under the leadership of one of Mother Seton's early companions,

professed their loyalty to Mother Seton's ideas and ideals by re-

fusing to don the cornette of the French community, a symbolic

gesture which indicated their unwillingness to give up the American

customs and practices which Mother Seton and Bishop Carroll had

insisted upon. With the consent of Bishop Purcell, these sisters broke with the Emmitsburg community and became an independent group, continuing to live the uniquely American form of religious life which Mother Seton and her companions had evolved.

When a priest of Nashville found that the constitutions of the Nazareth Sisters of Charity prohibited some of the works which he wished them to do, namely singing in the parish choir, he urged Bishop Miles to follow the example of Bishops Hughes and Purcell, and begin a community of his own. As is usually the case, the issue which brought the matter to the fore was not the only one involved. The priest was irritated when teachers in his school were removed and replaced without his consent and in general found the power of the Nazareth superiors over the sisters within the diocese irksome. He asked that those sisters who chose to do so would remain in Nashville as the nucleus of a new diocesan community, and in 1852, after some correspondence, this was accomplished.[142]

Five years later Bishop Martin J. Spalding described to Archbishop Purcell a visit he had paid to this "seceding branch," which was "getting on famously." He voiced an opinion which was becoming common among American bishops hard-pressed to provide for the needs of their flocks: "I was agreeably disappointed, and I begin to think that 'Secession,' after all, is not so bad. It is well that each diocese should have a motherhouse and a novitiate."[143]

Government

More and more bishops, following the example of Bishops Hughes, Purcell, and Miles, worked toward the development within their dioceses of communities which would be sensitive to local needs and could respond to them without having to consult authorities outside the diocese. Bishop Francis Patrick Kenrick wrote from Philadelphia to his brother, Bishop Peter Richard Kenrick of St. Louis in 1847, "I would have preferred to ask the Nuns of St. Ursula of Charleston to come here . . . but I fear that discipline may be not strictly observed, or that they are not entirely under the Bishop's control."[144] And Bishop Louis Rappe wrote to Bishop Purcell regarding a particular community, that he believed their inconstancy was due more to their system of government than to a lack of zeal or good will. So as not to be exposed to the same inconveniences in Cleveland, he says, he will choose for his house there an order which has its superiors at home.[145]

When the Josephite Sisters from various dioceses were invited in 1847 to a meeting at which some form of central government would be drawn up for the American sisters, the bishops of Buffalo, Philadelphia, Brooklyn, and Wheeling kept their sisters from attending. Each of these groups then became diocesan, under the immediate control of the local bishop.[146] Often, when expanding population figures necessitated the carving out of new dioceses, the sisters already teaching within the territory would be pressured to separate from their original community and become an autonomous group.

Some bishops, in their efforts to fashion sisterhoods which would be completely responsive to their demands, interfered repeatedly in the internal government of communities in their dioceses. Such was the case with Bishop de la Hailandiere, who often tampered with the lives of the Sisters of Providence.[147] He ignored their rule, moved sisters from one mission to another, closed and opened missions without consulting the superiors, forced them to accept unsuitable candidates, intercepted their mail, destroyed their reputation with priests and bishops, and refused them the sacraments. This was only one of the communities with whom he interfered; there were others as well.[148]

Domineering directors appointed by bishops sometimes took over most of the authority which should have resided in the sister superior. When Father Edward Joos assumed this power among the Monroe (Michigan) Sisters of the Immaculate Heart of Mary, Mother Theresa Maxis and some of the sisters moved to another diocese. Father Guy Chabrat tried to dissuade Rome from approving constitutions of the Loretto Sisters that did not give him as much power as he wished to have.[149]

The directors of the Franciscan Sisters in Milwaukee worked such havoc in the community that it is surprising it survived. They limited the number of new members to the number required for the domestic work of the seminary and the staffing of an orphanage; they convinced the original sisters that they should leave the community; they insisted that they help with crops when they preferred to prepare for teaching; and they gave them constitutions that were so stringent that the sisters took turns living according to their prescriptions.[150]

When Bishop Reynolds decided that only one religious community was needed in Charleston, the second community had to disband, its members joining various other Ursuline houses. The bishop

claimed ownership of the convent, which belonged to the sisters
but had never been deeded to them, because he was anxious to use
the site for his building projects. Though these Ursulines were
forced to disband their community, Bishop Reynolds felt that <u>he</u> had
been ill-used by them, and blamed them for trying to prove ownership of their property.[156] This was not the last time that sisters
would be deprived of their property by ecclesiastics who ignored
their rights.

Communities which relied upon abbots, provincials, or other
superiors of religious orders of men faced many of the same problems
which confronted those under diocesan authority. Among the communities which struggled many years before becoming relatively independent were the Benedictines, the Holy Cross Sisters, and the
Dominicans.

Abbot Boniface Wimmer, a Benedictine pioneer, was closely
associated with the first foundations of Benedictine nuns in
America. He appointed and dismissed superiors; he tried to sever
all ties with the Eichstatt motherhouse; and he urged the opening
of an American novitiate.[152] Mother Benedicta Riepp could see the
wisdom of many of his measures, but was obliged by her constitutions
to obtain approval from the Eichstatt motherhouse before carrying
them out. He urged complete separation from Eichstatt, but she
insisted on going through the proper channels to effect it. The
European superiors, in the meantime, were disturbed when they
learned that many adaptations in the rules had been made without
their permission. Mother Benedicta traveled to Eichstatt and to
Rome in an attempt to settle the many questions of adaptation to

American life which were points of contention between Wimmer, herself, and her Eichstatt superiors. For her forthright efforts to regularize the adaptations which were essential if the Benedictines were to prosper, she was removed from the office of superior, ostracized, and closely watched.[153] Harsh treatment seems to have been the lot of many of the sisters who honestly stated to their European superiors the need to adapt to American conditions.[154]

The Holy Cross Sisters at Notre Dame, called Marianites during this period, worked closely with the priests and brothers of Holy Cross. They encountered numerous difficulties in the working out of the details of their lives with their own superiors, the priest who was their director, the local bishop, and the European superiors who also claimed jurisdiction over them. Only by becoming completely autonomous were these sisters able to solve the problems which beset them.[155]

The provincial of the Dominican priests had jurisdiction over the Dominican sisters of Kentucky and Ohio. Since provincials were changed at least every four years, and sometimes oftener, there were shifting and sometimes contradictory interpretations of what the sisters should be doing. The problems which this situation caused for the sisters in the earlier period have been noted above in Chapter III. In the pre-Civil War period they persisted, though with less severity. Sometimes the provincial negated, by his adverse comments, petitions sent to Rome to alleviate the problems raised by confusion over their status. Thus Father James Whelan, provincial from 1854 until 1858, seems to have fought efforts to

adapt the earlier European form of religious life to American
needs. He wrote to the Master General of the Order, "I am sure it
is your wish to have no house rather than one not properly conducted."[156]

Economic Problems

The differences between European and American social classes
and economic conditions, which forced American religious communities
to find new methods of financing their works of charity, have been
discussed in Chapter III. Patterns established in the earlier
period were followed and developed in the pre-Civil War decades.
Works of charity for the poor had to be complemented by works for
which the sisters accepted payment of one kind or another. In some
cases state legislatures or city governments contributed funds to
support the sisters' services to the indigent. Wealthy patrons
like Mrs. Sarah Peter of Cincinnati gave of their fortunes, but
there were few Catholics in a position to do this. Women's auxi-
liaries of various kinds helped to support orphanages and hospitals,
as did European organizations like the Society for the Propagation
of the Faith, the Leopoldinen-Stiftung, and the Ludwig-Missions-
verein.

But most communities, whatever the works prescribed for
them in their constitutions, found it impossible to support themselves without the income which school tuition would bring. The
"select school" or "pay school" provided the funds which made the
"poor school" or "free school" possible. The greatest source of
income often was private lessons in music and art.[157] Communities

originally founded to serve the poor <u>gratis</u>, had to adapt to
American needs and attitudes. As Bishop Rosati wrote from St.
Louis in 1832:

> Here the idea of free public schools does not exist.
> The idea of a free school is that of a charity
> school, a school for the poor. Even the poor do not like
> to send their sons to such a school, for they consider
> it a disgrace. I know some well-to-do families in
> St. Louis who prefer to send their children to Protestant
> schools because they pay, than to the college or
> monastery because such schools are free.[158]

Communities newly begun or newly arrived learned from those
already established that American girls could not afford dowries.
Bishop Rese of Detroit wrote to Rome in 1835 of a double reason for
self-support, "Every religious order in America must unite the
active life to the contemplative; otherwise the Americans would
reject them, and we do not have means to support them in any other
way."[159] And the Ursuline, Sister Julia Chatfield, wrote from Ohio
to her French superiors, "Here, as elsewhere in America, novices
are received without dower; it is even rare for them to bring anything. So the religious establishments can hardly subsist except
through their pupils."[160]

Sisters in undeveloped areas like Oregon imitated the
earlier pioneers by working in the fields, making cheese, milking
cows, etc. in addition to administering a school. The Sisters of
St. Joseph of Carondelet found it necessary to apply for work in
stores and factories in order to supplement their income. During
the Mexican War they made shot-bags for a penny apiece.[161]

Other Problems

A final problem posed by the American situation, at least

for the non-English-speaking sisters, was the obvious one of lan-

guage. Fluent use of a foreign tongue was an advantage as well as

a disadvantage. Parents often boasted that their daughters had

learned French from native speakers.[162] The Minnesota Benedictines

and others discovered, however, that a knowledge of English was

indispensable if sons and daughters of the frontier were to be kept

under control in the classroom.[163] German religious communities

usually clung to the German language in their schools, prayers,

retreat conferences, etc. The practice of the Amityville Dominicans

was typical of many other communities as well. They insisted that

Irish (or American) postulants learn German, in the belief that

religious exercises and truths might lose something in trans-

lation.[164] Obviously, American girls who did not speak German would

not be inclined to enter a community of this type if an American one

were available. Nor did pastors care to have teachers in their

schools who did not know English, as Father John McElroy of St.

Mary's, Boston, indicated in a letter to Bishop Purcell:

> The qualifications of the Sister you mention will suit
> very well. I hope the others will be the same, I mean
> without foreign accent, having had their education in
> English, it matters not in what country, for the be-
> ginning this will be indispensable until the Sisters
> are known and their labors appreciated.[165]

Interaction With Society

The difficulties, crises, and adaptations discussed above

were for the most part internal affairs within religious communities

themselves and the Church of which they were a part. The general
public, however, knew little or nothing of these aspects of the
sisters' lives. Most Americans possessed some mental picture of the
nun, most likely a negative one, based on hearsay, reading, popular
myth, and other sources. But contact with nuns themselves, through
the nursing, teaching, or other charitable services which they performed, forced many to re-examine the images they held, and did
much to dispel ancient prejudices and promote positive attitudes
towards Catholicism.

Positive

Many had their first experience with sisters during the
epidemics which ravaged the country periodically. These women who
risked their lives in the service of their neighbors dispelled
prejudice in many cities. The simple heroism of the Sisters of
Charity who nursed in Boston during the cholera epidemic of 1832
evoked much admiration from the descendants of the Puritans.[166]
In San Francisco, where Irish Sisters of Mercy experienced bitter
hostility, the public attitude improved tremendously after a cholera
epidemic in which the sisters, the only people on the West Coast
with experience of the disease and knowledge of its remedies, saved
hundreds of lives. The Daily News of that city described their
services thus:

> They did not stop to inquire whether the poor
> sufferers were Protestants or Catholics, Americans or
> Foreigners, but with the noblest devotion applied
> themselves to their relief. One Sister might be seen
> bathing the limbs of the sufferer, another chafing the
> extremities; a third applying the remedies; while others
> with pitying faces were calming the fears of those
> supposed to be dying. The idea of danger never seems to
> have occurred to these noble women; self was lost sight

of.[167]

It was Archbishop Alemany's opinion that their work was the chief
factor in combatting nativism in his archdiocese.[168]

Zwierlein notes that "possibly no factor was so powerful
in disarming prejudice against Catholics in Rochester [New York] as
the establishment of St. Mary's Hospital in September, 1857."[169]
One who took part in nursing during the epidemics which plagued
Charleston during the 1850's wrote of the experience, "It was not
strange then that the people of Charleston should have been greatly
attached to these nuns, and honored the little black bonnet. In
truth the ladies of South Carolina called to a religious life think
no dress so respectable as that of the Sister of Mercy."[170] So great
was the esteem for these nuns that they were often called to the
bedsides of the sick even before the doctor was consulted.[171]

Public praise and gratitude were often expressed in newspaper articles. The Christmas, 1854, issue of the St. Paul
Democrat reminded readers of the sisters' nursing during a cholera
epidemic the preceding summer, and described the effect it had had:
"So it is all along the Mississippi River, many a man has cause to
bless these Sisters of Charity for a life which without their
assistance would have been lost . . . . We are no believers in the
Catholic religion but are willing to do them justice."[172]

Another newspaper which lauded the sisters' selfless
example was the Milwaukee Sentinel, which reminisced in its issue
of October 22, 1856, about the time six years earlier when the
Sisters of Charity had nursed a boatload of Swedish and Norwegian
immigrants stricken with typhoid:

> With no place where they could with safety be removed,
> with no nurses for these poor dying emigrants in a land
> of strangers, the community felt rejoiced that there
> were some unknown and unnoticed, for whom contamination
> and pestilence had no terrors. By their sick beds,
> amidst scenes often most trying, did the Sisters of
> Charity continue their work, when death's daily victims
> were counted by tens and twenties. The community,
> grateful and thankful for the noble spirit that knew
> no color or creed, offered through James H. Rogers,
> Esq., some compensation for services thus gracefully
> rendered. The compensation was respectfully declined.[173]

Public officials often expressed, in an official way, the

gratitude felt by their fellow citizens for the services of the

sisters. Thus the mayor of Augusta, Georgia wrote to the Charles-

ton Sisters of Mercy on Nov. 4, 1839, "Be assured that I heartily

unite with the Board in the expression of grateful thanks for the

signal kindness manifested by you in directing the efforts of the

Sisters of Charity to the relief of the afflicted of our city

. . . ."[174] The legislature of Louisiana expressed the gratitude

of the citizens of that state for the services of the sisters

during epidemics in a tangible way, when it granted a piece of

property near Donaldsonville to the Sisters of Charity for a

novitiate, where others might be trained for the same heroic life.[175]

Most railroads and steamboats asked no fare of Sisters of Charity,

so great was their appreciation for their work.[176]

Perhaps the greatest witness to the effect of the sisters'

lives on those whom they contacted was the number of conversions to

Catholicism which resulted. During the terrible epidemic of 1832

Bishop Rosati of St. Louis noted in his diary: "Every day some of

the Protestants desire the priest so that they might return to the

Holy Catholic Church before their death. Others who are well and

are not affected by the disease have also embraced the Catholic
Religion."[177] In the same year Dr. William Edmonds Horner, who
worked with the Sisters of Charity in alleviating the sufferings
of epidemic victims in Philadelphia, was drawn by their example
to examine and then embrace the Catholic religion. The apologia
which he later wrote to explain this step to his father crystallized
on paper sentiments which were shared by many.[178]

It was not just the heroism called forth by unusual crises
like epidemics which evoked praise for the sisters' work. Admiration greeted their more ordinary ministrations as well. Thus
Bishop Dubois could write of the New York Sisters of Charity who
cared for orphans, "The unselfish zeal of these nuns, their more-
than-motherly tenderness to the children entrusted to them, the
cleanliness, I would say almost the elegant plainness which they
preserve both in their schools and in their home, have gone far
towards lessening the prejudice of Protestants . . . ."[179]

It was through their schools that the greatest number of
persons encountered the sisters and came to know the qualities
which marked their daily lives. Here too, the sisters' work was
powerful enough to overcome and disarm the prejudices of many.
Perhaps the greatest testimony to the esteem in which the sisters'
schools were held is seen in the number of Protestants who sent
their daughters to the sisters for their education, and the change
of attitude which resulted from prolonged contact with them.
Mother Guerin's report of the gradual change of attitude in Madison,
Indiana describes a common experience:

> The Sisters were ridiculed; stones were thrown at them
> in the streets; they were insulted. But the most
> bigoted, the most prejudiced against them have already
> been appeased; two have even sent them their daughters.
> These children lose their prejudices in our schools,
> then parents are won over . . . . These poor little
> Protestants . . . who had been told everything that
> could make them hate and detest Catholics were all
> very much astonished in seeing and hearing us. They
> are completely changed after some months with us.[180]

There is abundant evidence of the popularity of the sisters'
schools among Protestant families. In Bishop England's school in
Charleston two-thirds of the two hundred pupils were Protestant.[181]
One-third of the girls in an Ursuline school in the wilds of Ohio
were non-Catholics.[182] An English traveller's report of his adventures "in the interior of America" in 1852 said this of education
in Cincinnati:

> In this country, the education of all the first classes
> of Protestants seems to be entrusted to the Catholic
> priests and nuns . . . . The parents say that their
> children are better taught and looked after than they
> would be in any other schools; the teachers say that
> they do not interfere with the religious opinions of the
> non-Catholic pupils; and that without such indiscriminate
> admission of all, they would not be able to support
> their establishments. Three-fourths of the boarders in
> many convents are Protestants.[183]

Frederick Marryat made similar observations.[184] With the opening
of free public schools, many Protestant children withdrew from the
more expensive sisters' schools.

Wealthy Protestants so valued the sisters' schools that
they contributed as readily as Catholics to finance them, and joined
their voices to those of Catholics when they urged religious
communities to open new schools in their towns. Thus Father Thomas
R. Butler could report to Bishop Purcell regarding a visit to
Chillicothe: "Mr. Anderson and I went among some of the principal

protestant folks, and found a very strong and general desire among them for the early opening of a school by the nuns--General Green will give us a contribution of $150 and will send his daughter to the Academy."[185] And Bishop Purcell wrote of the work of the sisters in Cincinnati: "The Protestants are forced to acknowledge the solidity of instruction given by these ladies. Consequently a goodly number of them have confided to them their children."[186]

In a letter to their Belgian motherhouse, the Sisters of Notre Dame de Namur described a tea party at which Protestants had vied with Catholics in raising funds for a parochial school. And a Protestant minister said of these sisters in a sermon in 1844: "Protestants always boast of their institutions; let them, if they can, show me among them an institution such as that of the Sisters of Notre Dame and I will believe their words."[187] Again and again the quality of the work of the sisters' school was attested to by Protestants as well as Catholics.[188]

One school which was singled out for high praise from many quarters was the ill-fated Mt. St. Benedict of Charlestown, Massachusetts. The daughters of Boston's most prominent families attended it in such numbers that two additional wings were added a few years after its inception.[189] Only an eighth of the students in this school were Catholic.[140]

When Catholic schools were attacked in Charlestown and in Louisville, it was the Protestant students and parents who defended them in the newspapers.[191] And Mother Guerin could note in a letter of 1849, "If others malign us, we have advocates in our little girls who defend us even in the presence of their ministers."[192] A group of parents whose daughters attended Mt. St. Benedict made a public

statement after the burning of that convent which said in part:

> It was important to us not to deceive ourselves, or
> to be deceived by others in a matter where the character
> and happiness of our children were concerned, and we
> have perfectly satisfied ourselves, that the Ursuline
> Community at Charlestown, was what it professed to be,
> a religious and virtuous community, who had abandoned
> the vanities of the world, and devoted themselves to
> the service of God and their fellow creatures and that
> their lives were pure and holy.[193]

Important for the record of the esteem in which the

sisters' schools were held is the number of people well known in

public life who supported them and entrusted their daughters to

convent schools for their education. The extant files reveal

that the daughters of the most important families in a town or

region--Protestant as well as Catholic--attended these schools.

Among families which patronized convent schools were those of

Senator Thomas Ewing, President Buchanan, Jefferson Davis,

Milwaukee's Mayor Solomon Juneau, and President Millard Fillmore.[194]

Charles Dickens praised the sisters' work during his visit to

America,[195] and John Greenleaf Whittier signed a petition to reim-

burse the Charlestown Ursulines for the destruction of their

school.[196] Among those who joined American religious communities

were the niece of Brook Farm enthusiast George Ripley and the grand-

daughter of Henry Clay. First postulant to join the San Rafael

Dominican community was Concepcion Arguello, daughter of the

governor of Baja California, a young lady whose legendary praises

have been sung by poets and historians of California.[197] General

Winfield Scott's daughter Virginia, converted to Catholicism by

Pierce Connelly and baptized in Rome, entered the Georgetown

Visitation Convent despite the remonstrances of her parents.[198]

Discussion in the Kentucky legislature of bills to in-
corporate the Nazareth and Loretto academies resulted in public
recognition of the good work being done in these schools. One Mr.
Bucker observed that Catholic female academies were the only ones
in the state deserving of public confidence and patronage. The
character and virtue of the nuns were beyond praise, according to
Mr. Hardin, who pointed out that several members of the legislature had themselves placed their daughters in Catholic schools.[199]

So highly esteemed were the convent schools, and so evident
the quality of the education which they gave, that even bigots
who feared their influence were forced to acknowledge their excellence. A deputation from the Congregational Union of England
and Wales wrote in its report for 1833, "They send out teachers
excellently qualified; superior, certainly, to the run of native
teachers . . . . They find little difficulty in obtaining the
charge of Protestant children . . . ."[200] Particularly fearful was
Lyman Beecher, whose lecture "A Plea for the West" emphasized the
effect which the constant example of Catholic teachers would have
on the minds of Protestant youth.[201] A newspaper called The
Presbyterian warned its readers in 1837 of the plans of pope and
clergy: "The principal means by which they expect to extend their
influence in our country, is the education of youth . . . . Their
efforts are especially directed to female education."[202] The excellence of Catholic schools was used as an impetus to spur Protestant efforts to combat Catholicism.[203]

Negative

During the period from 1829 to 1859, several events aroused
the antipathy towards Catholicism which had always been latent in
American Protestantism. Billington cites the giving of civil
rights to Catholics in England in 1829 and 1832, the trusteeism
controversy among American Catholics in the 1820's, the meeting of
the First Provincial Council of Baltimore in 1829, the influx of
Catholic immigrants, and the reform spirit of Protestant revivalism
as causes for the wave of hostility towards the Catholic Church
which swept the country in the decades before the Civil War. He
discusses these events, the sermons and anti-Catholic publications
which fanned the flames of hatred, and the political parties which
thrived on nativist platforms in The Protestant Crusade 1800-1860.[204]
His findings need not be repeated here. Anti-Catholic sentiment was
rampant in England and Ireland in the late 1820's and early 1830's.
"The period of most feverish and seditious activity in the history
of the Orange organization extends from about 1828 to 1835," notes
the historian of Orangeism.[205] Much of this activity spilled over
into America as well.

Most of the negative reactions towards nuns which are recorded during this period are closely bound up with the nativist
attitudes and prejudiced views of Catholicism which characterized
the climate of opinion of the times. Hostility towards nuns was
part of the general antipathy toward things Catholic, and was most
blatant among those who had little or no actual contact with them.
The public image of the nun, for those who had no contact with real
ones, was derived from what they heard and read. The country was

flooded with pamphlets, books, and newspaper articles which purported to reveal what really occurred behind convent walls. The
images portrayed in print were reinforced by the harangues of anti-
Catholic ministers who used the "Catholic threat" as a means to
get at the purses of their hearers, and by lectures given by so-
called escaped nuns and ex-priests. Those who accepted the image
of the nun as one who was a prisoner forced to submit to the
lascivious attentions of priests and to take part in immorality of
all kinds, including the murder of newborn babies, cannot really
be blamed for reacting as they did. It is no wonder that they
insulted nuns on the street, organized mobs to attack convent
property, tried to undermine the sisters' schools, and proposed
convent inspection laws to their legislatures, with the intention
of freeing nuns from their prisons.

Those who tried to undermine the sisters' works through unfavorable publicity and other strategies were a serious menace,
since sisters needed the financial support of the public in order
to survive. Mercy Sisters stepped off the boat in San Francisco
to a welcome of newspaper stories charging them with scandalous
conduct on shipboard: Sabbath-breaking and hard drinking. Other
articles attacked their reserve and supposed hostility towards
republican institutions. These stories did much to impede their
early work in California.206 The Visitandines found, when they
attempted to advertise the opening of their school in Wheeling,
West Virginia, that no newspaper would accept the advertisement.207
A Louisville Journal article of 1855 charged the Nazareth Sisters
with harsh treatment of a girl who had refused to go to confession.208

This newspaper also published Miss E.B. Miller's tales of religious pressures and severe discipline at the Nazareth boarding school.[209]

A conspiracy to destroy the Providence Sisters' school in Terre Haute was so successful that only one pupil returned to the school in the fall of 1842. The desperate situation of the sisters became even more serious when merchants demanded cash for all purchases.[210] In Madison, Indiana in 1845, ministers published derogatory newspaper articles and went to students' homes to persuade them not to return to the sisters' school. They even said they had seen the nuns climbing into the windows of a school at night in order to steal books, and accused them of kidnapping and murdering a child. Ladies pressured their friends not to allow their children to attend the Catholic school. One wrote to the mothers of the sisters' pupils:

> Dear Madam: Although I have not the honor of your acquaintance, the interest I take in your daughter prompts me to tell you that, if you leave her with the nuns, she will be lost. Twenty years from now she will remember the detestable principles she has imbibed there; and if she does not become a Catholic, she will at least defend the Sisters all her life and on all occasions.[211]

In Dayton, Protestants opened a school in opposition to that started by the Sisters of Notre Dame de Namur, and took away many of their pupils.[212]

Sisters of several communities came to expect open insult when they appeared on the streets. The School Sisters of Notre Dame were pelted with mud in Philadelphia, and slept in specially prepared robes at night that they might be decently clothed, should they be driven into the street by fire or mob action. They were taunted for their black clothing during their stagecoach ride from Pittsburgh to Milwaukee and molested by nativists who sang ribald songs outside their convent after they finally arrived in Milwaukee.[213] Here too, nativists shouted at them and threw stones, and children chalked white crosses on their backs.[214] In Baltimore they were stoned and called "papist," "cross-back," and "popelover."

The Josephites received similar treatment in Philadelphia,[215] as did the Providence Sisters in Madison, Ind. Sister St. Francis described the Madison experience thus: "The Protestants are enraged that the Sisters are in Madison. The first day they went with their pupils to Mass, children called after them, 'Oh, the old nuns.' One spat upon Sister Liguori . . . . Others threw stones at them."[216] When the Mercy Sisters from Providence, R.I. were on their way to a school near New Haven, they chanced to meet some Yale students, one of whom lifted one of the sisters up and carried her to a street corner some distance away. There he deposited her, and then went back to his friends to collect on the bet he had won.[217] In many places, because of the reputed immorality of convents, nuns were propositioned on the streets.[218] Episodes like these convinced the sisters that they should wear ordinary clothing when going out of their convents.

As anti-Catholic sentiment grew, fed by defamatory newspapers and magazines and the inflammatory harangues of ministers, more serious attacks on Catholic property, including sisters' convents and schools, were perpetrated by unruly mobs. Nationwide publicity focused attention on the convent as a symbol of the evils of Catholicism when Mount St. Benedict, the flourishing Ursuline

academy in Charlestown, Mass., was destroyed by a mob in 1834.

Since Billington discusses this incident in some detail, it is

only necessary to outline the sequence of events here.[219]

Miss Rebecca Reed, who had asked to be given a six months'

trial of the Ursuline life, was dismissed after four months. She

spread tales about the horrors of convent life that were believed

by many. Then one of the Ursulines, Sister Elizabeth Harrison, who

had been acting strangely and was tired from long hours of teaching,

left the convent and sought refuge with a Mr. Cutter, who lived

nearby. He took her to her brother's home, where she came to her-

self and, horrified at what she had done, begged to be returned to

the convent. She was allowed to return, but not before the story

of the "escaped nun" had spread throughout Boston. Newspaper arti-

cles suggested that she had been forced to return to the convent and

speculated about the punishment she must be undergoing. Many of the

sermons preached in Boston churches on Sunday, August 10, denounced

Catholicism; some of them focused on the evils of convents, using

the Charlestown one as an example. Lyman Beecher preached his

"Plea for the West" in three different churches on that day. On

Monday the selectmen of Charlestown toured the convent and were

convinced that Elizabeth Harrison truly wished to remain there.

Their report was to be published in Tuesday's paper, but on Monday

night a crowd gathered outside the Charlestown convent. A mob of

brickmen and truckers, in whose minds the school was connected with

its upper-class patrons, demanded to see the sister who was being

held prisoner. When their request was refused, they forced their way into the building, destroyed furniture, desecrated the chapel, and finally set fire to the whole building, forcing a dozen nuns and sixty pupils to flee in the night. Not satisfied with merely destroying the building, the mob then dug up the bodies of the sisters buried in the convent cemetery.[220] The property destroyed by this fire was valued at $50,000.[221]

A committee of prominent citizens appointed by the mayor to investigate the destruction of the convent attributed it primarily:

> to a widely extended popular aversion, founded on the belief that the establishment was obnoxious, to those imputations of cruelty, vice, and corruption so generally credited of similar establishments in other countries . . . fomented to hatred by representations injurious to the moral reputation of the members of that community . . . and also by reports that one of the sisterhood, Mrs. (Sister) Mary John . . . had been put to death or secretly imprisoned or removed.[222]

Protestant citizens who were dismayed at this action, which gave their city a national reputation for intolerance, met at Faneuil Hall on August 12 to discuss remedies. Among the resolutions which they drew up were the following:

> In the opinion of the citizens of Boston, the late attack on the Ursuline Convent in Charlestown, occupied only by defenceless females, was a base and cowardly act, for which the perpetrators deserve the contempt and detestation of the community . . . .
> We, the Protestant citizens of Boston, do pledge ourselves, collectively and individually, to unite with our Catholic brethren in protecting their persons, their property, and their civil and religious rights.[223]

A Protestant from Boston who sought an audience with Pope Gregory XVI while in Rome, later told of his humiliation when the pope asked, "Was it you who burned my convent?"[224]

Though there was an immediate nationwide reaction against this violation of basic American rights, many secretly rejoiced

that Catholics had been given what they deserved. The Concord,
New Hampshire Freeman, for example, was happy that "old Massachusetts is no longer disgraced by a nunnery and its accompaniments."[225]
The national publicity given to this event accustomed people to
the idea that one could express aversion to Catholicism by destroying Catholic property. Attention was focused particularly on
convents as centers of vice in which women were imprisoned, and as
part of the pope's plot to subvert American Protestantism through
education. Henceforth damage to convent property was a very real
possibility, and sisters had to live with the knowledge that their
homes might be attacked at any time. Mob violence did break out
rather frequently in the years following the Charlestown burning,
and often it was directed towards convents. Indeed, the very night
after the burning of Mt. St. Benedict, Boston mobs attacked
Catholic Church property on Franklin Street, burning the convent
fence, tearing up the grapery, and destroying the orchard and
garden.[226]

New Englanders harrassed the Sisters of Mercy at each convent they opened in that region. The windows in their Providence
convent were often shattered by mobs who came in the night.[227]
When the daughter of a prominent family became a Sister of Mercy,
public opinion held that the sisters had pressed her to join them
because they wanted her inheritance. So incensed were the people
that they decided to launch a massive attack on the convent.[228]
Men came in special trains from Boston, Salem, and Taunton to join
in the fun. When the mayor and governor refused protection, a
band of Irishmen, led by Bishop Bernard O'Reilly, guarded the

building. Mother Warde walked among the Irishmen, exhorting them

to use their firearms only in self-defense. When the bishop spoke

to the crowd and assured them he would protect the sisters with

his life if necessary, they withdrew. One of the rioters remarked,

> We made our plans without reckoning the odds we will
> have to contend with in the strong controlling force
> the presence of that nun commands. The only honorable
> course for us to follow is to retreat from this ill-
> conceived fray. I for one will not lift a hand to
> harm these ladies.[229]

One of the rioters, who was subsequently nursed by a Sister

of Mercy during the Civil War, told her that the heroism of Bishop

O'Reilly and the example of Mother Warde were responsible for his

conversion to Catholicism.[230] A similar incident occurred in

Hannibal, Missouri. Only after a committee had interviewed a local

girl who had entered the convent, and been assured that she wanted

to be a nun, was the threatened mob action called off.[231] In the

1850's college students at Yale and Harvard played a prominent

part in nativist activities in New Haven and Boston. It is said

that their recreation periods were spent in breaking the windows

of Catholic homes, churches, and convents, and insulting sisters

and priests on the streets.[232]

The Carmelite convent in Baltimore was threatened by

violence in 1839 when Sister Isabella Neale, who was mentally

deranged, left the convent through a window and was taken in by a

neighbor, warden of the local jail. Since Robert Breckenridge,

bigoted minister of a Presbyterian church nearby, had already in-

stilled a hatred of convents in his congregation, a crowd quickly

gathered as word of the "escaped nun" spread. The mayor, who had been taken through the convent and had spoken privately with each sister, tried in vain to convince the mob that all remained within the convent voluntarily. Several men, Presbyterians among them, guarded the convent for three days and nights until peace was finally restored.[233]

The Josephites of St. Louis aroused the anger of the people when they undertook the education of free Negro girls and prepared slaves to receive the sacraments. Whites surrounded their convent one night and tried to drive them out, but police dispersed the crowd. The mayor advised that the school be closed for a time, and it was.[234]

St. John's Orphan Asylum in Frederick, Maryland was burned to the ground in 1845 by arsonists who had cut the hoses of both fire companies. Fortunately, there were no lives lost, and the convent of the Sisters of Charity who staffed the orphanage was left untouched.[235] On June 6, 1848 a mob attacked the Ursuline convent in New Orleans, breaking doors and windows and shouting insults at the nuns,[236] and in 1854 there was an attempt to burn down the Ursuline convent in Galveston.[237]

Ursulines who took up residence in Columbia, S.C. were met by shouting and a deluge of stones. One man fired a pistol into the house, but shot off his own finger in the process. When the sisters appealed to the mayor for protection, he placed a guard around the house and even joined the patrol himself. The leading Protestants of the town then called a meeting and made certain that the sisters would never again be bothered.[238]

On the evening of their first Holy Thursday in America, the Good Shepherd Sisters of Louisville were startled by a group of bigots who tried to force their way into the convent. Their historian reports that the mob was prevented from entering "in a manner almost miraculous," but does not explain.[239] In many cities, when violence was threatened, prominent citizens took steps to insure that the peace would be kept.

When the Charlestown Ursulines tried to re-establish themselves in Roxbury, Mass., threatening handbills were circulated in the town and another attack was feared. Citizens formed a Committee of Vigilance which had six members on guard at all times, ready to spread the alarm in case of attack. Citizens also helped to protect an Ohio convent of the Sisters of Notre Dame when it was attacked by a mob in the early 1850's.[240] When the minister who edited the Charleston Observer tried to arouse his fellow Protestants to protest the arrival of Irish Ursulines, prominent non-Catholics quickly organized to silence the attackers.[241]

A mob which would burn down an orphanage, fire into a convent, or stone innocent women, must have been impelled by something more than the example of the Charlestown bricklayers. Promoters learned from the tales of Rebecca Reed, the Harrison incident, the large audiences attracted by speakers like Lyman Beecher, and the publicity given the Charlestown burning, that the tremendous public curiosity about convents and the rampant hatred of Catholicism had created a lucrative market for convent revelations of all kinds. Unscrupulous ministers learned that lectures and sermons which denounced convents filled their church coffers.

Anti-Catholic publishers began sponsoring "escaped nuns," whose published revelations were best-sellers. Public appearances helped to sell their books. Thus began the custom of placing "escaped nuns" next to "ex-priests" on the lecture platform to arouse the hatred of their audiences for Catholicism and enrich their backers, a practice which would continue into the twentieth century.

The most famous ex-nun of them all, and prototype of all who came after her, was Maria Monk, a girl who had suffered brain damage in childhood.[242] After her escape from a Montreal asylum for wayward girls, she came to New York with tales of her alleged experiences as a nun. Unscrupulous ministers there were not slow to see the uses to which the girl could be put. The Reverend J.J. Slocum, with the advice of the Reverend George Bourne and Theodore Dwight, undertook the task of writing up her story for publication, calling her book <u>Awful Disclosures of the Hotel Dieu Nunnery of Montreal</u>. The publication of this book in 1836, and of its sequels shortly thereafter, aroused a storm of controversy, with charges and countercharges on all sides. (Billington tells the story in detail.[243]) Miss Monk's public appearances provided more fuel for the fire. One of her most prominent backers was Samuel F.B. Morse. He wrote to his friend James Fenimore Cooper on May 27, 1836:

> I send for your perusal the second edition of Maria Monk's disclosures; I think the additional matter is very important and conclusive of the truth of her story. The fact that she has accompanied her volume with a plan of all the rooms in the convent is very strong in favor of her sincerity and integrity. Were she an imposter I cannot believe she would have dared to put forth a document of this kind, which, if materially incorrect, cannot

fail in the course of a few days from its
publication of exposing the whole cheat.[244]

On June 14, 1836 Cooper wrote to Horatio Greenough, "I am very much

afraid Morse is about to marry a certain Miss Monk, and when you

see him I beg you will speak to him on the subject." And in a

letter to Mrs. Cooper July 11 he said, "Morse is here and Monkish

as ever."[245]

Perhaps the best comment on Maria Monk is that given in her

daughter Lizzie's autobiography. Lizzie's sister visits her, and

reacts when Lizzie makes disparaging remarks about Catholics:

> But do you not know, that that book of our mother
> was all a lie? I know, that the Awful Disclosures
> of Maria Monk are all lies; SHE HERSELF TOLD ME SO.
> She wrote the book in order to make money. Some
> men put her up to it; but she never received one
> cent of the proceeds of the book; for these men kept
> all for themselves . . . . She did not write her
> book; in fact the book itself admits that she did
> not. She only gave certain alleged facts, which
> were dressed up by the men, who afterwards helped to
> cheat her out of the proceeds of her crime.[246]

Inspired no doubt by the popularity of Maria Monk's per-

sonal appearances, another fugitive nun, who called herself Sainte

Frances Patrick or Partridge, appeared on the New York lecture

platform in 1836. She pretended to have been an inmate of the same

convent which had housed Maria Monk, and corroborated her stories.[247]

These two, following in the footsteps of Rebecca Reed, proved be-

yond doubt the popularity and potential profit of the "escaped

nun" business. Maria Monk's book, which will be discussed below,

sold three hundred thousand copies before the Civil War, and went

through many additional printings after that, even though her

story had been discredited in the eyes of all objective observers.[248]

Many other young ladies were impelled, either from their own volition or as tools of unscrupulous backers, to step forward with their stories of convent life.

In the same year, Millie McPherson spread the tale of her escape from a convent in Bardstown, Kentucky. It was, she said, the indecent attentions of a priest, whom she named, which had moved her to seek an escape. The accused priest sued for libel and won, but was awarded only a penny for damages. When the trial was over, Miss McPherson dropped from sight, and there were those who believed that she had been abducted and murdered by priests.[249] Stories like that about Miss McPherson which appeared in one nativist newspaper would often be reprinted in others throughout the country and thus gave national prominence to every self-styled nun who appeared on a local platform.[250]

Lectures by escaped nuns gained added popularity during the 1850's, when the Know-Nothing party used them as part of its political campaign. During this decade a woman calling herself "Sister Agnes" went on tour with convent stories.[251] A Miss Jarrett of Memphis was supposedly kidnapped and imprisoned in a convent, where she was mistreated by Jesuits.[252] A lecture on convents scheduled to be given in Rochester on May 18, 1855 by a Miss Carlson was cancelled when the audience was found to contain only a few little girls.[253] Josephine Bunkley, who actually had been a novice with the Sisters of Charity of Emmitsburg, appeared in print and on the lecture platform in 1855.[254] There was an uproar in Austin, Texas when rumor held that a boarder at the Ursuline Convent who had died six months earlier had actually been smuggled out of the country and imprisoned in a French convent. The rumors were stopped only after the body had been disinterred and identified by the girl's father.[255]

Sometimes it was former priests, or those who pretended they had been priests, who spread scandalous stories about convents. By 1854, says McMaster, every city of any importance had its anti-Catholic preacher.[256] The Rev. Dr. Giustiniani gave a lecture on "Nunneries" in Rochester, N.Y. October 15, 1848, and the Rev. E. Leahey, "late a Monk of La Trappe, in France," gave a similar performance there in 1851. (Leahey, who did not scruple to use his wife for immoral purposes, ended his life in prison, convicted of murder.)[257] Most notorious was an Italian apostate priest and revolutionary named Alessandro Gavazzi, whose lectures were sponsored by the American and Foreign Christian Union.[258] Though his bitterest invective was reserved for papal nuncio Gaetano Bedini, he also accused the Sisters of Charity of being prostitutes the world over, and warned parents not to send their children to convent schools.[259] In a typical tirade he said to his audience:

> The demon . . . to introduce Catholicism into America
> uses nuns, real Eves, with their sweet engaging
> manners, their knowledge, and their attractions . . . .
> Guard against sending your children to their schools,
> and even against placing near them servants reared by
> the Sisters.[260]

Often it was a minister or other promoter of the nativist cause who lectured on the evils of nunneries. The American Protestant Vindicator, a bi-weekly newspaper begun by the Rev. W.C. Brownlee in 1834, employed agents, each with his own territory, to lecture against Catholicism and appeal for additional subscriptions to the newspaper. By 1840 six of these agents were employed full-time. Other anti-Catholic publications soon followed this example and sent out salesmen of their own. In 1844, the Rev. Charles Sparry employed thirty-three clergymen as lecturing agents to promote his magazine, the National Protestant.[261]

In some instances hostility to convents involved sisters in legal proceedings in which popular misconceptions about nuns and convents influenced the outcome. The first of these was the trial in 1834 of eight men accused of being leaders in the plot to burn down the Charlestown convent. Many aspects of the trial revealed the anti-Catholic sentiment of those conducting it. The Mother Superior of Mt. St.Benedict was cross-examined on the immorality of convent life, and when the whole travesty was over, all but one of the culprits was acquitted, to the great joy of all who thronged the courtroom.[262] Several petitions to the legislature asking reimbursement for the Ursulines' property loss were refused, and Bishop Fenwick was even required to pay a tax on the convent buildings after they had been destroyed.[263] When a House Committee of the Massachusetts legislature examined the reimbursement question in 1854, it reported that though the public belief in the immorality of the nuns was strong,

> during the time that has elapsed, no person has come
> forward before any of the numerous committees who have
> had the subject in charge to indicate the evidence of
> such crimes. From these considerations and a calm
> review of all the circumstances, your committee are
> led to the most settled conviction that no suspicion,
> even of impurity of life, attaches to the members of
> the Ursuline Convent of Charlestown. Justice requires
> that the Ursulines be paid for their loss.[264]

In 1852 a group of Pennsylvania ladies petitioned their state legislature to suppress convents in the state because they were centers of vice. The petition was referred to the legislature's Committee on Vice and Immorality, which never acted upon it.[265]

During the years when the Know-Nothing Party was most successful in state and national elections, particularly in 1854 and 1855, several bills aimed at the inspection of convents were introduced in state legislatures. Residents of Foxborough, Massachusetts petitioned that state's legislature for inspection of "convents, nunneries, or by whatever name they may be designated."[266] A "Nunnery Committee" was duly appointed to inspect "such theological seminaries, boarding schools, academies, nunneries, convents, and other institutions of like character as they may deem necessary."[267] Five members of this committee, accompanied by nineteen friends, descended upon the convent of the Sisters of Notre Dame de Namur in Roxbury in pursuit of their duties. Without warning, they entered and inspected classrooms and dormitories, opened closets, looked under beds, etc.[268] Both in Roxbury and in Lowell, committee members and their friends feasted on an elaborate dinner after their inspection tours, and at Lowell they enjoyed the favors of a certain Mrs. Patterson, all at the expense of the state. The publicity given to these junkets forced the legislature to dissolve the committee and expel its chairman from the assembly.[269]

Many petitions were presented to the Maryland Know-Nothing legislature of 1856 on behalf of those held captive in convents. One petition suggested that the Orphans' Court be given control of all the inmates' property, and that they be required to appear in court twice a year to voice any complaints they might have. The committee to which the petitions were referred decided that, since no particular case of injustice had been cited, it had no reason to examine convent practices.[270]

These are the kinds of experiences which marked the sisters interaction with those who lived beyond their convent walls. In general it can be said that those who had a first-hand acquaintance with sisters and their various works held them in high esteem. Those who knew the convent only through incendiary sermons and lectures, the tales of so-called ex-nuns, and anti-Catholic publications of all kinds saw the convent as a prison in which helpless women were subjected to cruel treatment and forced to submit to the indecent attentions of priests. At best, these people saw the convent as a tool of the hated Roman Catholic Church, a channel through which the corruptions of the Old World would seek entry into the New.

Roles Seen in the Literature

Some of the more popular of the anti-Catholic books which flooded England during the controversy over the Catholic Emancipation Bill of 1829 were distributed by American publishers in the 1830's. Among them were Scipio de Ricci's Female Convents. Secrets of Nunneries Disclosed and S. Sherwood's The Nun. The former book was said to be compiled from the papers of a reforming bishop of Pistoia and Prato, who died in the early years of the nineteenth century. The success of these books showed that there was a ready market for convent stories, and shrewd publishers were not slow to take advantage of it. They began to issue in book form tales of "escaped nuns" that had hitherto been repeated only in newspapers or on the lecture platform.

Beginning with the charges and countercharges that marked the Rebecca Reed incident, and reaching their zenith with Maria Monk's Awful Disclosures, these books were tremendously popular. As was noted above, 300,000 copies of Maria Monk's book were sold prior to the Civil War. The preface to an 1855 edition of Frothingham's Six Hours in a Convent, which was originally published in 1854, notes that after twelve very large editions, the public still wanted more. His book entitled The Convent's Doom sold 40,000 copies in the first week of publication.[271] Several American editions of Mrs. Sherwood's The Nun, an English import, had been published by 1835. Her works were so popular in this country that a sixteen-volume collected edition of them was brought out in 1855.[272] As early as 1836 the Catholic Telegraph was complaining that Protestants "have filled every village store, and cabin, with the 'Key to Popery,' 'Fox's Book of Martyrs,' 'Six Months in a Convent,' and other vile, mendacious works."[273] Books like these were cited as creditable authorities twenty-five, sixty, and more than eighty years later in campaigns against Catholicism.[274] Ruth Elson, in her study of the textbooks of the period, notes that spellers invariably included words like "nunnery," "abbot, monastick, papist, papal," in order to equip children to understand nativist literature.[275]

Works Studied

In the works about nuns published during this period, there
is an overlapping of fictional with autobiographical and historical
works. Some of the fiction writers follow the conventional
practice of insisting, as does the author of The School Girl in
France, that theirs is "not a work of fiction, but a collection of
facts, thrown together in one tale, with scarcely any additions,
and few other alterations than those which were absolutely necessary, in order to disguise names, places, and dates."[276] Others,
like Maria Monk, pretend to write autobiography while actually
writing fiction. The few books which give a positive view, or at
least try to correct misinformation, are those written to answer
the charges of people like Rebecca Reed and Maria Monk. Of the
twenty-eight books studied for this period, eleven are works of
fiction or romance per se, and seventeen purport to be autobiographical or historical accounts of convent life.[227]

Since stories about nuns were sometimes published in anti-
Catholic newspapers and magazines before being issued in book or
pamphlet form, and these media also exerted great influence on
popular ideas, stories printed in one magazine of this type, the
Baltimore Literary and Religious Magazine, and one newspaper, the
Downfall of Babylon, will be included as typical of many which
appeared at this time.

Before proceeding to a detailed study of the image of the
nun found in fiction, it might be well to note a few facts about
the authors of these stories. Four of the books were published
anonymously.[278] Five were written by ministers[279] and the

magazine was edited by ministers. Four were by men who claimed to be former priests,[280] and one of these men also edited the news-paper.[281] Four of the books were produced, ostensibly at least, by the two women who had lived in convents;[282] three were novelists;[283] one author was a businessman;[284] one an unimportant member of a prominent Boston family.[285] One of the books may per-haps be the creation of the ex-priest who edited the anti-Catholic newspaper that is being studied.[286]

All of these works repeated essentially the same image of the nun which was being projected from the pulpit and the lecture platform. A study of the ideas conveyed in the twenty-eight books and the representative magazine and newspaper reveals in abundant detail the role expectations for nuns which were held by large numbers of Americans during this period, expectations which were the cause of some of the acts of violence that have already been recounted. A more positive view of convent life is given in the books which were written to refute the stories told by Rebecca Reed, Maria Monk, and Josephine Bunkley.[287]

The works of fiction and romance are rather mild stories dealing with convent schools and romantic reconstructions of events leading up to the burning of Mt. St. Benedict; they must have appealed to the more respectable middle-class reader. They depict the imperceptible influence which sisters exert on students in boarding schools, and often have as heroes strong young men who scheme to rescue the maidens they love from convents in which they have been imprisoned. The autobiographical and historical accounts of convents were often used as instruments of propaganda,

and hence reflect the hatred of Catholicism which characterized
their promoters. Their descriptions of seduction, rape, torture,
murder, and other such niceties of life behind convent walls indicate a desire to appeal to the baser instincts of the lower classes.
The central scene in these books often uses the seduction theme of
the sentimental novel, but adds to it the emphasis on the strange,
the supernatural, and the macabre which is typical of the Gothic
novel.

As more and more convent stories appeared, authors were
hard put to reveal new "secrets" never before exposed to the public.
Hence they were loathe to let even the tiniest detail of convent
life go unrecorded. For those who pretended to be former nuns, reference to the minutiae of religious life was no doubt thought
necessary as "proof" that they really had been nuns. Apostate
priests like William Hogan, Samuel Smith, and S.J. Mahoney and
young women like Rebecca Reed and Josephine Bunkley, who did have
first-hand knowledge of the religious life, would be fertile
sources for information. No doubt the references to canon law,
details from the constitutions of particular communities, and
quotations from reforming saints which flesh out the plots of
these books, originated with informants like these. Many aspects
of convent life are caricatured or ridiculed in these books.

Apart from these exaggerations however, and the depictions
of immorality, the picture of the nun which emerges is in many
ways a realistic one. As we have seen, many convent practices had
originated centuries earlier, in another culture. Writers did not
have to stray very far from the truth in order to evoke strong

reactions to the "un-American" behavior patterns which actually
did characterize much of nineteenth-century religious life in the
United States. Let us examine convent life as it is depicted in
these publications, and compare it with the facts that have been
set forth above.

Cloistral Prescriptions

Many of the cloistral prescriptions which flowed from
canon law's insistence on enclosure for nuns are examined and
criticized in fictional accounts of convent life. The walls prescribed as tangible barriers between the convent and the world are
mentioned so often that they become a stereotyped part of the
physical appearance of a convent, and often figure prominently in
dramatic escapes, elopements, etc. To most writers, walls connote
a prison and involuntary detention. One of Mrs. Chaplin's characters remarks, "If these gates should be thrown open tomorrow by
the strong arm of the law, I do not think more than five nuns would
remain here of their own choice."[288] Another one of her characters
says that nuns "shut themselves out from the beautiful things of
God, and then growl at those whom they see through their prison
bars."[289] Nicholas Murray calls convents "prisons of confiding
girls,"[290] and in one of Frothingham's fictionalized accounts of
the events leading up to the burning of Mt. St. Benedict, the con-
spirators' aim is "to open the doors of a female prison."[291]

Several writers express suspicion about what convent walls
conceal. George Bourne, in explaining why "The Monastic System is
Destructive of Freedom, Morality, and the Republic" writes,

The gloomy external of those doleful mansions will
comport with the dark contrivances of iniquity which
are ever perpetrated in the interior--and the grates
and bars all bespeak the death-like living sepulchre
in which those children of crime and misery are entombed.[292]

McCrindell uses the same theme: "A thousand acts of oppression,

tyranny, and even cruelty, could have been perpetrated within

those walls and the girls wouldn't have known it."[293] Peter

Parley's Common School History, which had a total sales of seven

million, saw the enclosure of monasteries as a screen behind which

the inmates "often gave themselves up to luxurious pleasures.[294]

The grille which separated a sister from visitors in the

parlor, and the companion who was supposed to be present whenever

guests were received, were also described and criticized. The

Baltimore Literary and Religious Magazine, in its description of

the "Carmelite Convent in Baltimore," mentions the physical barriers

which would keep a nun from escaping from this convent--women can

only speak to the nuns through a grate, and even at that, a nun is

never left alone in the parlor when visiting with externs.[295] It

also stresses "the windows carefully closed, and curiously

grated."[296] In some issues the editor quotes from the decrees of

the Council of Trent and from canon law to prove that nuns are not

as free as American citizens should be.[297] Miss Bunkley says that

a sister's family may visit with her only in the presence of a

companion, and that the interview takes place "at an iron grating,

where the nun stands like a prisoner behind bars, which present an

impassable barrier."[298] The author of Pope or President also men-

tions the grille and the presence of a companion as characteristic.[299]

Another cloistral practice emphasized in the novels is the censorship of mail sent or received by sisters. This is mentioned in Sister Agnes, Frothingham's Six Hours in a Convent, and M'Gavin's book.[300] One of Mrs. Chaplin's boarding students say she doubts that more than five of the nuns would remain in the convent of their own free choice, but they cannot acknowledge their true feelings because only letters which praise the superior are allowed to be sent out of the convent.[301] The practice extends to boarding school students as well as nuns. The father of a boarder at a convent school in Washington wonders that her letters, which he knows are censored, contain no mention of herself, but are full of praise for the superior, whom she calls a "dear mother"--the term used by the Loretto Sisters to refer to their superior.[302] Mrs. Chaplin is no doubt basing this detail on Ciocci's quotation from the published prospectus of the Georgetown Visitation Convent which said, "All letters written and received by them [the students] are examined by the Directress previous to their delivery."[303]

The idea that separation from the world should also involve the severing of the natural ties of affection that bind the sister to her family is found in Sister Agnes. A novice longs to see her father, but then remembers that "nuns have no fathers." "He that loveth father or mother more than Christ is unworthy of him," says Scripture, and her confessor tells her that thoughts of her father reveal that she is still too attached to the world. She has too much carnal affection for him. In fact, all feelings of affection are to be rooted out, according to this author:

> Ere the convent can be happy, memory must be
> abolished, a parent's home must be blotted from
> the heart; the deep longings of woman after
> sympathy, and communion and affection, must be
> expunged from her nature--her soul must be chilled,
> converted into stone, or like a tree in winter,
> it must be stript of its verdure and beauty.[304]

For thoughtful nineteenth-century Americans who prized
freedom and independence, had an optimistic view of human nature,
and believed strongly in the individual's right and ability to
direct the course of his own life, convent walls and other
cloistral practices posed a basic question, particularly in the
face of Catholic assurances that convents were only for those who
willingly chose to be nuns. It is a question which attacks the
whole philosophy behind the law of enclosure and all of the minute
prescriptions for religious communities which flow from this
philosophy. The author of Sister Agnes explicitly raises the
question which is implicit in many of the other books when she
asks,

> But if the inmates of convents be happy, what possible
> harm can accrue from letting the world see their
> happiness--from overwhelming with confusion those who
> assert the contrary? If nuns desire above all things
> to remain in their paradises, why wall in, and bar,
> and bolt, and lock and guard those paradises more
> jealously than our gaols? If access be still denied,
> we cannot believe that there is no crime to hide;
> and we must persist in the attempt to have it as-
> certained, by law, whether frightful rumours be not
> true.[305]

The editor of Miss Bunkley's book voices the same sentiments.
"Are nuns, indeed, so invariably happy?" he asks. "Why, then,
are they insulted by their spiritual rulers by keeping them under
the very guards and precautions which magistrates employ to secure
external good behavior among the female inmates of prisons and

penitentiaries?"[306]

Tocqueville, in his comments on American manners in 1832,
stresses the novel way in which American girls are trained.
They are "far more the mistresses of their own actions than they
are in Catholic countries," he writes; "nowhere are young women
surrendered so early or so completely to their own guidance." The
American girl "thinks for herself, speaks with freedom, and acts
on her own impulse." "Even amidst the independence of early youth,
an American woman is always mistress of herself; she indulges
in all permitted pleasure without yielding herself up to any of
them; and her reason never allows the reins of self-guidance to
drop, though it often seems to hold them loosely." Americans,
knowing that "they could not prevent her virtue from being exposed
to frequent danger, . . . determined that she should know how best
to defend it; and more reliance was placed on the free vigor of
her will than on safeguards which have been shaken or overthrown."
"Far from hiding the corruptions of the world from her, they
prefer that she should see them at once, and train herself to shun
them." A girl who marries "voluntarily and freely enters upon
this engagement. She supports her new condition with courage,
because she chose it."[307]

Such was the American girl and young woman of 1832, be she
married or in the convent. Why wall in, indeed. Is it any wonder that the writers of the period attacked those aspects of convent life whose underlying assumptions contradicted this view of
womanhood; that women filled with the spirit of reform waged
campaigns to open up the nunneries; and that the evidence of walls,

grille, companion, and censorship of mail proved more powerful
than the testimony of nuns themselves when convent life was
examined?

Other characteristic traits of religious life--reasons
for entering the convent, the ceremony of taking vows, the
religious habit, prayer life, penance, the dowry and economic
arrangements--were also examined and commented upon in the books
which were popular during this time.

Reasons For Entering the Convent

Several possible reasons for joining the convent are
given. Hogan refers to the European economic situation when he
asserts that daughters of noble families impoverished by the French
Revolution prefer the convent to the marriage to a debauched
old nobleman that is their only other alternative.[308] Smith quotes
Robert Bellarmine, an Italian Jesuit cardinal who died in 1621, who
says that upon occasion the poor enter religious life in order to
improve their financial condition.[309] Murray suggests that young
ladies are induced to enter religion by romantic tales of beautiful noblewomen with exquisite taste, and a life that is heaven on
earth.[310] (He seems not to have read the convent stories that
were circulated in America at this time!) Disappointment in love
is another motive cited by Hogan, while a general disappointment
with life is favored by Chaplin, M'Gavin, and Murray.[311] Hawthorne uses the theme of the convent as a refuge for those who
are disappointed in life and love in The Blithedale Romance.[312]
M'Gavin says some choose the convent because they hope to find a
freer rein for vice there.[313] Some who enter are fleeing

domestic tyranny.[314] One of Mrs. Chaplin's characters sees the
economic security, the certainty of being taken care of for the
rest of one's life, as a reason why women enter the convent.[315]

The theme of the nun unwillingly professed, so popular
in European literature in earlier centuries, is repeated in books
avidly read in America. Culbertson tells of two hundred daughters
of the first families of Cuba who are induced to enter the convent
whether willing or not.[316] Murray says that in Europe he found
orphans and illegitimate children compelled to be nuns.[317] Miss
Bunkley's editor quotes Alphonsus Liguori's advice to nuns imprisoned against their will: "Make a virtue of necessity," he
says.[318] Chaplin tells of a nun who entered the convent because
her confessor told her to.[319] (It seems that few, if any, of these
reasons could actually have been decisive in an American girl's
choice of religious life, however influential they might have been
in Europe. This is one facet of convent life in which these
writers are not at all realistic.)

The Habit

The religious habit which marks the sister off from other
women in a rather conspicuous way causes hostile comment among
those who observe it. The Baltimore Literary and Religious
Magazine, in its article on Sister Olivia Neale, the deranged
Carmelite who walked out of her convent, mentions that she was
dressed in "the peculiar and shocking habit of her order."[320]
Samuel B. Smith gives an interesting explanation for the wearing
of the habit:

> The appearance of the Nuns clothed in their modest
> garb and veiled from the public gaze is imposing,
> and a superficial observer is led to believe that the
> interior corresponds with the exterior. Outwardly,
> or above the surface, the whole exterior form of the
> Monastic Show, moves with a solemn and imposing
> mien. The modestly adjusted dress, the downcast eye,
> the veil to hide the world from view, the attitude
> erect, the measured pace, the tout ensemble strikes
> the beholder with veneration.[321]

For Mrs. Chaplin, the black robe of the nun connotes mourning,

and is certainly not a guarantee that its wearers have eschewed

all womanly vanity concerning dress. One of her characters re-

ports that there is far more conversation about dress within the

convent than without. This is partly the result of a change in

the color of the cap worn by the sisters. "Every day," this pupil

reports,

> at recreation, we hear nothing but about the new
> white cap which has taken the place of the old black
> one. I have been asked by each one how it became
> her, and each one has told me from what order of
> foreign nuns the fashion came to this country. I
> think it worse to take pride in a hideous-looking
> garment than in a becoming one, because it is a
> mockery of religion, which is worse than a mere
> sacrifice to woman's vanity. The head-dress makes
> all the poor, pale nuns look as if arrayed for their
> burial.[322]

(That the habit does not always relieve the nun of that

concern about styles which characterizes her sisters in the world

becomes evident whenever a change in habit style is suggested.

We have already examined the dissensions which marked the Emmits-

burg sisters' change of habit and the reactions of the Nazareth

Sisters of Charity when a change in the color of their cap was

suggested. Of interest too is a letter from a Loretto sister to

Bishop Chabrat in which there is a long discussion of the relative merits of blue and black material for habits, and some interesting remarks on the best type of belt for nuns to wear:

> I think also it would be better for them to wear a belt the same as their habit, it would be more uniform and less remarkable, as they are so many different qualities of girdles among the Sisters which has been often been remarked some must be polished, and some fixed one way and some another I think there is even vanity in the girdles, besides if they look so much at the expense the girdle is more expensive than a belt of the same--50 cents for one bolt of leather.[323])

A basic Protestant reaction to the religious habit worn by sisters who are devoted to works of charity is expressed by a character in Barker's Cecilia . . . :

> There are thousands who daily dispense charities of various kinds; yet they do not term themselves Sisters of Charity, neither promenade the streets in a garb so antiquated and peculiar as to excite attention, or elicit encomiums on their marvelously holy lives and charitable deeds.[324]

This attitude is present, though not always explicitly stated, in many of the convent stories.

Reception and Profession Ceremonies

A highly romantic--but essentially accurate--description of the ceremonies of reception of the habit and profession of vows is included by many writers. "The pomp, show, and ceremony of 'taking the vail, [sic]' writes Nicholas Murray, "are so arranged as to exalt the heroism and piety of the maiden that takes it, and as, if possible, to induce other maidens to do likewise."[325] A typical description is that found in Pope or President, which pictures flattery, flowers, moist eyes, and an emphasis on the heroism of the girl who is taking the veil. Her "beautiful hair is all shorn from her head, by the merciless sisters . . . ."[326]

He emphasizes the nuptial character of the ceremony of the consecration of nuns with its references to the nun as the spouse of Christ, admitting no lover but Him. He also quotes Wiseman on spiritual espousals.[327] Mrs. Chaplin uses this imagery when Sister Leonore explains that she has given herself away as a "Bride of heaven," "and great rapture have I enjoyed in laying up everlasting treasure'," she insists.[328] Miss Bunkley quotes from the Pontificale Romanum the curse that is called down on those who would disturb these virgins or their property.[329]

Hogan repeats the traditional encomiums on the youthful beauty and wealth of the young woman.[330] The author of Important Facts describes the way the young lady throws herself on the ground after pronouncing her vows, thus symbolizing her death to all that is of the world, and the taking of the black habit.[331] Culbertson adds a procession through the streets to her description of an elaborate ceremony in Cuba.[332] In the sermon preached at the reception ceremony in Sister Agnes, the aspirant to religious life is reminded that even the holiest of earthly ties are dangerous, the fairest of earthly joys impure.[333]

Many descendants of the Puritans emphasize the appeal to the senses--through the use of incense, stained glass, wax tapers, flowers, rich vestments, organ music, etc.--in their descriptions of Catholicism; this also plays a large part in the descriptions of reception and profession ceremonies. McCrindell has her two school girls attend a profession ceremony and finds them very much affected by it.[334] The author of Important Facts quotes Mayor

Lyman of Boston, who says $1800 was spent on a vesture ceremony.[335]

Smith refers to the notion that the religious state is a special

state of life, superior to the married state:

> Nuns especially, from the supposed sanctity of their
> vocation, are taught to consider that they ought to
> aspire to a much higher state of perfection than
> that which characterizes the commonalty, or what
> they call worldlings, that is, the common people of
> the world, whose state of life is considered by them
> as much less perfect than that of the religious or
> Monastic state.[336]

Prayer

The prayer life of the sisters causes comment in some of

the books. In The Convent and the Manse, two girls are left

standing in the rain because the sisters are chanting vespers and

"their first duty is to finish their devotions. 'Heaven before

earth' is their motto . . . and nothing could be suffered to draw

even a domestic from her vespers." One of the girls contrasts

this attitude with that of Jesus, Who "was always ready to do the

smallest act of kindness." When told that the nuns' rule forbade

any earthly occurrence to interrupt their devotions, the same girl

remarks, "I presume that they would soon break through the rules

of their order, if the house were on fire. Selfishness would then

overcome bigotry." The sisters pray in Latin.[337] McCrindell's

schoolgirl is required to attend prayer service in French and

Latin both morning and evening. (The school she attends is in

France.)[338] Smith reports that many nuns are required to recite

the breviary worthily, attentively, and devoutly, or sin.[339]

Frothingham's hero, who has sneaked into a convent and successfully

gotten past six giants and a sleeping priest, nears the chapel

where, at two in the morning, the nuns are chanting office "in a
sleepy, drawling tone, their numerous voices repeating in a list-
less tone."[340] (As was noted above, the practice of rising in the
middle of the night did cause problems for teaching sisters.)

Penitential Practices

Several authors detail the penitential practices, done in
reparation for one's sins and those of others, which were common
in many religious houses. Needless to say, some of these are
exaggerated, and some are outright lies. The author of Sister
Agnes describes lashes on bare shoulders, fasting on bread and
water, making the stations of the cross on bare knees while being
flogged, lying prostrate at the threshold of the choir, and licking
a fifty-foot-long sign of the cross on the refectory floor.[341]
McCrindell's schoolgirls note that some sisters, after being absent
from meals for two or three weeks, return to the refectory looking
as if they have endured severe penance.[342] The Misses Reed, Monk,
and Bunkley speak of the practice of kissing the floor, which is
supposed to produce humility. This was done at least twenty times
a day, says the latter young lady.[343] Maria Monk also mentions
such penances as kneeling on hard peas and walking with them in
one's shoes; eating meals with a rope around one's neck; eating
things one doesn't like like eels or garlic; branding oneself with
a hot iron; standing with arms extended in imitation of a cross;
chewing a piece of windowglass to a fine powder; and wearing a
leather belt stuck with sharp metallic points around one's waist
and arms.[344] Chaplin includes among the penances she describes

nights spent in prayer, as does the author of <u>Pope or President</u>.[345]
In the latter book we are told that the few hours of sleep that are
taken are accompanied by the discomfort caused by a pillow of
thorns.[346] This author also reports that haircloth and scourges
are used, and Miss Bunkley supports his statement.[347] She quotes
St. Alphonsus Liguori's instructions on the use of the discipline,
as the scourge was called.[348]

 S.B. Smith describes the situation that actually did exist
among the Loretto sisters: they rose at 4 a.m.; went barefoot from
March to November; and performed difficult tasks like chopping wood,
hauling logs, manure, and stone.[349] Smith repeats the same facts in
another work, <u>Renunciation of Popery</u>.[350] In the Ursuline convent at
Charlestown as described by Frothingham in <u>The Convent's Doom</u>, a
"heavy penalty is afflicted [sic] if the inmates indulge a
smile."[351] Rebecca Reed says smiling is allowed only during recreation.[352] Culbertson voices the typical American reaction to
penances such as these: "the cruelties which they are taught to
endure as meritorious in the sight of Heaven, are inconsistent
with the spirit of the times; they belong to the darkest ages of
the world."[353]

Economic Situation

 The economic situation in America, which made it impossible for nuns to work among the poor <u>gratis</u>, and forced them to
support themselves and their works by charging tuition and finding
other means of supplementing their income, had repercussions on
the popular image that recurred in the fiction.

According to these books, one of the chief characteristics of convents is greed for money. Indeed, the primary occupation of many priests and nuns, if the books be believed, was that of trying to induce young heiresses to enter the convent and give their fortunes to the Church. Thus Sister Agatha in the book Sister Agnes acts as a governess but is really an undercover agent for the Jesuits, working to get her pupil--and that young lady's inheritance--into the convent. After the girl becomes a nun, she is hidden in a convent in Italy so that the community can claim her inheritance.[354] Frothingham has a priest in The Haunted Convent insist that a student become a nun because her father is rich and the convent will get his money.[355] Monks get head-money for every heiress they lure into the convent, according to S.J. Mahoney.[356] Letters are forged, and dying men and women badgered into signing away their property.[357] When a nun dies before coming into her inheritance, another nun is brought from Canada to substitute for her and claim her money.[358] The Sisters of Charity urge the sick whom they nurse to give them money for masses.[359] Not even a poor girl stopping at a convent to ask for prayers can escape the greedy demands of the nuns.[360]

The fact that sisters had to support themselves through the income from boarding schools led to accusations of greediness on that score. Smith notes in The Renunciation of Popery that the annual income of the school at Bardstown is $20,000.[361] (He does not bother, however, to list its expenses.) The only reason the sisters are kind to the pupils in their boarding schools, says one of Mrs. Chaplin's characters, is because of the money these schools bring in.[362] Nuns do not care for the poor in the hovels

of seaport towns, says Smith, nor are they ever seen in the Five

Points section of New York, because neither money nor publicity

would reward their work in places like these.[363] There is, of

course, a certain amount of truth in this. If sisters could have

afforded to spend a large percentage of their time among the poor,

they would have. But as we have seen above, circumstances forced

them to take up works that were more remunerative.

The Rev. Charles Sparry's account of convent finances in

the Protestant Annual offers a different view from those cited

above. Only rarely are American citizens asked to contribute to

the building or endowment of convents, he writes:

> As to the idea that females are educated in nunneries
> for the purpose of obtaining a support for their in-
> stitutions, it is not worthy serious notice, as it
> is well known that immense sums are annually sent
> from Catholic countries to their spies here, for the
> purpose of establishing their own religion, and of
> supporting such institutions as are best suited to
> educate the youth of our country in the creed of the
> church of Rome.[364]

Rebecca Reed held the same opinion.[365]

Foreign Attitudes and Customs

The tradition that the convent is a foreign, European

institution, inimical to English liberties and interests, is con-

tinued in the stories disseminated in the 1830's, '40's, and '50's.

Many of the tales and anecdotes take place in European settings.

Important Facts summarizes the history of religious life in

Europe and relates incidents that have taken place in convents in

the Azores, Madrid, and Cadiz. It also discusses the facts dis-

covered by Mayor Lyman of Boston during the time that he lived in

Rome.[366] The father of Isabella in The Convent and the Manse finds his objections to convents intensified by what he sees during a European trip.[367] Culbertson's tale of Rosamund has a Cuban setting, while Barker's Cecilia takes place in Canada. M'Gavin, in an appendix which purports to be about Catholicism in America, quotes from several European writers, who tell about European convents.[368] Nicholas Murray's book on Romanism at Home describes Catholicism as he saw it in Europe. He discovers, among other things, that the reason for the "vulgar appearance of nuns" is their lower class origins. "Italian nuns . . . needed not the walls of a nunnery to protect them from marriage," he reports.[369] McCrindell uses a Continental setting for The School-Girl in France, and the convent in Sister Agnes is an Irish one.

Several books refer to the fact that most of the nuns in America have come from Europe. Rebecca Reed reports that Bishop England "brought over a bevy of imported nuns."[370] Hogan says the nuns at a particular school "were said to be the most accomplished teachers in Europe."[371] Barker asks, "Why do not these very superior teachers disseminate knowledge at home?" and notes that Italians, Spaniards, and other inhabitants of Catholic countries are terribly ignorant.[372]

It is clear that convents are being associated with the alien culture of the Old World. The spotlight is focused on the monastery as it existed in periods of laxity and decline, not on the many fervent communities which bore fruit in holiness and virtue. There is implicit recognition of the fact that role definitions for nuns were derived from the European culture of previous centuries, and of the economic and social system which placed many girls in convents who would have chosen another way of life, had they been given the chance. Though the legislation of the Council of Trent was intended to correct abuses, social and economic patterns continued virtually unchanged, in some places, for centuries. Bishop Scipio Ricci's visitation records reveal the laxity which characterized some convents in his diocese in the eighteenth century, and there were Italian convents in the nineteenth century which were also in need of reform. (Indeed, it would remain true into the 1960's that Italian girls often entered the convent because their fathers had chosen this form of life for them.)[373] Mahoney quotes Ricci, and then reports what he himself saw in Pistoia and Rome--situations not very different from those of the eighteenth century.[374]

It is therefore not too surprising that Americans, who prided themselves on having a type of government and a way of life far superior to European forms, should seriously question whether an institution so bound up with European mores could survive in America. We have seen in Chapter III that European communities which started convents in America succeeded only if they adapted to American conditions. The many adaptations which became necessary as more and more European groups founded houses in America, prove that there is some truth in this contention. M'Gavin notes that most Americans would think "that convents and nunneries, being in their own nature so totally incongenial with all the principles of our social compact, could not possibly gain an ascendency in this republic." "It remains to be seen," he writes,

and the experiment will perhaps be tried by no
distant generation, whether the pollutions which have
defiled the convents of the old world, can exist amid
the purity of our own moral atmosphere; and the
scenes which have been acted in dungeons of Madrid
and Goa, can be renewed on the soil consecrated as
the home of freedom and the refuge of the oppressed.
To us as Americans, the inquiry is a deeply interesting one.[375]

M'Gavin attempts to show that the religious life is inimical to

the values that are most highly prized by America: social and

personal liberty, freedom and independence, civil and religious

liberty, morality, and national prosperity.[376]

These writers neglect to note one important fact, however.

If the American culture is different, so is the American girl. If

she is as independent and determined in her choices as Tocqueville

says, then she will not enter the convent unless she really wants

to. This will make a world of difference in the way she lives

religious life, and the corruptions of the Old World need not enter

in. There were defenders of Catholicism in this period who pointed

out some of the differences between European and American convents.

Rev. Charles Sparry felt constrained to answer them and wrote:

> One of the great delusions which pervades all classes
> of the American community is this--that Romanism is
> now, and in the United States, of a totally different
> character from its attributes in Europe or South
> America; and during the dark ages; and also, that
> although nunneries may have been the mere brothels
> of Roman priests, and filthy murderous dens in France,
> Italy, and Spain, prior to the reformation, yet in
> this country they are now abodes of piety, purity,
> and wisdom.[317]

Several of the writers place the sisters within the

aristocratic strata of European society, harking back to the days

when nuns were mostly members of the upper classes. Culbertson mentions two hundred girls "of the best families" who have been compelled to enter the convent in Cuba.[378] Hogan says that most of the nuns in European schools are usually descendants of the first families.[379] The superior of the convent school described by Mrs. Chaplin is said to have been of the highest rank in her own country and is called "the old duchess." She refers to ordinary Americans as "the lower order" or "the common people," and thus arouses the antagonism of her American pupils.[380] The practice of having lay sisters who perform menial tasks is another European custom which is depicted in these books. Hogan mentions the "lay sisters among Jesuits," who "are spies . . . but are sometimes bribed by the nuns for certain purposes." The lay sisters of the Sisters of Charity, he avers, get jobs as chambermaids or are disguised as boys in the senate, so as to ferret out the secrets of the country and of Protestant families and report them to the Jesuits.[381]

Works of Charity

In discussing the sisters' works, some writers make the basic distinction between nuns properly so-called and "sisters." Mrs. Chaplin carefully points out the difference between active and contemplative convents. At one point one of her characters says, "This is not a convent, but the house of the Sisters of the Heart of Mercy." Here the young lady was supposed to learn the rules and preparatory lessons before proceeding to a convent. At the convent school itself, life is very different. The girl sees no company, and the regime is very strict.[382] In Sister Agnes we

are told that the convent described is one of the "clausure,
strictly secluded." This explanation is added:

> Those of this class are usually occupied by young
> women of fortune; they are the more wealthy convents,
> whose inmates do not require to support them by
> educating the young; and there it is politic to place
> those who are in danger of changing their resolution
> of taking the veil, for they have not that communi-
> cation with the outer world which is afforded to
> nuns who receive pupils.[383]

Miss Bunkley says the house of the Sisters of Charity is not a
"close Convent," in which nuns are perpetually immured.[384]

We have seen that most communities, even those which led
a strictly contemplative life, had to support themselves. Because
of this need, and the scarcity of teachers in America, many turned
to teaching as a means of support and an apostolic work for their
neighbor. The large proportion of convents which ran boarding
schools according to the French plan is reflected in the convent
stories of the period, most of which feature convent boarding
schools rather prominently. In the course of the novels, various
aspects of these schools are examined.

One would have a difficult time drawing any conclusions
regarding curriculum and the quality of the education given from
these novels, so contradictory is the evidence. Rachel McCrindell
describes school work that begins at 6 a.m. and continues until
8 p.m., with only an hour's recreation, the memorization of
thirty or forty pages of history, and similar feats which suggest
a rigorous course of study.[385] Frothingham depicts a girl who
goes to a convent school in order to get a thorough education in
music and other accomplishments.[386] According to Hogan, sister-

teachers are usually "highly accomplished."[387] Mysteries of a
Convent also says convent schools offer a good education, and this
opinion is seconded by M'Gavin.[388] Mrs. Chaplin, however, dis-
parages the quality of the education offered. One of her characters suggests that "they no doubt spent most of their time in the
nunnery at ornamental branches, and in general reading." At the
convent school "French and Spanish, the piano and the pencil, light
English literature, and the embroidery-frame, divided the time . . . .
The playing and singing set on edge the teeth of any fine musician."
One girl is sent there to learn to make wax flowers and to embroider.
The teachers are incompetent: "She can play a few old-fashioned
marches and overtures, and read a little French; but she cannot
paint at all. I have a sister, fifteen years old, who could teach
Sister Mary for years to come." "Not one in ten of them," remarks
one student, "could teach in the public schools of the north."[389]
Maria Monk agrees with her.[390]

The French boarding-school system included close surveillance
of the students, and imposed heavy burdens on the sisters who
added this duty to a full teaching schedule. This custom is
commented on by several writers, who see in it a certain infringe-
ment upon individual rights. Rachel McCrindell says that the
students are watched at every moment;[391] Ciocci reports the same
thing of the Charlestown school;[392] and Frothingham mentions it in
connection with a Montreal boarding school.[393] In Mrs. Chaplin's
boarding school the sisters not only watch over every word, they
also hide the girls' clothes at night so they can't escape. "The
pupils were under the care of nuns ever watchful over their words,

looks, and actions," writes Mrs. Chaplin. "One nun slept in each room, if indeed the nuns ever slept, which the pupils thought very doubtful, for every whisper and every breath was heard."[394] Some of the cloistral practices which bind the nuns are required of their students as well. Ciocci cites the rules of the Charlestown school which prohibit talking after bedtime, and require censorship of mail. Few visitors are allowed, and there is always a sister present on the rare occasions when they are admitted.[395] M'Gavin also mentions censorship and rules which forbid communication with domestic friends.[396]

Since significant proportions of the students in convent schools were Protestants, it was customary to advertise that the religion of non-Catholic pupils would not be interfered with. This claim did not pass unnoticed by those anxious to discredit the schools. When a student in Convent and Manse says she has been assured her religion will not be interfered with, the nun to whom she is speaking answers, "Nor shall it be. You may believe in your heart what you please; but outwardly you must observe the rules of the convent." Then the nun tries through various arguments to persuade the girl to become a Catholic. Later the Lady Superior tries to win her over by lavishing affection on her.[397] In the French school described by McCrindell, the sisters pledged themselves not to interfere with the opinions of Protestants and "scrupulously avoided very intentional breach of that engagement."[398] Barker writes that nuns are far too polite to openly attack the religion of Protestant pupils, "yet secretly it is undermined . . . . Prizes are awarded for diligence and application; and these prizes are books, setting forth in winning language the doctrines of their church. I have seen one of these . . . . It was titled 'Alethea, or, a Defense of Catholic Doctrines.' Yet most diligently they deny any attempts toward proselyting the pupils intrusted to their care."[399]

These writers complain that the cost of convent schools limits their clientele to the daughters of wealthy families. Hogan tells of a school run by "Jesuit nuns" in which "the expenses of an education . . . were extravagantly high, but not beyond the reach of wealth and fashion." This school was "one of the most fashionable in the country," and a Protestant mother was yielding to "the malign influence of fashion" when she sent her daughter, "her earthly idol," there for her education.[400] McCrindell's students are sent to a French convent school to add "fashionable polish" to their education, and Chaplin notes that "it was . . . becoming quite genteel to send girls to a convent for education."[401] Mrs. Chaplin and Frothingham depict politicians who send their daughters to convent schools in order to win the Catholic vote. Frothingham's candidate promises to do all in his power to obtain remuneration for the destruction of the "convent of St. Ursuline" if elected.[402] M'Gavin notes that the price of tuition limits the clientele to those who have the most extensive opportunities to influence others.[403] Though it is true to a degree, this charge of catering to an elite does not accurately reflect the American situation, in which free schools existed side by side with select or pay schools.

Lyman Beecher's "Plea for the West" and his claim that
Catholics were pouring huge sums of money and armies of priests
and nuns into their campaign to take over the West, made the West
a popular setting for convent schools. The superior in Mrs.
Chaplin's novel had originally come from Europe with six other
nuns "to establish a convent in our great western valley."[404]
Smith describes "a Nunnery, in the United States, west of the
Alleghany mountains."[405] Rebecca Reed reveals that "an eminent
clergyman at the West" told her that "immense sums sent here from
Europe, go chiefly to establish Catholic colleges and Nunneries."[406]
Sparry also tells of immense sums being sent to establish schools
and nunneries "in the western country."[407]

The sisters' work of caring for orphans was disparaged by
Hogan, and also by Smith. They said the sisters only took in
orphans when they were old enough to work. The work the orphans
do makes it unnecessary to hire many servants, Hogan says. The
infirm, the lame, and the blind are not admitted.[408] Barker tells
the story of a woman whose orphans were refused admittance to a
Catholic orphanage because she had no money.[409] The devotion
shown by various communities in nursing victims of epidemics was
also disparaged, this time by Smith, who says they only nurse
because their rule obliges them to. Sisters of Charity care for
the dying, he says, only so that they can urge them to leave money
or masses. Benjamin Barker tells of a nursing Sister of Charity
who, when the patient resists her efforts to get him to become a
Catholic, refuses to nurse him any longer.[411]

Immorality

The more lurid of the books which purported to reveal the
truth about convents appealed to the baser instincts of the masses
at the same time that they fostered feelings of self-righteousness.
Hopkins has described the situation that prevailed in the pre--
Civil War decades thus:

> The popularity of such literature, apart from its
> anti-Catholicism, can also be attributed to the spirit
> of the age. The heavy hand of evangelical piety
> lay over the land. Anti-Catholic publications,
> like a number of those directed against slavery and
> alcoholic beverages, were a way of having your cake
> and eating it. The reader, in good conscience,
> could enjoy that most dangerous of virtues, righteous
> indignation while still experiencing the less noble
> sensations aroused by obscenity. In addition, this
> was the age of Poe when the macabre became a dominant
> theme in literature, art, and even architecture.[412]

The same themes of seduction, immorality, underground passageways,
torture, abortion, and infanticide recur monotonously in these
books. The seduction theme of the sentimental novel is intensified
through use of the trappings of the Gothic. The story of a
maiden's loss of her virtue was calculated to arouse horror in
American readers, while at the same time guaranteeing their avid
interest. Maria Monk apologizes, in her preface, for dealing with
delicate subject matter which might be offensive to some of her
readers, but insists that she must reveal the facts in order to
save children from ruin. It is better for society, she says, if
she reveals, rather than conceals, convent crimes.[413] It is to
the credit of the nun figure as seen in these novels that she is
usually sincere and virtuous at the start; the blame for her cor-
ruption is laid to scheming priests and monks. Many of the

heroines who are thus misused conform to the sentimental code by
fading away and dying after having been seduced.

The tale of seduction by one's confessor appears in several
of these books, most notably in Hogan's Auricular Confession and
Popish Nunneries. A young girl who has entered the convent sends
for him and reveals that she has been seduced by her confessor. "I
am in the family way, and I must die," she tells him, in true
sentimental fashion. Nor does she waste much time. When he returns
two weeks later, she is no more. "Cold clay contained all that
remained."[414] Many girls, according to Hogan, enter the convent
after having been seduced in the confessional while attending
boarding schools. They are taught vices and debauched by their
confessors. Two of the Charlestown Ursulines were "far advanced
in the family way," thanks to the efforts of their confessor, when
the convent burned down.[415] Many of the other books repeat Hogan's
tale, with little variation.[416] Given the fact that a grille
was required and used in any confessional in which women's confessions were heard, one can only conclude that these confessors
were a very athletic tribe. Some of the writers have an answer to
this objection. The seduction is only begun in the confessional;
it is consummated in an adjoining room. A lighted candle placed
on the altar, says Smith, is a warning to anyone who should
approach that the chaplain is busy. According to Maria Monk there
is a lattice between the novice and the priest during confession,
but this is not true of the professed sisters. They confess either
in the superior's room or another one.[417]

Frothingham has the hero of Six Hours in a Convent sneak
into the Charlestown convent in search of his sister and his be-
loved. He asks a nun who aids him whether the two girls are still
pure. They are, she replies, but she doesn't know how much
longer they will remain so. Another nun whose escape he abets is
no longer pure. The only future she has to look forward to is in
cheering the declining years of her father.[418]

Maria Monk and S.B. Smith refer to a doctrine which was
popular in certain quarters and did actually lead, in some instances, to immoral practices. Unsuspecting penitents, according
to Smith, are told that priests are not to be regarded as mere
men, but as Christ himself.[419] Maria Monk describes the experience
of a thirteen-year-old childhood friend in some detail:

> She was partly persuaded by the priest to believe
> he could not sin because he was a priest, and that
> anything he did to her would sanctify her . . . .
> A priest, she had been told by him, is a holy man,
> and appointed to a holy office, and therefore what
> would be wicked in other men, could not be so in
> him.[420]

When the girl told her mother about the priest's advances in the
confessional, her mother said "that as priests were not like other
men, but holy, and sent to instruct and save us, whatever they
did was right." Later, as a nun, Miss Monk reports that she was
taught to practice self-denial and mortify her feelings. "This
was to be done by opposing them, and acting contrary to them; and
what she proposed was, therefore, pleasing in the sight of God."
The superior told her that priests act "under the direct sanction
of God, and could not sin . . . . To refuse to do anything they
asked, would necessarily be sinful."[421] Priests ask improper and

revolting questions in the confessional, and thus plant the seeds
for later crimes, Miss Monk reports.

Statements like these were not simply products of Miss
Monk's imagination, however untrue they might have been. They
were based on reports of the actual practice in certain European
convents where the doctrine of quietism, a product of the seventeenth century's penchant for mysticism, was carried to its logical conclusion. This doctrine, as taught by the Spanish priest
Miguel Molinos, held, among other things, "that if souls in a high
state of prayer are tempted to commit the most obscene and
blasphemous actions, they must not leave their prayer to resist
the temptation; the devil is being allowed to humiliate them, and
if the actions are committed, they are not to be confessed as
sins."[422] As might be expected, scandals sometimes occurred when
this doctrine, or a variation of it, was taught by a spiritual
director.[423]

Such was the case with the convent of St. Catherine in
Prato and other monasteries in the diocese of Pistoia and Prato in
the eighteenth century. Nuns in the convent of St. Catherine sent
letters to the Grand Duke Leopold in the 1770's complaining of confessors who seduced their penitents, and even made mistresses of
them, while insisting that no sin was involved. The Jansenist
bishop of the region, Scipione Ricci, did his best to correct the
disorders that had crept in. The memoirs of this bishop, as
edited by the anti-Catholic historian Louis de Potter, included
copies of these letters, as well as the bishop's own reports of
what he had discovered during visitation of the convents in his

diocese.[424] This book, along with all books dealing with the decrees of the Synod of Pistoia which Ricci had called, was placed on the Index of Forbidden Books by the Catholic Church.[425] An English edition translated by Thomas Roscoe was published in London in 1829, and in 1834 an American edition appeared. These revelations of the immorality found in convents by a Catholic bishop, edited by a former Catholic, were taken by many American writers as proof that all convents were evil and should be abolished. What had actually happened fifty years earlier, in a few convents whose inhabitants had been deluded by quietism, provided a basis for stories of convent life that would continue in circulation in America for generations after the first editions appeared in the 1830's and 1850's.

After the initial seduction, these writers said, a nun would have no choice but to enter into a life of immorality. To add plausibility to the incidents they describe, they quote from the works of those who had called for the reform of religious communities during earlier periods of laxity. Thus S.B. Smith quotes Petrarch and Bellarmine, as well as Scipio Ricci.[426] M'Gavin also quotes Ricci and earlier reformers.[427] Many are the writers who repeat tales and charges of immorality.[428] Underground passages to the outside aid in the perpetration of various crimes. They are described in Awful Disclosures, Mysteries of a Convent, and M'Gavin's book. The last-named adds the detail that convents for men and women are always built near one another.[429]

Pregnancies inevitably occur to complicate convent affairs, according to these writers.[430] There are two solutions: abortion or murder (of either the mother or the child). Hogan tells of a nun told by her abbess to take some medicine which would induce an abortion. She knows it is poison, and refuses. In Europe, he says, lying-in hospitals are attached to every nunnery, but the use of abortion and murder make them unnecessary in America.[431]

Maria Monk and others give graphic descriptions of the techniques used in disposing of the bodies of murdered babies. In the cellar of her convent is a deep hole, twelve to fifteen feet in diameter, in which the bodies are put. A generous use of lime covers up all traces. In murdering babies, the sisters are doing them a favor, she has been told, because they will go straight to heaven. "Their little souls would thank those who kill their bodies, if they had it in their power," insists the superior.[432] Sparry tells of the bones of infants that were found in the ruins of an old convent "in a Catholic country."[433] Nor is it only infants and their mothers who are victims of the murders committed in these books. In Mysteries of a Convent, the superior murders the priest who is the highest superior of the Jesuits, and another nun, and then kills herself.[434]

Another unsavory aspect of convent life which is often linked to immoral practices is the use of cruelty and torture as punishment for refusal to comply with the requests of a priest, abbess, or other superior. Thus Maria Monk tells of a nun who is smothered and crushed to death--between two mattresses--because she refuses to condone the murder of innocent babies.[435] The heroine of Sister Agnes has red hot coals put on her feet as punishment for trying to escape. She finally chokes on a gag

while trying to resist the attentions of a priest and dies.[436]
(The use of a gag is borrowed from Maria Monk, who describes it
in detail.)[437] An article entitled "Help! Help! Oh! Lord!.
Help!" appeared in several issues of the Baltimore Literary and
Religious Magazine. It contains a statement signed by six citizens
of Baltimore who attest that on March 13, 1835 they heard female
screams emanating from the upper story of the Carmelite convent
in that city.[438]

There is much use in these books of dungeons and prison
cells as places of punishment for recalcitrant nuns. Frothingham's
narrator in Six Hours in a Convent remarks, "I had read of convents, and knew very well that they had secret cells, where prisoners could be placed."[439] Maria Monk makes much of the cells in
the basement of her convent, including detailed diagrams which
did not, however, correspond with the interior of the convent she
was purportedly describing. She finds nuns who have been imprisoned for years, some of them wealthy heiresses who refused
to sign their property over to the convent. Some are there only
temporarily because when the superior ordered them to sing,
fatigue kept them from complying. Barker tells of a sister who is
put into a dungeon for the birth of her baby.[440]

Positive Viewpoints

There were some publications which attempted to answer and
counteract the works of Rebecca Reed and Maria Monk. They pointed
out the contradictions, absurdities, and falsehoods found in these
books, and sometimes included page-by-page refutations of false
charges. Such was the case with the Lady Superior's reply to

Rebecca Reed's work.[441] William L. Stone and a Canadian publications committee demolished most of Maria Monk's statements.[442]
These works conveyed a more positive view of convent life, but
confined themselves chiefly to exposing errors; they made no
effort to depict the role of the nun as it actually was.

A more deliberate statement of a positive view of the role
of the nun is found in the published version of a sermon preached
by Bishop John England of Charleston at a reception ceremony in
his cathedral on May 19, 1835. England, founder of the first
Catholic newspaper in the country, and one of the most effective
defenders of Catholic doctrine, used the opportunity to present
a positive view of convent life. He was aware that his seven
hundred listeners were filled with misconceptions and false ideas
about convents, and examined the very points which had caused
the most controversy in the works of Rebecca Reed and others. The
published version of this sermon, though it probably had a very
small circulation, is a good source for the role definitions for
nuns that were found in Catholic writings of the period.

England's chief point of emphasis concerned that on which
the case against convents had been largely based: the fact that
no girl who is unwilling can be accepted by a religious community.
He quotes from the decrees of the Council of Trent and the constitutions of the Ursuline community, and also appeals to rational
argument to drive this point home. Several times during the course
of his sermon he pauses and asks the girl if she truly wants to be
a nun, and pleads with her to speak out if she is being coerced.[443]

The bishop is also very forceful in his descriptions of
the raison d'être of religious life, the reasons why a girl would
choose to become a nun. His explanation is based chiefly on St.
Paul's first epistle to the Corinthians. St. Paul contrasts the
situation of the married woman, who must be concerned about her
husband and her family, with that of an unmarried one, who can be
wholly taken up with the things of God, the practice of virtue,
and the alleviation of the sufferings of others. Bishop England
gives a long explanation of the Scriptural basis of religious life
and the three vows. He points out the great contribution which a
religious community makes to society through its works, and gives
the history of the Ursuline Order. The chief object of the
Ursuline Order, he says, is the sanctification of its own members,
and the education of female children.

We have noted above that the authors of the fictional works
on convent life include in their books many of the facets of religious life which were most important in the formal role definitions of canon law: prayer life, cloistral practices, the habit,
reception and profession ceremonies, penitential practices, and
works of charity. They also depict, in an unfavorable light, the
economic situation which faced American sisters, and the European
attitudes and manners which characterized many of them. Many of
the practices of convent life are caricatured and given false
interpretations; penitential practices, for example, are grossly
misrepresented. In two areas, the motives for entering religious
life and the depiction of immorality, these writers borrow
material from European convents of earlier centuries and give a

false picture of the American situation. It is evident that these stories had a profound influence on those who read them.[444] Positive statements like Bishop England's reached very few non-Catholics, though the refutations of the Lady Superior and William L. Stone did convince many fair-minded people.

Conclusion

Sisters' formal role definitions, arising from the European culture of an earlier century, caused problems for them, for the bishops under whom they worked, and for Americans who came in contact with them. The opinion that European religious life was incompatible with those values most prized by Americans was held not only by large numbers of American Protestants, but by bishops and religious superiors as well. The experiences of the sisters proved that some adaptations would have to be made if religious life was to prosper in America. Many believed the exaggerated or fabricated stories of convent life that were widely circulated; some took violent action as a result of them.

The evidence indicates, however, that despite the roles which canon law and their constitutions imposed on sisters, roles which proved unsuitable and caused great difficulty in America, despite the horrendous stories which were circulated about them, all fair-minded people who came into intimate contact with sisters and their works praised them. Even the enemies of religious life bore witness to the powerful influence which the sisters' lives exerted over those with whom they came in contact.[445] Students who had been prejudiced against them became their staunchest defenders, and men who attacked their convents were converted by their fearless reliance on God.

There is little in the popular stories of convent life
that could account for this phenomenon. It had nothing to do with
cloistral practices, the presence or absence of the religious
habit, or European attitudes. It transcended these external
trappings of the convent and flowed from that essence of religious
life discussed by Bishop England which was not dealt with in the
best-sellers, and yet constituted the real secret of female convents. Though some of the fictional works hint at the fact that
a girl might enter the convent in order to live the Christian life
in a more intense way and to be freer than her married sisters to
succor the needs of her neighbor, the actual picture they paint
is very different. To the extent that they leave out that essence
of religious life, these books fail to depict the role of the nun
as it was actually lived during this period. It would take far
wider contact with the actual work of nuns to change the public
attitudes towards them. This would be accomplished in the following decade.

CHAPTER V

1860-1870

Introduction

In the 1860's the communities which had already been
founded in America continued to grow and spread, though the war
created special problems for them, as it did for all Americans.
Eight religious communities, all of them stemming from European
motherhouses, began new foundations in America during this decade.

The nativism which had aroused so much antagonism towards
sisters in the preceding period abated, as the abolitionist
movement gained momentum and energies and thoughts were directed
toward the slavery question. With the coming of the Civil War,
there was an abrupt change in the attitude of the general public
towards the Catholic Church. The example of Catholic soldiers who
proved their patriotism by serving loyally in the war did much to
dispel prejudice, and daily contact with Catholics proved to many
that the charges of bigots were false. Members of religious
communities nursed on the battlefields, in army hospitals, and on
hospital ships and turned the tide of public sentiment from one of
suspicion, hatred, and bigotry to one of deep respect and admiration.

Formal Role Definitions of Canon Law

As far as canon law and the Church's formal role definitions for sisters are concerned, nothing was changed during this
period, though a few decisions were given in answer to questions
about the status of American communities. The questions regarding
simple and solemn vows, dispensations, and enclosure which had
been raised in the preceding decades continued to occupy a central
position. In 1860 Bishops Odin of Galveston and Rappe of Cleveland wrote to Rome asking whether the vows of the Ursulines were
simple or solemn.[2] In September, 1864, the question regarding
the vows of the Visitandine nuns, which had been debated for
twenty years, was answered once and for all by a decree of the
Congregation of Bishops and Regulars. After discussing many aspects
of the question and quoting the contradictory opinions of con-
sultors, the decree stated that nuns in five American Visitandine
convents--those at Georgetown, Mobile, Kaskaskia, St. Louis, and
Baltimore--could take solemn vows. All other sisters in America
must take simple vows, it said.[3] Though some bishops had asked
that solemn vows be allowed in America, and the superiors of all
ten American Visitandine convents had petitioned the pope for
this favor, Rome decided against it for two reasons: many bishops
wished sisters to staff schools in their dioceses, and cloistral
prescriptions would make this difficult; also, rules forbidding
entry to the cloister were repugnant to many non-Catholics, who
wanted civil authorities to have access to convents, to keep
sisters from being held in them against their will.[4]

Though one might assume that simple vows could be dispensed
by the local bishop, this was not the tenor of the letter which
Cardinal Barnabo wrote to Archbishop Purcell on December 19, 1865.
He held that all vows, solemn, simple, and even temporary, are
reserved to the Holy See, unless constitutions state the contrary.
He quoted the statement of Benedict XIV to the effect that bishops
should not concern themselves with dispensations of this kind.[5]
That this was not generally understood, and would have made life
extremely complicated for American sisters, can be deduced from
the letters which they wrote to their bishops requesting dispensations, several of which are quoted below.

In 1869 Pope Pius IX issued the constitution Apostolicae
Sedes, the last statement on enclosure before the codification
of canon law in 1918. It reaffirmed the regulations of Pope
Boniface VIII and the Council of Trent regarding enclosure for
those with solemn vows. Outsiders, even little girls, were forbidden to enter the cloister, and bishops were authorized to appeal
to civil authorities for assistance, when necessary, in enforcing
the law of enclosure. The pope can give permission for cloistered
sisters to receive pupils, the constitution said, but no pupils
may be admitted without his permission.[6]

These were the provisions of canon law which continued to
govern sisters' lives. As they strove to live out their roles in
the American milieu of the 1860's, they faced many of the same
problems which had caused tensions in the preceding periods. The
chief cause of conflict continued to be the constitutional restrictions which had been formulated for a culture very different from

that of America.

Problems Posed By The American Milieu

For many communities, tensions were eased after the
question regarding vows in America was settled by the decision of
September, 1864, which decreed that, with the exception of a few
Visitandine sisters, all others in America should take simple vows.
Enclosure restrictions were discussed by the bishops at the Second
Plenary Council of Baltimore in 1866; this must have cleared up
some misunderstandings on the part of the bishops, though guide-
lines were certainly not clearly drawn.

The idea of enclosure as an essential part of the life of
any sister who was truly a religious continued to prevail in Rome,
and hence in America. The decision of 1864 must have added to the
confusion in some quarters, since it left even strictly cloistered
communities with the same simple vows which were also professed
by uncloistered communities like the Josephites and the Sisters
of Mercy. Strict enclosure could no longer be equated with solemn
vows, and less strict with simple ones. Hence there were still
problems to be faced when sisters tried to live the fullness of
religious life in the American setting. The various manifestations
of the enclosure--remaining within the convent precincts, separation from the outside world by means of a grille, etc.--continued
to cause problems. Superiors were constantly asking their bishops
for permission to be dispensed from the cloistral prescriptions of
their constitutions.

Thus Bishop Henni wrote to the Racine Dominicans in 1862,
"Naturally the Sisters must have permission to walk to the schools.

I wish, however, that they would endeavor to keep their white habits concealed as much as possible on the street."[7] The Sisters of the Incarnate Word and Blessed Sacrament found the situation in Texas somewhat different from that in France. It was necessary for their superiors to visit one another to talk over various matters, and for people who conducted examinations and visited classes to come into the enclosure. Therefore Bishop Dubuis gave them permission for these things, and also to go into their exterior chapel when no priest or lay person was present.[8] The Amityville Dominicans got permission to leave the cloister in order to beg alms, nurse the sick, and care for children in orphanages. At their Williamsburg convent they went out of the cloister to teach, though there is no record of their having obtained permission for this.[9] Sister Mary Jacobins, SSND, wrote to Archbishop Odin of New Orleans, "We are sorry to intrude again upon your Lordship, but being desirous of undertaking nothing contrary to our rules of enclosure without the permission of Your Grace, we proceed, giving information of what we want . . . . We wish to know whether your Lordship will permit us to go to this store and examine this stove . . . . Such as this we have never before done."[10] Father Gilbert Raymond wrote to the same archbishop in behalf of the Ursulines, asking for dispensations, taking into consideration "the construction of the convent and the moral and almost physical impossibility of observing the primitive rule rigorously."[11] The Racine Dominicans got permission to attend a parish church until they could obtain a chaplain of their own.[12]

Various expedients were used in order to alleviate the hardships suffered because of cloistral prescriptions. The Atchison Benedictines sent their postulants to the stores and neighboring farmhouses to procure food.[13] The Amityville Dominicans had some postulants enter their community as Third Order members so that they could nurse and care for orphans.[14]

Some bishops deliberately sought communities which were flexible and uncloistered for the work of their dioceses. Bishop Dubuis found, upon his arrival in Texas in 1862, that both communities there were cloistered, and unable to teach in parish schools. He made a trip to Europe to find uncloistered sisters.[15] In Erie, Pennsylvania, Bishop Mullen persuaded the Benedictines to abandon cloistral seclusion and become an active teaching order.[16] Not long after the inception of their school in Selma, Alabama, the Religious of the Sacred Heart realized that the situation called for an uncloistered community, and hence the Mercy Sisters were asked to take over.[17] The 1862 constitutions of the Columbus Dominicans specifically stated that "Observance of the Rule and Constitutions" meant only that part binding on the Third Order, not the sections for priests and cloistered Dominicans.[18] Enclosure rules were in the omitted sections.

Sisters who associated strict enclosure with the fullness of the religious life--as the Church also did--sometimes endured crises of conscience when living in communities in which it was impossible to carry out cloister rules. Thus Sister Marie de St. Benoit, CSC, wrote to Father Stephen Rousselon that she could no longer stifle the cries of her conscience for having taken vows as a Holy Cross Sister. She had thought she was entering a cloistered community. She planned to join the Ursulines or another cloistered group, and failing that, to return to France. She had made too great a sacrifice in leaving the world, she said, to toy with her salvation and risk losing her soul in religion.[19] And when Mother Benedicta Bauer tried to persuade a friend from the Ratisbon mother-house to join her in Racine, she was told, "Sister Benigna . . . decidedly expressed herself thus: 'To America I will not go; either into a real convent or none at all.'" (Reports had reached Ratisbon about the impossibility of keeping strict enclosure in America.)[20]

Rigid interpretations of the prescriptions of constitutions continued to prevail in some quarters, and to keep sisters from taking an active part in the work of the Church. The wealthy Mrs. Sarah Peter, who brought a group of contemplative nuns to Cincinnati, asked if they might be permitted to speak to people through a grille and instruct them in spiritual matters. This request was refused because such a practice was contrary to the spirit of the community.[21] The Sisters of St. Mary of Namur found scant support for their schools in Lockport, New York. It was said that the priests there opposed them because they kept their rules, were controlled by their Belgian motherhouse, and were not Irish.[22] And a Mercy superior hesitated to accept pay schools because she felt this was not the work of her community.[23]

It is obvious that the call to nurse in the Civil War interrupted the regular routine of sisters' lives. Most saw the urgent need of their wounded brothers as an opportunity to carry out the counsels of the Gospels which took precedence over minute

rules and regulations of religious life. The necessary dispensa-

tions from rules which could not be kept during wartime were

usually forthcoming. A Josephite superior, for example, wrote

to the sister who was to be head nurse in a hospital, "I suppose

that you will be dispensed of a part of your prayers, and even

Mass and holy Communion through the week. Make a good meditation

in the morning. Offer up all the actions of the day, attend to

those poor people and I think our Lord will be satisfied."[24]

Later the same superior wrote to another group of sisters, "The

Bishop has already given the necessary dispensation . . . go to

Holy Communion when you can have that favor . . . . Make your

Meditation in the morning after your prayers and be not troubled

if you can say no other prayers of the Community, not even if you

are deprived of Mass on Sunday."[25]

Not all superiors were this understanding, however.

F.L. Olmsted tells of a hospital boat on which the sisters

chaplain clung to the letter of the law and kept them from fol-

lowing its spirit:

> The forty "Sisters" . . . had all struck for keys to
> their staterooms, and sat about on their large
> trunks, forbidden to stir by the Padre, who was in a
> high state of ecclesiastical disgust on the deck of
> the Knickerbocker, at not finding provision made
> for them, including a chapel.--Labored with the in-
> dignant old gentleman upon the unreasonableness of
> expecting to find confessionals, etc. erected on the
> battle-field, but to no purpose. There sat the forty
> "Sisters," clean and peaceful, with their forty um-
> brellas and their forty baskets, fastened to their
> places by the Padre's eye, and not one of them was
> allowed to come over and help us . . . . It was hard
> to have the "Sisters," who would have been so faith-
> ful, and who were so much needed, shut away from the
> sick men by the etiquette of their confessor.[26]

In Galveston, where the whole city praised Mother St.
Pierre Harrison for twice turning the Ursuline monastery into a
hospital, offering the sisters as nurses, and refusing all offers
of escape to safety during the shelling of the island, there was
another chaplain with an unrealistic attitude toward the counsels
of the Gospel. Father Joseph Anstaett wrote to Archbishop Odin
of New Orleans that Mother St. Pierre was wrong to offer the convent as a hospital and the sisters as nurses. This despite the
fact that her action saved the newly constructed building from
destruction. Mother St. Pierre had very indelicately extorted a
dispensation from the cloister, he said, and went to the hospital
against his will.[27]

Communities which added the active work of teaching to the
Divine Office which characterized contemplative communities continued to seek relief from the burdens it imposed on them. In
1866 all American Benedictines were dispensed from the obligation
to say the Divine Office on all ordinary days in the Church calendar.[28] And the section on the Divine Office seems to have been
one of those in their constitutions which the Columbus Dominicans
did not observe.[29]

The strict observance of minute prescriptions in outdated
constitutions often repelled American girls who joined American
branches of European communities. They failed to see the connection, for example, between opening doors in a particular manner
and the precepts of the Gospels. Nor was the postulant who was
told that the hem on her apron was too wide impressed with the
values which prevailed.[30] Even the bishop remonstrated when

Mother Frances Schervier insisted that no English-speaking novice should be professed until she could speak German. Only through the German tongue could the spirit of the Order be learned, she said, but Archbishop Purcell insisted that this would only cause sisters to become disgusted with the religious life.[31]

The idea that religious life was incompatible with American values continued to be held in some quarters. The European motherhouse of the Poor Handmaids had received shocking reports about the state of American convents. It was said that their members had the frontier spirit of self-sufficiency and informality, sure indications of a total lack of the decorum, virtue, and religious spirit that should characterize nuns. The ultra-conservative peasant mentality of the superior made her fear that the American spirit of generosity might enter her community through its American houses. She therefore took special care in preparing all those who would go to America. The historian of the community exemplifies the type of thing she feared with a telling quote from Father Hecker and His Friends which is worth repeating: "The first group of American boys making novitiate in Europe had been rather suspect for almost six months because, when addressed by a superior, they looked straight at him and gave him a direct answer."[32]

The provisions of canon law which stipulated the wearing of a religious habit continued to be set aside during the 1860's, though the habit came to inspire respect rather than disgust in American society during the war years. In many cases sisters continued to wear lay clothing when going out of their convents, though some abandoned this practice. The Mercy Sisters wore the broad-brimmed black straw bonnet, thick crepe veil, and ample cloak that had once been the fashionable walking dress of elderly women and widows. But styles which had been unobjectionable in an earlier period became outdated as time went on. This garb now made them conspicuous, and attracted as much attention as the religious habit would have. Fellow-travelers asked of the pioneer group en route to Bangor, Maine in 1865, "Is the corpse on this train?"[33] Sisters of many other communities also drew attention to themselves because of their outmoded fashions.[34] During the Civil War, the Kentucky Dominicans dropped their practice of wearing secular dress while travelling after two of their number, having aroused suspicion in their outdated clothing, were arrested as spies.[35]

The lack of secular clothing sometimes kept sisters within their convents. The Ursulines of Galveston, for example, preferred to have their own Mass exercise in their convent, when the priest could not come to officiate, rather than attend Mass at a church in the city. Their religious habits would have been a distraction to the congregation, they felt, and they lacked any less elaborate clothing.[36] One group, the Daughters of the Cross, were relieved when the captain of the ship taking them to America said he saw no inconvenience in their traveling in religious garb.[37]

Many sisters whose rules required adaptations for American conditions fell into the usual pattern of strained relationships with European superiors, bishops, and priest-directors. Sometimes there were disputes over just who should make the decisions which would govern the sisters' lives. The Holy Cross Sisters had problems of jurisdiction with European superiors, Father Sorin, who tried to govern them in America, and the bishops in whose dioceses they worked. The unusually capable American women who became their leaders found the interference of male members of their order, both European and American, extremely irksome. The sisters who held the positions of provincial and directress at Notre Dame left the American province and returned to France because of the tensions, and the American sisters petitioned for autonomy from the French house in 1861 and again in 1868. Mother Angela Gillespie went to France to insist that the constitutions be adapted to American conditions. Her reception there was somewhat less than cordial, and it was only the pleas of American bishops with Roman officials which won concessions for the sisters at St. Mary's.[38] The separation was finally accomplished in 1869, but this did not relieve the sisters of the watchful care of Father Sorin, who had closed the Holy Cross schools in Philadelphia in 1864 because of disagreements with Bishop Wood. (Similar disagreements had erupted between Sorin and Bishop Hughes in the preceding decade--with the same results.)[39] Bishop Wood wrote to Archbishop Purcell regarding these sisters:

> Their affairs have become so complicated, that is, their relations with their French superiors, that, for the peace of the Sisters and the safety of their institutions, I have been in a certain way compelled to take them under my own care at least for the present. The poor bishop of Fort Wayne has been sorely exercised with them. I hope France will let go, or become more reasonable, less impulsive and more charitable.[40]

The Daughters of the Cross also faced difficulties between their bishop and their European superiors. When they asked to borrow money and suggested that the motherhouse send them some young sisters who could learn English, the French superiors forbade the borrowing of money, and refused to allow anyone under forty to volunteer for the American mission. When the American foundress returned to France in order to clear up misunderstandings, she found little sympathy and no help. The only solution was to dissolve all ties with the French motherhouse and become independent. This was done in 1868.[41]

Sometimes it was simply the difficulties of distance and communication and the necessity for decision-making on the local level which caused a foundation to become independent of its motherhouse. This is the traditional practice in the Benedictine Order, and seems to have been the reason for the separation, in 1866, of the Columbus Dominicans from those in Kentucky.[42] A branch convent of the Amityville Dominicans became independent in 1869 because of a personality clash, a difference in diocese, and divergent interests.[43] The Ratisbon motherhouse encouraged its American foundations to become autonomous. The mother general wrote, "You people in America should become independent, and then you could adjust yourselves according to the regulations which exist in America."[44]

It is no wonder that bishops continued to form separate diocesan communities which would be responsive to local needs and untrammeled by foreign customs or recourse to distant superiors. In Rochester, New York, Bishop McQuaid used the removal of a hospital administrator as an excuse for requesting the withdrawal of the Sisters of Charity from a parochial school, "on account of their rules and irresponsibility to the bishop."[45] He persuaded the Josephite sisters to separate from their Buffalo motherhouse and become a diocesan community. Their rules were better adapted than those of other communities to the needs of his diocese, he felt, and he especially liked their founder's injunction to obey the bishop as their superior.[46] Years later he said of these sisters in a letter, "I get from them all the services I want without having recourse to distant superiors, without stumbling against rules made for other conditions."[47] When Bishop Wood succeeded to the see of Philadelphia in 1860, he decided to make the Franciscan Sisters in his diocese into a diocesan community. Those from the Philadelphia motherhouse who taught in various New York dioceses were encouraged for form separate communities, and did so.[48] Thus the trend begun by Bishop Hughes continued to gather momentum.

Sometimes disagreements between sisters and spiritual directors regarding their rules and their roles could only be solved by the withdrawal of one party to the argument. When this happened in the Racine Dominican community, it was solved in one instance by the removal of the spiritual director, and in another by the withdrawal of some of the sisters, who started their own community. In 1868, when disagreements were such that it seemed the Racine group would have to disband, the appointment of a new spiritual director saved the day.[49]

The Columbus Dominicans chafed under the strict regulations of the Irish provincial, Father William O'Carroll, of whom a
community biographer wrote, "a good and pious man, but did not
understand the people of the United States."[50] In 1865 the
Dominican Master General decreed that Dominican Sisters should not
be directed by Dominican priests, but should be under the jurisdiction of the local bishop instead.[51]

Another problem which some European communities faced in
America had to do with the age at which they accepted candidates.
The Sisters of Divine Providence found that girls in Texas matured
early and left school at the age of twelve. They felt that they
had to accept candidates at that age, and many who were accepted
left when they reached adulthood and thought better of their
adolescent decisions.[52] The Sisters of St. Mary of Namur accepted
candidates who were under sixteen because that was the age at
which girls went out to take jobs. If they accepted girls after
they had worked a few years, and it became known that they had
been servant girls, they thought the good name of their community
would be harmed.[53]

Some of the class-consciousness that had been so evident
in earlier comments about the various orders and congregations
is found in the correspondence of Archbishop Francis Patrick
Kenrick. He planned to bring Notre Dame sisters from Cincinnati
to Philadelphia, and said of the project, "My judgment is that they
will be better fitted to teach girls there in that suburb than
others in a higher state of life; but I was ill at ease lest, inviting the more advanced, I might appear to be looking for rivals

to the detriment of the ladies of the Sacred Heart."[54]

Most communities continued the practice of having pay schools and free schools in order to support themselves, and communities which were newly arrived adapted in the usual ways to this aspect of the American scene. The Sisters of St. Mary who came from Belgium were willing to seek a dispensation from the usual dowry when poor girls wished to enter their community.[55] When the school board refused to rehire the Benedictine Sisters in St. Joseph, Minnesota, they had to break their enclosure in order to go on begging tours, and supported themselves by doing the laundry for the neighboring community of monks.[56] State and city governments were sometimes willing to subsidize the work of the sisters. Thus Bishop Lamy of Santa Fe was able to report to Archbishop Purcell in 1866: "The Legislature of this poor Territory voted last week one hundred dollars a month for our hospital. It is not much but still it shows a good disposition."[57]

The severe financial problems which afflicted the South after the Civil War also affected religious communities. Begging tours became an inevitable part of the lives of some members. The Visitandines from Wheeling went East seeking money for a "Southern fund" with which to educate the daughters of impoverished Southern families. They wrote to Boss Tweed for a contribution, and received a hundred-dollar check by return mail. He came to visit them in Washington, and made out a list of people to whom they should write in New York. Each day he sent his orderly to personally deliver the letters they had written. He gave them a check of $1000 at the end of his first visit, and an order on a livery stable which enabled them to use a coach, horses, and driver for the time of their stay.[58]

The Mercy Sisters, who had previously been supported by their dowries, inquired of their Irish motherhouse and of Pope Pius IX for suggestions as to how they might support themselves when financial burdens became too crushing. The pope replied that he saw nothing wrong with their earning money by doing laundry work, etc. "So long as matters stood as they were re-presented in America," he wrote, "the good sisters should get their support by the ways they have."[59]

Roles Sisters Played

In many facets of their lives, sisters continued to play the same roles in this decade that they had during the previous ones. The American foundations of European motherhouses begun during the earlier period gradually became Americanized as adaptations, the addition of American members, the pressure of bishops, and other factors worked to lessen their foreign characteristics. European communities which began their first American foundations in the 1860's went through the same painful process of learning the language and adapting to American customs which their pre-decessors had struggled through. Many communities continued to insist that American candidates learn a foreign tongue in order to participate in community prayer and other exercises.[60] Some continued to make a distinction between lay sisters and choir sisters.[61]

Teaching

Teaching continued to be the work to which most sisters devoted themselves, and much of what was said of convent schools in the last chapter continued to be true, though the attacks on them were greatly mitigated. The Civil War imposed hardships of various kinds, and while it raged, sisters sometimes left their classrooms in order to nurse the wounded.

Though adaptations were made, many schools continued to be dominated by European customs and methods of education. The Benedictines in St. Joseph, Minnesota, for example, followed a German rule which permitted sisters to teach for only an hour at a time. The change of teachers at the end of each hour created such discipline problems that the sisters were not re-hired for the district public school in 1865.[62] The Sisters of St. Mary of Namur insisted that their pupils learn French and use books which followed French methods of pedagogy.[63]

These sisters followed the traditional practice of opening a pay school for what the superior called "the aristocratic class of our poor Catholics," as well as a free school.[64] The Sisters of Mercy did the same thing in Chicago, but those in St. Louis felt that teaching in a pay school was contrary to their constitutions, which stressed service to the poor. When the superior asked the advice of Archbishop Peter Richard Kenrick, he replied:

> I very much dislike seeing you or any other community giving up, or placing in comparative neglect the special objects of the Institute; but almost everywhere in this country where endowments are rare, candidates for the religious life almost without dowry, and public charity not always an available

resource, experience has shown that the school is a
necessary adjunct to religious institutes.[65]

Many communities continued to limit their enrollment to girls,

though the Racine Dominicans also accepted boys.[66]

With the widespread acceptance of the idea of free public

education, a gradual change in the Catholic educational system

began to occur. Bishop Timon of Rochester, New York tried to

abolish the system of free and pay schools as early as 1857, when

he wrote in his diary, "I desire to suppress Select Schools--they

oppose it--yield to keep both."[67] In 1861, while visiting a con-

vent school, he decided "that all things must be suspended except

a Parish School in which Select and Free shall combine." Two

years later he told a pastor "to have no Select School, but a

general one for all." And the following year he again insisted

that a pastor "put the two schools together."[68]

As always, the schools called forth both praise and blame

from the public, but now the former outweighed the latter. It

is evident that the actual evidence of the quality of education

given in convent schools had dispelled many of the falsehoods

that had been spread about them in the preceding decades. In

Ottumwa, Iowa, enemies of the Visitandines spread a rumor that a

girl who had died of cholera had been neglected by the sisters.

As a result, parents brought about an economic crisis by with-

drawing their children from the pay school. Having no other means

of support, the sisters had to close their free school as well,

and to try to begin life anew in another city.[69] Incidents like

this, however, were unusual in this period.

Those who sent their daughters to the sisters' schools, or
attended the elaborate exhibitions which characterized the commencement programs of the day were highly pleased with the work done.
The praise of a reporter for the Lockport, New York Daily Union
is typical:

> Each visit to this school strengthens and confirms
> the favorable opinion heretofore formed regarding
> St. Joseph's Academy . . . and the advantages it
> affords for acquiring a careful education in all that
> goes to make an accomplished young lady.[70]

And Bishop John Quinlan of Mobile could write to Archbishop Purcell,
"The good Ursulines of Tuscaloosa, from whose 'annual' commencement
I have just returned, are doing wonders there--The Protestants
were there in crowds and came away delighted, many determining
to send their children next year."[71]

An article in the April, 1868 issue of the Atlantic Monthly
entitled "Our Catholic Brothers," points out several ways in which
"Catholic schools have some advantages over most of ours." "Certainly these convent schools, which are now so popular, are free
from some of the objections and difficulties that lessen the usefulness of many of our fashionable private academies," writes the
author. He praises the excellent arrangements of a typical school,
the discipline, and even the salutary effect of the religious
habit on the pupils: "The garb of the nun, of the Christian
Brother, of the Sister of Charity, as well as the serenity, and
dignity of their demeanor, hold impudence in check, and teach
the young victims of successful speculation that there are distinctions other than those indicated by marble fronts and rose-
wood stairs."[72] The tenor of an article like this in such an

influential magazine indicates the reversal in public opinion which took place during this decade.

In addition to the teaching that was done by most communities, sisters continued to care for orphans, and in 1863, the Good Shepherd sisters were asked to take charge of a women's prison in Cincinnati, a work which they continued for ten years.[73]

Nursing

The work of charity which overshadows every other work done by American sisters in the 1860's is that of nursing. If the preceding decades were dominated by the tales of Rebecca Reed and Maria Monk and the burning of Mt. St. Benedict, the Civil War years brought countless stories of their work as "Angels of Mercy," nursing wounded soldiers on the battlefield, in hospitals, and on board transport ships. The sister, who had been the object of hatred, insult, and persecution, suddenly became the subject of the highest praise, with Lincoln, Grant, and Jefferson Davis joining soldiers of every rank in paying tribute to her virtues and selfless devotion.

Sisters had nursed wounded American soldiers in both the Revolution and the War of 1812 without fanfare, but by 1861 the situation had changed.[74] The Civil War came just after a period in which strong antipathies and infamous charges against sisters had received national publicity. It also occurred shortly after the Crimean War, in which Florence Nightingale had distinguished herself in nursing the wounded, and won the acclaim of the English-speaking world. She had been assisted by Catholic sisters from England and Ireland, and French Daughters of Charity had also nursed.[75]

To .assess the accomplishments of sister-nurses in the
Civil War, one must first examine the state of nursing at the time.
Gillgannon feels that the greatest accomplishment of the Crimean
War was that it gave the English-speaking world a chance to recognize nursing as an honorable profession.[76] Before this time,
nursing was left to rough women of the lower classes who were
typified by Dickens' characters, Sairey Gamp and Betsey Prig.[77]
A historian of nursing writes, "In the Protestant world, the mid-
seventeenth to the mid-nineteenth century was the Dark Age of
nursing."[78] He states that the very word "nurse" had fallen into
such disrepute that Mrs. Wardroper, matron of the hospital where
Florence Nightingale established her nurses' training school,
substituted the more honorable term "sister" for her supervisors.[79]
(This title is still used today in English hospitals, even for
male nurses who hold this position.)

The state of nursing in America is indicated by the
practice at Bellevue Hospital in New York City. There some of the
nursing care was given by prostitutes who, in the Five Points
Police Court, were given the option of going either to prison or
into the hospital service for ten days.[80] When the Civil War
began, Catholic sisters were almost the only women in America with
nursing experience. And nuns who were not trained as nurses had
at least the habits of obedience, discipline, and selflessness
which are essential for that occupation.[81]

Before Florence Nightingale's reforms in nursing education
changed the situation, it was considered improper and compromising

to one's modesty for a lady to nurse outside her home.[82] When

she was placed at the head of an institution for the care of sick

gentlewomen in distressed circumstances, for example, the ladies

on the board were puzzled by Miss Nightingale's social position

and asked, "Could a lady take orders, even from a committee of

other ladies; should a lady . . . nurse one who was not a lady;

was it nice for a lady to be present at medical examinations and,

worse still, at operations?"[83]

These views prevailed in America as well, particularly in

the South. Kate Cumming, matron of a Confederate hospital in

Tennessee, confided to her journal how sick she was of people who

said that nursing was an unrefined and immodest occupation for

ladies, and raised an interesting question:

> A very nice lady, a member of the Methodist Church,
> told me that she would go into the hospital if she
> had in it a brother, a surgeon. I wonder if the
> Sisters of Charity have brothers, surgeons, in the
> hospitals where they go? It seems strange that they
> can do with honor what is wrong for Christian
> women to do. Well, I cannot but pity those people
> who have such false notions of propriety.[84]

Massey reports that many parents, particularly in the South, re-

fused to allow their young unmarried daughters to nurse soldiers.[85]

When the American Civil War broke out, the Secretary of

War sent an appeal to Florence Nightingale. She was asked to help

organize the care of the sick and wounded, and immediately sent

all of the reports and forms she could find to the war office and

to Dorothea Dix, Superintendant of nurses.[86] It was only natural

that administrators, and sisters themselves, should think of the

services that sisters had performed in the Crimea, and should

arrange for the participation of sisters in the American war.

Mrs. Betty Ann Perkins, in her study of the work of sisters in the Civil War, summarizes the various ways in which sisters were called into service. Some were called by governors; others volunteered to their states; some turned over their hospitals for military use while continuing to staff them. In some places they went out to nurse when battles took place near their hospitals; others staffed hospital boats equipped by individuals or cities. A few of the sisters who had nursed in the Crimea also took part in the American war, among them the foundress of the Mercy Sisters' Cincinnati convent, Mother Teresa Maher, and two of her companions.[87] Others had been trained by Mother Frances Bridgman, an Irish nun famous for her work at Scutari.[88]

Father Edward Sorin, American founder of the Holy Cross Order who governed the institutions at Notre Dame, clearly saw the opportunity which the war provided to change the public attitude toward the Catholic Church and its religious orders. He wrote to the Holy Cross Sisters on October 22, 1861:

> An admirable opportunity . . . has been offered to show our love of the country, to gain new claims upon the esteem--nay, the gratitude of our people; and such claims as no one would reject . . . . Nor is it idle to show that our Institutions are not useless or totally dead to the vital interests of the land; for thus, and thus only, the eyes of many will be opened to the real spirit of religious communities. A little band of devoted Sisters, ministering like angels amidst the soldiery, will do away with prejudices; and show the beauty and resources of the Catholic faith to support man in all possible trials much more forcibly than volumes of arguments and evidences.[89]

In the early stages of the war, Archbishop Hughes had a different view, and was unwilling to have sisters from his diocese participate. He wrote to Archbishop F.P. Kenrick of Baltimore on

May 9, 1861,

> Our Sisters of Mercy have volunteered after the example
> of their Sisters toiling in the Crimean War. I have
> signified to them, not harshly, that they had better
> mind their own affairs until their services are needed.
> I am now informed indirectly that the Sisters of
> Charity in the diocese would be willing to volunteer
> a force of from fifty to one hundred nurses. To this
> last proposition I have very strong objections.
> Besides, it would seem to me natural and proper that
> the Sisters of Charity in Emmittsburg should occupy
> the very honorable post of nursing the sick and
> wounded . . . . But Maryland is a divided state, as
> New York isn't . . . . On these several points I
> would like much to know what your grace thinks and
> would advise.[90]

Hughes was no doubt wondering what would become of the numerous

works of charity staffed by the sisters if they left them.

Later he withdrew his objections, and allowed sisters from his

diocese to nurse the wounded.

Dorothea Dix, famous for her reforms in the care of the

insane, was appointed Superintendant of Women Nurses in 1861,

when she was over sixty years old. It was agreed that nurses

would be paid forty cents per day plus subsistence and transpor-

tation. Miss Dix required that nurses be healthy, over thirty,

and, says Adam, "plain almost to repulsion in dress, and devoid

of personal attractions." They were to renounce "colored dresses,

hoops, curls, jewelry, and flowers on their bonnets." They must

be in their own rooms at taps or nine o'clock unless occupied in

the wards; and could neither go to places of amusement in the

evening, nor walk outside with any patient or officer, except on

business.[9]

Miss Dix was not a good administrator. (Who could have

been, in that chaotic situation, in which lines of authority and sources of supply were not clearly defined?) She scolded doctors who shirked or drank with a very sharp tongue, and was the center of many disagreements between nurses and medical staff.[92] Miss Dix herself did not wish to have her life judged by her war work.[93] She particularly antagonized doctors by her discrimination against Catholics in general and sister-nurses in particular. Seldom would she approve a Catholic applicant if a Protestant were available.[94]

Most medical men opposed any use of women in the military hospitals, but they were particularly hostile to Miss Dix's recruits. Often they failed to distinguish between her hand-picked nurses and other women who attached themselves to the hospitals on one pretext or another. Jane Stuart Woolsey describes the situation well in Hospital Days:

> Was the system of women nurses in hospitals a failure? There never was any system . . . . Hospital nurses were of all sorts, and came from various sources of supply; volunteers, paid or unpaid; soldiers' wives and sisters who had come to see their friends, and remained without any clear commission or duties; women sent by State agencies and aid societies; women assigned by the General Superintendant of Nurses; sometimes, as in a case I knew of, the wife or daughter of a medical officer drawing the rations, but certainly not doing the work of a "laundress." These women were set adrift in a hospital, eight to twenty of them, for the most part slightly educated, without training or discipline, without company organization or officers.[95]

She quotes an officer in a neighboring hospital who wrote to her, "You will be interested to know that we are just now in the midst of a war among the women nurses, which has continued with varying intensity and fortunes, but with uniform clangor."[96]

If this was the situation in the hospitals, it is no wonder that doctors, many of whom had already had the experience of working with nuns in hospitals, did all that they could to obtain them for their military establishments. The experience described by Surgeon John Brinton was a typical one:

> The female nurse business was a great trial to all the men concerned, and to me at Mound City it soon became intolerable . . . . I determined, therefore, to try to get rid of them from the Mound City hospital. In answer to my request to the Catholic authorities of . . . South Bend, Ind., a number of Sisters were sent down to act as nurses in the hospital. Those sent were from a teaching and not from a nursing order, but in a short time they adapted themselves admirably to their new duties . . . . There were in all, I think, fourteen or fifteen of them. So I procured good nurses for my sick, and the whole tribe of sanitary "Mrs. Brundages" passed away. The sick patients gained by the change, but for a few days I was the most abused man in that department, for the newspapers gave me no mercy.[97]

And Dr. Henry Hollingsworth Smith, surgeon-general of the Pennsylvania Volunteers, wrote, "Whilst beset by applicants, every female nurse has been refused, Dr. Smith being unwilling to trust any but his old friends the Sisters of St. Joseph."[98]

Mary Livermore tried to find out why all of the doctors clamored for Sisters of Charity, and reported:

> "Your Protestant nurses are always finding some mare's-nest or other," said one of the surgeons, "that they can't let alone. They all write for the papers, and the story finds its way into print, and directly we are in hot water. Now, the 'Sisters' never see anything they ought not to see, nor hear anything they ought not to hear, and they never write for the papers--and the result is we get along very comfortably with them."[99]

Confederate nurse Kate Cumming summed up the general feeling in her diary after describing the noise of the "lady nurses": "I

thought that it was not strange that surgeons should prefer to
have Sisters of Charity to nurse their sick, for they know how
to keep quiet."[100]

Doctors were aware of Miss Dix's hostility towards sister-
nurses, as Dr. Smith's letter to a Josephite superior indicates:

> I have taken the liberty of advising them as to their
> new duties and suggesting points of conduct as they
> come into friendly competition with a party of females
> directed by Miss Dix. I intend them to win the
> good opinion and good will of all. I have told them
> to keep guard of their eyes and their tongues, which
> I am sure you will say is Fatherly advice.[101]

And Bessie Jones writes, in her introduction to Louisa May Alcott's
Hospital Sketches, "Miss Dix's prejudice against nuns and her
lack of jurisdiction over them were sources of great friction
between her and medical directors, surgeons, and wardmasters who
insisted on appointing only sisters of the Catholic Church."[102]

Miss Dix actually tried, shortly after her appointment, to
remove the sisters from military hospitals. The Cincinnati
Catholic Telegraph and Advocate had this to say about the removal
of sisters from Camp Dennison:

> The officers and men of the Tenth Regiment requested
> the Sisters of Charity to continue their valued services
> to the sick soldiers, but it seems that Miss Dorothy
> Dix is Adjutant General of the Hospitals and the
> soldiers have to bleed and die unconsoled by the nurses
> of their choice, unless she gives consent. The
> Sisters of Charity will not apply to Miss Dorothy Dix
> for leave to do good. Let the Secretary of War see
> to it; he does so handsomely to other things.[103]

The sisters in question returned to Cincinnati. Two years later
they faced another problem of the same kind. On October 26, 1863,
Sister Anthony, a sister-nurse whose work was acclaimed throughout the nation, wrote to Archbishop Purcell, "This day I received

a copy of the certificate which places us under the special
direction of Miss Dix. I thought it best to send you mine . . . .
I hardly thought you would be willing to leave us subject to
Miss Dix's whims."[104]

In the agreements entered into with those who requested
the services of the sisters, there was often a clause stating
that sisters would work directly under the supervision of the army
surgeons.[105] It is easy to see why they preferred to steer clear
of Miss Dix. When she and others, piqued at the obvious preference for sister-nurses, complained that Protestants were being
discriminated against, the non-Catholic Surgeon-General, William
A. Hammond, retorted that nuns were sought after in army hospitals
because they were good nurses.[106]

Finally, on October 29, 1863, a general order was sent out
by E.D. Townsend, Assistant Surgeon-General, at the request of
Secretary of War Stanton, giving final control over all nurses to
the Surgeon-General, and thus curbing Miss Dix's power. Some of
the sisters wished to leave their posts, but were urged by the
soldiers to remain. Sister Anthony wrote to Archbishop Purcell
on November 14, "I would not like to leave now. It would be
gratifying to the Presbetarian [sic] Ministers and Miss Dix's
Delegates for us to get out of the way. We are now so independent,
we can stay as long as we please."[107]

The type of work done by sisters in army hospitals is
summarized in a report of Surgeon-General J.K. Barnes:

> According to the testimony of all the medical
> officers who have referred to this point their best
> service was rendered in connection with extra
> diets, the linen-room and laundry. Male help was

> preferred in the wards, save in special cases of
> prostration and suffering where particular care was
> needful in the administration of dietetic or re-
> medial agents.[108]

The fastest writers went from ward to ward, taking down the last

requests and messages of the dying, then snipping a lock of hair

to send to the soldier's family.[109] Sisters also distributed

medicines and food. Mother Angela Gillespie established procedures

for hospital administration which became standard for navy nurses--

having a nurse at the head of each ward, with an assistant ward-

master and enlisted corpsmen under them.[110]

Gettysburg provides an example of what sister-nurses did

on the battlefields. Since it is only seven miles from Emmitsburg,

many sisters from the motherhouse there helped to nurse the

thousands wounded in the battle. They went out onto the battle-

field to care for those still lying there, and removed their

petticoats and tore them up for bandages when their supply ran out.

In the makeshift hospitals set up all over the town, they were

assigned to care for the Confederate wounded, since it was noticed

that many ladies of the town who were nursing ignored them.[111]

There is much evidence to indicate that sisters also

ministered to the spiritual needs of the soldiers. The famous

army scout, Captain Jack Crawford, has mentioned in his tribute

to the nuns of the battlefield,

> their . . . whispering words of comfort into the
> ears soon to be deafened by the cold implacable hand
> of death; . . . breathing words of hope of an im-
> mortality beyond the grave into the ear of some
> mangled hero . . . now holding the crucifix to re-
> ceive the last kiss from somebody's darling boy . .
> standing as shielding, prayerful angels between the
> dying soldiers and the horrors of death.[112]

Though exact statistics are lacking, reliable estimates hold that six hundred forty of the thirty-two hundred Civil War nurses were nuns, and these represented twenty separate communities of twelve religious orders.[113] They served in hospitals and camps, on battlefields and hospital ships in eighteen states and the District of Columbia.[114] Detailed studies of the places where sisters nursed, their communities, etc. have been done by Ellen Ryan Jolly and Betty Ann Perkins; their findings need not be repeated here, except as they have to do with topics pertinent to this study.[115]

It was a common experience for the sisters to meet bigotry and prejudice when they first arrived at a hospital. One sister-nurse has recorded a reaction that was repeated in many places:

> In the hospital at Louisville, so great was the prejudice that many of the ladies were bitterly opposed to what they called our usurpation of their work, though we had been called there by the government; and they showed us scant courtesy. We were only three Sisters in a house sheltering about five hundred wounded men; and most of these, too, were as little used to us and as prejudiced as the ladies; but we went about our work quietly, trusting that in growing familiar with our garb they would see that we were not different from other women and neither to be feared nor hated.[116]

The soldiers at the hospital in Beaufort, North Carolina, many of them New Englanders well-read in anti-convent literature, watched their sister-nurses very closely in order to catch any proselytizing that might be done. The steward of the hospital later confessed that he often watched them until one in the morning, expecting to find them poisoning patients, setting fire to offices, etc.[117] Obstacles were often placed in the sisters' way, and at some hospitals, pamphlets and leaflets filled with lies about convent life appeared on the patients' bedside tables several times a week.[118] When the Mercy Sisters first arrived in Beaufort, there were many rumors and theories about them. Some thought they were widows in search of their husbands' bodies; others female Jesuits or chief mourners.[119]

One soldier struck the sisters as they passed him, and upon seeing that they continued to nurse him, asked what they were and where their husbands were. The sister who answered surprised him by saying she was happy she had no husband, for if she did, she would not be able to take care of him.[120] A sister-nurse noted in her diary:

> Our smallpox patients appeared to think that the Sisters were not like other human beings, or they would not attend to such loathesome contagious diseases, which every one else shunned. . . . One said . . . "The boys often say they must be different from other people, for they do for us what no other person would do. They are not afraid of fevers, smallpox, or anything else."[121]

Many who came into contact with nuns for the first time during the war were frightened and puzzled by the religious habit, and revealed strange notions about those who wore it. One of the Sisters of Charity who nursed in Pensacola reported,

> On one occasion there were quite a number come to the hospital sick, and when we went into the wards they covered their heads with blankets and nothing would induce them to uncover them while we were in the wards for three or four days, as they were so frightened at our appearance or so "skerte" as they used to say, they were anxious to know to what regiment we belonged or if we had been engaged in any battles, for if ever we were, the "Yankeese" [sic] would be more afraid of us than any gun the boys could show them.[122]

A patient shrieked to the Mercy Sister who bent over him, "Great heavens! Are you a man or a woman? But your hand is a woman's hand; its touch is soft, and your voice is gentle--what are you?"[123]

And Sister Ann Cecilia, a Cincinnati Sister of Charity, noted in her diary:

> It is surprizing that our peculiar dress was a source of amusement to those who had never before seen a Sister of Charity or a Sister of any other order. We were frequently asked why we dressed so differently from other ladies. One boy told us the girls up at his place wore low necks and short sleeves, adding-- "You know them dresses make you look so funny."[124]

Another soldier thought the sisters' rosaries would make pretty watch chains.[125]

Two Sisters of Charity who wore their habits during a trip to central Georgia in 1863 caused consternation among people who had never seen religious garb before. Onlookers pushed against them to see if they were human, and asked if they were men or women. When one sister spoke, the crowd clapped and said, "She spoke! She spoke!"[126] When they sought shelter for the night at the home of a priest who had never seen a Sister of Charity, even he thought they must be imposters.[127] A backwoods mother who visited her wounded son at Wheeling Hospital asked of the sisters, "Be they Injuns?"[128]

Mary Livermore was very favorably impressed by the way sisters administered hospitals, but had to admit,

> I often sympathized with some of the sick men, who frequently expressed a wish for a reform in the "headgear" of the "Sisters." "Why can't they take off those white-winged sunbonnets in the ward?" asked one,. "Sun-bonnets!" sneered another . . . "They're a cross between a white sun-bonnet and a broken-down umbrella."[129]

After the first shock of the sisters' appearance wore off, and patients had a chance to watch them in action in the hospital wards, there was a gradual change in attitude which was remarked upon repeatedly in diaries, letters, speeches, and other accounts of the sisters' work. "Surely these ladies are working for God; money is not their motive" was a common refrain.[130] A Holy Cross sister reported, "Once I said to a sick soldier, who had learned to trust us in spite of his former dislike, 'So you really think we will go to Heaven, even if we are Catholics,' and he answered in all seriousness, 'Yes, I really do.'"[131] One characteristic which most impressed onlookers was the fact that the sisters made no distinction between friend and foe, Protestant and Catholic, in their ministrations.[132]

Sisters commanded such respect from both Union and Confederate armies that they were allowed to pass freely through the lines of either side. When Governor Morton of Indiana wished to obtain the sick and wounded who were being held in Richmond, he was able to do it only by using the Sisters as a passport.[133] In Baltimore, imposters donned the habit of the Daughters of Charity in order to enjoy some of their privileges.[134] Nor was this the only place where this happened.[135] When Bishop Verot took some Sisters of Mercy through the Union lines in a mule-drawn wagon, they were pursued for several miles by Union cavalry tracking down a rumor that he was transporting slaves dressed like nuns.[136]

Testimonials to the excellent work done by the nuns were showered on them from all sides, both during and after the war. Neal Gillespie, first graduate of Notre Dame, proudly wrote to his mother of the reactions to his sister, Mother Angela Gillespie,

and her companions:

> General Wallace and the officers of the brigade, who
> are all men of education and high standing and con-
> siderable influence at home, are delighted with the
> sisters . . . . When the Methodist chaplain, who is
> very zealous in the discharge of his duties, fails to
> make an impression on a hardened sinner, he requests
> M. Angela to pray for the sinner, and to talk to him
> herself . . . . She has . . . made the bigoted acknow-
> ledge the divine charity that burns in the hearts
> of the members of the Church, and recognize the
> superiority of the consolations given to the sick
> and dying by our Holy Mother Church.[137]

General Grant, watching Holy Cross sister Mother Augusta master a

difficult situation, once exclaimed, "What a wonderful woman she

is! She can control the men better than I can."[138] He often con-

sulted her about what should be done for the sick.[139] Lincoln is

said to have paid many visits to the sisters who nursed in the

military hospitals in and around Washington, visits marked by

the greatest friendliness and evident admiration for the sisters.[140]

A tribute to nuns that has been widely attributed to Lincoln,

however, was actually written by Lucius E. Chittenden and first

appeared in his Recollections of President Lincoln and His

Administration.[141]

Nor was it just the Union side whose great men praised the

sisters. Catching sight of some Mercy Sisters one day after the

war was over, Jefferson Davis approached them and said,

> Will you allow me, ladies, to speak a moment with
> you? I am proud to see you once more. I can
> never forget your kindness to the sick and wounded
> during our darkest days. And I know not how to
> testify my gratitude and respect for every member of
> your noble Order.[142]

During the battle for Richmond, when General McClellan's Reserve

Corps was encamped about three hundred yards from a convent of

the Emmitsburg Sisters, one officer gave his men orders to capture

Sisters of Charity if they could, for their hospitals needed

them.[143] Sister Anthony O'Connell of the Cincinnati Sisters of

Charity was personally acquainted with Generals Grant, Sherman,

Sheridan, McClellan, and Rosecrans, as well as Jefferson Davis.[144]

One soldier wrote of this remarkable woman in his diary:

> Amid this sea of blood she performed the most revolting
> duties for those poor soldiers. She seemed like a
> ministering angel, and many a young soldier owes his
> life to her care and charity. Happy was the soldier
> who, wounded and bleeding, had her near him to whisper
> words of consolation and courage. She was reverenced
> by blue and gray, Protestant and Catholic alike; and
> we conferred on her the title of the "Florence Night-
> ingale of America." Her name became a household word
> in every section of the North and South.[145]

The analogy to Florence Nightingale was made very early

in the war and used repeatedly thereafter. As early as the be-

ginning of June, 1861, the Cincinnati Commercial assured its

readers that the hospitals at Camp Dennison were in excellent

condition and added, "Sister Anthony and a number of Sisters of

Charity are acting as nurses and do much of the cooking for the

sick . . . . The services of these good women cannot be esti-

mated. They are the Florence Nightingales of America."[146]

And an article in the Chicago Tribune for December 17, 1861

described the change which usually accompanied the sisters'

arrival at a hospital thus:

> The Sisters of Mercy have taken hold of the hospitals
> in Jefferson City as nurses for the sick there, and
> will certainly, as far as they command the means, re-
> place the horrible filth, and squalor, and wretched-
> ness that filled them at my first visit, with a gentle,
> cheerful, abiding care and purity, and peace. Pray
> permit me, Standing so far from these women in

> ecclesiastical and theological ideas, to testify to
> their beautiful, holy and unselfish devotions where-
> ver I have found them in our hospitals, East or West.
> The doctors can find nowhere else such perfect nurses--
> so nice about the food--so reliable about the medicine--
> quiet as Quakers, yet cheerful and chatty whenever
> the undying womanly instinct is touched . . . . They
> give, asking nothing again, what no money can
> purchase.[147]

Doctors who heard about the smoothly operated system of the

sisters could not believe that forty women could live amicably

together, much less with an equal number of men, reported the

executive officer of one hospital.[148]

Walt Whitman assisted the Sisters of Charity in one of

their hospitals, but seems to have preferred nurses of another

sort. "Young ladies, however refined, educated, and benevolent,

do not succeed as army nurses, though their motives are noble,"

he wrote in the New York Times. "Neither do the Catholic nuns.

Among these home-born American young men, mothers full of motherly

feelings . . . are the true women nurses."[149]

One of the greatest compliments paid to sisters by their

Protestant brethren during the Civil War is found in the words of

those who asked, "Why have we no Protestant Sisters of Charity?"

This was the question raised in England when the splendid work

done by the French Daughters of Charity on Crimean battlefields

was praised, and it was repeated in America. Kate Cumming told of

a minister who said "he hoped some day we would have a sisterhood

in the church as was in the day of the apostles."[150] The wife of

General Lew Wallace wrote to her mother, "Nothing in our churches

equals the devotion of these women. When Protestant sisters get

time they go home, but the Sisters of the Holy Cross live among

238

the patients without thought of deserting infested places or avoiding contagion by flight."[151] And a soldier wrote from Gettysburg, "I think that the churches of all denominations should each send at least one Sister of Charity, to comfort and to bless these suffering men."[152]

In 1867 a New York Times article reflected the changed image of the nun which now dominated the country:

> We have every now and then attempts made in Pro-
> testant countries to establish a charitable order
> of women that shall do the work that is so admirably
> done in Catholic countries by the Sisters of Charity
> and other pious orders of the Church. During our
> great war the devotion of the women of America to the
> sick and wounded was spoken of far and wide. They
> nursed in the hospitals all over the country, and formed
> associations for aiding and comforting the helpless
> soldier wherever he might be found. But these
> organizations were special in their range, as well
> as temporary in their existence.[153]

The writer went on to speak of the need for permanent organizations to care for the sick and needy and then asked:

> Does not all this suggest to our great Protestant
> churches the necessity of establishing some order of
> holy women, whose labor shall be akin to that of the
> Sisters of Charity, or rather, . . . to that of the
> angels? If we cannot have such an order, we earnestly
> hope, for the sake of suffering humanity, that the
> Catholic Church will devote itself more than ever to
> enlarge the numbers and extend the beneficent labors
> of the sisters.[154]

Many doctors learned to appreciate the worth of sister-
nurses during the war and sought their help after it was over. It
was because of their fine work at Douglas Military Hospital in
Washington that the Sisters of Mercy were asked to take charge of
the Baltimore City Hospital (whose name was later changed to
Mercy Hospital). The hospital of the Sisters of Charity in Alton,
Illinois grew out of their nursing in an army hospital there.

Providence Hospital in Washington and St. Mary's in Cairo,

Illinois also grew out of wartime beginnings.[155] The American

Medical Association reported that as late as 1869, sisters were

the only organized group in America which realized the importance

of nursing.[156]

Some gave tangible recognition of the good done by the

sisters. In Galveston, after the war, representatives of both

armies entered the cloister of the Ursuline convent every Memorial

Day to decorate the grave of Mother St. Pierre Harrison, the

"Soldier's friend and Ministering Angel."[157] And the City of New

York gave the Mercy Sisters a tract of land on which to build an

establishment for the housing and education of girls whose fathers

had died in the war.[158]

An important accomplishment of sisters who nursed in the

Civil War was in the interests of women's emancipation. Other

women echoed the question of Miss Cumming quoted above, and by

the end of the war, many of the old restrictions against women

had begun to crumble. Where the sisters had led the way, other

women followed.[159] A Methodist Episcopal chaplain summed up the

situation, albeit in a condescending way, when he said,

> The war has brought out one fine result, it has
> shown that members of the weaker sex, though born
> to wealth and luxury, are ready to renounce every
> comfort and brave every hardship, that they may
> minister to the suffering, tend the wounded in
> their agony, and soothe the last struggle of the
> dying.[160]

In addition to their wartime nursing, a few communities

did emergency nursing during epidemics. In 1867 eleven Sisters of

Charity died during an epidemic in New Orleans, as did some

Kentucky Dominicans, who nursed in Memphis.[161] The following

year the Sisters of Mercy offered to nurse at the pesthouse when

smallpox broke out. Needless to say, their offer was accepted.[162]

Changes in Attitude After the Civil War

Charles Sewry concludes, from his study of alleged "Un-

Americanism" as a factor in anti-Catholicism between 1860 and 1914,

that "beginning with the Civil War, one of the strongest assets

that the Church has had in removing prejudice and lessening

suspicions of Catholic disloyalty has been the devoted and self-

sacrificing work of Catholic armed forces chaplains and members

of religious orders who have served as nurses."[163]

Many contemporary witnesses attest to the truth of Sewry's

conclusion. Bishop John Verot, who governed the Savannah diocese

and Florida, wrote to his people shortly after the war, "A good

number of crackers have seen our priests and our Sisters of

Charity for the first time in their lives in the towns and in the

camps where conscription called them, and they could not but carry

away a very favorable impression of what they saw with their own

eyes."[164]

Father Augustus Thebaud said of this period in his re-

collections:

> A complete revolution was taking place in the public
> opinion of the country. This change was even more
> marked in the popular estimate of the religious
> orders . . . . The former prejudices against con-
> vents, monasteries, ascetics of every denomination,
> gave way because of the charitable work to which they
> devoted themselves . . . . The female congregations,
> particularly, were respected by all classes of
> people. There was now no fear that their houses
> should be burned over their heads. They often ob-
> tained favors from their state and city governments

. . . . Their industrial, charitable, and academic
establishments, when they called on the public for
support, received from legislative and municipal
authorities generous appropriations, without which
they could often not have subsisted.[165]

Cardinal O'Connell recalled the change which took place

in New England, the scene of some of the most virulent attacks on

convents. When nuns passed in the streets, he said, Protestant

men often lifted their hats. "Here, at last, were the obvious

indications of a great transformation in the population, in the

old habits of mind and the old antipathies, with a . . . purer

sense of democracy in civil and social life."[166] He recorded an

abrupt change in attitude in a city in which sisters had formerly

been subjected to the indignities of the Nunnery Inspection

Committee:

> To the delight and surprise of the Catholics of
> Lowell, the Sisters of Charity of St. Vincent de
> Paul, who had done such noble work on the battle-
> fields and in the prisons, were invited by some
> of the principal Protestant citizens of Lowell
> to come and found a hospital and an orphan asylum,
> primarily for the benefit of the wounded and sick
> among the soldiers and for the children left
> orphaned, whose fathers had died in the war.[167]

Bishop John Lancaster Spalding went so far as to say,

"There was not a village throughout the land where some brave

soldier, not a Catholic, was not found to speak the praises of

her Catholic daughters, who, while men fought, stood by to staunch

the blood."[168] The same refrains are repeated by many other

writers.[169] Public opinion was now almost entirely in favor of

sisters. The 1868 Atlantic Monthly article on American Catholi-

cism mentioned above praises sisters in the very areas of their

lives which were most criticized in earlier decades. "All the

world approves and ever will approve" the Sisters of Charity,
Parton says. They are "still, self-contained, cheerful persons,"
and subsist on an annual salary of $200. He is especially im-
pressed by their economy and efficiency.[170]

Newspapers also praised the sisters' work. The reporter
who described the annual exhibition at an Ursuline academy for the
Cincinnati Commercial had to admit,

> We must confess our mistaken idea of nuns. We had
> pictured to ourselves a community of bilious old maids
> devoted to ecclesiastical scandal and spleen. We
> found them quiet, affable, intelligent, and gentle
> ladies, with numerous accomplishments, in no wise
> differing from their worldly sisters, save in dress
> and seclusion.[171]

A non-Catholic's letter to the editor of the Atchison Champion
was effusive in its praise of the Sister of Charity, who is
ministering angel to smoothe the pillow of the dying, ease the
pang of the sufferer, and relieve the necessities of the needy."[172]
Another letter in the same issue criticized the coverage which
the newspaper had given to the opening of a Benedictine convent
school, and insisted that "Americanism is Protestantism . . . .
In fact, Protestantism is education itself."[173] Subsequent issues
of the paper carried a sharp exchange on the values and weaknesses
of Catholicism. When it seemed that the sisters might be asked
to leave the city, they invited civic leaders to visit their convent, showed them samples of the work done there, and thus
silenced their critics.[174]

Though one or two convents were burned down during the
Civil War as part of the general destruction which accompanied
Sherman's march through the South, only one convent, that of the

Mercy Sisters in Manchester, New Hampshire, was deliberately burned down by anti-Catholic agitators during this period, and that took place before the war.[175]

There is thus abundant evidence to show that when Americans had personal contact with sisters, it was not their strange clothing or their stranger rules which impressed them most, but that essence of religious life not touched upon in fictional accounts of their lives, the intense living of the Christian virtues. And the impact of this powerful evidence overcame all of the negative impressions conveyed by sermons, newspapers, lectures, pamphlets, and novels in earlier decades.

Roles Seen in the Literature

One might expect this change in public attitude to be reflected in the fiction of the period, and to a certain extent it is. There is, of course, a sharp drop in the number of works published during the 1860's. A country torn by civil war and witnessing all of the horrors which this entails, has little time or money to spend on religious bigotry, much less on defaming women whose praises were being hymned on every side. The libraries whose collections were used in this study yielded only five works about nuns published in America during the 1860's. One other work which was published in that decade has not been located.[176] Two of these works were written by the prolific American novelist, Mrs. Julia McNair Wright.[177] Pamela Cowan, author of The American Convent as a School for Protestant Children, also seems to have been an American.[178] It is very possible that Mrs. Eliza Smith Richardson, author of The Veil Lifted, is an Englishwoman whose

work was published in America as well as England.[179] She claims to
have had experience of convent life. Enrichetta Caracciolo, whose
work on Neapolitan convents was translated from the Italian by
J.S. Redfield, claims to have been a Benedictine nun.[180]

All of these books could be said to be written in a
fictional style, though their authors insist that they are based
on facts. In both of Mrs. Wright's books we are assured that the
"story is composed almost entirely of fact. All the leading
incidents are sober truths."[181] "This book stands firmly on
facts," she assures her readers. "It contains no statements that
can be traversed. We send it forth as presenting some faint
picture of Romanism as it is today in these United States."[182]
These books repeat many of the charges made in the publications
of earlier decades, but with much less venom. The emphasis on
immorality which gained a wide audience for the works of Maria
Monk and William Hogan is almost entirely absent in them. To
this extent at least, they reflect the changed public image of the
nun. There would undoubtedly have been an outcry from war veterans
and others, had blatant charges of immorality been made against
sisters after the Civil War.

The young ladies in these tales enter the convent for a
variety of reasons, but the theme of the unwilling nun continues
to dominate. In Almost a Nun, we are shown a woman who has
destined her niece for the convent, where she feels she will make
"a charming Mother Superior," with "her beauty, her dignity, her
fine mind, her fortune, her family." The honor that would accrue
to her family is an important consideration:

What an advantage to us all to have her hold such a
place! And how much to the credit of us who should
be the means of placing her in it! Oh, to have one
of those devout, saintly sisters of our own flesh
and blood, and performing for us meritorious works,
and looking after our spiritual interests.183

This is a picture of convent life which is far different from

that found in the works of the preceding period. There is much

more emphasis on spiritual values and public esteem. When the

girl resists her aunt's attempts to get her into the convent,

chloroform is used. At the convent school where she is taken, she

meets an orphan whose aunt has also consigned her to the convent,

and a nun whose parents chose this vocation for her because, with

six daughters, "they had not sufficient fortune to establish so

many girls handsomely in life."184   Cowan also uses the character

of an orphan who is forced to become a nun.185   In Mysteries of

Neapolitan Convents, we find a girl who is put in the convent by

her widowed mother because she has no money with which to support

her.186

Among other motives for entering the convent which are

depicted in these books is the desire to "be a saint upon earth,

and take a place in heaven far enough in advance of all the

friends and relatives you have sacrificed."187   "Deciding to take

vows and the veil," writes Mrs. Wright of one of her heroines, "she

at once became a saint. Oh, short and broad and easy road to

heaven--a garb, a promise, a fixed routine of living; and lo! a

portal, said of salvation, opened wide."188 The convent is a

"refuge from the temptations of this world," and a place where

orphans, refractory girls, friendless children and others can

find security and love.189

Eliza Richardson is the only author in the group who describes the ceremonies in which young women become nuns, this despite her insistence that she will not describe the ceremony, since this has been done so often before.[190] She quotes from the letter of a girl who has just attended such a service. The emphasis is on the appeal to the senses. It is "gorgeous, magnificent," with exotic flowers, gold adornments, fragrant incense, and "sublime, ravishing" music.[191] Mrs. Wright mentions only that part of the ceremony in which the young girl is made to lie down in a coffin.[192] In the concluding chapter of her book Mrs. Richardson quotes passages from the works of various saints on spiritual marriage, spiritual espousals, and the reception ceremony.[193] It is almost as if she feels she must make this gesture toward the conventional ingredients of a convent story.

Many of the practices of convent life which were described in the books of the preceding decades are also depicted in the books of the 1860's, particularly in Eliza Richardson's book, which purports to be based on her own experiences in the convent. The fact that the sisters' mail is read is mentioned in one book.[194] Mrs. Richardson describes the injunctions against "particular friendships,"[195] and describes various penances: the most delicate nuns are given the most repulsive work to do; and some fanatics, in their emphasis on the importance of works, choose to scourge themselves, wear iron chains, etc.[196] This type also insists on adding more and more prayers to her schedule, in a frantic effort to store up merit for heaven.[197] The reader is referred to the lives of St. Rose of Lima and St. Catherine of Siena for other examples of such fanaticism in prayer and penance.[198] The emphasis here is on the fact that the sister herself chooses these penances. There is no indication that she is made to undergo them by someone else, and this represents a change from the earlier picture. At the end of Almost a Nun, as a concession to the convention, it seems, Mrs. Wright has a mischievous orphan tell of being punished by being put in a dungeon on a diet of bread and water for two days, but incidents of this kind are unusual in these books. Caracciolo tells of the cruelty of nuns toward the sick, the old, and the young, but it must be recalled that this book is about Italian convents, and hence is quite far removed from the American convent situation.

Mrs. Richardson makes much of the fact that a nun is taught to hate her family. "The worst spiritual enemies of a religieuse are her relatives," enjoins the novice-mistress.[199] A sister is not allowed to be with her mother when she is dying. Nor is the sister of a nun dying of tuberculosis allowed to come when she requests her presence. "Seculars cannot enter the rooms of consecrated nuns," she is told.[200] There actually was some basis for these charges in the rules of many communities which emphasized separation from the world, even from one's family, as an essential of religious life. In many communities sisters were not allowed to visit dying parents, nor were they ever allowed to visit their homes.

Mrs. Wright gives a rather romantic description of the appearance of nuns. One of hers is described as

clad in the coarse black weeds of her order . . . .
Her large black eyes had a peculiar mournfulness, and

> looked strangely forth from the white muslin folds
> bound closely over her brow; her features had been
> beautiful, but were sharpened by illness; her lips
> were pale, and her complexion colorless as that of
> a corpse . . . . The bright dresses of the girls
> formed a strange contrast to the narrow black robes
> and dead-white muslin folds of the members of the
> order.[201]

Another one of her nuns "was a small, shriveled, clear-voiced woman, in coarse black dress, broad black apron reaching to the hem of her gown, a rosary at her waist, a kerchief about her color- less face and a black hood on her head, the whole garb being un- suggestive of the saintly, except to prejudiced minds."[202]

Two of these writers depict greed for money as one of the characteristics of Catholics. In Almost a Nun, Catholic relatives of a Protestant orphan work for her conversion to Catholicism, so that her money could become the property of the Church. (The idea is that after she becomes a Catholic, she will of course join the convent as well.)[212] And Richardson charges the sisters with greed for the wealth of a youthful convert.[213]

Caracciolo ways there is a tendency towards insanity in the convent, and Richardson's twelfth chapter is called "The Insane Nun." She depicts a twenty-eight-year-old nun of lively imagination and temperament who becomes melancholic when she perceives the reality of convent life and is forced to give up all of her illusions about it.[214]

These convent stories are strikingly different from several of the most popular ones of the earlier period in that they do not picture convents as centers of vice. Only one, Caracciolo, refers to the scandals that supposedly take place in the confessional, and she is writing about Italy.

The convent school is depicted in three of the five books examined. In Almost a Nun, we are told that "in all the branches of a solid, thorough education, the convent school fell far below the average of Protestant schools. To cover this deficiency, the modern languages, music, drawing and a wonderful variety of fancy work occupied more than an ordinary share of attention. Pianos, melodeons, and a richly-toned organ were ready for the pupils."203 In Priest and Nun, the students are more concerned about clothes than about catechism, and a girl's Protestant mother says the priests and nuns have come between her daughter and her.204

In The American Convent as a School For Protestant Children, several charges are made against convent schools. The Protestant children must attend Catholic church services and catechism classes; they are not allowed to have Protestant bibles; the students' mail is read; and they are carefully watched, both day and night.205 Protestant students are shocked to learn that study, letter-writing, and card-playing are allowed on Sunday.206 A famous preacher analyzes Protestantism, pointing out its weaknesses.207 Protestant girls are made to recite the Catholic version of Luther's life, and the sisters walk with them in the garden, talking sweetly of Catholicism.208 A priest also has long religious discussions with them.209 A girl who has a beautiful voice learns to love singing in the church choir. She is introduced to a priest who also has a great interest in music, who will try to convert her to Catholicism.210 Many of these charges against convent schools were actually true, at least in some schools. This book is an improvement over others in that it does

use examples of things that did happen, rather than fabricate
lies in order to make a point.

Only one of these books shows sisters busy at another
work aside from teaching. In Priest and Nun, a sister is serving-
maid in a wealthy family. She returns to the convent after her
day's work, and there dons her religious habit.[211] Sisters take
jobs of this kind in order to spy out the secrets of important
people, it is alleged. They tamper with letters, listen at doors,
ransack drawers, etc. and then report anything of interest to
church authorities.[212] This is an absurd charge which would probably not have been believed in this period by intelligent people.

Conclusion

It is clear from the evidence presented in this chapter
that the public image of the nun--and of the church she represented--
underwent a dramatic change in the decade of the 1860's. This was
primarily due to the nursing of the sisters in the Civil War, which
gave thousands their first contact with nuns. It became evident to
all, that they were not mournful prisoners doomed by unhappy love
affairs to lives of sinful indolence, but happy, holy, efficient
women whose lives were dominated by the spiritual values of the
Gospel. Thus Americans changed their role expectations for nuns.
The positive value of many aspects of religious life which had
hitherto been ridiculed--the emphasis on obedience, discipline,
selflessness, silence, and the patient endurance of what is dis-
tasteful, for example--became evident amidst the daily pressures
of the military hospital. The contrast between the behavior of
the nuns and that of many of the other women nurses--whose values

had previously been considered superior to those of Catholicism--
gave pause to many onlookers. The many conversions to Catholicism
which resulted from wartime experiences speak for themselves.

The changed image of the nun which came out of the Civil
War is closely connected with changes in role definitions, changes
which were effected both by sisters and by the general public.
Many religious communities had adapted their constitutions in order
to conform more closely to the needs of the American situation, and
had thus brought them into closer touch with reality. Sisters
could never have nursed on the battlefields had they been held
to strict enclosure or required to follow minute prescriptions of
their constitutions. The chaplain who insisted on a regular
routine in the midst of battle only made himself look ridiculous.

The American public, for its part, devised more realistic
role expectations for nuns as a result of the Civil War. These
were now based on actual performance rather than the rantings of
anti-Catholic ministers, writers, and self-styled escaped nuns.
The gap between appearance and reality which had marked the public
image of the nun in the preceding period was almost completely
erased during the 1860's. The picture conveyed in the fiction was
not entirely in conformity with this changed public image, but in
its lack of venom and its depiction of some of the spiritual values
of religious life, it did reflect some of the changes which had
occurred.

CHAPTER VI

1870 - 1900

During the last decades of the nineteenth century, when immigrants poured into America's cities, the Catholic Church experienced a tremendous growth in numbers. She struggled to keep pace with the needs of all nationalities, and to preserve their cultural and religious heritage at the same time that she facilitated their Americanization. The Church looked to her religious communities of women to bear the greatest share of the burden of providing for the physical and spiritual needs of Catholic immigrants, and not in vain. Fifty-nine new foundations of religious women were begun in America during this period, and many additional missions were also opened by the communities which were already established. Thirty-nine of these new foundations sprang from European motherhouses; often European sisters came to succor the needs of their compatriots. Eight of the new communities originated in Canada, and twelve had distinctly American origins.[1] The Prussian May Laws and other restrictive legislation enacted during the years of the German Kulturkampf helped to swell the number of sisters who emigrated to America during the 1870's. Twenty-six new foundations were made in that decade, as compared with fifteen in the 1880's and eighteen in the 1890's.

Formal Role Definitions of Canon Law

There were several official statements of church policy
during this period which became a part of the Church's role definitions for nuns. The decrees passed by the American bishops at
the Third Plenary Council of Baltimore in 1884 encouraged the
establishment of normal schools where sisters could be properly
trained for the teaching profession, and placed all new congregations of women with simple vows under the jurisdiction of
their local bishops. The bishops also took note of the growing
importance of begging as a way of solving the financial needs of
religious communities, and warned that in some parts of the country
it had become an intolerable abuse that needed to be checked with
an iron hand.[2] In 1889, Rome added the requirements of living in
common and wearing a habit to the conditions which had to be met
before a group could obtain official recognition as a "religious"
community. (The earlier conditions will be recalled were strict
enclosure and solemn vows.)[3]

A development which had considerable influence on American
communities was the evolution of a uniform method for seeking
Rome's approval of a community's constitution. The accumulated
experience of centuries had made it clear that certain provisions
were necessary if congregations with simple vows were to prosper--
a clear line of demarcation between the authority of the bishop
and that of the religious superiors, for example. Roman authorities began to withhold their approval from constitutions which did
not have these provisions. Consequently, many congregations modified their constitutions, making them conform to Roman ideas of

religious life, in order to win papal approval for them. Sometimes they copied the prescriptions of constitutions which had already been approved. This practice of submitting constitutions to Rome had both good and bad results. Many communities, in preparing their rules for this scrutiny, omitted the sections which they knew could not easily be observed in America, and thus brought them into conformity with the informal role definitions which actually prevailed. Other communities however, in their anxiety to obtain this approval, added practices from European constitutions which were contrary to the spirit and needs of their American milieu. Many Dominican communities, for example, based their constitutions on those of the Dominican congregation of Stone, England, which contained provisions unsuitable for American needs. It was the constitutions of congregations with simple vows, not the institutes themselves, which Rome approved prior to 1900; the congregations themselves were merely tolerated as societies of pious women.[4]

In 1899 Pope Leo XIII addressed to Cardinal Gibbons the encyclical Testem Benevolentiae, which condemned "Americanism." The details of the controversy over the heresy called by this name are discussed elsewhere.[5] The encyclical is mentioned here for what it says about religious life. It condemns any who would say that the vows taken by members of religious orders narrow the limits of human liberty and interfere with Christian perfection and the good of human society, and hence are out of keeping with the spirit of the age. It also denounces those who say that religious orders are of little use to the Church, or who claim

more importance for active communities than for contemplative
ones. It notes that the idea of a society whose members work
for the Church without religious vows is not a new one, and warns
that such groups should not be esteemed more highly than religious
orders.[6] It was actually because the efforts of the Paulist
priests to meet the needs of the contemporary American Church
had been misinterpreted that the encyclical had been written. It
had no direct bearing on American communities of women, but it does
indicate a certain attitude toward the modernization and Americanization of traditional church practices, which should be noted.

In 1900 the centuries-long battle for the recognition of
congregations with simple vows as true "religious" in the eyes
of the Church was finally won. In that year the bull Conditae a
Christo, which has been called the Magna Charta for congregations
with simple vows, was issued. It came as the climax to a century
of development and experimentation which had proven the value and
the usefulness of such religious groups. Though they had existed
in the Church from the fourteenth century, they came to maturity
in the nineteenth, when five hundred seventy-one new congregations
of this type were founded.[7] Having recognized sisters with simple
vows as bona fide religious, Rome set up procedures for approving
both their institutes and their constitutions in the Normae issued
in 1901. These two documents, Conditae and the Normae, set forth
the role definitions for sisters which would be in force until the
promulgation of the new code of canon law in 1918.

One of the important problems of nineteenth-century
communities which was dealt with in the bull Conditae was that of

the jurisdiction of bishops and ecclesiastical superiors over
religious groups. There had been doubts about whether the superior
general of a community with missions in several dioceses should
have to submit to the decisions of local bishops, particularly
when those bishops wished the sisters in their dioceses to form
independent groups. Now provision was made for such congregations
to seek papal approval, which would remove them from the immediate
jurisdiction of local bishops. Rome had already abolished the
practice of having a priest as ecclesiastical superior because
of the problems this had caused.[8]

The new norms took cognizance of the need for the revision
of earlier cloistral prescriptions by mitigating the observance
of cloister. Congregations with simple vows were only to observe
a "partial cloister"; that is, a certain section of the convent
would be reserved exclusively for the use of the sisters. This
concession to the needs of active communities was not accompanied
by a corresponding change in basic attitudes, however. Many other
cloistral prescriptions were retained, including the requirement
that a sister have a companion whenever she went out of her
convent.

These two documents note types of work which are not
suitable for women religious and in doing so, reveal the Jansenistic attitudes which prevailed at the time. Among the works which
illbefit "virgins consecrated to God," they say, are the care of
babies, the nursing of maternity cases, the management of clerical
seminaries, and the staffing of co-educational schools. Since
operating and delivery rooms were thought to be especially

dangerous, they were to be staffed by physicians and trained
nurses rather than sisters. (Sisters were apparently less able
than trained nurses to withstand the temptations to which the
care of the sick would expose them.)[9]

Roles Sisters Played

In the last decades of the nineteenth century, most
Americans seem to have accepted the fact that sisters had a definite role to play in American society, though some continued to
resent them. The church used all of her resources to meet the
needs of the large numbers of Catholic immigrants who poured into
the country. Much of the actual burden was borne by religious
communities of women. They opened more and more schools, hospitals, and orphanages, and provided for the needs of working girls,
newspaper boys, delinquents, the aged, and others, and visited
prisons as well.

To many Americans, sisters represented the church of the
immigrant. Though they had become an accepted part of the American scene, many were foreign-born and continued to follow practices
which they had learned in European motherhouses. For example,
several communities used the German language, followed a German
diet, and adhered to German customs of various kinds until the
First World War. Other national communities had similar
practices.[10] When foreign-born sisters worked in national parishes
whose members were chiefly their own compatriots, their background
was a definite advantage. The Cenacle Sisters who established a
convent in New York in 1892 discovered, however, that their French
attitudes and customs were repugnant to Americans. It was several

years before any American girls joined their community. Only
after an Englishwoman was brought over to help them did they
begin to prosper.[11]

Though democratic attitudes were certainly gaining the
ascendency in many sectors of the American Church in the last
decades of the nineteenth century, certain communities continued
to be looked upon as "aristocratic." Bishop Foley wrote to
Archbishop Purcell in 1870 that parochial schools were needed in
Chicago, but he feared lest the previous situations and habits of
the Ursulines disqualify them for the type of living they would
have to endure, should they come to staff them.[12] J.T. Reilly
saw sisters in general as representatives of upper-class city ways,
and felt that they neglected the poor of the rural areas.[13]

The Religious of the Sacred Heart came to be thought of as
a community who restricted their schools to the wealthy upper
classes. One of their members answered this charge in a latter
to a friend:

> We are not so conceited or ill-informed as to imagine
> ourselves superior in any respect to other orders.
> But the bishops always invite us for what they
> especially style the "Upper Class of Catholics," hence
> in our Academies for young ladies we are supposed to
> be forming daughters of gentlemen in America, or
> "New Ireland," not teachers. For the latter we should
> have a distinct "Normal School."--Such we have at
> Wandsworth near London, at Santiago in Chile, etc.
> But we have never been called upon by any bishop in
> USA to do this work.[14]

The role that sisters played in society was definitely
an active rather than a passive one. Testem Benevolentiae to the
contrary, many felt that American life and the American Church
at this time had much greater need of active communities than of

contemplative ones. Only a very small number of sisters belonged
to contemplative groups. When two Poor Clare sisters from Rome
arrived in New York in 1875 and attempted to establish a convent
there, the archbishop refused to admit them because he "did not
consider their Order in keeping with the spirit of the age or
with the trend of the mind of the American people."[15] After
similar experiences in other dioceses, they finally settled in
Omaha, thanks to the kindness of a local philanthropist.

Teaching

The most familiar role played by the American nun was
that of teacher; the greater number of sisters were employed in
staffing schools. Much thought and attention were focussed on
Catholic schools during this period, both on the national level
and within Catholic circles. The Third Plenary Council of Baltimore stressed the importance of parochial schools and directed
about one-fourth of its decrees to this subject. The "School
Question," which involved questions of public aid to parochial
schools and charges of divisiveness, was one of the controversies
of the age.[16]

Sisters staffed two different types of schools during
these years. We have already noted the beginnings of the move to
replace select schools with parochial schools. This trend gained
momentum as the century wore on, spurred by the acceptance of the
idea of education for all, the influx of large numbers of Catholic
immigrants, and the decrees of the Third Plenary Council of Baltimore. It reflected changes which were taking place both in the
public and in the Catholic educational systems in this country.

The education of women beyond the rudiments of reading and writing had previously been restricted, in many instances, to the daughters of the wealthy. They were expected to return to their homes after graduation with those lady-like accomplishments which were proper for ladies of leisure. With the spread of public education and the passage of compulsory school attendance laws, children from lower socio-economic strata, whose needs were quite different, had also to be accommodated. The public and parochial schools which superseded private and select academies had to provide basic skills which would enable their graduates, girls as well as boys, to succeed in the business world. The Mercy Sisters in Brooklyn were typical of many communities in their adjustment to these changing needs. In 1894, after much urging, they relinquished their select schools and opened parochial schools where catechism and the three r's could be taught to "the ordinary boy and girl . . . the youth destined to form the rank and file of the workaday world."[17] Thus the system which had provided select and free schools in each center where sisters taught, was replaced by a much more democratic one in which most children attended parochial schools and only a small, elite group were educated at the private academies, many of them boarding schools, which religious communities continued to staff.

Mary McCarthy describes the very different spirit which characterized each type of school in her contrast between St. Stephen's parochial school in Minneapolis and the Sacred Heart boarding school she attended in Seattle. This section of Memories of a Catholic Girlhood is worth quoting at length because, though written of a later period, it epitomizes the school of the late

nineteenth century as well:

> [The Ladies of the Sacred Heart] were not <u>ordinary</u>
> nuns, it was scornfully explained to me, but women of
> good family, cloistered ladies of the world, just as
> Sacred Heart girls were not ordinary Catholics, but
> daughters of the best families. And my new subjects
> were not ordinary subjects, like spelling and arith-
> metic, but rhetoric, French, literature, Christian
> doctrine, English history. I was fresh from a
> Minneapolis parochial school, where a crude "citi-
> zenship" had been the rule, where we pledged allegiance
> to the flag every morning, warbled "My Country, 'Tis
> of Thee," . . . competed in paper drives and citywide
> spelling contests, drew hatchets for Washington's
> Birthday and log cabins for Lincoln's, gave to foreign
> missions for our brown and yellow brothers, feared
> the Ku Klux Klan, sold chances and subscriptions to
> periodicals, were taken on tours of flour mills and
> water works; I looked upon my religion as a branch
> of civics and conformity, and the select Sacred
> Heart atmosphere took my breath away. The very aus-
> terities of our life had a mysterious aristocratic
> punctilio . . . . I felt as though I stood on the
> outskirts and observed the ritual of a cult, a cult of
> fashion and elegance in thesphere of religion . . . .
> It was the France of the Restoration that was embalmed
> in the Sacred Heart atmosphere . . . . [18]

The opening of parochial schools necessitated a change in

the financial structure of the schools, since the fees paid by

the well-to-do no longer covered the cost of educating the poor,

though they did supplement the income of those communities whose

sisters also staffed parochial schools. The cost of operating

these schools involved heavy financial burdens for the Catholic

populace. Hence there were many attempts to get state aid for

these schools, and various co-operative plans were worked out.

There continued to be many places in which sisters taught in public

schools, particularly on the sparsely settled frontier, where

qualified teachers who could live on a minimal salary were rare.[19]

The Josephites' school in Tucson, for example, which opened in

1870, was the only one in the Territory for several years. In 1877 the legislature voted to give it $300 out of the territorial treasury.[20] Both the Poughkeepsie Plan and the Faribault Plan provided for the use of parochial school buildings and teachers by local school boards.[21] Sisters also taught in government schools which had been erected on Indian reservations.[22]

One finds, in the Catholic magazines of the 1890's, much discussion of the merits and faults of convent schools of the aristocratic type, and of the kind of education which they gave. The arguments reflect the opinions of the day about the role of women and the education most suitable for them. Champions of women's rights complained that the convent school prepares a woman for the religious life or marriage, but not for the state of "single blessedness" or for earning a living.[23] According to critics of convent schools, they stress the "accomplishments" of the finishing school: curtseying, managing a train, the niceties of speech, "culture," manners, piano, fancy needlework, Browning, Coventry Patmore, and all of the fads.[24]

Even the critics admitted, however, that there were some advantages to this type of education. Convent graduates have a gentler manner, are ennobled by their contact with fine women, and are sweet, simple, and frank. The sensible mother of the convent girl will accentuate her convent lessons and deprive "the plunge from seclusion to the world . . . of its first shock," insisted the defenders of the convent.[25] One member of the older generation looked with nostalgia to the golden age of the convent school and indicated some of the changes that had taken place:

Some convent girls are entirely spoiled by modern
education. The old days of finishing schools suited
me. Then a girl could play some brilliant pieces on
the piano--not too loud, unless she was "showing off";
she embroidered a little; she could courtesy à la Marie
Antoinette; they taught her to dance. And when she
got her diploma tied with a blue ribbon, she was
"finished." After that she never bothered herself
about books. She was never seen putting her gloves
on in the street; she made her retreats every year,
and she always spoke in a low voice. There was one
thing that might have been taught . . . which was
neglected--she did not learn how to cook.[26]

Some contrasted the convent school with the college. An
Irish critic had this to say of the quality of the education
given in Irish convent schools (which were surely similar to those
run by Irish nuns in America):

The nuns hitherto have taken education very lightly.
They have gone into the convent with just so much
knowledge as they received in a convent. They are forbidden newspapers, books, and reviews, almost entirely.
The years advance, but they stand still. They do not
realize that for women especially the world has
changed, so much that a woman's personality has changed
with it . . . . Many of our convents . . . are dominated
by a French mind and spirit, which are incapable of
understanding the different position and needs of
English-speaking women.[27]

This writer longed to see a Catholic college for women begun,
but could not see any way in which nuns could have anything to
do with college education, given the restrictions of cloistral
regulations:

Their circumstances forbid it. How could they hold
intercourse with the secular professor and all the
rest whom the affairs of the college would call into
being? I would have my college quite free from the
restrictions which hamper, as her clinging gown does,
the woman in religion . . . . My college will be a
far busier place and less retired than those homes,
by green pastures and pleasant waters, where
    "The Brides of Christ
    Lie hid, emparadised."[28]

The Religious of the Sacred Heart seem to have felt the brunt of attacks like these. The correspondent quoted above, who defended her community against charges of snobbery, defended its educational system as well. "Long before the Paulists were founded," writes Sister Elizabeth Ten Broeck to Father Daniel Hudson of Notre Dame,

> or "The C. Review" saw the light, our élève had annual lectures on British, American and Foreign Literature--on physics, botany and Astromony given by secular professors, who are at liberty to keep abreast of the times. And as the nuns assist at these, they need not be behind-hand in what concerns their vocation as instructresses. We have professors for the piano, harp, violin, etc. and for vocal music, and the organ . . . . True we have to employ French, Spanish, and Italian teachers for their respective languages, but with one exception . . . every superior is American born and bred . . . .[29]

Maurice Francis Egan conceded that the curriculum of convent schools was different from that of the colleges, but he was not at all sure that this was a disadvantage. Higher education, he said, should develop all of the talents which make a woman Christian and bring out her womanliness. There is no evidence that this is best done by the study of Latin and Greek. Our young women do not need a classical education, he asserted, but the intelligent development of their talents and a consciousness that their principal object ought not to be to make themselves attractive to men.[30]

Thus we see that sisters were deeply involved in the educational endeavors of the country on many levels. There was lively debate over the curriculum of the private academy, and some question as to whether cloistered nuns could keep abreast of contemporary developments in education. They hired qualified lay

professors to teach the subjects in which they themselves were
not competent, thereby providing for their students' needs while
admitting that cloister regulations limited their efficiency as
teachers. It would be a good half century before adaptations
would enable them to solve this problem in a realistic way.

Nursing

Sisters again proved their selflessness and concern for
their neighbor during the epidemics which struck during the last
decades of the nineteenth century. The years 1873 and 1878-9 saw
virulent plagues of yellow fever and cholera, particularly in the
South. In Memphis, Vicksburg, and Nashville, sisters remained
to nurse the stricken, some of them dying at their posts, while
thousands of the healthy fled the cities.[31] In 1884-5 Franciscan
Sisters nursed those stricken with smallpox in Philadelphia.[32]
The city of San Francisco expressed its gratitude to the sisters
who nursed the Spanish-American War veterans who returned home
with typhoid, by granting all sisters free transportation on buses
and streetcars in perpetuity.[33]

We have already mentioned the Catholic hospitals which developed from the work of sisters in the Civil War. By 1871 the
country boasted seventy hospitals staffed by sisters, and that
number increased fourfold by the end of the century.[34] Sisters
were often the first to open hospitals in frontier areas, and were
sometimes invited by civic groups to staff those which they had
built. The Baltimore city fathers, for example, asked Mercy
Sisters to take charge of the general hospital there in 1874.[35]
Railroads in the West and Southwest invited sisters to staff their

hospitals for the care of injured workers.[36] A few communities
opened special hospitals for the mentally ill, the tubercular,
and incurables.[37] Many of the German sisters who emigrated during
the Kulturkampf had previous hospital experience which proved
useful when they reached America. As the century wore to a close,
however, there was serious doubt as to whether the enclosure
rules and the Jansenistic attitudes which prevailed would allow
sister-nurses to keep abreast of modern advances in nursing and
medicine.

In order to understand the clashes which occurred during
this period between hospital sisters and the fast-changing culture in which they worked, it is necessary to review contemporary
developments in the nursing profession. The dearth of professional
nurses and the inferior quality of the hired help in charity
hospitals in the nineteenth century have already been noted.

The public outcry against the high death rate in English
hospitals in the Crimea, and the subsequent investigation into
all aspects of military medicine led the English-speaking world to
search for improved methods of hospital administration in the
latter half of the nineteenth century. In America, the Civil War
made doctors aware of the need for improvements in the training of
hospital personnel.

Rapid advances in the understanding of the principles of
asepsis and anesthesia, of anatomy and physiology, led to the development of more specialized techniques of caring for the sick.
Florence Nightingale established the first English nurses'
training school in 1860. Her reforms spread to America, and

resulted in the establishment of schools of nursing beginning in
1872.[38] Here future nurses learned not only modern bedside techniques, but also the principles of anatomy, physiology, and asepsis
on which they were based.

Though Catholic nursing communities had for centuries been
considered the leaders in their field, they failed to adapt to the
rapid changes in hospital administration and technique which revolutionized the nursing profession in the decades following the Civil
War. As more and more Catholic hospitals were opened, doctors had
a chance to observe and experience clashes between modern medical
ideas and the outdated practices of religious communities. Catholic
physicians heard the bitter exclamations of non-Catholic doctors
and resented the misguided zeal which impelled sisters to take
on works for which they were not qualified.[39] The apprenticeship
system of training, and the practice of assigning the most intelligent and best-educated sisters to teaching, and the less intelligent
ones to nursing, no longer sufficed. (This was not a uniquely
American situation. It existed as well in the European hospitals
in which many American sisters had received their training.)

Many of the problems which arose in Catholic hospitals
originated in the outdated constitutions which religious communities
continued to follow. During their times of prayer, it was charged,
the patients were entirely at the mercy of paid nurses, who were of
an inferior sort indeed.[40] The "dark habit and immense headdress"
were objected to because they "impede work and become a vehicle for
micro-organisms."[41] Penances, fasting, and other austerities
practiced in many communities sapped the strength of the sisters,

and they lived under unhygienic conditions. Nutting cites studies
which reveal that sister-nurses had a higher mortality rate than
any other group. In some orders, from seventy to one hundred
per cent of the deaths were from tuberculosis, she says, and most
died before reaching the age of fifty.[42]

Other problems arose because Jansenist ideas about the evil
propensities of material things, particularly the human body, had
made inroads in the minds of many churchmen and religious communities. Nowhere were the results more evident than in certain warped
attitudes which were imposed on sister-nurses. A French doctor who
gave many years to the work of nursing reform received the impetus
for his crusade during an operation on a newborn infant, when, as
he later reported, "Mother P., a woman in her forties, in handing
the instruments, turned her face away and held a hand before her
eyes in order not to see the field of operation. This singular
attitude caused me to reflect upon the manner in which the religious
sister regarded her functions as a nurse."[43] He did a case study
of sister-nurses, and summed up his findings thus:

> Little time given to the wards; much spent in re-
> ligious exercises. Little or no personal care given to
> patients, especially as concerned necessary attention
> to the genital zone; refusal to nurse venereal cases,
> lying-in women, and unmarried mothers. These were
> left entirely to the servant nurses . . . . My ob-
> servation of the nuns showed that the majority of them,
> aside from certain wealthy convents with a large dowry
> requirement, were recruited from the bourgeoisie, had
> had only a very limited primary education, and that
> their training for nursing was limited to a more or
> less bad routine, according as they had been trained
> under a more or less intelligent superior.[44]

It must be noted that these statements were made about the practice
in a French hospital, and were certainly not true of all American

ones. But many American hospitals were under the direction of the Daughters of Charity, who received their rules from their mother-house in Paris. Nor were the French the only national group tainted by Jansenistic attitudes. We have already noted the Normae which forbade sisters to have anything to do with maternity cases. Though these were formulated in 1901, they must represent the codification of ideas that were widely held prior to that time. It was not until 1936 that Dr. Anna Dengel succeeded in getting Rome's approval for her Medical Mission Sisters' obstetrical work in India. And there was still living in the 1960's a Daughter of Charity who as a young English midwife, had been refused admittance by both the English and French provinces of the Daughters of Charity because of her familiarity with matters which were con-sidered dangerous to the chastity of the consecrated virgin. (Fortunately, the American province was willing to accept her, despite her delivery room experience.)[45]

Such attitudes would obviously restrict the type of nursing that nuns might do in a hospital. Nutting describes their work thus: " [The nun] gave medicine and certain kinds of treatment, 'watched' in private duty, and supervised in hospitals (where she maintained discipline, system, and an atmosphere of refinement); she did not really nurse the patient except in a closely circum-scribed way, and the actual nursing . . . passed into the hands of the 'mercenaries, or lay attendants."[46] In some hospitals in which the sisters never did any menial services for the patients, such tasks were looked upon as somehow degrading. In the early days slaves performed the more menial tasks; later ambulatory patients and those who had recuperated took care of them.[47]

The scrupulosity of the sisters and the misguided zeal of their ecclesiastical superiors were sometimes revealed in rules which worked to the detriment of their patients. In some places, for example, doctors were not allowed to spend the night in the hospital unless they had a patient in very critical condition. Thus there was no competent medical advice available in the evenings.[48] Some sisters were charged with excessive zeal for the souls of their patients, calling the priest rather than the doctor when one was hemorrhaging, and even refusing to give medicine to children, on the pretext that "it is better for them to become angels."[49] Questions about who should have final authority over hospital personnel caused problems between sisters and doctors. One doctor said of sister-nurses, " [There was] meagre respect for administrative rules. The superior or prior came before the physician or the directors; the soul was more important than the body."[50]

Sisters were prohibited from studying anatomy, physiology, and similar subjects. Hence religious communities lagged behind when the movement to professionalize nursing made itself felt in America. In Europe, doctors who hoped to reform the hospital system saw laicization of the hospitals as the only way to accomplish it.[51]

American nursing sisters at first resisted doctors' attempts to establish nurses' training schools. They did not enroll in the courses that were offered, though some made every effort to attend lectures whenever they were free.[52] At Charity Hospital in New

Orleans, which was connected with the Medical College of Louisiana, there was intense interest in the science of medicine. The board decided to start a school of nursing, but did not discuss it with the Sisters of Charity until all plans had been made. The sisters resented this failure to consult them, and complained to the governor. The superior then refused to give her approval to the plan because if the school were opened, she would have to relinquish the absolute authority which she had hitherto exercised over all hospital personnel. To her, unity of authority was essential to proper discipline.[53] Ten years later, in 1892, the need for a nursing school was so evident that these objections were withdrawn. The director of nurses was placed under the authority of the superior, and there were seven sisters in the first graduating class.[54]

The extent to which obsolete rules could keep sisters from being proficient in their work is shown by an incident which occurred in Rome but could have taken place anywhere. When Pope Pius X himself invited sister-nurses to lay aside false modesty and come to the nursing school he had founded, to learn to be professional nurses, some replied that they could not attend the classes because their rules would not allow it.[55]

When the Spanish-American War broke out in 1898, the Daughters of the American Revolution took charge of the recruiting of nurses, under the chairmanship of Dr. Anita Newcomb McGee and Miss Ella Lorraine Dorsey. Recalling the sisters' generosity during the Civil War, Miss Dorsey wrote to the superiors of several religious communities asking for volunteers and enclosing qualification slips. All applicants were to be either graduate

nurses or women with hospital experience. They had to take an

oath of allegiance to the United States and accept $30 per month

remuneration. One hundred ninety-nine Sisters of Charity responded,

thirteen Mercy Sisters, twelve from the Holy Cross community,

eleven Josephites, and four members of an Indian community, the

Congregation of American Sisters.[56] These sisters nursed in the

Philippines, Cuba, and Puerto Rico as well as in army hospitals

in various parts of the United States.[57] Some of them were in charge

of hospital trains sent South to bring wounded or sick soldiers to

their homes in the North.[58] Other communities nursed sick and

wounded soldiers, many of whom had typhoid, in their own

hospitals.[59]

  The professionalization of nursing and the reluctance of

sisters to be a part of the nursing school movement created a

division between the sister-nurses and the trained nurses in army

hospitals. Alice Worthington Winthrop, who examined the official

War Department records, says that although these reports

> attest the fair average character of the Sisters'
> nursing, even those surgeons who are most enthusias-
> tic in their praise of the work of the orders, express
> their regret that the Sisters have not fallen into
> line with the system of training pursued in the best
> modern hospitals. This course may or may not be in
> every respect an advantage, and is often compensated
> for by the Sisters' long experience in their own hos-
> pitals, and by their discipline, their fidelity, and
> their self-forgetfulness. But it is nevertheless
> regarded by many surgeons as a misfortune that the
> Sisters have not had this method of training; and there
> is danger that its absence may militate against the employ-
> ment of the Sisters in the United States Corps of Nurses,
> which is likely to become a permanent organization in
> this country in future . . . . [All] agree that this
> formidable obstacle to the employment of the Sisters
> in a permanent corps would be completely overcome by

> the co-ordination of the Sisters' course of instruction
> for their nurses with that pursued in training nurses
> in the best-equipped non-sectarian hospitals . . . .[60]

Dr. S.P. Kramer, surgeon of the hospital at Camp Wikoff on Long

Island, felt differently about the sisters however. He compared

trained nurses with nuns and concluded:

> Whatever may be the case in civil institutions, in the
> field hospital the Sister of Charity is far superior.
> Sisters do good work. There is with them no bickering
> with the ward doctor, no fussiness, no refusing to
> perform menial work when necessary, no desire to
> "shine" as is the case with the "trained nurse." The
> Sister of Charity has no ambition but duty; she obeys
> all orders quietly, with a prompt, orderly and willing
> manner. No sacrifice is too great, no service too
> menial. It has been a matter of general comment here
> that the annex is a far superior hospital to the main
> branch, and to my mind this is largely due to the pre-
> sence of the Sisters of Charity in the former.[61]

The higher death rate of the sisters who nursed during the

few months that the war lasted has been blamed on the religious

habit, which produced conditions favorable for the growth and

retention of germs, and on the austerities which sapped the

sisters' strength and lowered their resistence. Surgeon-Major

William R. Hall had this to say of them:

> The only fault I had to find with the Sisters was that
> they would not rest, would not take care of their own
> health. After the long hours which their hospital
> service demanded, they devoted a portion of the time
> needed for rest to religious exercises. They arose so
> early in the morning for this purpose that they
> deprived themselves of necessary sleep, and by thus
> lowering their vitality, exposed themselves to disease.[62]

It is thus obvious that the situation of nursing sisters in

America changed for the worse during the last decades of the

nineteenth century. From being the only trained nurses in the

country, they were fast approaching the state of being the least

trained, because of rules and attitudes that kept them from

adapting to the needs of a swiftly changing profession.

Other Works

In addition to the teaching and nursing duties which occupied the majority of sisters, they ran homes for working girls,
orphans, newsboys and wayward girls, and visited prisons.[63] Because of Protestant campaigns to gain control of Catholic orphans
in order to rear them as Protestants, there was a serious need for
Catholic orphanages during this period, and many religious communities of women helped to meet this need. Catholic orphanages
attempted to provide job-training and an education which would fit
their charges to earn a living when they struck out on their own.[64]
In New York and other states, these institutions received a per
capita payment from the state which helped them to meet their
expenses.[65]

The abandoned infant and unwed mother were also cared for
in Catholic institutions, most notably at the New York Foundling
Hospital, whose practices set the pace for similar hospitals
throughout the country.[66] Between 1870 and 1900 twelve Catholic
infant homes and maternity hospitals were opened.[67] More of them
continued to open their doors into the twentieth century, despite
Rome's statement that work of this kind was unsuitable for consecrated virgins.

Sisters of the Good Shepherd continued their work of reforming delinquent girls, opening sixteen new houses in this period.
The Little Sisters of the Poor opened thirty-four homes for the
aged poor between 1870 and 1900. The Santa Maria Institute in
Cincinnati, the first Catholic settlement house, was founded in

1897 to help Italian immigrants,[68] and several day nurseries were
opened in the 1890's to care for the children of working mothers.[69]
Thus sisters were busy in works of charity of many kinds. Wherever
there was a need, some group of selfless, dedicated women came
to the fore to meet it as best they could.

Finances

Sisters financed their good works in various ways. Some
charged those who could afford to pay for their services, and were
thus enabled to serve the poor gratis. Others received charitable
donations from individuals or groups. Sometimes the state or city
governments paid sisters for their care of the indigent. Railroads
and other organizations which invited sisters to staff their hospitals usually paid their expenses. In most parochial schools, the
parish paid the sisters a stated salary every month. When this
was too little to support them, or a pastor fell behind in his
payments, they had to supplement their income in various ways:
through music lessons, bazaars, church work, and similar expedients.
The bishops' disapproval of excessive begging, expressed at the
Third Plenary Council of Baltimore, indicates that this practice
must have been widespread. The Mercy Sisters in Baltimore opened
a dress shop and a flower shop in order to earn money for the
support of their works for the poor; in 1904 they opened a public
laundry.[70]

Problems Posed by the American Milieu

Since canon law definitions for sisters did not change
noticeably until 1900, it was to be expected that attempts to adapt

twelfth century prescriptions to nineteenth-century needs would continue to cause tension. The rapid advances in education, science, technology, and medicine which characterized the post-Civil War era made the need for adaptation even more acute. We have already noted the handicaps under which sister-nurses and cloistered sister-teachers worked, as a professionalization of which they were not a part revolutionized fields in which they had previously been the leaders. Doubtless the forty-seven European communities which established their first American foundations during this period experienced more conflict than those groups which had already become acculturated. Those who worked among their own compatriots endured less culture shock than European sisters who had to deal with Americans.

In any case, this was a period when the obsolete practices enshrined in the constitutions of many communities could not be glossed over. The acute need to revise their constitutions was keenly felt by many groups, and most of them did something about it. Many communities received the impetus to rewrite their constitutions from Rome's policy of encouraging religious congregations to apply for papal approval of their constitutions. Often those burdens which were most intolerable were removed or mitigated in the rewriting. Sometimes the good sense of a priest-advisor enabled sisters to view age-old customs from a twentieth-century perspective. It was doubtless through the experience gained in these years of studying and revising constitutions which convinced Roman authorities of the necessity for the changed attitudes towards enclosure and simple vows which are evident in Conditae a Christo.

Until the promulgation of that decree, however, the old rules for enclosure continued in force, and religious communities struggled as they had before to reconcile European constitutions with American needs, to somehow combine the strenuous works of the active life with the austerities of the contemplative way. The history of the struggle of the various Dominican communities which were offshoots of Holy Cross Convent, Ratisbon, Bavaria, illustrates the evolution experienced in greater or lesser degree by many communities during these decades.

The American communities which stemmed either directly or indirectly from Ratisbon followed the prescriptions of their Second Order constitutions as closely as they could, even though they were obliged to open schools. The recitation of the Divine Office combined with the strenuous work of teaching had caused problems for American Dominicans from the first, as we have seen in Chapter III. During the last decades of the nineteenth century it became evident that something had to be done. One by one these communities gave up the idea of becoming cloistered Second Order nuns and sought Dominican affiliation as Third Order sisters. This was often done at the insistence of bishops or chaplains, who wished to correct the impossible situation which prevailed when constitutions prescribed practices which could not be kept without causing grave inconvenience and even physical harm. In 1871 the Dominican Master General, A.V. Jandel, wrote to one chaplain who had asked his opinion,

> It seems to me a sheer impossibility for the Sisters
> to take upon themselves the strenuous burdens of a
> cloistered life to which the Sisters of the Second
> Order are obliged, together with the labor of the

> active life to which the American Sisters devote
> themselves. It seems sufficient if the Sisters
> content themselves with the obligations and the duties
> of the Third Order as so many congregations of our
> Order here in Europe who devote themselves to edu-
> cation and works of mercy.[71]

When the sisters finally agreed to be content with Third Order

status, their chaplain told them, "Don't regret the change any

longer--you have been cured of an incurable illusion."[72] Most

of these communities rewrote their constitutions, many of them

using those of a congregation in Stone, England as a model. They

substituted the Little Office of the Blessed Virgin for the Divine

Office, modified the fasts, and removed the grilles from their

chapels and parlors.

The Visitandines found, when they installed a grille

in the parlor of their new convent in Tacoma, that people resented

having to talk to them through "that pigeon hole." And in Rock

Island, Bishop Spalding refused to allow them to install a grille

until their school was well-established.[73] Other sisters bound by

enclosure rules also sought dispensations from them. Thus the

Ursulines in Galveston sought and received from Pope Pius IX a

dispensation from the cloistered life so that they could staff

parochial schools.[74] Archbishop Wood wrote to the superior of a

Franciscan group, "We grant the usual permission to dispense the

Sisters from Fast and Abstinence when you think it prudent or

necessary."[75] Archbishop Riordan gave the San José Dominicans per-

mission to go out when they were in need of fresh air.[76] (Many

communities applied to the bishop for permission every time it was

necessary to go out of their convents.)[77]

Lay Sisters

The practice of dividing their members into two classes, lay sisters and choir nuns, caused serious problems in this period, as more American girls joined communities which had brought this aristocratic custom with them from Europe. American bishops who proudly extolled the virtues of American Catholicism worked to abolish this undemocratic custom, but European superiors were not always sympathetic to the American viewpoint, and a painful struggle was often the result.

Archbishop Ireland tried for many years to abolish this custom among the St. Paul Josephites, whose lay sisters or "servants of the sisters" wore a black cape and headdress different from those of the choir sisters, and ranked below them in dining room, chapel, and elsewhere. "It's a wonder they don't burn the house down," was his comment on this practice. It was not until the twentieth century, and only after a trip to Rome, that his efforts to abolish it were successful.[78] The Savannah Josephites, who had only a few lay sisters, integrated them in the 1880's.[79] In 1895 the Mercy Sisters of Omaha petitioned the bishop to allow their lay sisters to remove the full white calico apron that they had hitherto worn over their habits, even in the chapel, as a badge of their position.[80] The Benedictines of Minnesota abolished some of their distinctions between lay and choir sisters in the 1880's, but later Bishop Zardetti tried to restore them. The sisters were able to drag their feet until John Ireland came into power.[81]

Among the Dominican Sisters, the practice of having lay sisters who wore a distinguishing dress caused a great deal of

tension. The diary entries of Mother Pia Backes for the 1890's
contain numerous references to this problem. On August 21, 1890,
she wrote, "To my amazement, I have heard that the Lay Sisters are
contemplating asking for the white scapular and the black veil . .
. . They give me much matter for thought."[82] If one priest insisted that the custom be continued, another advised that it be
given up. In 1898 she records, "Sister Y . . . , a Lay Sister,
wrote me that she would prefer to be in a convent where there is
no distinction in dress."[83] And as late as 1904 she is still
writing, "Concerned about Enclosure, Breviary, and Lay Sisters"--
a refrain that recurs throughout her diary.[83]

The inability of Europeans to understand the repugnance
which class distinctions inspired in America is reflected in a
letter of 1871 from the Dominican Master General, A.V. Jandel, to
an advisor of the Racine Dominicans:

> You are quite right . . . to disapprove of the abuse
> which has been introduced in consequence of which choir
> and lay sisters are classified merely according to age
> and profession, and where there does not even exist the
> distinction of the habit--a thing quite unusual; in-
> deed, quite unheard of in our Order. Therefore, the
> Sisters known as "Conversae" should tactfully be in-
> duced to wear the white veil and black scapular in the
> church and in the house.[84]

The following year the lay sisters at Racine dutifully resumed
their distinctive dress. A generation later however, in 1891, it
was the Master General who suggested that these distinctions should
be abolished because they pertained to the Second Order and not
the Third.[85]

Habit

     The religious habit assumed a greater importance after 1889,
when "Ecclesia Catholica" made it one of the essential characteristics of bona fide religious. The element of public witness in the
religious habit was emphasized, though ironically, true religious
were supposed to be cloistered, and thus incapable of giving much
public witness. Fortunately, the work of sisters in the Civil War
made it possible for them to wear the habit in public without fear
of persecution. Only gradually, however, did sisters take advantage
of this change in public opinion. Custom is slow to die in religious
communities, and the years of persecution and intolerance were not
immediately forgotten. Until 1907 the Mercy Sisters of Omaha, for
example, wore what their rule book described as "a cottage bonnet
of fine twilled woolen stuff or straw with a veil of thick silk
gauze or crepe tied on it according to the season,"[86] when they
went out of their convents.

     The Amityville Dominicans put a black skirt over their
white habit and a tight-fitting bonnet on their heads, pinned a
short veil to the bonnet, and then covered the whole outfit with a
long black shawl whenever they went out. Later a change in their
regular habit enabled them to wear it on the street.[87] As sisters
began to wear their habits on the street, face veils came into style
in several communities. These were drawn over the face whenever
sisters attended public church services or went out of their convents. The Benedictines wore them until after breakfast on
communion days.[88] Sometimes neighborhood children ran after them
shouting "Nunnie, Nunnie, lift up your veil!"[89]

The wearing of heavy habits, often of wool, in the heat of summer, caused great discomfort for many sisters. Occasionally something would be done to alleviate their suffering, as happened with a group of Franciscans. Their mother general visited her American mission in August, 1896, a very hot month during which six hundred fifty-one people died of heat prostration in a single week. This convinced her that the community should use a lighter weight material during the summer months.[90] The disadvantages of the habits were noticed by doctors who worked with sisters in caring for the sick and wounded during the Spanish-American War. Alice Worthington Winthrop reports:

> As a rule, the surgeons condemn the woolen habit of the Sisters. It was unnecessarily heavy and warm in the severe heat to which they were exposed; and modern science teaches that it is most favorable for the growth and retention of disease germs, thus rendering it a menace to the health of nurse and of patient as well. The orders would naturally be unwilling to make changes in the essential character of their habits, endeared to them by their symbolic meaning and by historical associations; but there seems to be no good reason why the material of which they are composed should not be altered,-- why woolen stuffs should not be replaced by linen and cotton, especially as these may be frequently washed and can be renewed at less cost. The Apostolic Delegate, Archbishop Chapelle, expressed himself to the writer . . . as greatly in favor of this adaptation or modification of the Sisters' habit.[91]

Thus the religious habit was seen, on purely scientific grounds, as an impediment to the good works the sisters wished to perform.

Constitutional restrictions on the works which could be undertaken by a given community continued to cause trouble, especially where work with young boys was concerned. The idea that there was something improper about sisters having anything to do with boys over the age of ten or twelve continued to prevail in many places in the American church, but sheer necessity forced

some ecclesiastics to re-examine the "boy question." The first

Catholic normal school in the country was founded in Milwaukee in

1871 specifically to train male lay teachers for upper-grade boys.[92]

And in 1880 Bishop Baltes issued an order forbidding sisters to

teach boys over twelve--a severe blow to the small country schools

in which two sisters divided the grades between them.[93] Father

Dominicus Scheer told the San José Dominicans that they should

neither conduct boys' sodalities nor teach boys over fourteen.[94]

But a priest in Jacksonville, Illinois found that male teachers

were too rough with boys, and sought sisters even for those over

twelve years of age. (No community in the Alton diocese would

undertake such dangerous work, possibly because the bishop had

forbidden it.)

There were some signs that a new viewpoint was beginning

to prevail, however, and surely the success of the few communities

who taught older boys had something to do with it, as did the

movement to replace the class system of free and pay schools with

unified parochial schools. A parish could not afford to run two

schools, one for boys and one for girls, and to hire two sets of

teachers to staff them. In 1875 Bishop McCloskey of Louisville

removed a priest from his position as ecclesiastical superior of the

Nazareth Sisters of Charity for telling a pastor that the sisters

could teach only children of their own sex.[95] Though the Cleve-

land Ursulines had to give up St. Bridget's School in 1889 because

Bishop Horstmann would not allow them to teach boys, Bishop Gilmour

give them the necessary permission the following year.[96] And even the Emmitsburg Sisters of Charity were allowed to teach boys in the two lowest grades at St. Peter's, Milwaukee from 1877 until 1895, though their rule forbade it.[97] The Visitandines accepted boys at first at their school in Rock Island, Illinois, but stopped taking them as soon as their finances improved. They aroused the antagonism of the people when they refused to take boys in Tacoma in 1891.[98] At Altoona the older boys were taught by laymen, but a Cincinnati Sister of Charity reports, "It was amusing to see well-grown boys coming to us, declaring that they were only seven or eight years old."[99] And a priest in Springfield, Illinois who wished to unite the boys' and girls' schools taught by Notre Dame sisters and Holy Cross brothers, found that the Springfield Dominicans were willing to teach in the combined school.[100] When the Cleveland Ursulines were asked to open a boarding school for young boys, they felt it was one of those adaptations to local circumstances of which their foundress would approve, and accepted.[101] In 1871 a priest was able to get permission from the mother general of the Sisters of Notre Dame de Namur for her sisters to teach boys' classes in Lawrence, Massachusetts,[102] but twenty years later this same community preferred to withdraw its sisters from schools in Arlington and Chelsea, Massachusetts, rather than teach boys.[103]

Problems with Bishops

Bishops who wished to control the religious communities in their dioceses continued to cause problems during this period. Sometimes they disagreed with community superiors over the type of work sisters should do. There was trouble at St. Francis Seminary in Milwaukee, for example, when the superior wished to withdraw some sisters who did housework there, and train them for teaching.[103]

This was also a problem with the Holy Cross Sisters, without whose

help Notre Dame would have had to close.[104] Both Roman authorities

and the local bishop supported this community's insistence that

its members not become involved in laundering altar linens, de-

corating altars, and other forms of church work.[105]

Bishops continued to prefer diocesan communities which would

be under their direct control and free from foreign entanglements.

They were sometimes very aggressive in the means they used to

achieve this goal. When the mother general of the Precious Blood

sisters refused to cut the ties that bound their Ruma, Illinois

convent to its European motherhouse, Bishop Baltes ordered the

sisters out of his diocese and removed the Blessed Sacrament from

their chapel.[106] The newly-appointed Bishop John Ireland gave a

speech at the dedication of a new motherhouse in Winona, stressing

the importance of Americanizing the Church, and then told the sis-

ters they could remain in his diocese only if they would take no

more German members and become a diocesan community under his

direction. Because the sisters would not agree to this, their new

motherhouse became an academy, and they had to start building a

motherhouse anew, this time in Milwaukee.[107] Ireland had also

forced the closing of a Benedictine convent in Shakopee, Minnesota,

a decision which later proved an unwise one, as even he was forced

to admit.[108]

It was a theologian rather than a bishop who approached

Sister Blandina Segale and listed all of the reasons why her

sisters in Santa Fe should become independent of their Cincinnati motherhouse. She thus records the arguments that he used:

> You are so far from the Motherhouse, and the local
> Superior is restricted by rule in many ways; awaiting
> answers to permissions asked is a slow process . . . .
> Few understand the needs of our southwestern missions.
> Only those who are actively engaged in the work are
> fit judges.[109]

Sister Blandina was not convinced.

When given a free hand, bishops and other directors who did
not understand the principles of the religious life could work
havoc in communities under their control. In Buffalo, Bishop
Ryan made the different convents of the Mercy Sisters independent
in the 1870's, and took upon himself the task of transferring
sisters and superiors from one house to another. He learned
through experience that this would not work, and finally reunited
the houses under a central government.[110] When Bishop Dominec
tried to do the same thing to the Mercy Sisters in Pittsburg, they
insisted that their rule could not be changed in this way without
permission from Rome. Rome advised them to remain as they were
until the diocese was divided.[111]

It was for protection of this kind against the whims of
well-meaning but inexperienced or inept bishops that many communities
sought papal approval of their constitutions. Once approved, the
constitutions could not be changed without Rome's permission.
Communities which were "exempt" were removed from the control of
local bishops and given a Cardinal Protector to look after their
affairs. This exemption was especially necessary for communities
which had houses in several dioceses. A part of the procedure of
applying for papal approval involved the sending of letters of
recommendation and praise from the bishops of all dioceses in which

a community had houses. Father Pacificus Neno, who was the Roman

agent for the Philadelphia Josephites, warned them of the diffi-

culties they might encounter in their struggle for papal approval:

> Your congregation would pass from the jurisdiction of
> the Bishops to the immediate jurisdiction of the Sacred
> Congregation. In such a case you would find the
> greater obstacle in the Bishops themselves, who want to
> have you under their control exclusively.[112]

He was right. Archbishop Wood refused to approve their petition.

This was the tactic of bishops who did not want the sisterhoods

under them to be released from their control. Bishop McCloskey

of Louisville, for example, forced two mothers general of the

Loretto Sisters to withdraw their petitions for papal approval of

their constitutions.[113] And at one point in the long history of

his disagreements with this community, he placed the sisters under

an interdict when they refused to follow his orders.[114] Hence an

anomalous situation existed. Rome had provided a way out for

communities whose local bishops insisted on interfering in their

internal affairs, but had made papal approval contingent on the

acquiescence of these same bishops.

In studying the ways in which sisters were hampered in their

good works by the restrictions of their constitutions, one is

struck by the excruciatingly slow pace of the process by which these

obstacles were removed, and by the incredible amount of tension,

suffering, and embarrassment endured by these very good, well-

intentioned women during the interim. When Rome did finally move

to alleviate these sufferings, as with Conditae a Christo and the

provision for papal approval, the result was only a partial solution.

Interaction With Society

Positive

Though the Catholic school question and other aspects of
American Catholicism were widely debated in the press and in political campaigns during these years, and Catholicism was bitterly
attacked in influential magazines like Harper's, one finds almost
no derogatory remarks about nuns. This negative tribute to the
esteem in which they were held speaks volumes. Sisters met with
both friendly and hostile reactions, but the evidence seems to
indicate that they were generally respected, though bigots still
persecuted them when they had the opportunity. Several instances
might be cited to indicate the positive reactions which nuns
evoked among those who encountered them, and the public tribute
that was occasionally given to them.

Josephite Sisters traveling to Tucson by covered wagon in
1870 were accustomed to stop for the night at ranches along the way.
Sister Monica Taggart's diary (upon which several plays and tele-
vision programs have been based) gives an amusing account of the
reactions at one ranch house:

> The ranchman . . . invited us to dinner . . . .
> There were several ranchmen there from the neighbor-
> ing stations, but no women. There are few women in
> this country. After dinner they became sociable. We
> retired to the stable . . . and they followed.
> Some of them proposed marriage to us, saying we would
> do better by accepting the offer than by going to
> Tucson, for we would all be massacred by the
> Indians. The simplicity and earnestness with which
> they spoke put indignation out of the question, as
> it was evident that they meant no insult, but our
> good. They were all native Americans. For that afternoon
> we had amusement enough.[115]

Others also looked upon nuns as potential wives. A line in the St.

Paul Daily Press of September 12, 1872 notes, "Just as if women

were not already scarce enough for wives and mothers out that way

the Roman Catholics are building a large nunnery at Detroit Lake,

Becker County."[116]

The Holy Cross Sisters who went to Utah in 1875 made a

point of calling on Brigham Young. He apologized for not being

able to give them financial help, since this would cause trouble

among his followers, but urged them to stay and open a school. He

told Mother Augusta that he would make her one of his celestial

brides, so that she could be certain of a place in heaven. There-

after, whenever he saw her on the street, he stepped down from

his carriage to shake her hand and inquire about her health.[117]

The esteem that the sisters had earned during the Civil

War was attested to in 1874, when the Lincoln monument at Spring-

field was unveiled. President Grant asked that two members of a

religious community do the unveiling as a token of gratitude for

wartime services. At the last moment, it was learned that the

nearest community had declined the honor rather than leave their

enclosure. General Sherman remembered the efficient nursing of

the Dominican Sisters in Memphis and remarked, "If I had my Sisters

of St. Dominic near, they would not disappoint me." The Chicago

Tribune reported what happened next:

> The Reverend P.J. Macken . . . said: "Why, I have
> Sisters of Saint Dominic from Kentucky teaching in
> my school . . . in Jacksonville. I am sure they
> would come with the permission of Bishop Baltes."
> "Where is the Bishop?" asked President Grant. "We'll
> get the permission. Sherman, order a special train
> while I wire the Bishop." In a very short time
> President Grant received a telegram authorizing

> Sister Josephine Meagher . . . to take a companion
> [Sister Rachel Conway] and depart at once for
> Springfield . . . . [118]

The sisters rode in the second carriage, just behind the one

carrying President Grant and the other generals.[119]

When the Little Sisters of the Poor opened a home for the

aged poor in Washington, D.C. in 1874, they were given permission

to solicit alms in federal office buildings--a permission that had

never before been granted to anyone. And Congress greeted a

petition for financial aid for these sisters with applause. A

law was duly passed which granted them $25,000 toward the cost

of their building. Later they received a like sum for an addition

for aged Negroes.[120]

An article in an 1897 issue of Cosmopolitan projected the

image of the nun which had come to prevail in many quarters

> To no woman, perhaps, is accorded wider recognition
> than to the sister of charity. Familiar, in her
> ministrations, to the afflicted of mind and of body:
> the soldier wounded on the field of battle, the
> prisoner under sentence of death, the orphan, the
> foundling, the outcast--recognizing neither race, color,
> creed nor conditions of servitude--the sister of charity
> is known to all men. She is the inspiration of the
> poet, the painter, the romancer, and even skepticism
> does not withhold respect, while her contribution to
> human ameliorization is lost in the history of
> civilization.[121]

As always, the testimony of sisters' lives was powerful

enough to overcome former prejudices among many who came into con-

tact with them. Sister Blandina Segale tells of a girl, well-read

in anti-convent literature, who watched her very closely and then

asked to become a Catholic, saying, "Maria Monk and Edith O'Gorman

may talk and have books published against convents--but what I saw

this afternoon has counteracted all I have ever read derogatory to convents and sisters."122

In Duluth in the late 1880's, men pushed the Benedictines off the sidewalk and made crude remarks when they passed them on the street. Much of the prejudice against them died out, however, when they opened a hospital and people came to know them personally. Three men who came to the hospital one day with a sincere desire to free the sisters imprisoned there, were astounded at the joy and contentment of those with whom they spoke. The following day a large gift from an anonymous donor arrived at the hospital.123

Joel Chandler Harris was delighted to have his daughters educated in a convent school and wrote to one of them:

> My regards to Sister Bernard, and say to her, that I am glad and grateful that she is praying for a special favor to me. I think I know what it is, and the idea is growing more pleasing to me every day. Say to her that if she had been raised a Protestant she would know how hard it is to root out of the mind the prejudice and doubts and fictions that have been educated into it. This is the task I am engaged in now. There are only small and insignificant weeds in my mind at this time, but I want to have them all cleared out and thrown over the fence in the trashpile.124

Even such an unlikely person as Samuel Clemens entrusted his daughter to a convent school. He wrote to his wife in the early 1890's,

> I am very very glad Jean is in a convent. I was astonished at myself that I had never thought of a convent. And away deep down in my heart I feel that if they make a good strong unshakable Catholic of her I shan't be the least little bit sorry . . . . If I had it I would not trade it for anything in the earth. If I ever change my religion I shall change to that.125

Among those who gave the ultimate testimony of their belief in the validity of the religious life by taking it upon themselves, was Rose Hawthorne Lathrop, daughter of Nathaniel Hawthorne. She founded a group of Dominican sisters called the Servants for the

Relief of Incurable Cancer and devoted her life to the care of the sick poor.[126] Una Hawthorne, who cared for orphans and destitute children in London, had earlier been dissuaded by Rose from becoming an Anglican nun.[127] In a letter to Rose which was published in her community's magazine, Christ's Poor, Samuel Clemens wrote, "Certainly if there is an unassailably good cause in the world it is this one undertaken by the Dominican Sisters of housing, nourishing and nursing the most pathetically unfortunate of all the afflicted among us . . . ."[128] Clemens contributed generously to this community and encouraged others to do so as well. Rose Hawthorne's friend, Susan Swift, a Salvation Army brigadier, also became a Catholic and a nun.[129] Katherine Drexel, daughter of Philadelphia financier and philanthropist Francis A. Drexel, founded the Sisters of the Blessed Sacrament in 1891 to care for the needs of the Indians and the Negroes, and devoted her large fortune to this cause until her death at the age of ninety-six in 1955.

Negative

Anti-Catholic movements have recurred in cycles in America's history, alternating periods of calm with seasons of extremely active hostility and bitterness. Though the outstanding record of Catholic service in the Civil War did much to lessen the traditional prejudice against Catholics, there were many who were still tainted by it. Attacks on convents and on sisters had become a standard device of anti-Catholic propaganda during the 1830's and 1850's, and it was to be expected that they would be used again when hostility to Catholicism broke out in the 1890's. In areas where bigotry against Catholics was strong, the usual tactics of

propaganda, lectures by ex-nuns and ex-priests, and harrassment
of many kinds were used.

After an "escaped nun" gave a lecture on the immorality of
convents in Milwaukee in 1873, the Christian Statesman published
a long article describing further horrors of convent life. The
indignant Catholics of the city entered a libel suit against the
editor. During the trial, which dragged on for several months,
witnesses were often asked insulting questions. The Catholics
finally won the case. The editor apologized, and a retraction
was published in an obscure part of the newspaper.[130]

The Manitowoc Franciscans faced a lawsuit when the family
of one of their sisters demanded that she return home. The judge
ruled that the girl could choose her own life-style, but a mob
outside the courthouse captured her when she came out. They handed
her over to her mother, who imprisoned her in her home for several
months, but finally allowed her to return to the convent.[131] A
woman who had been a Glen Riddle Franciscan for twelve years lost
a suit against this community for back pay.[132]

Many people believed and acted upon the stories which were
circulated about convents. Two children arrived at a Benedictine
boarding school in Bismark, North Dakota, with two lengths of
clothesline. Their parents had told them to use them to make their
escape, should the stories they had read about convents prove to be
true.[133] Preacher White of Jacksonville, Illinois, scattered
flyers saying "Beware of the painted hypocrites who have come
among you, they may be known by the disguise they wear!" in a
place where children would pass on their way to a convent school.

Both Protestants and Catholics were so indignant that the preacher had to leave town for a while.[134]

The Ursulines in Columbia, South Carolina, reported in 1888 that bigotry was rampant; the Methodist minister had a meeting against them and the Presbyterians tried to keep them from having a school. The editor of the newspaper published articles about every school except theirs. In addition to these troubles, the sisters were unsuccessful in their efforts to get remuneration from Congress for the convent which had been burned down during Sherman's march through the South.[135]

The American Protective Association, the anti-Catholic political organization which was so strong in the 1890's, included attacks on convents in its campaign against Catholicism. W.J.H. Traynor, its president, said in presenting the aims of the group, that the ʳixth aim was "to secure the regular inspection of convents by civil officers."[136] Convents were attacked in numerous publications which poured from A.P.A. offices, and in lectures given by so-called ex-priests and escaped nuns. These publications will be discussed below, along with the literature of the period.

The Dark Lantern Society of Omaha brought in Margaret Shepherd to lecture there in 1897. She had never been a nun, but had been committed for being a prostitute and an alcoholic to a good Shepherd home in Bristol, England.[137] Edith O'Gorman, who actually had been in a convent, and many others who hadn't, travelled around the country, rousing the anger of Catholics and sometimes reaping a harvest of rotten eggs and tomatoes for their pains. Many of these renegades worked more harm than good for the

A.P.A., generating charges of embezzlement and falsehood that could not be overlooked. State branches finally demanded that they be dropped from A.P.A. campaigns, and in 1895 the national convention resolved "that whenever an ex-priest or ex-nun is lecturing, or claims to be lecturing under the auspices of the A.P.A. we denounce and show him up."[138]

"Escaped nuns" were used in many cities to discredit the Good Shepherd convents in particular, and others in general. Good Shepherd sisters were especially ripe for attack because their chief work was the care and reform of delinquent girls. The courts often committed delinquents to their houses rather than to the prisons. It was natural that criminals thus referred should seek to escape, or be willing to fabricate stories of cruelty and immorality, for which they would be paid. By publishing charges of whipping, indecencies, and drunken superiors, the A.P.A. succeeded in 1891 in getting the Michigan legislature to appoint a committee to inspect the Good Shepherd Convent in Detroit. The committee members found the management "excellent and highly commendable," but this did not silence the attackers.[139] In 1898 they brought suit against this convent for alleged imprisonment.[140]

Scandalous stories were circulated in Omaha in 1892 about a Catholic orphanage and the Good Shepherd, Poor Clare, and Sacred Heart convents. The superior of the orphanage invited its attackers to come and inspect it at any time. They did, were served a delicious dinner, and left singing the praises of the institution.[141] The A.P.A. stopped the sisters' visits to the poorhouse and jail, and had a Miss Crowley who had taught successfully at the Omaha

public high school for twelve years, fired from her job. She was
charged with recruiting for convents by having her students read
Scott's "Marmion." When a pupil asked if nuns were still walled
in, she replied that the only convent basement she had ever seen
had only contained coal. In the Southwest, the A.P.A. claimed
that the Southern Pacific Railway discharged all shopworkers who
refused to contribute to the Sisters of Charity.[142]

Legislative Acts

In the last decades of the nineteenth century, many aspects
of the "school question" were hotly debated. Anti-Catholic groups
objected strenuously when various compromises like the Poughkeepsie
Plan and the Faribault Plan allowed the combining of Catholic
and public schools. In some states   the wearing of
religious garb by public school teachers was tested in the courts.
Such was the case in Pennsylvania, where a compromise plan for
the schools of Pittsburgh and Gallitzin was implemented in 1893.
The Junior Order of United American Mechanics and the Patriotic
Order of the Sons of America campaigned against the employment
of nuns in public schools. In 1894 the Board of Education passed
a resolution forbidding the wearing of religious garb by public
school teachers. The battle was carried to the state supreme court,
which sustained the lower court's decision allowing the wearing
of religious garb by public school teachers. Mr. Justice Dean
pointed out that many county and state superintendants of education
were ministers, and the court noted that "in a popular government
by the majority, public institutions will be tinged more or less
by the religious proclivities of the majority."[143] Most subsequent

decisions on this subject have followed the one set forth here in Hysong vs. Gallitzin, which held that symbols of religious devotion worn by nuns could not be regarded as the kind of sectarianism prohibited by the Constitution.[144]

The wearing of religious garb by public school teachers can be prohibited by statute, however. So the Pennsylvania legislature passed a Religious Garb Bill in 1895 which forbade the wearing by public school teachers, of religious garb, insignia, etc. which would indicate membership in any sect. The constitutionality of this law was upheld in 1910 on the grounds that it was directed against acts and did not interfere with religious sentiments.[145] In 1895, a bill forbidding the use of religious insignia or garb by teachers in the public schools was passed by the lower house of the Minnesota Legislature, but not by the senate.[146] In 1898 State Superintendant Charles R. Skinner ruled against the wearing of religious garb by public school teachers in New York.[147] The twentieth century was to see many other court tests of the wearing of religious garb in public schools, as complaints were made in the various states in which it was done. The A.P.A. also lobbied for other types of legal action. In 1894 its members tried to get through the constitutional convention in New York an amendment prohibiting the granting of public funds to sectarian charities.[148]

Roles Seen in the Literature

The nun seen in the fiction of this period is much like the one in earlier works, with these differences: she is used for the first time as a character in serious American fiction, and there is far less venom in the descriptions of popular writers and

propagandists. In the novels of F. Marion Crawford, William
Dean Howells, and Henry James, the nun-figure is no longer a
paradigm for the evils of Catholicism, but comes into her own in
American literature as an integral part of plot and setting. Those
who use the nun as a vehicle for their attacks on the Catholic
Church reflect changed public attitudes in their gentler treatment
of her.

Twelve books which featured nuns as major or minor characters
during this period, and one magazine which published sensational
stories about convents, have been examined.[149] Six of these books
convey a deliberately negative impression of the nun; and six use
the nun character in much the same way that Continental writers
had long been doing.

Several of the anti-Catholic books purport to be revelations
of the secrets of convent life in the tradition of Maria Monk and
Rebecca Reed. Edith O'Gorman's Convent Life Exposed was written
by a woman who had been a Sister of Charity from 1863, when she
arrived with two trunks and a dog, until 1865. (Miss O'Gorman
spread her stories on the lecture platform as well, until her name
came to be almost as well-known as that of Maria Monk.) Members of
the community to which she had belonged felt that there was no
need to refute charges as patently false as hers.[150] Charles
Chiniquy, whose The Priest, the Woman, and the Confessional went
through twenty-four editions between 1874 and 1888, and whose Fifty
Years in the Church of Rome was translated into ten languages,[151]
had been a priest in Canada for twenty-five years. The author of
Secrets of Convent and Confessional, Mrs. Julia McNair Wright, was

the minister's wife whose earlier works on convents were examined in Chapter V. Hudson Tuttle, spiritualist, scientist, and novelist, was the author of Secrets of the Convent. Margaret Shepherd, mentioned above, published the stories she told on the lecture platform in My Life in the Convent. Cornelia Harmon was written by Justin Dewey Fulton, a Baptist minister who devoted much of his time to the conversion of Roman Catholics. The American Protective Association Magazine contained various articles attacking convents.[152]

Several of these books are fictional works which are purportedly based on facts. Their authors insist that the reason for revealing ugly truths is to save those who might otherwise become the unwitting victims of the system which is being exposed. Miss O'Gorman asserts that there is not a single statement in her book which can be refuted. She wants to enlighten those whose children might attend convent schools, and be beguiled by appeals to their senses.[153] Tuttle avers that he has toned down the facts, lest his readers be shocked by his revelations (p. 3). Mrs. Wright says her book "is designed to reveal the mischief and the mystery of this dark and dangerous organization [the Catholic Church] to the eyes of the American people" (p. xi). "A thin veil of fiction is cast upon the face of the monster lest all should turn away from the hideous reality and refuse to gaze," she writes (p. xi).

More positive attitudes towards nuns are reflected in Henry James' The American[154] and Portrait of a Lady;[155] Howells' A Chance Acquaintance[156] and Their Wedding Journey;[157] F. Marion Crawford's Casa Braccio;[158] and Peter McCorry's Mount Benedict;

or, the Violated Tomb. A Tale of the Charlestown Convent.[159] In
the novels of Howells and James, the convent is part of the foreign
culture which is being contrasted with that of America. Both of
Howells' novels are set in Canada; the convent is part of the
romantic French Canadian setting which he describes in some detail.
James describes convents in Paris and in Rome, but what he says
would be true of the convents of European communities in America as
well. In The American, he uses the convent in typical romantic
fashion, as the recourse of a woman who has had an unhappy love
affair. He himself said of this book, in rereading it decades
after he wrote it, "I had been plotting arch-romance without knowing
it."[160] Portrait depicts the European convent school, and the
virtues and defects which characterize at least one of its graduates.
Casa Braccio is one of the Italian romances of that prolific
and popular expatriate writer of the turn of the century, F. Marion
Crawford. Crawford, himself a Catholic, was astonished at the
hostile criticism which his romance elicited from American
Catholics. McCorry's book uses direct quotations from the trial
of the Charlestown rioters to show the extent to which the Ursulines
of Mount St. Benedict were the victims of bigotry and prejudice.

The Nun Herself

The nuns depicted in these books offer some contrast to
those in earlier American works. They are described as virtuous,
gentle, childlike women, pale and sad, devoid of personality, who
work and pray for their neighbor, and willingly submit to the penances
and mortifications imposed on them. Several writers describe
sisters as virtuous women; James uses the epithet which would

become standard for complimentary references to nuns in the twentieth century: "the good sisters."[161] Peter McCorry defends the Ursulines of Mount St. Benedict for their piety, learning, virtue, and devotion to Christian education (p. v). Howells praises the good works which nuns have been performing in Canada since 1692.[162] James' nuns in Portrait are "tranquil, virtuous women. Many of them are gentlewomen born; some of them are noble" (p. 434). "Their attitude expressed a final reserve and their faces showed the glaze of prudence." They have "a kind of business-like modesty," are "very meek," speak "gently," and "softly" and blush frequently (p. 193f.). Their eyes are modestly cast down at the carpet (p. 194).

Even the anti-Catholic writers are forced to pay tribute to the high esteem in which nuns are held during this period--and to conform to the expectations of a Victorian audience. There is not a single direct charge of sexual immorality on the part of nuns in these works. Both Fulton and Tuttle repeat the heretical Quietist doctrine that "a priest cannot commit sin,"[163] and Tuttle asserts that "all novices are the brides of Jesus Christ, and as all priests are one with Jesus, it follows by unanswerable logic that all novices are brides of all priests."[164] Nothing comes of these assertions, however, except a perfectly harmless party at which priests and nuns are present. And Fulton is quick to say, "It is not asserted or believed that all priests and nuns are un-chaste" (p. 13). In any indirect charges of sin--Miss O'Gorman's tale of attempted seduction, for example (p. 106f.), it is the nun who is the innocent victim. Fulton expounds the idea that, since Church theory originated in the East, it is to be expected that the harem would be an important part of its practice (p. 59). But all of these are general statements; their authors do not venture to describe any instances in which the theories are put into practice, though genteel readers were no doubt expected to fill in lascivious details for themselves.

Much of the imagery that is used to describe the nun in the books of Howells and James connotes the dehumanization of the person. To Isabel, in Portrait, Mother Catherine's attitude seems "to represent the surrender of a personality, the authority of the Church" (p. 453). James emphasizes this quality in his description of "the impersonal aspect of their stiffened linen and of the serge that draped them as if nailed on frames" (p. 193). In the first edition of the book the serge is "inexpressive serge."[165] One of Howells' nuns has a "statue-like sadness about her,"[166] and in general they have "still mask-like faces" set in a "stiff framework of white linen."[167] Fulton tells us that "The abbess wished her nuns to be childlike. These were" (p. 124). Howells refers to them as "quaint black birds with white breasts and faces" who flock into the chapel;[168] their characteristic gait is gliding. Their movements are "constrained and ordered" with clockwork precision.[169]

It is the destruction of personality which Crawford emphasizes as well. His Sister Maria Addolorata is told that during her religious life she will repeat such acts as prayers, mortifications, sleepless nights, the endurance of cold and heat "for half a century, sum them up, and offer them to God as a meet and fitting sacrifice--the destruction, by fine degrees of petty suffering, of one woman's whole life, almost from the beginning, and quite to the end, with the total annihilation of all its human possibilities of love, of motherhood, of reasonable enjoyment and legitimate happiness" (p. 39).

Many writers dwell upon the drying-up of the affections which they take to be the meaning of the vow of chastity. Miss O'Gorman's confessor tells her that the doubts she has about leaving her mother and crushing all of her affections are temptations. She must choose between God and her mother, he says, since it is not possible for her to serve both (p. 12). The APA Magazine reveals that a girl who has entered the convent can no longer show any affection, even to her own sisters.[170] Sisters are warned against developing "particular friendships" with other sisters, says Edith O'Gorman (p. 82).

Crawford, Howells, and James all feel that the renunciation of the opportunity to love and to be loved is one of the greatest sacrifices required by the religious life. "Poor Soeurs Grises! " writes Howells,

> the power of your Church is shown far more subtly and mightily in such as you, than in her grandest fanes or the sight of her most august ceremonies, with praying priests, swinging censers, tapers and pictures and images, under a gloomy heaven of cathedral arches. There, indeed, the faithful have given their substance; but here the nun has given up the most precious part of her woman's nature, and all the tenderness that clings about the thought of wife and mother.[171]

He admits, however, that his American characters may be biased in their attitudes toward the convent: "Perhaps they did not judge wisely of the amount of self-sacrifice involved, for they judged from hearts to which love was the whole of earth and heaven . . . ."[172]

And in <u>The American</u>, Mrs. Bread says of the Carmelites, "They give

up everything, down to the very name their poor old nurses called

them by. They give up father and mother, brother and sister,--

to say nothing of other persons" (p. 315).

The majority of Americans in the nineteenth century believed

that a woman finds her highest fulfillment in the home, where she

reigns as wife and mother. In view of this belief, and the fact

that sisters were asked to give up not only the love of a husband

and children, but their affection for their families and the love

of friendship as well (thanks to a warped interpretation of the vow

of chastity), it is not surprising that they should be depicted

as pale shadows of the mature human beings they could have become,

had they lived normal lives. In stressing the importance of deep

interpersonal relationships for the development of the mature per-

sonality, these writers anticipated the findings of contemporary

personality theory.

Almost all of the nuns are depicted as pale and sad.[173]

Fulton's nuns have "pallid cheeks, vacant countenances, lackluster

eyes, and attenuated figures" (p. 124), and Crawford's heroine is

destined "to be a veiled shadow amongst veiled shades, a priestess

of sorrow among sad virgins" (p. 8). Howells has "an elderly

sister with a pale kind face" give Isabel March a white rose in

<u>Their Wedding Journey</u>; it becomes a symbol for the life of the nun:

> A thrill of exquisite compassion for it trembled
> through her heart, as if it had been the white, cloistered
> life of the silent nun; with its pallid loveliness, it
> was as a flower that had taken the veil. It could
> never have uttered the burning passion of a lover for
> his mistress: the nightingale could have found no thorn
> on it to press his aching poet's heart against; but sick
> and weary eyes had dwelt gratefully upon it; at most it

might have expressed, like a prayer, the nun's
stainless love of some favorite saint in paradise.
Cold and pale, and sweet.--was it indeed only a flower,
this cloistered rose of the Hotel Dieu? (p. 302-3)

Not all of the nuns in these novels are pale and sad,
however. When Newman, the hero of The American, visits the convent,
"a robust lay sister with a cheerful complexion" directs him to the
chapel (p. 320). Fulton's nuns put on a "pantomime of pretended
cheerfulness" (p. 124), and Chiniquy explains why. One of the
secret rules of the convent, he says, is "always, especially in
the presence of strangers, to have an appearance of joy and
happiness" so as to encourage young girls to join the community
(p. 55).

Howells' Canadian sisters do not live in the real world.
The two nuns whom Kitty Ellison looks upon in the courtyard beneath
her window are "but figures in a beautiful picture of something
old and poetical," not real human beings (p. 91). But "she loved
and pitied them . . . the same as if they had been real. It could
not be that they and she were in the same world: she must be
dreaming . . . ."[174] The convent scene in Chance Acquaintance
is one of "pensive romance" (p. 93), a "bit of opera" (p. 105).
The "quiet, gliding nuns with white hoods and downcast faces" she
"unerringly relegated to an appropriate corner of her world of
unreality" (p. 97).

In 1892 Howells gave a brief picture of a nun who is very
different from the pale, sad shadow of his earlier novels. At
the end of A Hazard of New Fortunes,[175] Margaret Vance, whose individual efforts to help the poor had brought only misunderstanding
and frustration, appears in the garb of a nun. She smiles

"joyfully, almost gayly" at the Marches, who feel that "the peace
that passeth understanding has looked at them from her eyes."
They have no doubt that she is at rest, now that "she can do all
the good she likes." She hurries on her way with a "free nun-
like walk" (p. 429). In the context of all that has preceded this
final episode of the book, this is high praise indeed. Other means
of solving the social ills of the times have produced violence,
bloodshed, and death, as aggressive action provoked hostile reaction.
But in the religious life, alleviation of the sufferings of others
brings fulfillment, happiness, and peace.

     Henry James uses the traditional idea of religious life
as a state of perfection. The sisters in Portrait, particularly
the elder of the two, give lip service to the idea that having
entered a state of perfection, they have in face become perfect.
When Osmond says "You're very complete," the sister agrees: "Oh,
yes, we're complete. We've everything, and everything's of the
best" (p. 195). When it is remarked that Pansy has no faults, the
elder sister asks, "As for faults, how can we give what we have
not? Le couvent n'est-ce pas comme le monde, monsieur" (p. 196).
When the bespectacled sister says "We are never tired," however,
her young companion, the "junior votaress," feels constrained to
murmur, "Ah, my sister, sometimes" (p. 197). The Countess Gemini
becomes irritated at Osmond's insistence that "Pansy will never
know any harm" because she is "a little convent-flower." She rejects
this unrealistic, hothouse view and insists that the weaknesses of
human nature will be present wherever there are people: "Speak to
me of the convents!" she says, "You may learn anything there. I'm

a convent-flower myself. I don't pretend to be good, but the nuns do!" (P. 216)

The description in The American of the austere life of the Carmelite is a far cry from the tales of luxury, wealth, and pleasure told by the writers of anti-convent propaganda. "Of all the nuns in Christendom the Carmelites are the worst," says Mrs. Bread. "You may see they are not really human, sir; they make you give up everything--forever" (p. 285). She describes what this entails in a later scene:

> There is no rule so strict as that of the Carmelites. The bad women in the reformatories are fine ladies to them . . . . They sleep on the ground . . . . They are no better . . . than tinckers' wives . . . . They get up on winter nights and go off into cold places to pray to the Virgin Mary. (p. 315)

Surprisingly enough, when one considers the earlier practice, J.D. Fulton is the only one of these writers who claims that religious communities are greedy for wealth (p. 17, 24). Mrs. Wright, however, stresses the obvious wealth of the community she is discussing when she describes the luxurious appointments of the convent, including its "thick velvet carpet" (p. 24). Miss O'Gorman describes sumptuous meals with ale and porter to drink, the best beefsteak for breakfast, etc. (p. 28). Madame Merle injects a note of worldliness into the plain but cheerful atmosphere of Pansy Osmond's convent in Portrait. On rather slim evidence she concludes, "Mother Catherine has a very good room . . . . I assure you I don't find the poor sisters at all monastic. Mother Catherine has a most coquettish toilet-table, with something that looked uncommonly like a bottle of eau-de-Cologne" (p. 450).

Reasons for Entering the Convent

The reasons for entering the convent, these books suggest, are an unhappy love affair which impels one to put herself beyond the reach of similar sufferings forever, or obedience to an all-powerful father. Edith O'Gorman tells of a fellow nun who entered the convent after her fiancé's death (p. 82) and other girls also enter because of some "heart distress."[176] Kitty Ellison hears in her dreams the "slim, pale nun crying out, in a lamentable accent, that all men were false and there was no shelter save the convent or the grave."[177]

In The American, Henry James bases his use of the convent as a "dusky old-world expedient" (p. 282) on Turgenev's Nest of the Gentry. Claire de Cintré obeys her mother's command to break her engagement to Christopher Newman, and then chooses to enter the convent rather than live in the world, beside him but not with him (p. 280). This decision ends the attempts of her mother and brother to improve the family fortunes by marrying her to a wealthy nobleman.

In dealing with Claire's decision, James repeats many of the stereotypes which were the standard clichés of convent fiction. Claire sees the convent as a refuge from "the hateful, miserable world" (p. 278) where she will find "peace and safety" (p. 279). "It is to be out of the world, where . . . troubles . . . come to the innocent, to the best. And for life--that's the blessing of it. They can't begin again" (p. 279). Newman reacts with horror to this decision:

The idea struck Newman as too dark and horrible for belief, and made him feel as he would have done if she had told him that she was going to mutilate her beautiful face, or drink some potion that would make her mad . . . . That this superb woman . . . should turn from him . . . to muffle herself in ascetic rags and entomb herself in a cell, was a confounding combination of the inexorable and the grotesque. (p. 279)

Howells also sees the convent as an escape from a hostile world. In recounting the story of the siege of Quebec, when "the sisters were driven out into the world they had forsaken forever, and went from their cloistered schoolrooms and their innocent little ones to the wards of the hospital," Kitty Ellison comments, "What a sad, evil, bewildering world they had a glimpse of!"[178] She imagines other reasons for entering the convent as well:

some Indian maiden lured to the renunciation by the splendor of symbols and promises seen vaguely through the lingering mists of her native superstition; or some weary soul, sick from the vanities and vices, the bloodshed and the tears of the Old World, and eager for a silence profounder than that of the wilderness into which she had fled.[179]

Edith O'Gorman says that she entered the convent on her confessor's advice. It is better to be a bride of Christ and live in the pure light of holiness, he had told her, than to be married to a mere man (p. 9). F. Marion Crawford sets Casa Braccio in the cultural milieu of the Italy of the 1840's. He depicts a girl whose father has decreed that she shall be a nun, even though she would rather marry. This is a patriarchal society in which the father's word is law, and a daughter would not think of disobeying his decree (p. 5).

Margaret Fuller Ossoli, who witnessed a reception ceremony in Italy in which the girl seemed also to be doing her father's bidding, objected to this practice of forcing girls into the convent.[180] The worldly young lady gave the impression "that it was one of those arrangements made because no suitable establishment could otherwise be given her . . . . The effect on my mind was revolting and painful to the last degree," she wrote (p. 272).

> Were monastic seclusion always voluntary, and could it be ended whenever the mind required a change back from seclusion to common life, I should have nothing to say against it; there are positions of the mind which it suits exactly, and even characters that might choose it all through life; certainly, to the broken-hearted it presents a shelter that Protestant communities do not provide. But where it is enforced or repented of, no hell could be worse; nor can a more terrible responsibility be incurred than by him who has persuaded a novice that the snares of the world are less dangerous than the demons of solitude. (p. 272)

Margaret Fuller's reactions to the reception ceremony are interesting because they take into account the usual description given by novelists and contrast it with the reality. "It was a much less effective ceremony than I expected from the descriptions of travellers and romance-writers," she wrote. "There was no moment of throwing on the black veil; no peal of music; no salute of cannon" (p. 272).

The reception and profession ceremonies are described in the usual way in a few of these books, but not with the elaborate detail which was previously considered necessary. It is perhaps because the usual descriptions of these ceremonies has become stereotyped that these writers can omit details. The APA Magazine, in an article called "The Romish Spider Catches Another Fly," describes the beauty of an heiress who has recently joined the convent,[181] and Fulton and Miss O'Gorman use the nuptial imagery of the bride of Christ.[182]

Cloistral Practices

Many of the cloistral practices required by canon law are remarked upon in these books. The grille which symbolizes and enforces the nun's separation from the world is mentioned in three of them. Fulton and Crawford place a double grating in the parlor of their Carmelite convents.[183] For readers who cannot imagine what such a grating might look like, Fulton even furnishes a drawing (p. 356). The APA Magazine discloses under the headline "A Crime Against Humanity," that Carmelites are only allowed to see their mothers through a grille.[184] In The American, Christopher Newman walks up to the grille in the Carmelite chapel and tries to look through it, "but behind it there was darkness, with nothing stirring" (p. 320).

The prison imagery traditionally associated with the walls of a convent is used over and over. Fulton describes the high wall around his convent and notes that its "heavy, sullenlooking gates seemed as if borrowed from a jail" (p. 123). Tuttle also mentions a "massive wall" and "heavy iron gate" (p. 36). He says of his heroine, "She was as excluded from the world as though locked in a penitentiary . . . the walls of the convent were as impregnable as Gibralter, and the iron gate frowned as forbiddingly on him as he passed" (p. 70). Miss O'Gorman speaks of the "convent prison in which I was thenceforth to be entombed," and says the "gloomy walls of the cloister" were like a "living sepulchre" (p. 12). Crawford also uses prison imagery, and has his heroine ask herself what good life was, if it had to be lived in a tomb (p. 36f.). In the convent, young girls are "self-doomed to youthful death," says

Howells.[185] They live "mute blank lives" in "narrow cells"
"amidst the unhomelike comfort of their convent."[186]

The convent is seen as a prison or a tomb, in which young
women are buried alive. In The American, Christopher Newman feels
that Claire Cintré is going to "entomb herself in a cell" (p. 279)
"behind locks and bars" (p. 220). "Madame de Cintré is buried
alive," he cries. "The door of the tomb is at this moment closing
behind her" (p. 296). The convent is in the Rue d'Enfer, in "a
region of convents and prisons, of streets bordered by long dead
walls" (p. 356). A "high-shouldered blank wall" surrounds the
convent, "pale, dead, discolored" (p. 356). It is "a dull, plain"
edifice which "reveals no symptoms of human life; the place looked
dumb, drear, inanimate" (p. 356). "The woman within was lost
beyond recall, and . . . the days and years of the future would
pile themselves above her like the huge immovable slab of a tomb."
Madame de Cintré could look forward to a "'life-time' passed
within prison walls" (p. 355), in "a stony sepulchre" (p. 322).
Claire's last request to Newman is that he will "Let me go alone--
let me go in peace. I can't call it peace--it's death. But let me
bury myself" (p. 243).

When Isabel Archer of Portrait visits Pansy Osmond in the
convent to which her father has sent her for a retreat, we are
told that "the old Protestant tradition had never faded from
Isabel's imagination" (p. 435). She dislikes the convent, despite
its clean, cheerful rooms, and it produces on her "the impression
of a well-appointed prison" (p. 448). The parlour is vast and
cold, very empty and very soundless (p. 448-9). As she is led to

Pansy's room, Isabel notes that everything is solid and bare,
light and clean. "So," she thought, "are the great penal establishments" (p. 450).

James is too skillful a writer to present a one-sided
picture. He adds another dimension with his description in The
American of the Carmelite convent on the Avenue de Messine. This
convent adjoins "one of the prettiest corners of Paris" (p. 319).

> The quarter has an air of modern opulence and convenience
> which seems at variance with the ascetic institution,
> and the impression made upon Newman's gloomily irritated
> gaze by the fresh-looking, windowless expanse . . .
> was less exasperating than he had feared. The place
> suggested a convent with modern improvements--an asylum
> in which privacy, though unbroken, might be not quite
> identical with privation, and meditation, though mono-
> tonous, might be of a cheerful cast. (p. 319)

The practices which follow from the attitude that nuns
must constantly be watched, lest they fall, are reflected in the
references to the censorship of mail[187] and to the companion who is
supposed to be present whenever a sister is speaking to a visitor
in the parlor.[188] In the convent created by Tuttle, three nuns
watch in order to make sure that the most minute regulations are
followed at all times (p. 72).

Jansenistic attitudes towards the body are revealed in a
few of these stories. Miss O'Gorman asserts that sisters are not
allowed to touch the orphan children in their care (p. 42). She
also says that sisters are told that it is wrong to look at a man's
face (p. 38). Nor are they allowed to shake hands with men.[189]
Crawford describes the absurd situation which occurs when the
abbess of an Italian Carmelite convent becomes ill. A doctor
comes, is allowed the great liberty of feeling her pulse, and is

even able to get her to lift her face veil and open her mouth.
But he must tell another sister what should be done for her, since
he cannot touch her himself (p. 74). After the abbess takes to
her bed, her brother the cardinal finally persuades her to allow
the doctor to stand in the doorway of her room, with his back to
her, and ask questions about her health. "Many an old Italian
doctor," notes Crawford, "can tell of even stranger and more absurd
precautions observed by the nuns of those days" (p. 105). The
evidence we have gathered from the history of nursing and other
sources indicates that these statements are based on actual
practice, not merely the imaginative creations of writers.

Prayer

Tuttle and O'Gorman describe long prayers, many of them in
Latin, which sisters are obliged to say.[190] Miss O'Gorman goes into
some detail in her description of the prayer life of her community.
There is an hour's meditation, early in the morning, during which
the sisters are supposed to kneel. Many faint before the hour is
over (p. 27). Crawford speaks of the "wearily nasal chant of the
sisters" (p. 36) and Howells says their voices have a "strange,
metallic clang" when they sing, and they pray with "rather harsh
voices."[191]

James describes the sound of the sisters' voices chanting
their prayers in much the same way that other writers have, though
with more skill. The funereal theme recurs:

> Suddenly there arose from the depths of the chapel,
> from behind the inexorable grating, a sound of a
> strange, lugubrious chant, uttered by women's voices.
> It began softly, but it presently grew louder, and
> as it increased it became more of a wail and a dirge.

It was the chant of the Carmelite, their only human
utterance. It was their dirge over their buried
affections and over the vanity of earthly desires . .
. . The chant kept on, mechanical and monotonous, with
dismal repetitions and despairing cadences. It was
hideous, it was horrible . . . . The thought came over
him that this confused impersonal wail was all that
either he or the world she had deserted should ever
hear of the voice he had found so sweet. (p. 321)

Madame Urbain de Bellegarde asks Newman, "Did you hear the chanting?

They say it's like the lamentations of the damned. I wouldn't

go in; one is certain to hear that soon enough" (p. 323). "It's

a wonder they have any heart for singing," Mrs. Bread had said;

this description indicates that they hadn't (p. 316).

The Habit

The religious habit worn by the Carmelites also carries

connotations of death. "They wear old brown cloaks . . . that

you wouldn't use for a horse blanket," reports Mrs. Bread. "They

wear a shroud under their brown cloaks and a rope around their

waists . . . ." (p. 315). The lay sister "with the high-colored

cheeks" has "a fan-like frill to her coiffure" (p. 321). Madame

Urban de Bellegarde sighs, "Poor Claire--in a white shroud and a

big brown cloak! That's the toilette of the Carmelites, you know.

Well, she always was fond of long, loose things" (p. 323).

Howells describes the uniform "ungraceful gowns of coarse gray,

the blue checked aprons, the black crape caps" of the Canadian

sisters.[192]

Penitential Practices

Three of the writers of this period--Tuttle, O'Gorman, and

Fulton--plagiarize Maria Monk and other earlier writers when they

describe the penances which are supposedly imposed by superiors.
Miss O'Gorman tells of being made to eat a worm and to hold her
hands in hot lime (p. 24, 51). Tuttle repeats several penances
which involve peas: kneeling on peas during church services or
for several hours at a time, and putting thm in one's shoes and
walking up and down stairs (pp. 57, 74, 191). He also mentions
the cap studded with needles and the gag which keeps the sufferer
who is made to wear it from crying out (p. 91). Fulton tells of
a nun who is made to chew a piece of window glass into a fine powder in expiation for having rinsed her teeth with water before
going to communion, while Tuttle tells of putting broken glass in
one's shoes. For talking without permission, a sister is allowed
to have only the apple-parings from the superior's dessert for
her dinner.[193] Tuttle describes a nun who is forced to swallow
salt, and then kept from drinking any water (p. 74), and of one
made to lick the dust from her superior's shoes (p. 93). Another
is told to sleep on the cellar floor for a month (p. 57). Fulton
writes of sisters mopping the floor with their tongues (p. 41).
The practice of kissing the floor is mentioned by Mrs. Wright (p. 24).
Scourging with a discipline and wearing a haircloth shirt are
described by Tuttle. Fulton's heroine tells of the chapter of
faults, at which one accuses oneself of such faults as eating between meals, "having walked too heavily, making too much noise in
shutting the doors," etc. (p. 149). Miss O'Gorman also describes
this traditional monastic practice (p. 29).

Sadistic brutality is described by Tuttle and Fulton.
Fulton tells of a nun who is dragged along the floor by her hair,

thrown into a dungeon, and kicked, because she revealed a secret.
Her hair is tied to nails fastened into the wall and she is kept
without food for two days (p. 133). Another nun imprisoned in a
cell shrieks for help. The bishop hears her but is told that she
is insane. She denies it and charges that the sisters throw cold
water on her to keep her from shrieking (p. 99). Tuttle tells of
several nuns imprisoned in basement cells, one of whom says they
have killed her baby (p. 91, 103, 140f.). He also depicts the
disposal of the body of a nun who has been poisoned, in a hole
where many other bodies have also been thrown (p. 104, 141).

It is chiefly in the sections on penances that anti-
Catholic writers present grotesque caricatures of convent practice.
They take a sadistic delight in inventing ever stranger and more
painful tortues with which to rack the bodies of the poor women
whom they have doomed to meaningless existences. An accomplished
writer like James, on the other hand, who has no interest in
giving his readers cheap emotional thrills at the expense of
restraint, verisimilitude, and artistry, merely mentions the austerity
of the Carmelite life without including exaggerated details. (See
for example, the quotation cited on page 307).

Works of Charity

A strictly contemplative Carmelite convent is used in Casa
Braccio and in The American, but most of the other convents described in these books have some active apostolate like teaching.
Miss O'Gorman describes her experiences on the staff of an
orphanage. The orphans are cruelly treated, she says, made to run
barefoot in the snow for exercise, subjected to corporal punishment,

and served unappetizing food in meagre amounts (p. 57f.). The older ones help the younger to dress in the morning "because the sisters are forbid touching them" (p. 42).

Fulton describes sisters whose chief work is the infiltration of Protestant families for purposes of subversion. He pictures a nun who lays aside her habit and dresses like a servant-girl in order to nurse a wealthy woman in her last illness (p. 91). Novices are sent as governesses into Protestant families, he says, and are given permission to attend church services with the family, so that no one will suspect their identity. They are thus in a position to learn the secrets of Protestants and to subtly sway the children's interests towards Catholicism (p. 128).

Most of the communities described in these books conduct schools, and it is chiefly through criticism of them, rather than direct attacks on nuns themselves, that hostile writers attack Catholicism. Nor is this surprising since, as we have seen, many Protestant families learned, through their experiences with convent schools, to hold sisters in high regard and to esteem the Catholic Church. The debate over the education of women which enlivened contemporary magazines provided a basis for criticisms of convent academies which did not open the writer to charges of bias. Even in their critiques of these schools, however, they are forced to acknowledge the high reputation which they enjoy. Miss Shepherd, for example, unwittingly stresses the good points of these schools while deprecating their lack of a teacher-training program:

> The general impression among Protestants is that girls
> receive a far superior education in a convent school
> to that in any Protestant institution. This is, however,
> a great mistake. A convent education cannot, under

ANY circumstances, be called a practical one, and
will never fit the pupil in after years (should necessity
require it) to teach in any advanced school. Most of
the time is devoted to accomplishments, and the sisters
will find out just what particular accomplishment (if
any) the pupil may have an aptitude for, and will ac-
cordingly cultivate it. The education, as a whole, is
superficial. (p. 7)

Tuttle and Fulton have similar criticisms.[194]

Miss O'Gorman claims that more time is spent in prayer
than in learning at these schools, and a superficial show of
accomplishments is the aim. One sister might teach as many as
one hundred eighty or two hundred children, she says (p. 65).
Tuttle admits that the lessons in needlework are incomparable, but
claims that for the rest there is only a smattering of French,
Italian, reading, music, drawing, and painting. He feels that co-
education rather than seclusion is the best way to prepare a girl
to meet temptation (p. 38). Fulton asserts that the subjects
taught in convent schools turn the mind from healthy pursuits to
subjects which are ill-suited to the needs of the soul. The Bible
is thought to be unsafe for young girls because of its "impure
tendencies," he claims (p. 44). Many of these writers charge that,
despite assurances that a girl's religion will not be interfered
with, subtle pressures are brought to bear on Protestant students
to induce them to become Catholic. Tuttle claims that nine-tenths
of the many Protestant pupils in convent schools become Catholics.[195]

Gilbert Osmond of Portrait of a Lady has a different view
of the convent school. He sees it as the perfect vehicle for the
education of his daughter Pansy. "The Catholics are very wise
after all," he says. "The convent is a great institution: we
can't do without it; it corresponds to an essential need in

families, in society. It's a school of good manners; it's a school
of repose." "Convents are very quiet, very convenient, very
salutary" (p. 434-5).

The qualities which Osmond prizes most highly in a convent
education are those emphasized in the characterizations of nuns
themselves discussed above: dehumanization and separation from
the evils and the realities of the everyday world. Pansy is a
flower child, devoid of emotion, personality, and talent, docile
and submissive and pathetically eager to please others, her father
above all. Her one brief venture in personal initiative--her preference for Edward Rosier--is effectively crushed by a further
confinement in the convent. One who accepts the psychologists'
theory that the personality matures through the assertion of one's
own will and the facing and surmounting of conflicts, can readily
agree with Osmond's conviction "that she would always be a child"
(p. 292). It is for this that her convent school has prepared her.
But let us take a closer look at James' depiction of the school
and of its product, Pansy Osmond.

The convent school curriculum includes languages taught
by native speakers, drawing, and gymnastics (p. 195). Convent
graduates become good Christians and charming young women with
impeccable manners, we are told (p. 196), but the most important
values taught are submissiveness, docility, and obedience to
authority. "For everything they must ask leave. That's our
system. Leave is freely granted, but they must ask it," says
Sister Catherine (p. 195). Thus the practices which flowed from
the sisters' vow of obedience were imposed on their students as

well.

In Pansy Osmond we are given the perfect specimen of the
"convent girl." Though Madame Merle thinks that much of her personality is her own, and not due to her convent training, Osmond
insists that it's the combination of nature and nurture which
has produced his charming convent flower (p. 206). The first
thing to be noted about Pansy, for whom James uses a great deal
of flower imagery, is that she is a hothouse flower. She typifies
those qualities described by Tocqueville which distinguish European
girls from American ones. She reminds Isabel of "an ingenue in a
French play" (p. 233) and of "the ideal jeune fille of foreign
fiction" (p. 233). She is "like a sheet of blank paper" (p. 233).
This is a flower which has been cultivated apart from the noxious
atmosphere of the everyday world, with its polluted air, excesses
of heat and cold, and evil influences of many kinds. Her father
says that she "will never know any harm" (p. 216). She is innocent
and "pure as a pearl" (p. 206, 233), "a pure white surface successfully kept so; she had neither art nor guile, nor temper, nor talent--
only two or three small exquisite instincts" (p. 262). Edward Rosier

> was sure Pansy had never looked at a newspaper and that,
> in the way of novels, if she had read Sir Walter Scott
> it was the very most. An American jeune fille--what
> could be better than that? She would be frank and gay,
> and yet would not have walked alone, nor have received
> letters from men, nor have been taken to the theatre
> to see the comedy of manners. (p. 305)

She had, in fact, seen "nothing but roofs and bell-towers" from
the convent windows while in Rome (p. 263).

Pansy has been trained to have no will of her own. "She
was evidently impregnated with the idea of the submission which

was due to any who took the tone of authority; and she was a
passive spectator of the operation of her fate" (p. 199). "I
,obey very well," she cries, "almost with boastfulness" (p. 199).
However much this might accord with a culture in which the father
decides whether his daughter shall enter the convent or marry,
and chooses her husband for her, Isabel, the supreme exemplar of
the self-reliant American woman, feels that it leaves something to
be desired. "She could be . . . an easy victim of fate. She would
have no will, no power to resist, no sense of her own importance;
she would easily be mystified, easily crushed; her force would be
all in knowing when and where to cling" (p. 262). Isabel sees
that Pansy is a weak person who is extraordinarily anxious to
please (p. 334) and "very limited" (p. 337). The irony of the
situation lies in the fact that Isabel, who is the opposite of
Pansy and the essence of independence and personal initiative has,
through the most independent decision of her whole life, placed
herself in a position of dependence on Osmund that is almost the
same as Pansy's. Osmond is certain that since Pansy "wishes above
all to please" (p. 346), and to please him, she will allow him to
dispose of her life in any way he wishes, even though this means
giving up the man she loves (p. 346). Her convent training has
prepared her for this, as it prepared other young women to enter
the convent at their father's bidding.

The emphasis on good manners, on never showing one's emotions,
never being surprised, is also an important part of the convent
training Pansy has received. When Osmond tells her he plans to
marry Isabel Archer, she is neither surprised nor alarmed, which

"proves that her good manners are paramount" (p. 292). Isabel thinks Pansy so accomplished in this line that she could even give lessons in deportment to the Countess Gemini (p. 293).

Pansy is always pictured as being very child-like. "That she would always be a child was the conviction expressed by her father, who held her by the hand when she was in her sixteenth year and told her to go and play while he sat down" (p. 292). She is very small for her age, and wears dresses that are too short for her (p. 292). She is "innocent and infantine" (p. 233).

We see in the literature then, some repetition of the cliches of convent novels and some new developments. The trend away from charges of immorality noted in the last chapter continues to restrain writers hostile to sisterhoods, but they make increased use of sadistic penances and brutality. In many of the details of these depictions--apart from the more unusual penances--the picture of convent life is realistic. The grille, convent walls, companion, belief in religious life as a state of perfection, attitudes toward human love, long Latin prayers, chapter of faults, Jansenism, and traditional penitential practices were all a part of convent life. Distortions in the actual teaching of the Church regarding many of these practices existed among nuns themselves, just as they did among those who wrote about them, though the latter tended to caricature the realities. The essential supernatural motivation which impelled a girl to enter a convent is not dealt with in these works, however; hence the picture drawn is only a partial one. Only in the character of Margaret Vance do we catch a brief glimpse of a nun to whom convent life brings fulfillment and joy.

Howells, James, and to a lesser extent Crawford, bring the
nun into the mainstream of serious American literature, and in doing
so they repeat many of the themes which were traditional in Continental literature. The lament of the unwilling nun was common from
the thirteenth century on.[196] Regret at the stunted personality
development which must result from the deprivation of human love
had been common in the fourteenth, eighteenth, and nineteenth
centuries.[197] The theme of the girl who enters the convent because
she wishes to flee the world and its troubles was first stated in
the eighteenth century.[198] Eighteenth-century romanticists pictured the convent as a prison or a tomb and used lachrymose and
sepulchral details to reinforce this image.[199] By releasing the
nun-figure from the grip of the propagandists and making her an
integral part of the plot and setting of American literature, these
writers have prepared the way for the fuller treatment which she
would be given in twentieth-century American fiction.

Conclusion

We have noted the abrupt change in the public image of the
nun which occurred during the 1860's. The woman who had previously
been considered the epitome of evil was then so idealized that she
became an angel whose superhuman virtues left little room for human
failings. In the last three decades of the nineteenth century,
the pendulum swung back to the middle. The nun was seen as a good
person, but one whose life-style interfered with her competence
in her work. Because the nun was accepted as a respectable person,
it was now possible for Catholics as well as non-Catholics to
examine her life and work in a rather objective way. One could

lament the failure of sister-nurses to keep up with contemporary developments in medicine without incurring charges of bigotry. Perhaps it was the public as well as private awareness of the ways in which obsolete cloistral regulations harmed those whom they were supposed to help that finally induced Rome to change these regulations.

It was because "convent disclosures" were no longer widely read or believed that serious writers could now include the nun among the characters in their novels. They were inclined to use her in the ways in which she had typically been used in Continental literature. The earlier convent novels had made the details of convent life familiar to all. Howells and James were able to draw upon that background knowledge of their readers even when they did not explicitly refer to it. They probed a little more deeply into the possible psychological effects of the practices which had been described and sometimes caricatured in previous American novels. Only in Howells' vignette of Margaret Vance, however, do we glimpse the inner spiritual realities which give meaning to the external details of convent life. It remained for twentieth-century American writers to create nuns who were individuals rather than stereotypes and to deal with the real secrets of convent life.

Perhaps it was only after the mitigation of the strictest cloistral regulations that nuns could become a familiar part of the American scene and writers like James T. Farrell, J.F. Powers, J.D. Salinger and others would be interested in probing the realities of their lives. Less talented writers would continue to repeat in the twentieth century the stereotyped nun-figure which has become traditional in Western literature.

CHAPTER VII

CONCLUSION

It was the hypothesis of this paper that a study of the role of the nun in American society, and her interaction with her milieu, would reveal a cultural clash between European and American values. This study contains abundant evidence that such was actually the case. The Church's formal role definitions for nuns continued, throughout the period studied, to be based on a twelfth-century view of woman as an immature, inferior, and evil being, incapable of directing her own life and requiring constant surveillance lest she fall. The type of religious life frozen into canon law regulations was the outgrowth of an aristocratic society with an economic system in which fathers sometimes consigned their daughters to convents for financial rather than religious reasons.

This system of religious life was based on an abstract ideal of monasticism which embodied as essentials many practices which were actually the products of medieval culture. Thus salvation was insured by one's adherence to formal role definitions which did not change significantly for over seven hundred years. Had they embodied only general directions for living the Christian Gospel, this might have sufficed, but unfortunately, they embodied instead practices designed to keep unwilling nuns separated from the world outside their convent walls.

Given the fact that more than three-fourths of the communities established in America prior to 1900 were from European or Canadian motherhouses, whose members were unfamiliar with American ways, one could expect that serious difficulties would face most sisters who tried to live according to the Church's traditional expectations for nuns in America. Small wonder that conflict occurred when these role definitions were imposed on a dynamic society whose system of government, values, and attitudes towards women were quite different from those of medieval Europe; that Roman cardinals, bishops, nuns, and American Protestants all voiced the opinion that religious life based on traditional values was incompatible with the American way of life. Because of the differences between these two cultures, sisters in America faced countless battles with their superiors in Europe and their bishops and ecclesiastical superiors in America at the same time that they were confronting frontier conditions and hostile fellow townsmen. They were constantly compelled to seek dispensations from their constitutions and to live with the knowledge that, try as they would, it was impossible in America to adhere strictly to the abstract ideal of what a nun should be.

We have noted the basic patterns that marked the interaction of sisters with American society. In the early years, the disparity between the European values which characterized traditional forms of religious life and the realities of the American milieu were such that five of the six foundations attempted by Europeans failed, while all six communities founded by Americans survived into the 1970's. They did so chiefly because of their ability to

adapt to the necessities of their American culture, particularly
those of the economic system. Several of them resisted their
advisers' efforts to import European nuns to teach them how to be
"real" religious.

In the pre-Civil War decades, particuarly the 1830's and
1850's, bigotry towards Catholics and hostility to convents--based
on unfavorable role expectations derived from anti-Catholic publications and speeches--sparked violent attacks on nuns and convents.
No doubt it was chiefly because they were representatives of the
Catholic Church that nuns were attacked, but the charges against
them focussed on their supposed immorality, and on practices that
smacked of an aristocratic European culture. Published tales of
convent horrors helped to form the unsavory public image which impelled many to attack convents and convent schools. Nuns themselves, with their commitment to the values of the Gospels, earned
the respect of all who came in contact with them. Unfortunately,
however, cloistral rules sometimes kept them from giving that public
witness to the values of Christianity which would have broadened
their sphere of influence, and from serving their neighbor in all
of his needs. One of the indigenous American communities chose
during this period to take on French customs and a French rule,
but several sisters refused to give up their American heritage and
founded separate communities instead.

The Civil War provided that opportunity for widespread
contact with nuns which would bring about a dramatic change in
public opinion and force all right-minded men to acknowledge their
virtues. Some of the theories of public opinion experts are

corroborated by this Civil War experience. Actual association
with groups hitherto looked upon with hostility can change one's
whole attitude to those groups, they say. (See page 9   above.)
So can strong invalidating evidence and the failure of important
expectations. We have cited many instances, and not just those
connected with the Civil War, in which contact with sisters
brought about a complete change in attitudes towards nuns.

After the Civil War, the role expectations of the general
public were conformed more closely to the actuality. Writers no
longer dared to accuse nuns of immorality. Those hostile to them
concentrated on undermining those works which were earning high
praise in many quarters, particularly the convent schools. In the
last decades of the nineteenth century, sisters continued to be
held in high esteem, except by bigoted groups like the A.P.A.,
but their admirers regretted that obsolete practices hampered their
effectiveness in their work and damaged their health as well. Because nuns were now an accepted part of the American scene, serious
writers could use them in their fiction and probe the effects which
convent practices might have on the personality. They also pointed
to a need for change. One of them hints at the joyful meaning
that religious life, properly interpreted, can have for one who
chooses it.

Father Jerome Murphy-O'Connor, a contemporary scripture
scholar, holds that one of the essential characteristics of the
Christian life according to St. Paul is its quality of witness
through good works.[1] It was this essential attribute of the
Christian which was made difficult, if not impossible, by the rules

which governed religious communities in the nineteenth century.
True, these were often dispensed with, and some adaptations were
made, but how much more clearly sisters would have witnessed if
they had not been hampered by cloister rules. One can only admire
the selfless women who managed to witness to Christian values
despite the tensions and frustrations of an alien way of life which
took its toll in personal suffering, early death, and a less
effective response to the needs of the Church. Finally, in 1900,
the Church, in response to changed conditions in many countries,
modified its rules for nuns. Not until the 1960's, however, were
American sisters free to shape a form of religious life that responded to all of the needs of their culture, and even then, attitudes from the past curtailed some of the adaptations which were
proposed.

If any lesson for the future can be learned from the past
experience of American nuns, it is that the only commitment which
can remain static for the religious life is the commitment to
live according to the Christian gospels. All other aspects of the
sister's life, including the way in which she supports herself
and the type of apostolic work she does must be determined by the
needs and the realities of the constantly changing society of which
she is a part. Intelligent people on the scene are best able to
make decisions about specific details of religious life, not outsiders who live in another country or another world.

As we have noted on page 1 of Chapter I, it is precisely
this kind of adaptation which is called for in the decree on the
renewal of religious life which was issued by the Second Vatican

Council. This decree called for the revision of the constitutions of all religious communities, that they might be brought into conformity with the culture of the modern world and the needs of the Church today. It finally freed sisters from the trammels of the past and made it possible for them to adapt completely to modern needs for religious life. The central core around which sisters have been directed to build their lives is the message of the Christian gospel, and they have been urged to study the needs and the culture of the contemporary world in order to witness to gospel values in the best possible way. For the first time in centuries, they are free to live a contemporary form of Christianity. It is to be hoped that they can learn from the lessons of the past to keep their lives free from all that would keep them from adapting to the dynamic society of the present.

FOOTNOTES FOR CHAPTERS ONE AND TWO

1. Walter M. Abbott (ed.), The Documents of Vatican II, trans. Rev. Joseph Gallagher (New York: Guild Press, American Press, 1966), 466-482. This document was issued on October 8, 1965.

2. Ibid., p.468-69.

3. Ibid., p.479.

4. See for example what has happened since 1966 to the Glenmary Sisters, the Sisters of the Immaculate Heart of Mary, and the Benedictine Sisters of Tulsa, Oklahoma.

5. Though strictly speaking nuns are religious women who profess solemn vows, or who belong to an order whose vows are normally solemn, and sisters are religious women who profess simple vows, these two terms will be used interchangeably in this dissertation.

6. Ray Allen Billington, America's Frontier Heritage (New York: Holt, Rinehart and Winston, 1966) has a good bibliography on this topic on pages 293-95.

7. Ibid., p.215-17.

8. Alexis de Tocqueville, Democracy in America, ed. Phillips Bradley (New York: Vintage, 1959), II, 210.

9. Ibid., p.209.

10. Ibid.

11. Ibid., p.212ff.

12. Werner J. Cahnman and Alvin Boskoff (eds.), Sociology and History, Theory and Research (New York: Free Press, 1964), p.1-3.

13. Ibid., p.8.

14. American History and the Social Sciences (New York: Free Press, 1964), p.16.

15. Ibid., p.16.

16. For discussions of symbolic interactionist sociology see Arnold M. Rose, Human Behavior and Social Processes (Boston: Houghton Mifflin, 1962) and Glenn Vernon, Human Interaction (New York: Ronald, 1965).

17. Sullivan's theories are discussed in his Conceptions of Modern Psychiatry (Washington: Wm.Alanson White Psychiatric Foundation, 1945).

18. Asylums (New York: Doubleday Anchor, 1961).

19. Slavery (New York: Grosset & Dunlap, 1959), p.124n.

20. Neil Gross, Ward S. Mason, and Alexander W. McEachern, Explorations in Role Analysis: Studies of the School Superintendency Role (New York: John Wiley & Sons, 1958), p.163.

21. Ibid., p.248.

22. Vernon, p.133.

23. Frederick L. Bates, "Position, Role, and Status: a Reformulation of Concepts," Social Forces, XXXIV (1956), p.315.

24. Jackson Toby, "Some Variables in Role Conflict Analysis," Social Forces, XXX (1952), p.324.

25. Milton Rokeach, "Attitude Change and Behavioral Change," Public Opinion Quarterly, XXX No.4 (Winter, 1966-67), p.530.

26. Joseph T. Klapper, "The Effects of Mass Communications," Reader in Public Opinion and Communication, Bernard Berelson and Morris Janowitz, eds. (New York: Free Press, 1966), p.474-77; and Gordon Allport, The Nature of Prejudice (Cambridge, Mass.: Addison-Wesley, 1954), p.493-4.

27. Harwood L. Childs, Public Opinion: Nature, Formation, and Role (Princeton, N.J.: Van Nostrand, 1964), p.119.

28. Theodore Newcomb, Ralph Turner, and Philip E. Converse, Social Psychology The Study of Human Interaction (New York: Holt, Rinehart & Winston, 1965), pp.444 and 82-89.

29. Childs, p.138.

30. Allport, p.22-23, 57.

31. Literature, Popular Culture, and Society (Englewood Cliffs, N.J.: Prentice-Hall, 1961), p.xi.

32. Ray Allen Billington, The Protestant Crusade, 1800-1860 A Study of the Origins of American Nativism (New York: Macmillan, 1938), p.45.

33. Billington.

34. Betty Ann Perkins, "The Work of the Catholic Sister-Nurse in the Civil War" (Unpublished master's thesis, the University of Dayton, 1967).

35. Sister Mary Augustina Ray, American Opinion of Roman Catholicism in the Eighteenth Century (New York: Columbia University Press, 1936).

36. Rene Metz, What is Canon Law?, trans. Michael Derrick (The Twentieth-Century Encyclopedia of Catholicism. New York: Hawthorn Books, 1960), p.29ff.

37. H. A. Ayrinhac, General Legislation in the New Code of Canon Law (New York: Benziger, 1923), p.70.

38. S. B. Smith, Elements of Ecclesiastical Law (New York: Benziger, 1881), p.43.

39. Theodore Roemer, The Catholic Church in the United States (St. Louis: Herder, 1950), p.321.

40. Simone de Beauvoir, The Second Sex, trans. H. M. Parshley (New York: Knopf, 1953).

41. The Church and the Second Sex (New York: Harper and Row, 1968).

42. Ibid., p.167.

43. Quoted by Simone de Beauvoir, p.98.

44. Eileen Power, Medieval English Nunneries c.1254 to 1535 (Cambridge: University Press, 1922), p.29ff.

45. Sister Gretchen Hessler, "The Nun in German Literature, " (unpublished Doctoral thesis, the University of Illinois, Urbana, 1944), p.15.

46. Quoted in Power, p.344.

47. "Circa Pastoralis" (1566); "Decori et Honestati" (1570); and "Deo Sacris" (1572).

48. See Charles Bachofen, A Commentary on the New Code of Canon Law (St. Louis: Herder, 1929), pp.57, 22, 226.

49. Sister Mary Olivia Ferguson, "Frances de Bermond and the Cloistering of the Ursulines," (unpublished Master's thesis, University of Notre Dame, Ind., 1961), pp.15, 77.

50. Ibid., and James R. Cain, The Influence of the Cloister on the Apostolate of Congregations of Religious Women (Lateran University, Rome, 1965), p.37ff.

51. Perhaps the repeated failure of regulations designed to keep religious permanently apart from the world is somehow connected with its interruption of that rhythm of retirement into nature for reflection and contemplation apart from the distractions of cities, and subsequent return with a clarified outlook, which has been celebrated for centuries in the literary tradition of the pastoral. Cf. Leo Marx, The Machine in the Garden (New York: Oxford, 1964) and "Pastoral Ideals and City Troubles" (paper read at the Smithsonian Institution, Washington, D.C., February 16, 1967).

52. Clement Orth, The Approbation of Religious Institutes (Washington, Catholic University Press, 1931), p.54.

53. The effect of cloistral regulations on American congregations is studied by James Cain.

54. Henry C. Semple, The Ursulines in New Orleans 1727-1925 (New York: Kennedy, 1925), p.3.

55. Sister Mary Christina Sullivan, Some Non-Permanent Foundations of Religious Orders and Congregations of Women in the United States (1793-1850) (Vol.XXXI of Historical Records and Studies. Edited by Thomas F. Meehan. New York: The United States Catholic Historical Society, 1940), pp.11.

56. Treaty of the Company of the Indies with the Ursulines, Semple, pp.167ff.

57. Letter of Sister Mary Magdeleine Hachard to her father, Feb.22, 1727, quoted by Semple, p.187.

58. Ibid., p.196.

59. Ibid., p.230.

60. Rev. James Burns, The Principles, Origin and Establishment of the Catholic School System in the United States (New York: Benziger, 1912), p.68.

61. Gabriel Gravier (ed.), Relation du Voyage des dames Religieuses Ursulines de Rouen à la Nouvelle-Orleans avec une introduction et des notes par Gabriel Gravier (Paris: Maisonneuve, 1872), p. 5, 6.

62. Ibid., p.118.

63. Quoted in Martin J. Spalding, Sketches of the Life, Times and Character of the Rev. Benedict Joseph Flaget, First Bishop of Louisville (Louisville: Webb and Levering, 1852), p.158.

64. Quoted in Semple, p.27.

65. Ibid., p.25.

66. "Early Convent Projected," American Catholic Historical Researches, VIII (October, 1891), p.178.

67. Arthur Riley, Catholicism in New England to 1788 (Washington: Catholic University Press, 1936), p.30. See also Historical Records and Studies, XXX (1939), p.154-55, which tells of Lydia Langley of Groton, who became a sister of the Congregation of Notre Dame in 1696; Mary Ann Davis of Salem, who became an Ursuline in Quebec in 1700; and Mary Dorothea Jeryan, who became a nun in the same convent in 1722.

68. Quoted in American Catholic Historical Researches, X (June, 1893), p.42.

69. Quoted in United States Catholic Historical Magazine, I (April, 1887), p.214.

70. American Catholic Historical Researches, XXVI, p.240.

71. American Catholic Historical Researches, XXIV (1907), p.101 quotes this from Proceedings of the Delaware Historical Society, I, p.28.

72. Rev. Thomas Phelan, Catholics in Colonial Days (New York: Kenedy, 1935), p.170.

73. Martin I. J. Griffin, "Washington's Masonic Apron and the Ursuline Nuns of Nantes," American Catholic Historical Researches XXIV (October, 1907), p.368.

74. "London Nun," Catholic Weekly Instructor; or Miscellany of Religious, instructive, and entertaining knowledge, I, No.2 (June 22, 1844), p.24.

75. Dumas Malone, Jefferson and His Times (Boston: Little, Brown, 1948), Vol. III, p.6.

76. Thomas Jefferson, Papers ed. by Julian P. Boyd; Lyman H. Butterfield and Mina R. Bryan associate editors (Princeton: Princeton University Press, 1950-65), Vol. XI, p.612.

77. Ibid., Vol. XII, p.112 quoting letter of Sept.10, 1787.

78. Ibid., Oct.4, 1787, Vol. XII, p.202.

79. Ibid., Mar.8, 1787, Vol. XI, p.203.

80. Ibid., Mar.28, 1787, Vol. XI, p.252.

81. Malone, P.207.

82. Annabelle Melville, John Carroll of Baltimore (New York: Scribner's, 1955), p.102.

83. Quoted ibid.

84. Paul Leicester Ford, The Writings of Thomas Jefferson Collected and edited by P. L. Ford (New York: G. P. Putnam's Sons, 1892-99), Vol. VI, p.455.

85. (Washington: Catholic University, 1932), p.xxx.

86. Medieval English Nunneries c. 1254 to 1535 (Cambridge: University Press, 1932).

87. Ibid., p.25-42.

88. Byrne, p.161-84.

89. Power, p.501ff.

90. The Quebec Act: A Primary Cause of the American Revolution (New York: The United States Catholic Historical Society, 1936).

91. (Chicago: Loyola University Press, 1962).

92. Cited in Riley, p.16.

93. (Philadelphia: D. W. Clark, 1855).

94. (London, 1769).

FOOTNOTES FOR CHAPTER THREE

1. Visitandines, Emmitsburg Sisters of Charity, Loretto Sisters, Sisters of Charity of Nazareth, Kentucky Dominicans.

2. The Carmelites of Port Tobacco, Maryland.

3. The Religious of the Sacred Heart.

4. Charles A. Bachofen, A Commentary on the New Code of Canon Law (St. Louis: Herder, 1929), III, 470-71.

5. A. Boudenhon, "Dowry," The Catholic Encyclopedia (1913 ed.), V, p.146.

6. T. M. Kealy, "Dowry," The New Catholic Encyclopedia (1966 ed.), X, p.1028-29.

7. January 16, quoted in Annabelle M. Melville, John Carroll of Baltimore (New York: Scribners, 1955), p.170.

8. Thorpe to Carroll, Oct.18, 1788, quoted Melville, Carroll, p.170.

9. Joseph B. Code, Great American Foundresses (New York: Macmillan, 1929), p.39.

10. Sister Anne Hardman, English Carmelites in Penal Times (London, 1936), p.109; Code, op. cit., p.44; Charles Warren Currier, Carmel in America (Baltimore: Murphy, 1890), p.65.

11. Code, p.45.

12. Carroll to Antonelli, Sept.19, 1792 quoted in Peter Guilday, The Life and Times of John Carroll, 1735-1815 (New York: Encyclopedia Press, 1922), p.490.

13. Ibid.

14. Mar. 1, 1793 quoted in Currier, p.80.

15. Antonelli to Carroll, Sept.29, 1792 quoted in Guilday, p.490.

16. Quoted Melville, p.172-73.

17. Sister Mary Christina Sullivan, Some Non-Permanent Foundations of Religious Orders and Congregations of Women in the United States (1793-1850) (Vol. XXXI of Historical Records and Studies. Edited by Thomas F. Meehan. New York: The United States Catholic Historical Society, 1940), p.13, 19.

18. Ibid., p.19.

19. Quoted p. 13 Sullivan, from The Centinel of Liberty and George-town and Washington Advertiser, Mar. 8, 15, 26, 1799.

20. Code, 186.

21. Ibid., p.188.

22. George Parsons Lathrop and Rose Hawthorne Lathrop, A Story of Courage. Annals of the Georgetown Convent of the Visitation (Boston: Houghton Mifflin, 1894), p.156.

23. Ibid., p.201

24. Marechal to Propaganda Fide, Feb.18, 1823; Lathrop, op.cit., p.281ff; Giuseppe Andrea Bizzarri (ed.), Collectanea in usum Secretariae sacrae congregationis Episcoporum et Regularium (Rome: Typographia Polyglotta, 1885), p.724.

25. Sullivan, p.22ff.

26. Ibid., p.43; John Gilmary Shea, History of the Catholic Church in the United States (New York: John G. Shea, 1886-92), III, 163.

27. Sullivan, p.41.

28. An Account of Louisiana, being an Abstract of Documents in the offices of the Departments of state and of the Treasury (Philadelphia), p.33, quoted in American Catholic Historical Researches, VIII (Oct., 1891), 188.

29. Henry C. Semple (ed.), The Ursulines in New Orleans, a Record of Two Centuries, 1729-1925 (New York: Kenedy, 1925), p.54ff.

30. Ibid., p.60-61.

31. Quoted ibid., p.62.

32. Ibid., p.75.

33. Guilday, p.485.

34. Quoted Code, p.99.

35. Henri Lavedan, The Heroic Life of Saint Vincent de Paul, trans. Helen Younger Chase (New York: Longmans, 1929), p.209.

36. Charles I. White, Life of Mrs. Eliza A. Seton... (Baltimore: John Murphy & Co., 1856), p.240.

37. Quoted in Melville, p.162.

38. Quoted in Annabelle M. Melville, Elizabeth Bayley Seton 1774-1821 (New York: Scribner's, 1951), p.161.

39. Ibid., p.211.

40. Quoted ibid., p.164.

41. Quoted ibid.

42. Quoted in Sister Marie de Lourdes Walsh, The Sisters of Charity of New York 1809-1959 (New York: Fordham University, 1960), I, p.19.

43. Ibid., p.21.

44. Quoted Melville, Seton, p.165.

45. Ibid., p.223f.

46. Ibid., p.194.

47. Philip E. Dion, "The Daughters of Charity, their Early United States History," Saint Vincent De Paul ed. Arpad F. Kovacs (Jamaica, N.Y.: St. John's University Press, 1961), p.107ff.

48. Code, p.125.

49. Quoted in Paul Camillus Maes, Life of Rev. Charles Nerinckx, with a Chapter on the Early Catholic Missions in Kentucky (Cincinnati: Robert Clarke & Co., 1880), p.257-58.

50. William Howlett, Life of Rev. Charles Nerinckx, Pioneer Missionary of Kentucky and Founder of the Sisters of Loretto at the Foot of the Cross (Techny, Ill.: Mission Press, 1915), p.57; John Gilmary Shea, "Pioneer of the West--Rev. Charles Nerinckx," American Catholic Quarterly Review, V (1880), p.508.

51. Maes, p. 249.

52. Quoted in Rev. John Rothensteiner, "Father Charles Nerinckx and His Relations to the Diocese of St. Louis," St. Louis Catholic Historical Review, I (1918), p.157-75.

53. Maes, p. 277.

54. Margaret B. Downing, Chronicles of Loretto (Chicago: McBride, 1897), p.27-28.

55. Quoted in Maes, p. 508.

56. Ibid., p. 508-9.

57. Duchesne to Barat quoted in Sister M. Lilliana Owens, "Loretto Foundations in Louisiana and Arkansas," Louisiana History, II (Spring, 1961), p.207-8 from Louis Baunard, Life of ... Sophie Barat, transl. Georgiana Fullerton (Paris), p.290.

58. Nerinckx to Dear Mother et al. Nov. 1, 1820, Francis Clark; Carl Russell Fish, Guide to Materials for American History in Rome and Other Italian Archives (Washington: Carnegie Institution, 1911), p.144; Finbar Kenneally, United States Documents in the Propaganda Fide Archives, First Series, Volume I (Washington: Academy of American Franciscan History, 1966), p.402.

59. Quoted in Sister M. Lilliana Owens, Loretto in Missouri (St. Louis: Herder, 1965), p.20.

60. Flaget to Rosati, Sept.11, 1824, St. Louis Archdiocesan Archives.

61. Ibid.

62. John T. Gillard, The Catholic Church and the American Negro (Baltimore: St. Joseph's Society Press, 1929), p.136.

63. Ibid.

64. Sister Roseanne Murphy, "A Comparative Study of Organizational Change in Three Religious Communities" (Unpublished Ph.D. dissertation, Notre Dame University, 1965), p. 116ff.

65. Quoted Howlett, p. 394.

66. Melville, Seton, p. 161ff.

67. David to Bruté, 1811 trans. in Melville, Seton, p. 190.

68. David to Bruté, Apr. 21, 1814, NDUA.*

69. Carroll to David, Sept. 17, 1814.

70. Murphy, p. 129.

71. Anna Blanche McGill, Sisters of Charity of Nazareth (New York: Encyclopedia Press, 1917), p. 26.

72. Ibid., p. 32.

73. Code, p. 232.

74. Anna C. Minogue, Pages from a Hundred Years of Dominican History (New York: Pustet, 1921), p. 48; June 6, 1823 quoted in Code, p. 236.

* NDUA refers to Notre Dame University Archives here and throughout these footnotes.

75. Code, p. 236; Minogue, p. 49-50.

76. Minogue, p. 66.

77. Ibid., p. 46.

78. Ibid., p. 49.

79. Sister M. Natalie Kennedy, "A Pioneer Religious Venture in Ohio" (unpublished Master's thesis, University of Notre Dame, 1936), p. 19.

80. Code, p. 240.

81. Katherine Burton, Make the Way Known (New York: Farrar, Straus & Cudahy, 1959), p. 27.

82. For an account of this see Victor Francis O'Daniel, The Right Rev. Edward Dominic Fenwick O.P. (Washington: Dominicana, 1920), p. 135ff.

83. Oct. 23, 1824, quoted in Minogue, p. 60.

84. Smith to Fenwick, Sept. 26, 1829 NDUA.

85. Minogue, p. 69-70.

86. Burton, p. 3.

87. Louise Callan, The Society of the Sacred Heart in North America (New York: Longmans, Green, 1937), p.47-48.

88. Ibid.

89. Callan, p. 58-59.

90. Ibid., p. 59.

91. Ibid., p. 65, 80.

92. Ibid., p. 170, 176; Marjory Erskine, Mother Philippine Duchesne (London: Longmans, Green, 1926), p. 225.

93. Callan, p. 173.

94. Ibid., p. 175ff.

95. Ibid., p. 134.

96. Mother M. Benedict Murphy, Pioneer Catholic Girls' Academies (New York: Columbia University Press, 1958), p. 95.

97. New Orleans Ursulines, Sacred Heart nuns, Loretto Sisters, Emmitsburg Sisters of Charity.

98. M. M. Murphy, p. 95.

99. Sister Mary Ellen Keenan, "French Teaching Communities and Early Convent Education in the United States, 1727-1850" (Unpublished Master's thesis, Catholic University of America, Washington, 1934), p. 65.

100. M. M. Murphy, p. 134.

101. Ibid., p. 149.

102. William R. Taylor, Cavalier & Yankee (Garden City: Doubleday, 1963), p. 110.

103. M. M. Murphy, p. 146.

104. Ibid., p. 52.

105. Diary, 1828, quoted in M. M. Murphy, p. 150.

106. Elinor Tong Dehey, Religious Orders of Women in the United States (Cleveland, n.p., 1930), p. 54.

107. Code, p. 165.

108. M. M. Murphy, p. 260.

109. Ibid., p. 233.

110. Emmitsburg Sisters and Loretto Sisters.

111. Emmitsburg Sisters, Visitandines, Dominicans, Loretto Sisters.

112. Carmelites, Loretto Sisters, Visitandines, Nazareth Sisters of Charity, Dominicans, Sacred Heart nuns, New Orleans Ursulines.

113. Quoted in Walsh, p. 33 from "Souvenir of Centennial Celebration," n. p.

114. Callan, p. 69.

115. Louise Callan, Philippine Duchesne (Westminster, Md.: Newman, 1957), p. 278.

116. "Documents," St. Louis Catholic Historical Review, II, p. 207.

117. Walsh, p. 21.

118. Quoted in Walsh, p. 33 from Stranger's Guide to New York City, footnote, p. 203.

119. Henry DeCourcy and John Gilmary Shea, The Catholic Church in the United States (New York: Dunigan, 1856), p. 81.

120. J. Herman Schauinger, Cathedrals in the Wilderness (Milwaukee: Bruce, 1952), p. 128.

121. Sullivan, p. 44.

122. William Flint Thrall, Addison Hibbard, and C. Hugh Holman, A Handbook to Literature (New York: Odyssey Press, 1960), p.215.

123. Sister Mary Muriel Tarr, Catholicism in Gothic Fiction (Washington: Catholic University Press, 1946), p. 44.

124. Devendra Varma, The Gothic Flame (New York: Russell, 1957), p. 170ff. and passim.

125. Sister Mary Mauritia Redden, The Gothic Fiction in the American Magazines (1765-1800) (Washington: Catholic University Press, 1939), p. 57.

126. p. 603-7, 657-61; cited p. 130 Redden.

127. Ibid., p. 131.

128. Gentlemen and Ladies Town and Country Magazine, 1790, p. 23-27, cited Redden, p. 132.

129. p. 629-37, 696-702, cited Redden, p. 132f.

130. p. 117-20, cited Redden, p. 133ff.

131. Rural Magazine, Rutland, Vt., 1796, p. 110-117, cited Redden, p. 35f.

132. Philadelphia Minerva, 1796, Vol. II No. 89, cited Redden, p.136.

133. Philadelphia Minerva, 1797, Vol. III, No. 124, cited Redden, p. 136.

134. Philadelphia Minerva, 1797, Vol. III No. 136, cited Redden, p. 140.

135. Ibid., p. 159.

136. Sister Marie Leonore Fell, The Foundations of Nativism in American Textbooks, 1783-1860 (Washington: Catholic University Press, 1941).

137. (Philadelphia: Bradford & Inskeep).

138. Ibid., p. 1.

139. (Bliss & White, 1827), from 4th Edinburgh ed.

140. Tarr, p. 121.

141. (Boston: Wells and Lilly, 1820).

142. Ibid., p. 142.

143. Joel Barlow, Advice to the Privileged Orders (New York: Childs & Swain, 1792), Vol. I, p. 19.

144. Melville, Seton, note 104 p. 307.

145. Letter I (New York: Doubleday Dolphin, 1782 ed.), p. 18.

146. Cf. Ray Allen Billington, The Protestant Crusade, 1800-1860 (New York: Macmillan, 1938), Ch. 1; and Sister Mary Augustina Ray, American Opinion of Roman Catholicism in the Eighteenth Century (New York: Columbia University Press, 1936), passim.

FOOTNOTES FOR CHAPTER FOUR

1. Elinor Tong Dehey, Religious Orders of Women in the United States (Cleveland: n.p., 1930), passim.

2. Charles Augustine Bachofen, A Commentary on the New Code of Canon Law (St. Louis: Herder, 1929), p. 7.

3. Katherine Burton, Make the Way Known: The History of the Dominican Congregation of St. Mary of the Springs (New York: Farrar, Straus & Cudahy, 1959), p. 27 and passim; Mother Mary Clarissa, With the Poverello: History of the Sisters of St. Francis (New York: Kenedy, 1948), p. 27; Letter of Sister Benedicta to Bishop Guy Chabrat, Sept. 1, 1840, UNDA; Eugene Crawford, Daughters of Dominic on Long Island (New York: Benziger, 1938), p. 303; /Sister Dympna Flynn/ Mother Caroline and the School Sisters of Notre Dame in North America (St. Louis: Woodward & Tiernan Co., 1928), p. 120; Sister M. Grace McDonald, With Lamps Burning (St. Joseph, Minn.: St. Benedict's Priory Press, 1957), p. 18;/Sister M. Octavia/ Not With Silver or Gold (Dayton, 1945), p. 116.

4. Centenary of the Convent of the Visitation, Mount de Chantal 1848-1948 (Wheeling, W. Va., 1948), n.p.

5. Peter M. Abbelen, Mother M. Carolina Friess (St. Louis: Herder, 1893), p. 106.

6. McDonald, p. 30, 43.

7. Flynn, p. 47ff.

8. Sister Mary de Lourdes Cohmann, Chosen Arrows: An Historical Narrative (New York: Pageant Press, 1957), p. 328; also several conversations.

9. Sister Mary Eleanore /Brosnahan/, On the King's Highway (New York: Appleton, 1931), p. 172; Sister Mary Eunice Hanousek, A New Assisi: Milwaukee Franciscans 1849-1949 (Milwaukee: Bruce, 1948), p.26; Burton, p. 59; Sister M. Dolorita Mast, Through Caroline's Consent: Life of Mother Teresa of Jesus Garhardinger, Foundress of the School Sisters of Notre Dame (Baltimore: Institute of Notre Dame, 1958), p. 185; and in many other places.

10. Helen Bailly de Barberey, Elizabeth Seton tr. and adapted from the Sixth French ed. . . . by Joseph B. Code (New York: 1927), p. 303.

11. Sister Helen Angela Hurley, On Good Ground (Minneapolis:
     University of Minnesota Press, 1951), p. 8ff.

12. Katherine Burton, So Surely Anchored (New York: Kenedy, 1949),
     p. 79f.; "Letters bearing on the foundation of the Sisters of
     Notre Dame de Namur in America," Records of the American
     Catholic Historical Society, XI, 1900, p. 325.

13. Sister Maria Kostka Logue, Sisters of St. Joseph of Philadelphia:
     A Century of Growth and Development, 1847-1947 (Westminster,
     Md.: Newman Press, 1950, p. 106.

14. Sister Helen Louise Nugent, Sister Julia (New York: Benziger,
     1928), p. 166; Peter Leo Johnson, Crosier on the Frontier: A
     Life of John Martin Henni (Madison: State Historical Society of
     Wisconsin, 1959), p. 105; Sister M. Michael Francis, The Broad
     Highway: a History of the Ursuline Nuns in the Diocese of
     Cleveland 1850-1950 (Cleveland: Ursuline Nuns, 1951), p. 200.

15. Quoted by Mother Mary Aloysius Doyle in Memories of the Crimea
     (London: Burns & Oates, 1897), p. 21.

16. "American Religious Foundations," American Ecclesiastical Review,
     XIX (1898), p. 455; Hanousek, p. 25; Brosnahan, p. 186; Sister
     Mary Agnes McCann, The History of Mother Seton's Daughters: The
     Sisters of Charity of Cincinnati, Ohio, 1809-1923 (New York:
     Longmans, Green, 1917-1923), II, p. 111f.; Sister Julia Gilmore,
     Come North (New York: McMullen, 1951), p. 91; Octavia, p. 146;
     Joseph B. Code, Great American Foundresses (New York: Macmillan,
     1929), p. 155.

17. Sister M. Xavier Farrell, Happy Memories of a Sister of
     Charity (St.Louis: Herder, 1941), p. 74; Crawford, p. 305;
     McDonald, p. 61; Hurley, p. 222; Michael Francis, p. 217.

18. Hurley, p. 12.

19. Thomas Low Nichols, Forty Years of American Life: 1821-1861
     (New York: Stackpole Sons, 1937), II, p. 268.

20. Rev. Thomas Campbell, Mary Aloysia Hardey (New York: America
     Press, 1910), p. 118.

21. Quoted Mary Ellen Evans, The Spirit is Mercy (Westminster, Md.:
     Newman, 1959), p. 96. Some idea of the status of the Mercy
     Sisters can be gained from the description of the reception
     ceremony establishing this community in England. Lady Barbara
     Eyre, who was taking the habit, wore "a full court dress worth
     a hundred guineas, besides valuable diamonds. Her train went
     below the last step when she was at the top." The convent
     received a note from Her Majesty's hairdresser which said: "By
     desire of the Countess Constantia Clifford, Monsieur Trufitt

will wait on the Sisters of Mercy . . . to adjust a court headdress." Sister M. Bertrand Degnan, _Mercy Unto Thousands: The Life of Mother Catherine McAuley_ (Westminster: Newman, 1957), p. 253f.

22. Jeremiah J. O'Connell, _Catholicity in the Carolinas and Georgia, 1820-1827_ (New York: Sadlier, 1879), p. 68.

23. Sister Mary Christina Sullivan, _Some Non-Permanent Foundations of Religious Orders and Congregations of Women in the United States (1795-1850)_ (Vol. XXXI of _Historical Records and Studies_. Edited by Thomas F. Meehan. New York: The United States Catholic Historical Society, 1940), p. 55.

24. June 21, UNDA.

25. Oct. 31, 1849, UNDA.

26. Flynn, p. 30.

27. Mother Theodore Guerin, _Journals & Letters of Mother Theodore Guerin_, ed. Sister Mary Theodosia Mug (St.Mary of the Woods, Indiana: Providence Press, 1942), p. 46.

28. Father Charles McCallion to Bishop Purcell, Aug. 4, 1845, UNDA.

29. Sara-Alice Quinlan, _In Harvest Fields by Sunset Shores_ (San Francisco: Gilmartin, 1926), p. 49.

30. (New York: Pantheon, 1959), pp.24-30.

31. Sister Mary Borromeo Brown, _The History of the Sisters of Providence of Saint Mary-of-the-Woods_ (New York: Benziger, 1949), I, p. 64.

32. Mug., p. 54.

33. Brown, p. 73.

34. Mug., p. 64.

35. Brown, p. 233.

36. _Ibid._, p. 151.

37. Quoted Brown, p. 206.

38. Mug., p. 319.

39. John O'Grady, _Catholic Charities in the United States_ (Washington: National Catholic Welfare Conference, 1930), p. 378ff.; Sister

Monica, The Cross in the Wilderness: A Biography of Pioneer Ohio (New York: Longmans Green, 1930), p. 72.

40. Sister Francis Catherine, Convent Schools of French Origin in the United States, 1727-1843 (Philadelphia: University of Pennsylvania, 1936), p. 220.

41. Howard Mumford Jones, America and French Culture, 1750-1848 (Chapel Hill: University of North Carolina Press, 1927), p. 475; Mother M. Benedict Murphy, Pioneer Roman Catholic Girls Academies (New York: Columbia University Press, 1958), p. 127ff.; James A. Burns, The Principles, Origin and Establishment of the Catholic School System in the United States (New York: Benziger, 1912), p. 225.

42. The Dominicans of San Rafael (San Rafael: Grabhorn Press, 1941), p. 42; Frederick Marryat, A Diary in America (1839), p.221.

43. Sister Maria Concepta, The Making of a Sister-Teacher (Notre Dame, Ind.: University of Notre Dame Press, 1965), p. 25.

44. Mother Mary Clarissa, p. 77.

45. "Convent of the Visitation," American Catholic Historical Researches 1905-1911 ed. Martin I. J. Griffin (Philadelphia, 1884-1912), XI, p. 128.

46. Quoted Concepta, p. 25.

47. "Letters," RACHS, p. 332.

48. Mag., p. 43.

49. Concepta, p. 36.

50. Brown, p. 360.

51. Murphy, p. 106.

52. Concepta, p. 25.

53. "Convent of the Visitation," p. 128.

54. Ibid.

55. Gohmann, p. 272; Logue, p. 135; Katherine E. Conway, In the Footprints of the Good Shepherd New York: 1857-1907 (New York: Convent of the Good Shepherd, 1907), p. 56.

56. Clarissa, p. 33; Brown, p. 197.

57. Burns, p. 288; Burton, Make the Way Known, p. 49.

58. Sisters of Charity, Emmitsburg, 1809-1959 (Emmitsburg: St. Joseph Central House, 1959), p. 264.

59. Sister M. Felicity O'Driscoll, "Political Nativism in Buffalo, 1830-1860," Records of the American Catholic Historical Society, XLVIII (1937), p. 292; Peter Leo Johnson, "Sisters of Charity and the Immigrant Hospital on Jones Island," Salesianum, XL (1945), p. 167f.

60. "American Religious Foundations," Amer Eccles. Rev., XX (1899), p. 457f.

61. Sisters of Charity, p. 264.

62. Sister M. Eulalia Herron, The Sisters of Mercy in the United States (New York: Macmillan, 1929), p. 124ff.

63. Hurley, p. 77.

64. Ann Doyle, "Nursing by Religious Orders in the United States," American Journal of Nursing, XXIX (July, Aug., Sept., 1929), p. 967f.; O'Grady, p. 185.

65. Ibid., p. 168; Conway, p. vi.

66. O'Grady, p. 216f.

67. Hanousek, p. 25; Sister M. Meleta Ludwig, Chapter in Franciscan History: Third Order of St. Francis of Perpetual Adoration, 1849-1949 (New York: Bookman Associates, 1950), p. 106.

68. Logue, p. 148.

69. Hanousek, p. 46; Octavia, p. 125.

70. Charles Warren Currier, Carmel in America (Baltimore: Murphy, 1890), p. 273ff.

71. Giuseppe Andrea Bizzarri (ed.), Collectanea in usum Secretariae sacrae congregationis Episcoporum et Regularium (Rome: Typographic Polyglotta, 1885), p. 725; Finbar Kenneally, United States Documents in the Propaganda Fide Archives: a Calendar, First Series, Volume I (Washington: Academy of American History, 1966), p. 323.

72. Bachofen, p. 472; Kenneally, p. 323.

73. Mar. 30, 1854, Kenneally, p. 111f.

74. Kenrick to Propaganda Fide, Mar. 13, 1855, Kenneally, II p. 140; June 6, 1855 Kenneally II, p. 140.

75. Acta Sanctae Sedis in compendium opportune redacta et illustrata 1865-66 Vol. 1, (Rome: Propaganda Fide, 1872), p. 710.

76. Purcell to Bishop Peter Paul Lefevere, Detroit, UNDA.

77. Baraga to Purcell, Nov. 5, 1857, UNDA.

78. St. Palais to Purcell, Jan.7, 1858, UNDA

79. Spalding to Purcell, Nov. 12, 1857, UNDA.

80. Kenrick to Purcell, Nov.28, 1857, UNDA.

81. Rappe to Purcell, Nov. 3, 1857, UNDA.

82. Blanc to Purcell, Nov. 23, 1857, UNDA.

83. Lefevere to Purcell, Nov. 12, 1857, UNDA.

84. n.d. UNDA.

85. F. P. Kenrick to Purcell, May 12, 1858, UNDA.

86. Bizzarri, p. 725.

87. Bachofen, p. 474.

88. Bizzarri, p. 725.

89. Burton, Make the Way Known, p. 60ff.

90. Dominicans, p. 31.

91. Flynn, p. 120.

92. McDonald, p. 18.

93. Hardey, p. 175.

94. Katherine Burton, Bells on Two Rivers (Milwaukee: Bruce, 1965), p. 15.

95. McDonald, p. 30.

96. McCann, p. 75.

97. Monica, p. 228.

98. Michael Francis, p. 117.

99. May 31, June 10, June 16, UNDA.

100. Flynn, p. 46; Mary E. Mannix, Memoirs of Sister Louise,
     Superior of the Sisters of Notre Dame with Reminiscences of the
     Early Days of the Order in the United States (Boston: Angel
     Guardian Press, 1907), p. 130; Carlos Castaneda, The Church
     in Texas Since Independence, 1836-1950 Vol. VII of Our Catholic
     Heritage in Texas 1519-1936 (Austin: Von Boeckmann-Jones,
     1936-50), p. 294.

101. Sister Mary Xavier Holworthy, Diamonds for the King (Corpus
     Christi: Incarnate Word Academy, 1945), p. 32.

102. McDonald, p. 44.

103. Ibid., p. 300.

104. Degnan, p. 193f.

105. Peter Condon, "Constitutional Freedom of Religion and the Revivals
     of Religious Intolerance," Historical Records and Studies,
     Vol. IV Pt. 2 (1906), p. 210; Abbelen, p. 100; Flynn, p. 48;
     Margaret Williams, Mother Hardey: A Religious of the Sacred
     Heart and First American-born Superior (New York: Manhattanville
     College, 1945), p. 4.

106. Sister M. Lucida Savage, Congregation of St. Joseph of
     Carondelet (St. Louis: Herder, 1923), p. 35.

107. Abbé Rivaux, Life of Mother St. John Fontbonne, Foundress and
     first Superior-General of the Congregation of the Sisters of St.
     Joseph in Lyons (New York: Benziger, 1887), p. 224.

108. Sister Mary Ildephonse Holland, Lengthened Shadows (New York:
     Bookman Associates, 1952), p. 69.

109. Abbelen, p. 125.

110. Quinlan, p. 148.

111. Brown, p. 67.

112. Guerin, p. 281.

113. Sullivan, p. 64.

114. Burton, Bells, p. 11.

115. "Letters," RACHS, p. 332-3.

116. Brown, p. 75.

117. Clarissa, p. 23.

118. Anna Blanche McGill, Sisters of Charity of Nazareth (New York: Encyclopedia Press, 1917), p. 68.

119. McDonald, p. 35.

120. Currier, p. 247.

121. Burton, So Surely Anchored, p. 79ff.

122. "Letters," RACHS, p. 325.

123. Mannix, p. 130.

124. Brown, p. 593.

125. Michael J. Hynes, History of the Diocese of Cleveland, Origin and Growth, 1847-1952 (Cleveland: Chancery Office, 1953), p. 83; Flynn, p. 213.

126. Holworthy, p. 321.

127. Sister Eulalia Herron, "Work of the Sisters of Mercy in the United States," American Catholic Historical Society of Philadelphia Records , Vol. 33 (June, 1922), p. 146.

128. Sisters of Notre Dame de Namur, American Foundations of the Sisters of Notre Dame de Namur (Philadelphia: Dolphin, 1928), p. xiv.

129. Sister Maria Alma Ryan, "Foundations of Catholic Sisterhoods in the United States," American Catholic Historical Society of Philadelphia Records, Vol. 52,(1941), p. 96.

130. Ibid., p. 99; Sisters of Charity, op. cit., p. 19; Frederick John Easterly, The Life of Rt. Rev. Joseph Rosati, C.M. First Bishop of St. Louis, 1789-1843 (Washington: Catholic University Press, 1942), p. 148.

131. Ryan, p. 227.

132. Sister Marie de Lourdes Walsh, The Sisters of Charity of New York, 1809-1959 (New York: Fordham University Press, 1960), Vol. I, p. 82.

133. Cecil Woodham-Smith, Florence Nightingale (New York: McGraw-Hill, 1951), p. 93.

134. Mar. 12, 1838, UNDA.

135. de Barberey, p. 467.

136. McCann, p. 100ff.

137. Walsh, p. 127.

138. Mar. 8, 1846, UNDA.

139. John R. Hassard, Life of the Most Reverend John Hughes, D. D. First Archbishop of New York (New York: Appleton, 1866), p. 289ff.

140. Walsh, p. 130ff.

141. Joseph B. Code, Bishop John Hughes and the Sisters of Charity (Miscellanea Historica, 1949), p. 43; Hughes to Propaganda May 14, 1847, UNDA.

142. Gilmore, p. 42ff.; Victor F. O'Daniel, The Father of the Church in Tennessee (New York: Pustet, 1926), p. 448.

143. Mar. 26, 1856, UNDA.

144. Francis E. Tourscher, The Kenrick-Frenaye Correspondence, 1830-1862 (Lancaster: Wickersham Printing Co., 1920), p. 246.

145. July 10, 1848, UNDA.

146. Sister Evangeline Thomas, Footprints on the Frontier (Westminster: Newman, 1948), p. 60.

147. Brown, p. 148, 227ff., 262.

148. Ibid., p. 378ff., 262, 348.

149.. Sister M. Rosalita, No Greater Service (Detroit: St. Mary's Academy, 1948), p. 123ff.; Kenneally, II, p. 7; Chabrat letter to Paquin, Dec. 22, 1841, UNDA.

150. Hanousek, p. 26, 46ff.

151. Sullivan, p. 60; Gohmann, p. 272; Letter Reynolds to Purcell, September 11, 1847, UNDA.

152. Sister Mary Faith Schuster, The Meaning of the Mountain (Baltimore: Helicon, 1963), p. 20; Sister M. Regina Baska, The Benedictine Congregation of St. Scholastica: Its Foundation and Development, 1852-1930 (Washington: Catholic University Press, 1935), p. 35; McDonald, p. 12.

153. McDonald, p. 10ff.

154. Flynn, p. 49.

155. Etienne Catta and Tony Catta, Basil Anthony Mary Moreau transl.
Edward L. Heston (Milwaukee: Bruce, 1955), passim; Sister M.
Rita Heffernan, A Story of Fifty Years from Annals of the Sisters
of Holy Cross, 1865-1905 (Notre Dame, Ind.: Ave Maria Press,
1905), p. 61; Concepta, p. 19; Brosnahan, p. 211.

156. Burton, Make the Way, p. 62 and passim.

157. Concepta, p. 44f.

158. Robert Trisco, The Holy See and the Nascent Church in the Middle
Western States (Rome: Gregorian University, 1962), p. 286.

159. Ibid., p. 308.

160. Monica, p. 61.

161. Sister Mary Dominica, Willamette Interlude (Palo Alto: Pacific
Books, 1959), p. 190 and passim; Rivaux, p. 218.

162. Concepta, p. 30.

163. McDonald, p. 54.

164. Clarissa, p. 191; Crawford, p. 135; "Sisters of the Third
Order of St. Francis 1855-1928," American Catholic Historical
Society of Philadelphia Records, XL (1929), p. 41.

165. Sept.21, 1849 quoted in McCann, p. 74f.

166. Sisters of Charity, p. 19.

167. Quoted Herron, Amer.Cath. Hist. Soc. Records, p. 125.

168. Mary Teresa Austin Carroll, Leaves from the Annals of the
Sisters of Mercy, Vol. III (New York: Shea, 1895), p. 483.

169. Frederick J. Zwierlein, Life and Letters of Bishop McQuaid Vol. I
(Rochester: Art Print Shop, 1925-27), p. 234.

170. "American Religious Foundations," AER, XX, p. 457.

171. Ibid., p. 458.

172. Quoted Hurley, p. 77.

173. Quoted by Johnson, p. 167f.

174. Quoted Peter Guilday, *Life and Times of John England First Bishop of Charleston 1786-1842* (New York: America Press, 1927), II, p. 168.

175. Ryan, p. 142.

176. Nichols, p. 278.

177. Quoted Easterly, p. 147.

178. Logue, p. 22.

179. Quoted Walsh, p. 93.

180. Brown, p. 365; see also Gohmann, p. 272; Trisco, p. 296; Flynn, I, p. 146; Brown, pp. 528, 589, 679.

181. Daniel Sargent, *Our Land and Our Lady* (New York: 1937), p. 218.

182. Nichols, p. 270.

183. J. Richard Beste, *The Wabash: or Adventures of an English Gentleman's Family in the Interior of America* (London: Hurst & Blackett, 1855), I, p. 222.

184. *Ibid.*, p. 221.

185. July 5, 1845, UNDA.

186. Joseph Aloysius Griffin, *Contribution of Belgium to the Catholic Church in America (1523-1857)* (Washington: Catholic University, 1932), p. 184.

187. Mannix, p. 70f.

188. Sister M. Natalie Kennedy, "A Pioneer Religious Venture in Ohio," (unpublished master's thesis, University of Notre Dame, 1936), p. 40; A. Reed, *A Narrative of the Visit to the American Churches by a Deputation from the Congregational Union of England and Wales* (1835), p. 78; Murphy, p. 143; Thomas, p. 58; Louise Callan, *The Society of the Sacred Heart in North America* (New York: Longmans, Green, 1937), p. 437; Elmer E. Brown, *The Making of our Middle Schools* (New York: Longmans, Green, 1903), p. 329.

189. Sullivan, p. 46; Carleton Beals, *Brass-Knuckle Crusade* (New York: Hastings House, 1960), p. 32; Richard S. Fay, *An Argument Before the Committee of the House of Representatives, upon the petition of Benedict Fenwick and others . . .* (Boston: Eastburn, 1835), p. 7.

190. Gustavus Myers, History of Bigotry in the United States ed. and rev. by Henry M. Christman (New York: Capricorn, 1960), p. 84.

191. Sister Anges Geraldine McGann, Nativism in Kentucky to 1860 (Washington: Catholic University, 1944), p. 121; Fay, p. 38ff.

192. Brown, SMB, p. 589.

193. Fay, p. 38f.

194. Murphy, p. 149ff.

195. Beals, p. 83.

196. Edward Wagenknecht, John Greenleaf Whittier (New York: Oxford University Press, 1967), p. 188.

197. Dominicans, p. 11ff.

198. Charles Elliott, Delineation of Roman Catholicism (New York: George Lane, 1841), p. 415f.

199. Sister Columba Fox, The Life of the Right Reverend John Baptist Mary David, 1761-1841 Bishop of Bardstown and Founder of the Sisters of Nazareth (New York: United States Catholic Historical Society, 1925), p. 215ff.

200. Quoted Sister Mary St. Patrick McConville, Political Nativism in the State of Maryland 1830-1860 (Washington: Catholic University, 1928), p. 96.

201. (Cincinnati: Truman & Smith, 1835), p. 92ff.

202. Quoted McGann, p. 2.

203. Brown, Elmer, p. 255.

204. (New York: Macmillan, 1938).

205. Rev. H. W. Cleary in History of Orangeism, p. 362, quoted in Condon, p. 149.

206. Carroll, p. 475ff.

207. Centenary of the Convent of the Visitation, Mount de Chantal 1848-1948 (Wheeling, W. Va., 1948), n.p.

208. McGann, p. 121.

209. Gohmann, Political Nativism in Tennessee to 1860 (Washington: Catholic University, 1938), p. 156; W. Darrell Overdyke, The

Know-Nothing Party in the South (Baton Rouge: Louisiana State University, 1950), p. 269.

210. Brown, SMB, p. 218.

211. Ibid., p. 575.

212. Sisters of Notre Dame de Namur, p. 46.

213. Flynn, I, pp.39, 51, 92.

214. Covelle Newcomb, Running Waters (New York: Dodd, Mead, 1947), p.193.

215. Rivaux, p. 223.

216. Brown, SMB, p. 365.

217.. Carroll, p. 338.

218. Beals, p. 126.

219. See Billington, Chapter III for further details.

220. Condon, p. 152ff.; Fay, op. cit., throughout; Robert H. Lord et al., History of the Archdiocese of Boston (New York: Sheed & Ward, 1944), II, p. 15ff.; Benjamin Hawkes, "Letters," US Catholic Historical Magazine, III (1890), p. 274.

221. Condon, p. 152.

222. Quoted Condon, p.166.

223. Documents Relating to the Ursuline Convent in Charlestown (Boston: Samuel N. Dickinson, 1842), p. 6.

224. Condon, p. 230.

225. Quoted ibid., p. 168 from June, 1835 newspaper.

226. Francis J. Connors, "Samuel Finley Brese Morse and the Anti-Catholic Political Movements in the United States," Illinois Catholic Historical Review Vol. X, No.2 (Oct., 1927), p. 103.

227. Condon, p. 211.

228. Carroll, p. 399.

229. Code, Foundresses, p. 372.

230. Herron, p. 160.

231. Overdyke, p. 229.

232. Connors, p. 119.

233. Currier, p. 212f.

234. Thomas, p. 52-3.

235. McCann, p. 20.

236. John Gilmary Shea, History of the Catholic Church in the United States (New York: John G. Shea, 1886-92), IV, p. 273.

237. Sister Mary Angela Fitzmorris, Four Decades of Catholicism in Texas, 1820-1860 (Washington: Catholic University, 1926), p. 88.

238. Lydia Stirling Flintham, "Leaves from the Annals of the Ursulines," Catholic World, LXVI (1897), p. 330.

239. Conway, p. 58.

240. Billington, pp. 87, 311.

241. Sullivan, p. 54.

242. Billington, p. 101.

243. Ibid., p. 98ff.

244. James Fenimore Cooper, Correspondence of James Fenimore-Cooper ed. by his grandson (New Haven: Yale University Press, 1922), I, p. 358.

245. Ibid., pp. 358, 362.

246. Mrs. L. St. John Eckel /Mrs. Lizzie St. John Harper/ Maria Monk's Daughter; an Autobiography (New York: United States Publishing Co., 1874), p. 170.

247. Billington, p. 103ff.

248. Ibid., p. 108.

249. Ibid., p. 320, note 1.

250. Overdyke, p. 170.

251. Billington, p. 310.

252. Gohmann, Nativism, p. 156.

253. Zwierlein, I, p. 189.

254. Overdyke, p. 235.

255. Ibid., p. 273.

256. John B. McMaster, "The Riotous Career of the Know-Nothings," Forum XVII (1894), p. 531.

257. Zwierlein, I, p. 151ff.

258. Billington, p. 301ff.

259. McMaster, p. 531.

260. Brown, p. 705.

261. Billington, pp.171; 87ff.

262. Ibid., p. 87ff.

263. Condon, p. 168.

264. Mass. House Report, Document No. 160 1854 quoted by Myers, p.91.

265. James F. X. O'Connor, "Anti-Catholic Prejudice," American Catholic Quarterly Review I (Jan., 1876), p. 13ff.

266. Charles Hale, A Review of the Proceedings of the Nunnery Committee of the Massachusetts Legislature . . . (Boston: Boston Daily Advertiser, 1855), p. 9.

267. Billington, p. 414.

268. Hale, p. 17; Billington, p. 414.

269. Billington, p. 415.

270. Laurence F. Schmeckebier, "History of the Know-Nothing Party in Maryland," Johns Hopkins University Studies in History and Political Science XVII, No. 4-5 (April-May, 1899), p. 33.

271. Billington, p. 348.

272. Myers, p. 93.

273. Alfred G. Stritch, "Political Nativism in Cincinnati, 1830-1860," Records of the American Catholic Historical Society of Philadelphia, XLVIII (1937), p. 232 quoting the Feb. 25, 1836 edition.

274. Myers, p. 92.

275. Guardians of Tradition: American Schoolbooks of the Nine-teenth Century (Lincoln: University of Nebraska, 1964), p. 53.

276. Rachel McCrindell, The School-Girl in France, or The Snares of Popery (New York: Wellman, 1845), p. v.

277. See Appendix A for a list of the books studied.

278. Important Facts!! History of Convents, With an account of the Order of Ursuline Nuns; . . . n.p., n.d.; Pope or President? Startling Disclosures of Romanism as revealed by its own writers . . . (New York: Delisser, 1859); A Noted Methodist Preacher, The Mysteries of a Convent (Philadelphia: Peterson, 1854); A Clergyman's Widow, Sister Agnes; or The Captive Nun: Sketches of Convent Life (New York: Riker, Thorne, 1854).

279. Charles Sparry, The Protestant Annual... (New York: C. Sparry, 1847); Kirwan /Nicholas Murray/, Romanism at Home. Letters to the Hon. Roger B. Taney . . . (New York: Harper, 1852); Thomas Ford Caldicott, Hannah Corcoran . . . (Boston: Gould & Lincoln, 1853); George Bourne, Lorette. The History of Louise, Daughter of a Canadian Nun . . . (New York: Charles Small, 1834); Maria Monk, Awful Disclosures of the Hotel Dieu of Montreal (New York, 1836) - actually written by the Rev. J. J. Slocum; see Billington, p. 101.

280. Rafaele Ciocci, Iniquities and Barbarities Practiced at Rome in the Nineteenth Century (Philadelphia: Peterson, n.d. /1845?/); William Hogan, Popery! As it was and as it is; also Auricular Confession; and Popish Nunneries (Hartford: Silad Andrus & Son, 1853); S. J. Mahoney, Six Years in the Monasteries of Italy... (Hartford: S. Andrus & Son, 1844); Samuel B. Smith, Renunciation of Popery (Philadelphia: L. Johnson, 1833).

281. S. B. Smith.

282. Josephine M. Bunkley, Miss Bunkley's Book. The Testimony of an Escaped Novice from the Sisterhood of St.Joseph, Emmettsburg . . . (New York: Harper, 1855); / Bunkley/ The Escaped Nun . . . (New York: De Witt & Davenport, 1855); Rebecca Theresa Reed, Six Months in a Convent . . . (Boston: Russell, Odiorne, & Metcalf, 1835); Reed, Supplement to "Six Months in a Convent" . . . (Boston: Russell, Odiorne & Co., 1835).

283. Benjamin Barker, Cecilia; or, The White Nun of the Wilderness. . . (Boston: F. Gleason, 1845); /Mrs. Jane (Dunbar) Chaplin/, The Convent and the Manse (Boston: John P. Jewett, 1853); Harry Hazel /Justin Jones/ (Boston: F. Gleason, 1845).

284. William McGavin, The Protestant . . . 2 v. (Hartford, 1833). .

285. Charles Frothingham, The Convent's Doom . . . and The Haunted Convent, (Boston: Graves & Weston, 1854); Frothingham, Six Hours in a Convent . . . (Boston: Graves & Weston, 1855).

286. The story was published in Smith's newspaper before being published separately, and there is no evidence that Rosamund Culbertson actually existed.

287. Mary Edmond St. George, An Answer to Six Months in a Convent. . . (Boston, 1835); The Truth Unveiled; or, A Calm & Impartial exposition . . . of the Terrible Riots in Philadelphia . . . (Philadelphia: M. Fithian, 1844); Awful Exposure of the Atrocious Plot Formed by Certain Individuals against the Clergy and Nuns of Lower Canada, through the Intervention of Maria Monk (Montreal: Jones, 1836); William L. Stone, Maria Monk and the Nunnery of the Hotel Dieu (New York: Paulist Press).

288. p. 148.

289. Ibid., p. 141.

290. p. 206.

291. Convent's Doom, p. 14.

292. McGavin, p. 714.

293. p. 200.

294. Sister Marie Leonore Fell, The Foundations of Nativism in American Textbooks, 1783-1860 (Washington: Catholic University, 1941), p. 111f.

295. Vol. I, No.5, (May, 1835), p. 130.

296. Ibid., p. 129ff.

297. Ibid., Vol. 5, No. 1, (Nov., 1839), p. 481ff; Vol. 5, No.10 (Oct., 1839), p. 437.

298. p. 290f.

299. p. 112.

300. p. 135; 17; 713.

301. p. 148.

302. Ibid., p. 122.

303. p. vi.

304. p. 134f.; 75.

305. p. 4.

306. p. 149; 284.

307. Alexis de Tocqueville, Democracy in America ed. by Richard
D. Heffner (New York: New American Library, 1956), p. 233ff.

308. p. 246.

309. Downfall of Babylon (Philadelphia) Vol. I, No. 2 (1834),
p. 6.

310. p. 206.

311. p. 141; 713; 79.

312. The Complete Novels and Selected Tales of Nathaniel Hawthorne
ed. by Norman Holmes Pearson (New York: The Modern Library,
1937), p. 573.

313. p. 713.

314. Murray, p. 78ff.

315. p. 14.

316. p. 130.

317. p. 78ff.

318. p. 284.

319. p. 107.

320. p. 436.

321. Downfall of Babylon, Vol. I, No. 3, p. 14 quoting Mrs. Sherwood's
The Nun.

322. p. 42; 148.

323. Sister Benedicta to Bishop Guy Chabrat, Sept. 1, 1840, UNDA.

324. p. 150.

325. p. 79.

326. p. 82.

327. p. 86; 92.

328. p. 107.

329. p. 49f; 286.

330. p. 239.

331. p. 6.

332. p. 132.

333. p. 132.

334. p. 208ff.

335. p. 7.

336. Downfall of Babylon, Vol. 1, No. 2, p. 8.

337. Chaplin, p. 41; 44; 46.

338. p. 22.

339. Renunciation of Popery, p. 21.

340. Six Hours, p. 37f.

341. p. 188f.; 196; Miss Bunkley also describes this practice, p. 41, as does Miss Reed, p. 82.

342. p. 221.

343. Reed, p. 76; Monk, p. 175; Bunkley, p. 69f.

344. p. 175ff.

345. p. 107.

346. p. 109.

347. Ibid.

348. p. 291f.

349. Downfall, Vol. I, No. 4, p. 13.

350. Renunciation, p. 11.

351. p. 14.

352. p. 76.

353. p. 133.

354. p. 5; 284.

355. p. 26.

356. p. 165.

357. Six Hours, p. 13.

358. Mysteries of a Convent, p. 61.

359. Smith, Downfall, Vol. 8, No. 39, p. 159.

360. Chaplin, p. 144.

361. p. 10.

362. p. 140.

363. Downfall, Vol. 8, No. 39, p. 159.

364. p. 110.

365. Supplement, p. 205.

366. p. 2ff.

367. Chaplin, p. 123.

368. p. 717f.

369. p. 78f.

370. p. 205.

371. p. 237.

372. p. 152.

373. Conversation with Sister Anne Schaudenecker, Mar. 15, 1970.

374. p. iii-v; 54.

375. McGavin, pp.677; iiif.

376. Ibid., p. 713ff.

377. p. 49.

378. p. 132.

379. p. 246.

380. pp. 112; 146; 147

381. pp. 240; 473.

382. pp. 40; 86.

383. p. 109.

384. p. 187.

385. p. 22.

386. Six Hours, p. 16.

387. p. 246.

388. p. 45f; 716.

389. pp. 72, 87, 134, 136, 116, 141-2.

390. p. 13.

391. p. 22.

392. p. vi.

393. Haunted Convent, p. 22.

394. pp. 149; 86.

395. p. vi.

396. p. 713.

397. Chaplin, p. 88; 142.

398. p. 21.

399. p. 152-3.

400. p. 237-8.

401. p. 10; 115.

402. Chaplin, p. 72; Haunted Convent, p. 21f.

403. p. 716.

404. Ibid., p. 114.

405. Smith, Downfall, Vol. I, No 1, p. 2.

406. p. 205.

407. p. 110.

408. p. 10ff.; 10.

409. p. 150.

410. Downfall, Vol. VIII, No. 39, p. 159.

411. p. 149.

412. Vincent Hopkins, "A Common Protestant Image of the Catholic Church: The Development of a Stereotype," In the Eyes of Others, ed. Robert W. Gleason (New York: Macmillan, 1962), p. 19.

413. p. 4.

414. p. 241.

415. Ibid., p. 247; 473.

416. Hazel, p. 43; Mysteries, p. 34; Barker, p. 50; Culbertson, p. 133; Bunkley, Miss Bunkley's Book, p. 100ff.

417. p. 32; 109.

418. p. 34; 43.

419. p. 10.

420. p. 19.

421. p. 20; 47; 75.

422. Ronald Knox, Enthusiasm (New York: Oxford University Press, 1950), p. 313.

423. See for example Reuben Parsons, Studies in Church History (New York: Pustet, 1896-1901), Vol. IV, Centuries XVII-XVIII, p. 304.

424. de Ricci, Scipio, Female Convents. Secrets of Nunneries Disclosed . . . compiled by Louis de Potter, edited by Thomas Roscoe (New York: Appleton, 1834).

425. Index Librorum Prohibitorum (Vatican: Typis Polyglottic, 1938), p. 375.

426. Downfall, Vol. I, No. 2, p. 6.

427. p. 717ff.

428. Sparry, p. 110; Culbertson, p. 133ff.; Monk, passim; Important Facts, p. 7.

429. McGavin, p. 717.

430. Hogan, p. 241, 283; 473; Barker, p. 50; Smith, _Downfall_, Vol. I, No. 2, p. 6.

431. p. 241, 283.

432. p. 49.

433. p. 109.

434. p. 110.

435. p. 102.

436. p. 451; 385.

437. p. 177.

438. p. 131-2.

439. p. 29.

440. Monk, p. 141; Barker, p. 50.

441. St. George.

442. Stone, _Awful Exposure_.

443. John England, "Discourse at the Habiting of an Ursuline Nun..." in _Bishop England's Works_ ed. Ignatius Aloysius Reynolds (Baltimore: John Murphy, 1849), Vol. IV, p. 191ff.

444. See pp.133 and 141 above.

445. See, for example, pages 131 and 145 above.

FOOTNOTES FOR CHAPTER FIVE

1. Elinor Tong Dehey, Religious Orders of Women in the United States (Cleveland: n.p., 1930), p. 576ff.

2. Finbar Kenneally, United States Documents in the Propaganda Fide Archives: a Calendar, First Series, Volume II (Washington: Academy of American Franciscan History, 1966), p. 255, 259.

3. Giuseppi Andrea Bizzarri (ed.), Collectanea in usum Secretariae sacrae congregationis Episcoporum et Regularium (Rome: Typographia Polyglotta, 1885), p. 723ff.; M. J. Spalding to Purcell, October 1, 1865, UNDA.

4. Clement R. Orth, The Approbation of Religious Institutes (Washington: Catholic University Press, 1931), p. 65.

5. UNDA.

6. Valentine Schaaf, The Cloister (Cincinnati: St. Anthony Messenger, 1921), p. 116f.

7. Quoted by Sister Mary Hortense Kohler, Life & Work of Mother Benedicta Bauer (Milwaukee: Bruce, 1937), p. 208-9.

8. Sister Mary Xavier Holworthy, Diamonds for the King (Corpus Christi: Incarnate Word Academy, 1945), p. 111.

9. Eugene Joseph Crawford, Daughters of Dominic on Long Island (New York: Benziger, 1938), p. 69, 250.

10. August 29, 1863, UNDA.

11. October 6, 1861, UNDA.

12. Kohler, p. 240-41.

13. Sister Mary Faith Schuster, The Meaning of the Mountain (Baltimore: Helicon, 1963), p. 87; Sister M. Regina Baska, The Benedictine Congregation of St. Scholastica: Its Foundation and Development, 1852-1930. (Washington: Catholic University Press, 1935), p. 89.

14. Crawford, p. 250.

15. Sister M. Generosa Callahan, History of the Sisters of Divine Providence, San Antonio, Texas (Milwaukee: Bruce, 1955), pp. 7, 16, 42.

16. Baska, p. 47.

17. Louise Callan, The Society of the Sacred Heart in North America (New York: Longmans, Green, 1937), p. 554.

18. Sister M. Natalie Kennedy, "A Pioneer Religious Venture in Ohio," (Unpublished Master's Thesis, University of Notre Dame, 1936), p. 36.

19. November 30, 1861, UNDA.

20. Kohler, p. 233.

21. Anna Shannon McAllister, In Winter We Flourish: Life & Letters of Sarah Worthington King Peter, 1800-1877 (New York: Longmans, Green, 1939), p. 301; Theodore Maynard, Through My Gift (New York: Kenedy, 1951), p. 219.

22. Mary Louise Corcoran, Seal of Simplicity . . . (Westminster, Md.: Newman, 1958), p. 233ff.

23. Sister Mary Isidore Lennon, Milestones of Mercy (Milwaukee: Bruce, 1957), p. 27f.

24. Quoted by Sister Maria Kostka Logue, Sisters of St. Joseph of Philadelphia . . . (Westminster: Newman, 1950), p. 121.

25. Ibid., p. 126.

26. Frederic Law Olmsted, Hospital Transports. A Memoir of the Embarkation of the sick and wounded from the peninsula of Virginia in the summer of 1862 . . . (Boston: Ticknor and Fields, 1863), p. 113-14.

27. October 25, 1861. UNDA.

28. Sister M. Grace McDonald, With Lamps Burning (St. Joseph, Minn.: St. Benedict's Priory Press, 1957), p. 202.

29. Kennedy, p. 36.

30. Kohler, pp. 219ff.; See also Callahan, p. 21.

31. Maynard, p. 211.

32. Quoted by Rev. George T. Meagher in With Attentive Ear and Courageous Heart . . . (Milwaukee: Bruce, 1957), p. 176.

33. William Leo Lucey, The Catholic Church in Maine (Francestown, New Hampshire, 1957), p. 198; Sister Mary Innocentia Fitzgerald, Historical Sketch of the Sisters of Mercy in the Diocese of Buffalo, p. 40.

34. Corcoran, pp.88, 116f.; Sister Mary Eunice Hanousek, A New Assisi . . . (Milwaukee: Bruce, 1948), p. 68; Annals of the Monastery of Our Lady of Charity . . . at Baltimore, Maryland from August, 1864 to January, 1895 (Baltimore: Foley Brothers), 23; McDonald, p. 65; Baska, p. 88; Maol-Iosa (pseud.), Franciscan Missionary Sisters of the Sacred Heart . . . (Peekskill: Mt. St. Francis, 1927), p. 32.

35. Anna C. Minogue, Pages from a Hundred Years of Dominican History (New York: Pustet, 1921), p. 111.

36. Letter of Mother Marie de St. Stanislaus, to Bishop Odin, December 10, 1861, UNDA.

37. Sister Saint Ignatius, Across Three Centuries . . . (New York: Benziger, 1932), p. 195f.

38. Anna Shannon McAllister, Flame in the Wilderness . . . (Paterson: St. Anthony Guild Press, 1944), p. 214ff.

39. Sister Mary Eleanore Brosnaham, On the King's Highway (New York: Appleton, 1931), p. 269ff.

40. April 22, 1863, UNDA.

41. St. Ignatius, 190-212.

42. Katherine Burton, Make the Way Known . . . (New York: Farrar, Straus & Cudahy, 1959), p. x.

43. Crawford, pp.83, 113-14.

44. Quoted Crawford, p. 83.

45. Quoted Frederick J. Zwierlein, Life and Letters of Bishop McQuaid, Vol. II, p. 77.

46. Ibid., p. 84.

47. Ibid., p. 113.

48. Dehey, p. 426f.

49. Kohler, p. 265ff.; 287.

50. James Reginald Coffey, Pictorial History of the Dominican Province of Saint Joseph, U.S.A. (New York: Holy Name Society, 1946), p. 54.

51. Burton, p. 74; Minogue, p. 119.

52. Callahan, p. 83.

53. Corcoran, p. 141.

54. Francis E. Tourscher, The Kenrick-Frenaye Correspondence, 1830-1862 (Lancaster: Wickersham Printing Co., 1920), p.247.

55. Corcoran, p. 140.

56. McDonald, p. 61.

57. February 5, 1866, UNDA.

58. Centenary of the Convent of the Visitation, Mount de Chantal, 1848-1948 (Wheeling, W. Va., 1948), n.p.

59. Quoted by Mary Ellen Evans, The Spirit is Mercy (Westminster: Newman, 1959), p. 95.

60. Crawford, p. 135; Maynard, p. 211; Hanousek, p. 46.

61. McDonald, p. 61; Maol, p. 10; Sister Mary Hortense Kohler, Rooted in Hope . . . (Milwaukee: Bruce, 1962), p. 122.; Christine Sevier, From Ratisbon Cloisters . . ., p. 101; Sister Helen Angela Hurley, On Good Ground (Minneapolis: University of Minnesota Press, 1951), p. 222.

62. McDonald, p.60.

63. Corcoran, p. 122.

64. Ibid., p. 121, 162.

65. Lennon, p. 28.

66. Kohler, Mother Benedicta, p. 222; Corcoran, p. 142; Peter Leo Johnson, Crosier on the Frontier . . . (Madison: State Historical Society of Wisconsin, 1959), p. 112; Robert H. Lord et al. History of the Archdiocese of Boston (New York: Sheed & Ward, 1944), Vol. II, p. 622.

67. Quoted in Zwierlein, Vol. I, p. 136.

68. Ibid., p. 138-9.

69. Katherine Burton, Bells on Two Rivers (Milwaukee: Bruce, 1965), p. 16.

70. Quoted Corcoran, p. 180f.; See also p. 134.

71. July 11, 1868, UNDA.

72. James Parton, "Our Catholic Brothers," Atlantic Monthly, XXI (April, 1868), p. 569f.

73. Margaret Rives King, Memoirs of the Life of Mrs. Sarah Peter (Cincinnati: R. Clarke, 1889), p. 345.

74. Ann Doyle, "Nursing by Religious Orders in the United States," American Journal of Nursing, XXIX (July, 1929), p. 778; Ambrose Kennedy, Speech of Hon. Ambrose Kennedy of Rhode Island in the House of Representatives Monday, March 18, 1918 (Washington: Government Printing Office, 1918), p. 37.

75. Sister Mary McAuley Gillgannon, "The Sisters of Mercy as Crimean War Nurses," Unpublished Ph. D. dissertation (University of Notre Dame, 1962) has the full story of the nursing by nuns in the Crimean War.

76. Gillgannon, p. 1.

77. Gillgannon, p. 12.

78. Victor Robinson, White Caps the Story of Nursing (New York: Lippincott, 1946), p. 108.

79. Ibid., p. 123f.

80. Sylvia G. Dannett (ed.) Noble Women of the North (New York: Yoseloff, 1959), p. 60.

81. Logue, p. 124; Stewart Brooks, Civil War Medicine (Springfield, Ill.: Charles C. Thomas, 1966), p. 53; Robinson, p. 183.

82. Gillgannon, p. 12.

83. Cecil Woodham-Smith, Florence Nightingale (New York: McGraw-Hill, 1951), p. 71.

84. Kate Cumming, A Journal of Hospital Life in the Confederate Army . . . (Louisville: Morton, 1866), p. 178.

85. Mary Elizabeth Massey, Bonnet Brigades (New York: Knopf, 1966), p. 43f.

86. Woodham-Smith, p. 255.

87. Ellen Ryan Jolly, Nuns of the Battlefield (Providence: Providence Visitor, 1927), p. 276ff.

88. Sister John Francis, CSC in conversation and "Mound City Hospital Staffed by Sisters of the Holy Cross," Jacksonville (Ill.) Courier Journal, Oct. 22, 1961.

89. Edward Sorin, Circular Letters (Notre Dame, 1885), p. 305-6.

90. Quoted by George Barton, Angels of the Battlefield (Philadelphia: Catholic Art Publishing Co., 1897), p. 6-7.

91. George W. Adams, Doctors in Blue (New York: Henry Schuman, 1952), p. 177.

92. Helen E. Marshall, Dorothea Dix, Forgotten Samaritan (Chapel Hill: University of North Carolina Press, 1937), p. 220f.; Adams, p. 178.

93. Marshall, p. 227.

94. Marshall, p. 218; Brooks, p. 54.

95. Quoted Logue, p. 123.

96. Ibid.

97. John Hill Brinton, Personal Memoirs (New York: Neale Publishing, 1914), p. 43ff.

98. Quoted Logue, p. 121.

99. Mary A. Livermore, A Woman's Story of the War (Worthington, 1888), p. 224.

100. Cumming, p. 19.

101. Quoted Logue, p. 126.

102. Louisa May Alcott, Hospital Sketches ed. Bessie Z. Jones (Cambridge: Belknap Press of Harvard, 1960), p. xxxi.

103. June 29, 1861 issue, p. 4, quoted by Betty Ann Perkins, "The Work of the Catholic Sister-Nurse in the Civil War," Unpublished Master's thesis (University of Dayton, 1967), p.40-41.

104. Quoted Perkins, p. 51.

105. See for example, Benjamin J. Blied, Catholics and the Civil War (Milwaukee: n.p., 1945), p. 120.

106. William Quentin Maxwell, Lincoln's Fifth Wheel . . . (New York: Longmans, Green, 1956), p. 68.

107. Quoted Perkins, p. 53.

108. Joseph K. Barnes, (ed.) Medical and Surgical History of the War of the Rebellion (Washington, G.P.O., 1870), Vol. I of Part III, p. 958.

109. Major D. P. Conyngham, "The Soldiers of the Cross . . ."
     Unpublished manuscript, UNDA.

110. Patrick R. Duffy, "The Navy Nurses' Hundredth Birthday,"
     Columbia (October, 1966),

111. Patriot Daughters of Lancaster, Hospital Scenes after the
     Battle of Gettysburg, July, 1863 (Philadelphia, Ashmead, 1864),
     p. 53; Perkins, p. 29; Jolly, p. 62ff.

112. Quoted by Dehey, p. xxix-xxx.

113. Jolly,p. 241.

114. Kennedy (Ambrose), p. 8.

115. Jolly and Perkins in the works cited above.

116. Brosnahan, p. 251-53; Also Lennon, p. 22.

117. Mary Teresa Austin Carroll, Leaves from the Annals of the Sisters
     of Mercy (New York: Shea, 1895), Vol. III, p. 163.

118. Sister Eugenia Logan, "Angels of Mercy," Indianapolis Star
     magazine (October 16, 1966), p. 20; J.S. Hyland, Progress of
     the Catholic Church in America . . . (Chicago: J. S. Hyland,
     1897), p. 434; Logue, p. 122.

119. Conyngham, n.p.

120. Robinson, p. 177.

121. Eleanor C. Donnelly, Life of Sister Mary Gonzaga . . .
     (Philadelphia, 1900), p. 117.

122. Michael V. Gannon, The Cross in the Sand (Gainesville: University
     of Florida Press, 1967), p. 181.

123. Carroll, Vol. III, p. 163.

124. Quoted Perkins, p. 47.

125. Ibid.

126. Barton, p. 87.

127. Robinson, p. 176.

128. Perkins, p. 83.

129. Livermore, p. 219.

130. Sister Mary Agnes McCann, History of Mother Seton's Daughters. . . (New York: Longmans, Green, 1917-23), II, p.235.

131. Brosnahan, p. 252.

132. Conyngham, Ch. 26.

133. Perkins, p. 54-55.

134. Sisters of Charity, Emmitsburg, 1809-1959 (Emmitsburg: St. Joseph Central House, 1959), p. 90.

135. Norah Smaridge, Hands of Mercy: Story of the Sister Nurses of the Civil War (New York: Benziger, 1960), p. 13.

136. Gannon, p. 174.

137. Dec. 13, 1861 quoted in McAllister, Flame, p. 176-78.

138. Superior Generals, Volume II of Centenary Chronicles of the Sisters of the Holy Cross (Paterson, St. Anthony Guild Press, 1941), p. 68.

139. Brosnaham, p. 244.

140. Thomas E. Kissling, "600 Sister-Nurses Served North, South in Civil War," Chicago New World, April 21, 1961, n.p.

141. Ibid.

142. Carroll, p. 166.

143. Barton, p. 88.

144. Ambrose Kennedy, p. 34.

145. Ibid., p. 33

146. Quoted Perkins, p. 39-40.

147. Quoted Perkins, p. 96. Other tributes are quoted in Logue, p. 124; Conyngham, passim; Dehey, p. xxix; "Sisters of Charity in the War," Ave Maria XXXIX (Dec. 15, 1894), p. 664; Cumming, p. 22; Kennedy, passim.

148. Sara Trainer Smith (ed.), "Notes on Saterlee Military Hospital, West Philadelphia, Penn." American Catholic Historical Society Records, VIII (1897), p. 408.

149. Smaridge, p. 30; New York Times article, December 11, 1864, included in Walt Whitman, The Wound Dresser.

150. Cumming, p. 114.

151. Dec. 18, 1861; Wallace Collection, photostatic copy in possession of Sister John Francis.

152. Quoted by Emily Bliss (Thacher) Souder, _Leaves from the battlefield of Gettysburg; a series of letters from a field hospital_ (Philadelphia: C. Sherman, 1864), p. 34.

153. Quoted in "Sisters of Mercy and Charity," _Ave Maria_, III (August 24, 1867), p. 538-39.

154. _Ibid._

155. John O'Grady, _Catholic Charities in the United States_ (Washington: National Catholic Welfare Council, 1930), p. 194.

156. M. Adelaide Nutting, and Lavinia L. Dock, _A History of Nursing . . ._ (New York: Putnam, 1935), Vol. II, p. 366.

157. Lydia Stirling Flintham, "Leaves from the Annals of the Ursulines," _Catholic World_, LXVI (1897), p. 325.

158. Sister M. Eulalia Herron, _The Sisters of Mercy in the United States_ (New York: Macmillan, 1929), p. 39.

159. Olga Hartley, _Woman and the Catholic Church Yesterday and Today_ (London: Burnes, Oates, Washbourne, 1925), p. 220; Dannet, p. 53; Massey, p. 63; Cumming, p. 421.

160. Quoted Conyngham, n.p.

161. _Sisters of Charity_, p. 264; Minogue, p. 129.

162. Herron, p. 133.

163. Charles Louis Sewry, "The Alleged 'Un-Americanism' of the Church as a Factor in Anti-Catholicism in the United States, 1860-1914," Unpublished Ph.D. dissertation (University of Minnesota, 1955), p. 159.

164. Gannon, p. 181.

165. Augustus Thebaud, _Three-Quarters of a Century (1807-1882)_ . . . ed. Charles G. Herbermann (New York: U.S.Cath. Hist.Soc.,)p.297.

166. William Cardinal O'Connell, _Recollections of Seventy Years_ (Boston: Houghton, Mifflin, 1934), p. 45.

167. _Ibid._

168. John L. Spalding, Life of Archbishop Spalding (New York: Catholic Publication Society, 1873), p. 305.

169. Carlos Castaneda, The Church in Texas Since Independence, 1836-1950 Vol. VII of Our Catholic Heritage in Texas 1519-1936 (Austin: Von Boeckmann-Jones, 1936-50), p. 289; Sister M. Gabriel Denham, Educational Influence of M. Catherine McAuley, Unpublished master's thesis (University of Notre Dame, 1928), p.25; Brosnahan, p. 251-3; Perkins, pp.98-126; "Sisters of Charity in the War," p.664-5.

170. Parton, p. 449.

171. July 12, 1860 quoted by Sister Monica, The Cross in the Wilderness (New York: Longmans, Green, 1930), p. 153.

172. December 24, 1863, quoted Schuster, p. 35.

173. Quoted Schuster, p. 36.

174. Ibid.

175. Sister M. Edmund Croghan, Sisters of Mercy in Nebraska, 1864-1910 (Washington: Catholic University Press, 1942), p. 13; Matthew Page Andrews, comp. The Women of the South in War Times (Baltimore: The Norman, Remington Co., 1920), p. 276.

176. Ned Buntline /Edward Zane Carroll Judson/, The Beautiful Nun, (Philadelphia: T. B. Peterson & Brox., 1866).

177. Julia McNair Wright, Almost a Nun (Philadelphia: Presbyterian Publication Committee, 1868); Priest and Nun . . . (Philadelphia: Crittenden & McKinney, 1869).

178. Pamela H. Cowan, The American Convent as a school for Protestant Children (New York: Thos. Whittaker, 1869).

179. Mrs. Eliza Richardson, The Veil Lifted (Boston: Hoyt, 1869), p. 139, 153.

180. Enrichetta Caracciolo, The Mysteries of Neapolitan Convents transl. J. S. Redfield (Hartford: A. S. Hale, 1867).

181. Almost a Nun, p. 3.

182. Priest and Nun, p. 3.

183. p. 52-3.

184. Ibid., p. 213, 223.

185. p. 132.

186. n.p.

187. Wright, _Almost a Nun_, p.111.

188. _Priest and Nun_, p. 30.

189. Wright, _Almost a Nun_, p. 54; _Priest and Nun_, p. 37.

190. p. 12.

191. p. 13-14.

192. _Almost a Nun_, p. 112-13.

193. p. 222f.

194. Richardson, p. 67.

195. p. 71.

196. p. 32, 105.

197. p. 103.

198. p. 108.

199. p. 28.

200. pp. 56, 180, 177.

201. _Almost a Nun_, p. 201, 103.

202. _Priest and Nun_, p. 26.

203. p. 206-7.

204. p. 11, 25.

205. p. 36, 40, 42, 61.

206. p. 42, 45.

207. p. 49.

208. p. 70.

209. p. 88.

210. p. 172.

211. pp. 80, 82, 85.

212. p. 42.

213. p. 63.

214. p. 142f.

FOOTNOTES FOR CHAPTER SIX

1. Elinor Tong Dehey, Religious Orders of Women in the United States (Cleveland: n.p., 1950), p. 576ff. and passim.

2. Peter Guilday, A History of the Councils of Baltimore: 1791-1884 (New York: Macmillan, 1932), p. 234.

3. Sister Mary Clare, "The Nun," Catholic World, CL (February, 1940), p. 588; James R. Cain, The Influence of the Cloister on the Apostolate of Congregations of Religious Women (Rome: Pontifical University of the Lateran, 1965), pp.56-7.

4. Benjamin F. Farrell, The Rights and Duties of the Local Ordinary Regarding Congregations of Women Religious of Pontifical Approval (Washington: Catholic University, 1941), pp. 36f.

5. Particularly in Thomas T. McAvoy, The Great Crisis in American Catholic History 1895-1900 (Chicago: Regnery, 1957).

6. Ibid., pp.387ff.

7. Francis J. Callahan, The Centralization of Government in Pontifical Institutes of Women with Simple Vows (Rome: Gregorian University, 1948), p. 34.

8. Ibid., p. 51.

9. Charles A. Bachofen, A Commentary on the New Code of Canon Law (St. Louis: Herder, 1929), p. 67-8.

10. Mother Mary Clarissa, With the Poverello (New York: Kenedy, 1948), p. 191; Sister M. Grace McDonald, With Lamps Burning (St. Joseph, Minn.: St. Benedict's Priory Press, 1957), p. 314; Eugene Joseph Crawford, Daughters of Dominic On Long Island (New York: Benziger, 1938), p. 135; Sister M. Octavia, Not With Silver and Gold (Dayton, n.p., 1945), p. 325.

11. S.Hayes, Women of the Cenacle (Milwaukee: Convent of Our Lady of Cenacle, 1952), p. 84.

12. Oct. 15, UNDA.

13. Collections and Recollections in the Life and Times of Cardinal Gibbons (McSherrystown, Pa.: The Author, 1890-1904), III, p. 188ff.

14. Sister Elizabeth Ten Broeck to Fr. Daniel Hudson, Apr. 6, 1890, UNDA.

15. St. Clare and Her Order (London: Mills & Boon, 1912), p. 241.

16. See Robert D. Cross, The Emergence of Liberal Catholicism in America (Cambridge: Harvard U. Press, 1958), Chapter 7; Alvin Stauffer, "Anti-Catholicism in American Politics, 1865-1900," (unpublished Ph.D. dissertation, Widener Library, Harvard University, 1933), pp. 217ff.; Sister Mary Angela Carlin, "The Attitude of the Republican Party toward religious schools," (unpublished master's thesis, Catholic University, 1948), pp. 1ff.; McAvoy, Ch. 2.

17. Sister Mary Josephine Gately, The Sisters of Mercy . . . 1831-1931 (New York: Macmillan, 1931), p. 299.

18. (New York: Harcourt Brace, 1957), pp. 103-4.

19. Richard J. Gable, Public Funds for Church and Private Schools (Washington: Catholic University Press, 1937), p. 654; McDonald, p. 78ff.; W.J.H. Traynor, "The Aims & Methods of the APA," North American Review CLIX (July, 1894), p. 72.

20. Sister Dolorita Marie Dougherty, Sister Helen Angela Hurley et al. Sisters of St. Joseph of Carondelet (St. Louis: Herder, 1966, p. 295.

21. Cross, pp. 140f.; Mary Louise Corcoran, Seal of Simplicity (Westminster, Md.: Newman, 1958), p. 209.

22. Gately, p. 271, 437; Dougherty, pp. 124-5, 341.

23. F. C. Farinholt et al., "The Public Rights of Women," Catholic World LIX (June, 1894), p. 301.

24. Maurice Francis Egan, "Sunday Nights with Friends. The Convent Graduate," Ave Maria XXXVIII (June 16, 1894), pp. 660f.; Daniel Dorchester, Romanism versus the Public School System (New York: Phillips & Hunt, 1888), p. 271ff.; Katherine Tynan, "The Higher Education for Catholic Girls," Catholic World LI (August, 1890), p. 275.

25. Egan, p. 660ff.; Dorchester, p. 275.

26. Egan, pp. 661-2.

27. Tynan, pp. 616-17.

28. Ibid., pp. 620-21.

29. Apr. 6, 1890, UNDA.

30. Maurice Francis Egan, "Chats with Good Listeners," Ave Maria XXXV (July 23, 1892), p. 101.

30. Gately, p. 271, 437; Dougherty, pp. 124-5, 341.

31. Gately, p. 322, 350; Anna C. Minogue, Pages from a Hundred Years of Dominican History (New York: Pustet, 1921), pp. 130ff.; Dougherty, p. 75.

32. "Sisters of the Third Order of St. Francis 1855-1928" American Catholic Historical Society of Philadelphia Records XL (1924), p. 232.

33. Sister M. Teresita, "Mother Dolores" Review for Religious XV (Sept., 1956), p. 244.

34. Ann Doyle, "Nursing by Religious Orders in the United States" Amer. Journal of Nursing XXIX (Aug.,1929), pp.959, 967ff; John O'Grady, Catholic Charities in the United States (Washington: NCWC, 1930), p. 195.

35. Gately, p. 295.

36. O'Grady, pp.198-9; Sister M. Helena Finck, Congregation of the Sisters of Charity of Incarnate Word of San Antonio, Texas (Washington: Catholic University of America, 1925), p. 92.

37. O'Grady, p. 208.

38. Stella O'Connor, "Charity Hospital at New Orleans: . . . 1736-1941" Louisiana Historical Quarterly XXXI (1948), p. 70.

39. Thomas Dwight, M. D., "The Training Schools for Nurses of the Sisters of Charity" Catholic World LXI (May, 1895), p. 190.

40. Abby Howland Woolsey, A Century of Nursing with Hints Toward the Organization of a Training School . . . (New York: Putnam, 1950), p. 26; M. Adelaide Nutting, and Lavinia L. Dock, A History of Nursing . . . (New York: Putnam, 1935), Vol. I, p. 503.

41. Nutting, Vol. IV, p. 83.

42. Ibid., Vol. 3, pp.36ff.; Vol. $, p. 133.

43. Ibid., Vol. 3, p. 284.

44. Ibid., Vol. 3, p. 290.

45. Conversation with Sister Mary Lourdes, D. C. April, 1966.

46. Nutting, Vol. I, p. 503.

47. O'Connor, p. 71.

48. Dwight, p. 190.

49. Nutting, Vol. 4, p. 82.

50. Quoted Nutting Vol. 3, p. 290. See also Woolsey, p. 27 for Florence Nightingale's reflections on this.

51. Nutting, Vol. 3, p. 290.

52. Dwight, p. 192.

53. O'Connor, pp.73-4.

54. Ibid., p. 76.

55. Nutting, Vol. 4, p. 113.

56. Senate Documents, 3877, First Session, Fifty-sixth Congress, XXXV nos. 389-425, 299 (1899-1900; Mary Magdalen Wirmel, "Sisterhoods in the Spanish-American War" U.S. Cath.Hist. Soc. Records and Studies xxxii (1941), p. 32.

57. George Barton, "A Study of Self-Sacrifice" Amer. Cath.Hist. Soc. of Philadelphia Records, XXXVII (1926), pp.117f.; 151f.

58. Dehey, p. 277; Barton, p. 176.

59. Alice Worthington Winthrop, "Work of the Sisters in the War With Spain," Ave Maria IL (1899) p. 427; Frank T. Reuter, Catholic Influence on American Colonial Policies 1898-1904 (Austin: University of Texas Press, 1967), p. 12.

60. Winthrop, p. 429.

61. Barton, pp.166-67.

62. Winthrop, p. 62.

63. Gately, p. 268.

64. O'Grady, p. 110.

65. Ibid., pp.101ff.

66. Ibid., pp. 132f.

67. O'Grady, pp.139-40.

68. Ibid., p. 289f.

69. Ibid., pp.311f.

70. Sister Mary Innocentia Fitzgerald, Historical Sketch of the Sisters of Mercy in the Diocese of Buffalo (Buffalo: Mount Mercy Academy, 1943), p. 57.

71. Quoted Sister Mary Hortense Kohler, Life and Work of Mother Benedicta Bauer (Milwaukee: Bruce, 1937), p. 323.

72. Ibid., p. 328.

73. Katherine Burton, Bells on Two Rivers (Milwaukee: Bruce, 1965), pp.24, 85.

74. Ettie Madeline Vogel, "The Ursulines in America" Researches of the American Catholic Historical Society I (1884), p. 232.

75. "Sisters of the Third Order of St. Francis" p. 151.

76. Rev. Mother Pia Backes, Her Days Unfolded, trans. Mother Bernadina Michel (St. Benedict, Oregon: Benedictine Press, 1953), p. 62.

77. Sister Mary Xavier Holworthy, Diamonds for the King (Corpus Christi: Incarnate Word Academy, 1945), p. 69.

78. Sister Helen Angela Hurley, On Good Ground (Minneapolis: University of Minnesota Press, 1951), pp. 222, 233.

79. Dougherty, p. 97.

80. Sister M. Edmund Croghan, Sisters of Mercy in Nebraska, 1864-1910 (Washington: Catholic University of America Press, 1942), p. 41; see also Sister M. Michael Francis, The Broad Highway . . . (Cleveland: Ursuline Nuns, 1951), p. 217; Maol-Iosa (pseud.), Franciscan Missionary Sisters of the Sacred Heart . . . (Peekskill, N.Y.: Mt. St. Francis, 1927), p. 6; Sister Mary Faith Schuster, The Meaning of the Mountain (Baltimore: Helicon, 1963), p. 80.

81. Schuster, p. 80.

82. Backes, p. 112.

83. Ibid., pp. 135, 137, 191, 254 et passim.

84. Kohler, p. 323.

85. Sister Mary Hortense Kohler, Rooted in Hope (Milwaukee: Bruce, 1962), p. 122.

86. Croghan, p. 41.

87. Crawford, pp. 304, 306.

88. McDonald, p. 140; Ludwig, p. 430.

89. Kohler, Rooted, p. 78.

90. Maol, p. 10.

91. Winthrop, p. 429.

92. Sister Dympna Flynn, Mother Caroline and the School Sisters of Notre Dame in North America (St. Louis: Woodward & Tiernan, 1928), p. 213f.

93. Congregation of Sisters Adoreres of the Most Precious Blood (Techny, Ill.: Mission Press, 1938), p. 64.

94. Backes, p. 170.

95. McCloskey to Purcell, Aug.30, 1875, UNDA.

96. Sister Michael Francis, p. 200f.

97. Peter Leo Johnson, Crosier on the Frontier . . . (Madison: Wisconsin State Historical Society, 1959), p. 112.

98. Burton, pp. 24, 32.

99. Sister M. Xavier Farrell, Happy Memories of a Sister of Charity (St. Louis: Herder, 1941), p. 53.

100. James M. Graham, Dominicans in Illinois: A History of Fifty Years, 1873-1923 (Springfield, Ill.: Edw. F. Hartmann Co., 1923), p. 145.

101. Michael Francis, p. 200f.

102. Sisters of Notre Dame de Namur, American Foundations of the Sisters of Notre Dame de Namur (Philadelphia: Dolphin Press, 1928), p. 301.

103. Sister M. Mileta Ludwig, Chapters in Franciscan History . . . (New York: Bookman Associates, 1950), p. 188.

104. Father Wm. Corby to James F. Edwards, Oct. 2, 1894, UNDA; Sister J. to Edwards, Dec. 9, 1894, UNDA.

105. Superior Generals, Centenary Chronicles of the Sisters of the Holy Cross, Vol. II (Paterson, New Jersey: St. Anthony Guild Press, 1941), p. 96.

106. Congregation of Sisters Adorers . . . p. 30.

107. Sister M. Francis Borgia, He Sent Two (Milwaukee: Bruce, 1965), p. 93-4.

108. McDonald, p. 95f.

109. Sister Blandina Segale, At the End of the Santa Fe Trail (Milwaukee: Bruce, 1948), p. 167.

110. Fitzgerald, p. 67.

111. Sister M. Eulalia Herron, The Sisters of Mercy in the United States (New York: Macmillan, 1929), p. 170.

112. Sister Maria Kostka Logue, Sisters of St. Joseph of Philadelphia . . . (Westminster, Md.: Newman, 1950), p. 173.

113. Sister Patricia Jean Manion, Only One Heart (Garden City: Doubleday, 1963), p. 272; Ludwig, p. 329.

114. Manion, p. 285 et passim.

115. Sister Monica Taggart, "Diary of the Journey of the Sisters of St. Joseph to Tucson, Ariz. 1870" St. Louis Cath. Hist. Rev. II (Apr-July, 1920), p. 110; Dougherty, p. 290f.

116. Quoted Hurly, p. 144.

117. Superior Generals, p. 79.

118. Quoted Graham, p. 92.

119. Minogue, p. 114.

120. Rev. John F. McShane, Little Beggars of Christ (Paterson, N.J.: St. Anthony Guild Press, 1954), pp. 43-44.

121. Lida Rose McCabe, "The Everyday Life of a Sister of Charity," Cosmopolitan XXIII (1897), p. 289.

122. Segale, pp. 50-51.

123. McDonald, pp. 112-13.

124. Mrs. Julia Collier Harris, Life and Letters of Joel Chandler Harris (New York: Houghton Mifflin, 1918), p. 351-2.

125. Clara Clemens, My Father, Mark Twain (New York: Harper, 1934), p. 100.

388

126. Katherine Burton, *Sorrow Built a Bridge* (New York: Longmans, Green, 1937); Theodore Maynard, *A Fire Was Lighted* (Milwaukee: Bruce, 1948); James J. Walsh, *Mother Alphonsa; Rose Hawthorne Lathrop* (New York: Macmillan, 1930).

127. Burton, *Sorrow*, p. 108.

128. Quoted Walsh, pp.171-2.

129. Burton, *Sorrow*, p. 157.

130. Flynn, p. 233f.

131. Sister Florence Kientz, *Alverno . . . Franciscan Sisters 1866-1919* (Washington: Catholic Educational Press, 1919), p.44.

132. "Sisters of the Third Order of St. Francis," p. 226ff.

133. McDonald, pp.84-5.

134. Graham, p. 74.

135. Mother St. Charles Wid to James F. Edwards, Notre Dame, Feb. 7, 1882; Oct. 22, 1888, UNDA.

136. Quoted from St. Louis *Globe Democrat* Dec. 16, 1894 by Croghan, p. 124.

137. Croghan, p. 120.

138. Gustavus Myers, *History of Bigotry in the United States* ed. and rev. by Henry M. Christman (New York: Capricorn Books, 1960), p. 186.

139. Sister Alicia Andres, "The A.P.A. Movement in Michigan," unpublished master's thesis (Washington: Catholic University, 1955), p. 88.

140. *Ibid.*, p. 54.

141. Croghan, p. 113.

142. Stauffer, p. 404.

143. Carl Zollman, *American Civil Church Law* (New York: Columbia University Press, 1917), pp. 98-99.

144. Ashley Gorman, "Teachers Wearing Religious Garb," *Wayne Law Review* III (Winter, 1956), p. 60; Stauffer, p. 364; J. T. Reilly, p. 197; Gable, p. 281.

145. Reilly, p. 197; Zollman, p. 99.

146. Donald L. Kinzer, An Episode in Anti-Catholicism: the APA (Seattle: University of Washington, 1964), pp. 164ff.

147. James A. Burns, Growth and Development of the Catholic School System in the United States (New York: 1912), p. 266.

148. Sister Mary Teresa, The Fruit of His Compassion (New York: Pageant Press, 1962), p. 373.

149. See appendix for a list of the books studied.

150. Sister Blanche Marie McEniry, Woman of Decision (New York: McMullen, 1953), p. 110; O'Gorman, (Hartford: Connecticut Pub. Co., 1871).

151. Stauffer, p. 21; Chiniquy, Fifty Years (New York: Agora Pub. Co., 1885); Wright, (Cincinnati: National Pub.Co., 1876).

152. Shepherd, (Toledo, 1938); Tuttle, (Philadelphia: Carter Pub. Co., 1892); Fulton (Somerville, Mass.: Pauline Propaganda, 1898); APA Magazine, (San Francisco) 1895-7.

153. O'Gorman, p. iii.

154. (New York: Holt, Rinehart & Winston, 1962).

155. (Boston: Houghton Mifflin, 1956).

156. (New York: Grosset & Dunlap, 1901).

157. (Boston: Houghton Mifflin, 1916).

158. F. Marion Crawford, (New York: Macmillan, 1894).

159. (Boston: Patrick Donahoe, 1871).

160. Preface to the New York edition of The American (New York: Charles Scribner's Sons, 1907), p. ix.

161. Portrait, pp.193, 194, 196, 198, 435, 448; The American, p. 321.

162. Wedding Journey, p. 252.

163. Tuttle, pp.8, 82; Fulton, p. 14.

164. pp. 16, 82.

165. Portrait (New York: New American Library, 1881 ed.), p. 211.

166. Chance Acquaintance, p. 27.

167. C.A., p. 105.

168. Ibid., p. 92.

169. W.J., p. 255.

170. A.P.A. Magazine, Vol. I, No. 1, p. 31.

171. W.J., p. 256-7

172. Ibid., p. 256.

173. Ibid., pp. 255, 302; C.A. p. 127.

174. C.A., p. 91.

175. (New York: Bantam Books, 1960), p. 425.

176. APA Vol. I, No.1, June, 1895, p. 31; Tuttle, p.81.

177. C.A., p. 241.

178. Ibid., p. 128.

179. W.J., p. 258.

180. Margaret Fuller Ossoli, At Home and Abroad . . . (Boston: Roberts, 1874).

181. Vol. III, No. 4 (Nov., 1896), p. 1583.

182. Fulton, p. 135; O'Gorman, p. 75f., 9.

183. Fulton, p. 124; Crawford, p. 97.

184. Vol. I, No. 1, Sept. 18, 1896, p. 346.

185. W.J., 1 p. 256.

186. Ibid., pp. 304, 256.

187. Fulton, p. 124; O'Gorman, p. 70.

188. APA, I, p. 31; O'Gorman, p. 73.

189. Quoted in Wright, pp.571f.

190. Tuttle, p. 72.

191. <u>C.A.</u>, pp. 188, 255.

192. <u>W.J.</u>, p. 255.

193. Fulton, p. 126.

194. Fulton, p. 38; Tuttle, pp.25, 38.

195. Tuttle, p. 10; Wright, p. 17; Chiniquy, p. 54.

196. Sister Gretchen Hessler, "The Nun in German Literature" Unpublished Ph.D. dissertation,(Urbana, University of Illinois, 1944), p. 37.

197. <u>Ibid</u>., pp.38, 92, 102, 112, 172, 189, 239.

198. <u>Ibid</u>., pp. 89, 99.

199. <u>Ibid</u>., pp. 132, 174.

FOOTNOTE FOR CHAPTER SEVEN

1. Jerome Murphy-O'Connor, "Religious Life as Witness," <u>Supplement to Doctrine and Life</u>, XVII (1967), 124.

BIBLIOGRAPHY

Unpublished Materials

Archives of the University of Notre Dame - various
    letters and United States documents in the
    Propaganda Fide Archives on microfilm.

Andres, Sister Alicia. "The APA Movement in
    Michigan." Unpublished Master's Thesis,
    Catholic University of America, 1955.

Baumgartner, Mildred Florence. "The Ave Maria Index."
    University of Notre Dame. 1947-49.
    (Typewritten.)

Byrne, Paul R. "American Catholic Quarterly Review
    Author and Subject Index to Volumes 1-49,
    1876-1924." University of Notre Dame.

Conyngham, Major D.P. "The Soldiers of the Cross;
    Heroism of the Cross, or, Nuns and Priests on
    the Battlefield." University of Notre Dame.
    (Typewritten.)

Denham, Sister M. Gabriel, OM. "Educational Influence
    of M. Catherine McAuley." Unpublished Master's
    Thesis, University of Notre Dame, 1928.

Egler, Raymond Ottman. "The Rule of St. Benedict as
    Adapted to American Conditions." Unpublished
    Master's Thesis, University of Notre Dame, 1936.

Ferguson, Sister Mary Olivia, OSU. "Frances de
    Bremond and the Cloistering of the Ursulines."
    Unpublished Master's Thesis, University of Notre
    Dame, 1961.

Gillgannon, Sister Mary McAuley, RSM. "The Sisters
    of Mercy as Crimean War Nurses." Unpublished
    Ph.D. dissertation, University of Notre Dame,
    1962.

Hessler, Sister Gretchen. "The Nun in German
    Literature." Unpublished Ph.D. dissertation,
    University of Illinois, 1944.

Keenan, Sister Mary Ellen. "French Teaching Commun-
    ities and Early Convent Education in the United
    States, 1727-1850." Unpublished Master's thesis,
    Catholic University of America, 1934.

Kennedy, Sister M. Natalie. "A Pioneer Religious
    Venture in Ohio." Unpublished Master's
    thesis, University of Notre Dame, 1936.

McGray, Sister Mary Gertrude. "Evidence of Catholic
    Interest in Social Welfare in the United
    States between 1830 and 1850." Unpublished
    Master's thesis, University of Notre Dame, 1937.

Murphy, Sister Roseann, SNDdeN. "A Comparative Study
    of Organizational Change in Three Religious
    Communities." Unpublished Ph.D. dissertation,
    University of Notre Dame, 1965.

Perkins, Betty Ann. "The Work of the Catholic Sister-
    Nurses in the Civil War." Unpublished Master's
    thesis, University of Dayton, 1967.

Sewry, Charles Louis. "The Alleged 'Un-Americanism'
    of the Church as a Factor in Anti-Catholicism
    in the United States, 1860-1914." Unpublished
    Ph.D. dissertation, University of Minnesota,
    1955.

Stauffer, Alvin Packer. "Anti-Catholicism in American
    Politics, 1865-1900." Unpublished Ph.D. disser-
    tation, Harvard University, 1933.

Materials in the collection of Francis Clark,
    University of Notre Dame.

Materials in the collection of Sister John Francis, CSC,
    Holy Cross Hospital, South Bend, Indiana.

WORKS ON THE HISTORY OF RELIGIOUS COMMUNITIES

Abbelen, Peter M. Mother M. Caroline Friess. St. Louis:
    Herder, 1893.

"Accounts of the Voyage of the Ursulines to New Orleans
    in 1727," United States Catholic Historical
    Magazine, I (1887), 28-41.

The American Foundations of the Sisters of Notre Dame
    de Namur. Philadelphia: Dolphin Press, 1928.

"American Religious Foundations," American Ecclesiastical Review, XVII-XXI (1897-1899), various pages.

Annals of the Monastery of Our Lady of Charity of the Good Shepherd of Anges, at Baltimore, Md. from August, 1864 to January, 1895. Baltimore: Foley Brothers, n.d.

Backes, Rev. Mother Pia. Her Days Unfolded. Translated by Mother Bernadina Michel. St. Benedict, Oregon: Benedictine Press, 1953.

Bailly, Madame de Barberey. Elizabeth Seton. Translated from the Sixth French Edition and adapted by Rev. Joseph B. Code. New York: Macmillan, 1927.

Baska, Sister M. Regina, OSB. The Benediction Congregation of St. Scholastica: Its Foundation and Development, 1852-1930. Washington: Catholic University of America, 1935.

Borgia, Sister M. Francis. He Sent Two. Milwaukee: Bruce, 1965.

Boyle, Sister Electa. Mother Seton's Sisters of Charity in Western Pennsylvania. Seton Hill, Pennsylvania, 1946.

Brosnahan, Sister Mary Eleanore. On the King's Highway. New York: Appleton, 1931.

Brown, Sister Mary Borromeo. The History of the Sisters of Providence of Saint Mary-of-theWoods. Vol.I, 1806-1856. New York: Benziger, 1949.

Burton, Katherine. Bells on Two Rivers. Milwaukee: Bruce, 1965.

_____ Make the Way Known. New York: Farrar, Straus & Cudahy, 1959.

_____ So Surely Anchored. New York: Kenedy, 1949.

_____ Sorrow Built a Bridge. New York: Longmans, Green, 1937.

Callahan, Sister M. Generosa. History of the Sisters of Divine Providence, San Antonio, Texas. Milwaukee: Bruce, 1955.

Callan, Louise. Philippine Duchesne. Westminster,
Md.: Newman, 1957.

_____ The Society of the Sacred Heart in
North America. New York: Longmans, Green, 1937.

Carroll, Mary Teresa Austin. Leaves from the Annals
of the Sisters of Mercy. New York: Shea, 1895.

Catta, Etienne and Tony. Basil Anthony Mary Moreau.
Translated by Edward L. Heston. 2 vols.
Milwaukee: Bruce, 1955.

Centenary of the Convent of the Visitation, Frederick,
Maryland, 1846-1946. Convent of the Visitation,
1946.

Centenary of the Convent of the Visitation, Mount de
Chantal, 1848-1948. Wheeling, W. Va., 1948.

Clarissa, Mother M. and Sister Olivia. With the
Poverello. New York: Kenedy, 1948.

Code, Rev. Joseph B. Bishop John Hughes and the Sisters
of Charity. Miscellanea Historica reprint., 1949.

_____ Great American Foundresses. New York:
Macmillan, 1929.

_____ "A Select Bibliography of the Religious
Orders and Congregations of Women Founded Within the Present Boundaries of the United States
(1727-1850)," Catholic Historical Review, XXIII
(1937), 331-351.

Conway, Katherine E. In the Footprints of the Good
Shepherd, New York, 1857-1907. New York: Convent
on the Good Shepherd, 1907.

Corcoran, Mary Louise. Seal of Simplicity. . ..
Westminster, Md.: Newman, 1958.

Crawford, Eugene Joseph. Daughters of Dominic on Long
Island. New York: Benziger, 1938.

Croghan, Sister M. Edmund. Sisters of Mercy in
Nebraska, 1864-1910. Washington: Catholic
University of America Press, 1942.

Currier, Bishop Charles Warren. Carmel in America.
Baltimore: Murphy, 1890.

Degnan, Sister M. Bertrand. Mercy Unto Thousands . . .
    Westminster, Md.: Newman, 1957.

Dehey, Elinor Tong. Religious Orders of Women in the
    United States. Rev. ed. Hammond, Ind.: W.B.
    Conkey Co., 1930.

"Destruction of the Charlestown Convent," United States
    Catholic Historical Society Records and Studies,
    XIII (1919), 106-119; XII (1918), 66-75.

Dion, Philip E. "The Daughters of Charity, Their
    Early United States History," St. Vincent de
    Paul, edited by Arpad F. Kovacs. Jamaica, N.Y.:
    St. John's University Press, 1961.

Documents Relating to the Ursuline Convent in
    Charlestown. Boston: Samuel N. Dickinson, 1842.

The Dominicans of San Rafael. San Rafael: Grabhorn
    Press, 1941.

Donnelly, Eleanor C. Life of Sister Mary Gonzaga of
    the Daughters of Charity of Saint Vincent de Paul,
    1812-1897. Philadelphia, 1900.

Dougherty, Sister Dolorita Maria, Sister Helen Angela
    Hurley, et al. Sisters of St. Joseph of
    Carondelet. St. Louis: Herder, 1966.

Downing, Margaret B. Chronicles of Loretto. Chicago:
    McBride, 1898.

"Early Convent Projected," American Catholic Historical
    Researches, VIII (October, 1891), 178.

Eckenstein, Lina. Woman under Monasticism. New York:
    Russell & Russell, 1963.

England, John. "Discourse at the Habiting of an
    Ursuline Nun . . . ," Bishop England's Works,
    edited by Ignatius Aloysius Reynolds, Baltimore:
    John Murphy, 1849.

Evans, Mary Ellen. The Spirit is Mercy. Westminster,
    Md.: Newman, 1957.

Farrell, Sister M. Xavier. Happy Memories of a Sister
    of Charity. St. Louis: Herder, 1941.

Fay, Richard S. An Argument before the Committee of
    the House of Representatives, upon the Petition
    of Benedict Fenwick . . .. Boston: J. H.
    Eastburn, 1835.

Finck, Sister M. Helena. Congregation of Sisters
of Charity of the Incarnate Word of San
Antonio, Texas. Washington: Catholic University Press, 1925.

Fitzgerald, Sister Mary Innocentia. Historical
Sketch of the Sisters of Mercy in the Diocese
of Buffalo. Mount Mercy Academy, 1943.

Flintham, Lydia Stirling, "Leaves From the Annals of
the Ursulines," Catholic World, LXVI (1897),
319-39.

Flynn, Sister Dympna. Mother Caroline and the School
Sisters of Notre Dame in North America. St.
Louis: Woodward & Tiernan, 1928.

Gately, Sister Mary Josephine. The Sisters of Mercy . . .
1831-1931. New York: Macmillan, 1931.

Gilmore, Sister Julia. Come North. New York:
McMullen, 1951.

Gohmann, Sister Mary de Lourdes. Chosen Arrows.
New York: Pageant Press, 1957.

Gowen, Marguerite Horan & Sister M. Mercedes. "Sisters
of Notre Dame de Namur Philadelphia 1856-1956,"
Records of the American Catholic Historical
Society, LXVIII (Mar., June, 1957), 29-45.

Graham, James M. Dominicans in Illinois: A History of
Fifty Years, 1873-1923. Springfield, Ill:
Edward F. Hartmann, 1923.

Graves, William. Life and Times of Mother Bridget
Hayden. St. Paul, Kansas: Journal Press, 1938.

Gravier, Gabriel, editor. Relation du Voyage des dames
Religieuses Ursulines de Rouen à la Nouvelle-
Orleans avec une introduction . . .. Paris:
Maisonneuve, 1872.

Griffin, Martin I.J. editor. "Convent of the Visitation," American Catholic Historical Researches,
XI (1894), 128.

Guerin, Mother Theodore. Journals and Letters of Mother
Theodore Guerin. St. Mary-of-the-Woods, Indiana:
Providence Press, 1937.

Hale, Charles. A Review of the Proceedings of the
    Nunnery Committee of the Massuchusetts
    Legislature. Boston: Boston Daily Advertiser,
    1855.

Hanousek, Sister Mary Eunice. A New Assisi.
    Milwaukee: Bruce, 1948.

Hardman, Sister Anne, SND. English Carmelites in
    Penal Times. London, 1936.

Hawkes, Benjamin. "Letters," US Catholic Historical
    Magazine, III(1890), 274.

Hayes, S. Women of the Cenacle. Milwaukee: Convent of
    the Cenacle, 1952.

Hedges, S. B. "Father Hecker and the Establishing of
    the Poor Clares in the United States." Catholic
    World, LXI (June, 1895), 380-86.

Hefferman, Sister M. Rita. A Story of Fifty Years.
    Notre Dame: Ave Maria, 1905.

Herron, Sister M. Eulalia. The Sistersof Mercy in the
    U.S. New York: Macmillan, 1929.

Hester, Sister M. Canticle of the Harvest. New York:
    Kenedy, 1951.

"History of the Establishment of the Carmelites in
    Maryland," US Catholic Historical Magazine, III
    (Jan., 1890), 65-71.

Holworthy, Sister Mary Xavier. Diamonds for the King.
    Corpus Christi, Texas: Incarnate Word Academy,
    1945.

Hurley, Sister Helen Angela. On Good Ground.
    Minneapolis: University of Minnesota Press, 1951.

Immaculata, Sister M. Sisters of the Immaculate Heart
    of Mary. New York: Kenedy, 1921.

Johnson, Peter Leo. Daughters of Charity in Milwaukee,
    1846-1946. Milwaukee: St. Mary's Hospital, 1946.

_____ "Sisters of Charity and the Immigrant
    Hospital on Jones Island," Salesianum, XL
    (1945), 162-68.

Kientz, Sister Florence. Alverno: . . . Franciscan
    Sisters 1866-1919. Washington: Catholic Educa-
    tion Press, 1919.

Kohler, Sister Mary Hortense. Life and Work of Mother Benedicta Bauer. Milwaukee: Bruce, 1937.

_____ Rooted in Hope. Milwaukee: Bruce, 1962.

Larkin, Gertrude M. "First New England Nuns," Historical Records and Studies, XXIX (1938), 49-57.

Lathrop, George Parsons & Rose Hawthorne Lathrop. A Story of Courage. Boston: Houghton Mifflen, 1894.

"Letters bearing on the foundation of the Sisters of Notre Dame de Namur in America," American Catholic Historical Society of Philadelphia Records, XI (1900), 320-37.

Lincoln, Sister Angela. Life of the Rev. Mother Amadeus . . .. New York: Paulist Press, 1923.

Logue, Sister Maria Kostka. Sisters of St. Joseph of Philadelphia: a Century of Growth and Development, 1847-1947. Westminster: Newman, 1950.

Long, Sister M. Brideen. Annotated Bibliography of Research Studies on the Education of Sisters. Washington: Sister Formation Conference, 1964.

Lord, Rev. Robert H. "Religious Liberty in New England: the Burning of the Charlestown Convent, 1834," Catholic Historical Records and Studies XXII (1932).

Ludwig, Sister M. Mileta. Chapter in Franciscan History . . . 1849-1949. New York: Bookman Associates. 1950.

Manion, Sister Patricia Jean. Only One Heart. Garden City: Doubleday, 1963.

Mannix, Mary E. Memoirs of Sister Louise . . .. Boston: Angel Guardian Press, 1907.

Maol-Iosa (pseud.). Franciscan Missionary Sisters of the Sacred Heart in the United States 1865-1926. New York: Kenedy, 1927.

Maria Concepta, Sister. The Making of a Sister-Teacher. Notre Dame, Ind.: University of Notre Dame Press, 1965.

Mary Teresa, Sister, RDC. The Fruit of His Compassion. New York: Pageant Press, 1962.

Mast, Sister M. Dolorita. Through Caroline's Consent. Baltimore: Institute of Notre Dame, 1950.

Maynard, Theodore. A Fire Was Lighted. Milwaukee: Bruce, 1948.

_____ Through My Gift. New York: Kenedy, 1951.

Melville, Annabelle M. Elizabeth Bayley Seton 1774-1821. New York: Scribner's, 1951.

Member of the Community. Foundation and Progress of the Sisters of the Adoration of the Most Precious Blood. O'Fallon, Mo., 1925.

Members of the Province. Congregation of Sisters Adorers of the Most Precious Blood. Techny, Ill.: Mission Press, 1938.

Michael Francis, Sister M., OSU. The Broad Highway. Cleveland, Ursuline Nuns, 1951.

Minogue, Anna C. Loretto: Annals of a Century. New York: America Press, 1912.

_____ Pages from a Hundred Years of Dominican History. New York: Pustet, 1921.

Monica, Sister, OSU. The Cross in the Wilderness. New York: Longmans Green, 1930.

Mousel, Sister M. Eunice. They have Taken Root. New York: Bookman's Associates, 1954.

Mug, Sister M. Theodosia. Life & Letters of Sister Francis Xavier. St. Mary-of-the-Woods, Providence Press, 1934.

Mug, Sister M. Theodosia, editor. Journals and Letters of Mother Theodore Guerin. St. Mary-of-the-Woods, Ind.: Providence Press, 1942.

McAllister, Anna Shannon. Flame in the Wilderness. Paterson, N.J.: St. Anthony Guild Press, 1944.

McCann, Sister Mary Agnes. History of Mother Seton's Daughters. New York: Longmans Green, 1917-23. 3 volumes.

McCarthy, Sister M. Barbara, SSJ. A Covenant with
Stones. Paterson, N.J.: St. Anthony Guild
Press, 1939.

McDonald, Sister M. Grace, OSB. With Lamps Burning.
St. Joseph, Minn.: St. Benedict's Priory
Press, 1957.

McEniry, Sister Blanche Marie. Woman of Decision.
New York: McMullen, 1953.

McGill, Anna Blanche. Sisters of Charity of Nazareth.
New York: Encyclopedia Press, 1917.

McKenna, Sister Mary Lawrence, SCMM. Women of the
Church: Role and Renewal. New York: Kenedy,
1967.

McShane, Rev. John F. Little Beggars of Christ.
Paterson, N.J.: St. Anthony Guild Press, 1954.

Newcomb, Covelle. Running Waters. New York: Dodd,
Mead. 1947.

"New England Nuns," Historical Records and Studies,
XXX (1939), 154-55.

"New England's First Nun." America, XLIV (Dec. 13,
1930), 244.

Nugent, Sister Helen Louise. Sister Julia (Susan
McGroarty). New York: Benziger, 1928.

Octavia, Sister M. Not with Silver and Gold. Dayton,
1945.

Owens, Sister Lilliana, "Pioneer Days of the Lorettines
in Missouri, 1823-41," American Catholic Historical Society of Philadelphia Records, LXX
(Dec., 1959), 67-87.

Petre, Edward Robert. Notices of the English Colleges
and Convents Established on the Continent after
the Dissolution of Religious Houses in England.
Norwick: Bacon & Kennebrook, 1849.

Power, Eileen. Medieval English Nunneries c. 1254 to
1535. Cambridge: University Press, 1922.

Quinlan, Sister Anthony. In Harvest Fields by Sunset
Shores. San Francisco: Gilmartin Co., 1926.

Rivaux, Abbe. _Life of Rev. Mother St. John Fontbonne_. New York: Benziger, 1887.

Rosalita, Sister M. _No Greater Service_. Detroit: St. Mary's Academy, 1948.

Ryan, E.A. "The Sisters of Mercy," _Theological Studies_, XVIII (June, 1957), 258.

Ryan, Sister Maria Alma. "Foundations of Catholic Sisterhoods in the US to 1850," _American Catholic Historical Society Records_, LII-LIV (March, 1941 – June, 1943).

Ryan, Sister Mary Philip. _Amid the Alien Corn_. St. Charles, Ill.: Jones Wood Press, 1967.

St. Clare and Her Order. Edited by the author of "The Enclosed Nun." London: Mills & Boon, 1912.

Saint Ignatius, Sister. _Across Three Centuries_. New York: Benziger, 1932.

Savage, Sister M. Lucida. _Congregation of St. Joseph of Carondelet_. St. Louis: Herder, 1923.

Schuster, Sister Mary Faith, OSB. _The Meaning of the Mountain_. (Benedictine Studies No. 6) Helicon: Baltimore, 1963.

Segale, Sister Blandina. _At the End of the Santa Fe Trail_. Milwaukee: Bruce, 1948.

Semple, Henry C. (ed.) _The Ursulines in New Orleans_. New York: Kenedy, 1925.

Sevier, Christine. _From Ratisbon Cloisters_. Farmingdale, N.Y.: Nazareth Trade School Press, 1917.

Sharkey, Sister M. Agnes. _New Jersey Sisters of Charity_. New York: Longmans Green, 1933.

Sherwood, Grace. _The Oblates' Hundred and One Years_. New York: Macmillan, 1931.

A Sister of Mercy. "Sisters of Mercy, Chicago's Pioneer Nurses and Teachers, 1846-1921," _Illinois Catholic Historical Review_, III (1921), 339-70.

Sisters of Charity, Emmitsburg, 1809-1959. Emmitsburg: St. Joseph Central House, 1959.

Sisters of Charity of the Blessed Virgin Mary. In the Early Days--Pages from Annals. Herder, St. Louis, 1912.

"Sisters of Mercy and Charity," Ave Maria, III (August 24, 1867), 538-9.

Sisters of Notre Dame de Namur. American Foundations of the Sisters of Notre Dame de Namur. Philadelphia: Dolphin Press, 1928.

"Sisters of the Third Order of St. Francis, 1855-1928," American Catholic Historical Society of Philadelphia Records, XL-XLI (1929-30).

Sorin, Very Rev. Edward. Circular Letters. Notre Dame 1885.

Styles, William A. L. "Pioneer American Nuns," Ave Maria, LV (1942), 167-70.

Sullivan, Sister Mary Christina. "Some Non-Permanent Foundations of Religious Orders and Congregations," US Catholic Historical Society Records and Studies, XXXI (1940) 7-118.

Superior Generals. Volume II of Centenary Chronicles of the Sisters of the Holy Cross. Paterson, N.J.: St. Anthony Guild Press, 1941.

Taggert, Sister Monica. "Diary of the Journey of the Sisters of St. Joseph to Tucson, Ariz. 1870," St. Louis Catholic Historical Review, II (April-July, 1920), 101-113.

Teresita, Sister M. "Mother Dolores," Review for Religious, XV (Sept., 1956), 238-46.

Thomas, Sister Evangeline. Footprints on the Frontier. Westminster, Md.: Newman, 1948.

Tranchepain, Rev. Mere St. Augustin de. Relation du voyage des premieres Ursulines a la Nouvelle Orleans et de leur etablissement en cette ville. New York: Shea, 1859.

Vincentia, Sister Mary, SND. Their Quiet Tread. Milwaukee: Bruce, 1955.

Vogel, Ettie Madeline, "The Ursulines, in America," Records of the American Catholic Historical Society, I (1884), 214-53.

Walsh, James J. Mother Alphonsa, Rose Hawthorne Lathrop. New York: Macmillan, 1930.

_____ These Splendid Sisters. New York: J.H. Sears & Co., 1927.

Walsh, Sister Marie de Lourdes. The Sisters of Charity of New York 1809-1959. New York: Fordham University Press, 1960. 3 Volumes.

White, Charles I. Life of Mrs. Eliza A. Seton, Foundress and First Superior . . . Daughters of Charity . . . . 2nd rev. ed. Baltimore: John Murphy & Co., 1856.

Williams, Margaret. Mother Hardey. New York: Manhattanville College, 1945.

WORKS ON THE HISTORY OF NURSING

Alcott, Louisa May. Hospital Sketches. Edited by Bessie Z. Jones. Cambridge: Belknap Press of Harvard University Press, 1960.

Barnes, Joseph K. (ed.) Medical and Surgical History of the War of the Rebellion. Washington: GPO, 1870.

Barton, George, Angels of the Battlefield. Philadelphia: Catholic Art Publishing Company, 1897.

_____ "A Study of Self-Sacrifice," American Catholic Historical Society of Philadelphia Records, XXXVII (1926), 104-92.

Brinton, John Hill. Personal Memoirs. New York: Neale Publishing Co., 1914.

Bucklin, Sophronia E. In Hospital and Camp. Philadelphia: J. E. Potter & Co., 1869.

Cumming, Kate. Kate: The Journal of a Confederate Nurse. Edited by Richard Barksdale Harwell. Baton Rouge: La. State University Press, 1959.

Dannett, Sylvia G. (ed.) Noble Women of the North. New York: T. Yoseloff, 1959.

Dietz, Lena Dixon. History and Modern Nursing. Philadelphia: F.A. Davis, 1961.

Doyle, Ann, "Nursing by Religious Orders in the United States," American Journal of Nursing, XXIX (July, Aug., Sept., 1929).

Doyle, Mother Mary Aloysius, SM. Memories of the Crimea. London: Burns & Oates, 1897.

Duffy, Patrick R., CSC. "The Navy Nurses Hundredth Birthday," Columbia, (Oct., 1966).

Dwight, Thomas. "The Training Schools For Nurses of the Sisters of Charity," Catholic World, LXI (May, 1895), 187-92.

John Francis, Sister. "Mound City Hospital Staffed by Sisters of the Holy Cross," Jacksonville (Ill.) Courier Journal, Oct. 22, 1961.

Jolly, Ellen Ryan. Nuns of the Battlefield. Providence: Providence Visitor Press, 1930.

Jones, "Americans, Wounded, Attended by Ursuline Nuns," American Catholic Historical Society Researches, XXVI (Apr., 1909), 240.

Kennedy, Ambrose, Speech of Hon. Ambrose Kennedy of Rhode Island in the House of Representatives, Monday, March 18, 1918. Washington: GPO. 1918.

Kissling, Thomas E. "600 Sister-Nurses Served North, South in Civil War," The New World, Chicago, April 21, 1961.

Leslie, Shane. "Forgotten Passages in the Life of Florence Nightingale," Dublin Review, CLXI (Oct., 1917), 179-98.

Livermore, Mary A. My Story of the War. Hartford: A. D. Worthington, 1889.

Logan, Sister Eugenia, SP. "Angels of Mercy," Indianapolis Star magazine, October 16, 1966, p. 18.

Marie Loretto, Sister, "Visiting Nursing as Done by
    Sisters in the United States--A Survey of the
    field," Catholic Charities Review, XXIV (1940),
    41-44.

Marshall, Helen E. Dorothea Dix, Forgotten Samaritan.
    Chapel Hill: University of North Carolina Press,
    1937.

Massey, Mary Elizabeth. Bonnett Brigades. New York:
    Knopf, 1966.

Maxwell, William Quentin. Lincoln's Fifth Wheel: the
    Political History of the United States Sani-
    tary Commission. New York: Longmans Green,
    1956.

Nutting, M. Adelaide and Lavinia L. Dock. A History of
    Nursing. New York: Putnam, 1935. 4 volumes.

O'Brien, Msgr. Frank A. Forgotten Heroines. Lansing,
    Mich.: Michigan Historical Commission, 1916.

O'Connor, Stella, "Charity Hospital at New Orleans: . . .
    1736-1941," Louisiana Historical Quaterly,
    XXXI (1948), 1-109.

Olmstead, Frederic Law. Hospital Transports. Boston:
    Tickner & Fields, 1963.

Patriot Daughters of Lancaster. Hospital Scenes after
    the Battle of Gettysburg, July, 1863.
    Philadelphia: Ashmead, 1864.

Robinson, Victor. White Caps, the Story of Nursing.
    Philadelphia: J. B. Lippincott, 1946.

Scanlon, John, "The Yellow Fever Epidemic of 1878 in the
    Diocese of Natchez," Catholic Historical Review,
    XL (Apr., 1955), 27-45.

Sellew, Gladys and Sister M. Ethelreda Ebel, OSF. A
    History of Nursing. St. Louis: C. V. Mosby Co.,
    1955.

Senate Documents, 3877, First Session, Fifty-sixth Con-
    gress, XXXV nos. 389-425, 299, 1899-1900.
    Washington : GPO, 1900.

Simkins, Francis Butler and James Welch Patton, The Women
    of the Confederacy. New York: Garrett and
    Massie, 1936.

Smaridge, Norah. Hands of Mercy. New York: Benziger, 1960.

Smith, Sara Trainer, (ed.) "Notes on Saterlee Military Hospital, West Philadelphia, Penna." American Catholic Historical Society Records, VIII (1897), 399-449.

"A Soldier of the Revolution, Prisoner in Canada, Cared for by Nuns," American Catholic Historical Researches, XXIV (Apr., 1907), 101.

Souder, Emily Bliss(Thacher). Leaves from the Battle-field of Gettysburg. Philadelphia: C. Sherman, 1864.

[Stanley, Mary]. Hospitals and Sisterhoods. 2nd ed. London: J. Murray, 1854.

Strachey, Lytton. Eminent Victorians. New York: Putnam, 1918.

Walsh, James J. The History of Nursing. New York: Kenedy, 1929.

Whitman, Walt. Memoranda during the War. Bloomington: Indiana University Press, 1962.

Winthrop, Alice Worthington, "Work of the Sisters in the War with Spain," Ave Maria, XLIX (1899), 385-88, 426-30.

Wirmen, Mary Magdalen, "Sisterhoods in the Spanish-American War," US Catholic Historical Society Records and Studies, XXXII (1941), 7-69.

Woodnam-Smith, Cecil. Florence Nightingale. New York: McGraw-Hill, 1951.

Woolsey, Abby Howland. A Century of Nursing with Hints Toward the Organization of a Training School . . .. New York: Putnam, 1950.

Young, Agatha Agnes (Brooks) Young . The War and the Crisis. New York: McDowell, Obolensky, 1959.

WORKS ON CANON LAW

Abbott, Walter M. (ed.) The Documents of Vatican II.
Translated by Rev. Joseph Gallagher. New York:
Guild Press, 1966.

Acta Sanctae Sedis in Compendium Opportune Redacta et
illustrata. Vol I (1865-66), Rome: Propanda Fide,
1872.

Ayrinhac, H. A. General Legislation in the New Code of
Canon Law. New York: Benziger, 1923.

Bachofen, Charles Augustine. A Commentary on the New
Code of Canon Law. 3 volumes. St. Louis: Herder,
1929.

Barrett, John D. A Comparative Study of the Councils
of Baltimore and the Code of Canon Law.
Washington: Catholic University Press, 1932.

Barry, Garrett F. Violation of the Cloister. Washington:
Catholic University, 1942.

Bizzarri, Giuseppe Andre (ed.). Collectanea in usum
Secretariae Sacrae Congregationis Episcoporum et
Regularium. Rome: Typographia Polyglotta SC de
Propaganda Fide, 1885.

Boudinhon, A. "Dowry," The Catholic Encyclopedia, (1913),
V 146-7.

Cain. James R. The Influence of the Cloister on the
Apostolate of Congregations of Religious Women.
Rome: Pontifical University of the Lateran, 1965.

Callahan, Francis J. The Centralization of Government
in Pontifical Institutes of Women with Simple
Vows. Rome: Gregorian University, 1948.

Concilii Plenarii Metropolitana Baltimorensi Decreta.
Baltimore: John Murphy, 1875.

Farrell, Benjamin F. The Rights and Duties of the Local
Ordinary Regarding Congregations of Women
Religious of Pontifical Approval. Washington:
Catholic University Press, 1941.

Gallen, Joseph F. "Cloister of Congregations," Review
for Religious, XV (November, 1956), 282-94.

Kealy, T. M. "Dowry," New Catholic Encyclopedia, (1966), IV 1028-9.

Kenneally, Finbar, OFM. United States Documents in the Propaganda Fide Archives. 2 volumes. Washington: Academy of American Franciscan History, 1966.

Lanslots, Don Ildephonse, OSB. Handbook of Canon Law for Congregations of Women under Simple Vows. New York: Pustet, 1919.

Meta, Rene. What is Canon Law? New York: Hawthorn Books, 1960.

Orth, Clement R., OMC. The Approbation of Religious Institutes. Washington: Catholic University Press, 1931.

Papi, Hector. Religious in Church Law. New York: Kenedy, 1924.

Schaaf, Valentine. The Cloister. Cincinnati: St. Anthony Messenger, 1921.

Smith, Dr. S. B. Elements of Ecclesiastical Law. New York: Benziger. Volume I, 1881. Volume II, revised, 8th ed. 1891.

_____ Notes on the Second Plenary Council of Baltimore. New York: P. O'Shea, 1875.

WORKS OF POPULAR AND SERIOUS LITERATURE

American Protective Association Magazine, Volumes 1-3 (1895-97).

Baltimore Literary and Religious Magazine, edited Robert J. Breck-
    inridge and Andrew B. Cross. Volumes 1-7, 1835-41.

Barker, Benjamin. Cecilia; or, The White Nun of the Wilderness.
    Boston: F. Gleason, 1845.

Bourne, George. Lorette; the History of Louise, Daughter of a
    Canadian Nun: Exhibiting the Interior of Female Convents.
    New York: Charles Small, 1834.

Bunkley, Josephine M. Miss Bunkley's Book; the Testimony of an
    Escaped Novice from the Sisterhood of St. Joseph, Emmettsburg.
    New York: Harper, 1855.

Caldicott, Thomas Ford. Hannah Corcoran . . . . Boston: Gould &
    Lincoln, 1853.

Caracciolo, Enrichetta. The Mysteries of the Neapolitan Convents.
    Translated from the fourth Italian edition by J. S. Redfield.
    Hartford: A. S. Hale & Co., 1867.

/Chaplin, Mrs. Jane (Dunbar)/ The Convent & the Manse. Boston:
    John P. Jewett & Co., 1853.

Chiniquy, Charles. Fifty Years in the Church of Rome. New York:
    Agora Publishing Co., 1885.

Ciocci, Rafaele. Iniquities and Barbarities Practiced at Rome in
    the Nineteenth Century. Philadelphia: T. B. Peterson, 1845.

Cowan, Pamela H. The American Convent as a School for Protestant
    Children. New York: Thomas Whittaker, 1869.

Crawford, Francis Marion. Casa Braccio. 2 volumes. New York:
    Macmillan, 1895.

Culbertson, Rosamond. Rosamond. Introduction and notes by Samuel
    B. Smith. New York: Leavitt, Lord & Co., 1836.

/Damon, Norwood/ The Chronicles of Mount Benedict; a Tale of the
    Ursuline Convent . . . . Boston, 1837.

The Escaped Nun; or, Disclosures of Convent Life; and the Confes-
    sions of a Sister of Charity. Giving a more minute detail of
    their inner life, and a bolder revelation of the mysteries and
    secrets of nunneries, than have ever before been submitted to
    the American Public. New York: DeWitt & Davenport, 1855.

Fairfield, Sumner L. The Sisters of St. Clara. Portland: Dodd
    & Smith, 1825.

Frothingham Charles W. The Convent's Doom; a Tale of Charlestown
in 1834. Boston: Graves & Weston, 1854, 5th ed.

_____ The Haunted Convent. Boston: Graves, 1854.

_____ Six Hours in a Convent; or, the Stolen Nuns.
16th ed. Boston: Graves & Weston, 1855.

Fulton, Justin Dewey. Cornelia Harmon Rescued from a Convent, or
The Way Out. Revised and enlarged. Somerville, Mass.:
Pauline Propaganda, 1898.

Gavin, Anthony. The Great Red Dragon; or The Master-Key to Popery.
Philadelphia: W. D. Clark, 1855.

_____ Observation on a Journy /sic7 to Naples.
London: Samuel Roycroft, 1691.

Hawthorne, Nathaniel. The Complete Novels and Selected Tales. Ed.
Norman H. Pearson. New York: The Modern Library, 1937.

Hazel, Harry /Justin Jones7. The Nun of St. Ursula, or, the Burning
of the Convent. A Romance of Mount Benedict. Boston: F.
Gleason, 1845.

Hogan, William. Popery! As it was and as it is; also Auricular
Confession; and Popish Nunneries. Hartford: Silas Andrus, 1853.

Howells, William Dean. A Chance Acquaintance. Cambridge: Osgood, 1873.

_____ A Hazard of New Fortunes. New York: Bantam, 1960.

_____ Their Wedding Journey. Boston: Houghton
Mifflin, 1872.

Important Facts!! History of Convents, With an account of the Order
of Ursuline Nuns; also, a narrative of events which preceded
the Conflagration of the Nunnery at Charlestown, Mass. N.p. N.d.

James, Henry. The American. New York: Holt, Rinehart, & Winston, 1962.

_____ Portrait of a Lady. Boston: Houghton Mifflin, 1956.

Kirwan /Nicholas Murray7. Romanism at Home. New York: Harper, 1852.

Lennox, Mrs. Charlotte Ramsey. The Sister. London: Dodsley, 1769.

/McCorry, Peter7 Mount Benedict; or, The Violated Tomb; a Tale of
Charlestown the Convent. Boston: Patrick Donohoe, 1871.

/McCrindell, Rachel7 The School-Girl in France, or The Snares of
Popery; a Warning to Protestants against Education in Catholic
Seminaries. New York: J. K. Wellman, 1845.

McGavin, William. The Protestant. 2nd American edition from the 9th
Glasgow edition. 2 volumes. Hartford: Hutchison & Dwier, 1833.

Mahoney, S. Six Years in the Monasteries of Italy. Hartford: S.
Andrus & Son, 1844.

Monk, Maria. Awful Disclosures of the Hotel Dieu Nunnery of
Montreal. New York: Howe & Bates, 1836.

The Mysteries of a Convent, by a Noted Methodist Preacher. Philadelphia: T. B. Peterson, 1854.

O'Gorman, Edith. Trials & Persecutions of Miss Edith O'Gorman,
Otherwise Sister Teresa de Chantal, of St. Joseph's Convent,
Hudson City, New Jersey. Hartford: Connecticut Publishing
Co., 1871.

Pope or President? New York: R. L. Delisser, 1859.

Reed, Rebecca. Review of Lady Superior's Reply . . . . Boston:
Russell, Odiorne & Metcalf, 1835.

_____ Six Months in a Convent . . . . Boston:
Russell, Odiorne, & Metcalf, 1835.

_____ Supplement to "Six Months in a Convent," . . .
Boston: Russell, Odiorne & Co. 1835.

Ricci, Bishop Scipio de. Female Convents. Secrets of Nunneries
Disclosed. Compiled by Louis de Potter; edited by Thomas
Roscoe. New York: Appleton, 1834.

/Richardson, Mrs. Eliza (Smith)/ The Veil Lifted; or, the Romance
and Reality of Convent Life. Boston: H. Hoyt, /1869/.

St. George, Sister Mary Edmond. An Answer to Six Months in a Convent
Exposing its falsehoods and manifold absurdities, by the Lady
Superior. Boston: J. H. Eastburn, 1835.

Sansay, Mrs. Leonora. Laura. Philadelphia: Bradford & Inskeep, 1809.

Shepherd, Margaret nee "Sister Magdalene Adelaide". My Life in
the Convent. Toledo, 1938 ed.

Sister Agnes; or, The Captive Nun; Sketches of Convent Life. By a
Clergyman's Widow. New York: Riker, Thorne & Co., 1854.

Slocum, Rev. J. J. Further Disclosures by Maria Monk . . . .
Boston: Crocker & Brewster, 1837.

Smith, Samuel B. The Downfall of Babylon, or, The Triumph of Truth
over Popery. Volume I, 1834.

_____ Renunciation of Popery. 3rd ed. Philadelphia:
L. Johnson, 1833.

Sparry, Rev. Charles. The Protestant Annual; exhibiting the Demoralizing Influence of Popery, and the Character of its Priesthood. New York: C. Sparry, 1847.

Stone, William L. Maria Monk and the Nunnery of the Hotel Dieu. New York: Paulist Press, n.d.

The Truth Unveiled. Philadelphia: M. Fithian, 1844.

Tuttle, Hudson, Secrets of the Convent. Philadelphia: Carter Publishing Co., 1892.

/Wood, Mrs. Sally Sayward (Barrell) Keating/ Julia and the Illuminated Baron . . . . Portsmouth, N.H.: U.S. Oracle Press.

Wright, Julia McNair. Almost a Nun. Philadelphia: Presbyterian Publication Committee, 1868.

_____ Priest and Nun . . . . Philadelphia: Crittenden and McKinney, 1869.

_____ Secrets of the Convent and Confessional. Cincinnati: National Publishing Co., 1876.

GENERAL WORKS

"An Account of Louisiana, being an Abstract of Documents in the offices of the Departments of state and of the Treasury," Catholic Historical Researches,VIII (Oct., 1891), 188.

Allibone, Samuel A. Critical Dictionary of English Literature and of British and American Authors. Philadelphia: Lippincott, 1858-71.

Allport, Gordon W. The Nature of Prejudice. Cambridge, Mass.: Addison & Wesley, 1954.

"Articles of the Capitulation of Havanna . . . " US Catholic Historical Magazine, I (April, 1887), 214.

Awful Exposure of the Atrocious Plot formed by Certain Individuals Against the Clergy and Nuns of Lower Canada through the intervention of Maria Monk. Montreal: Jones & Co., 1836.

Barlow, Joel. Advice to the Privileged Orders in the Several States of Europe. New York: Childs and Swain, 1792.

Barry, Colman J. "Some Roots of American Nativism," Catholic Historical Review, XLIV (July, 1958), 137-46.

Bates, Frederick L. "Position, Role and Status," Social Forces, XXXIV (1956), 313-21.

Beals, Carleton. Brass-Knuckle Crusade; the Great Know-Nothing Conspiracy: 1820-1860. New York: Hastings House, 1960.

Beauvoir, Simone de. The Second Sex. Translated H. M. Parshley. New York: Knopf, 1953.

Beecher, Lyman. A Plea for the West. Cincinnati: Truman & Smith, 1835.

Benson, Lee. "An Approach to the Scientific Study of Past Public Opinion," Public Opinion Quarterly, XXXI, No. 4 (Winter, 1967-68), 522-67.

Beste, J. Richard. The Wabash . . . . London: Hurst & Blackett, 1855.

Billington, Ray Allen. America's Frontier Heritage. New York: Holt, Rinehart & Winston, 1966.

_____ The Protestant Crusade, 1800-1860. New York: Macmillan, 1938.

_____ "Tentative Bibliography of anti-Catholic Propaganda in the U.S.," Catholic Historical Review, XVIII (1933), 492-513.

Blakely, Paul, S.J. "Uncle Remus and the Convent School," America, XIX (Sept. 28, 1918), 609.

Boyd, Julian P. (ed.) The Papers of Thomas Jefferson. Princeton, N.J.: Princeton University Press, 1955. Volume XI.

Brown, Elmer Ellsworth. The Making of our Middle Schools. New York: Longmans, Green, 1903.

Burke, W.J. and Will D. Howe. American Authors and Books. Augmented and revised by I. R. Weiss. New York: Crown, 1943.

Burns, James A. Growth & Development of the Catholic School System in the United States. New York: Benziger, 1912.

_____ The Principles, Origin and Establishment of the Catholic School System in the United States. New York: Benziger, 1912.

Byrne, Sister Mary of the Incarnation, CDP. The Tradition of the Nun in Medieval England. Washington: Catholic University, 1932.

Cahnman, Werner J. and Alvin Boskoff, (eds.) Sociology and History, Theory and Research. London: Collier-Macmillan Limited, 1964.

Castaneda, Carlos. The Church in Texas since Independence, 1836-1950. Volume 7 of Our Catholic Heritage in Texas 1519-1936. Austin: Van Boeckmann-Jones, 1958.

Childs, Harwood L. Public Opinion: Nature, Formation, and Role, Princeton, J.J.: Van Nostrand, 1964.

Christina, Sister M. "Early American Convent Schools," Catholic Educational Review, XXXIX (Jan., 1941), 30-35.

Clay, Henry. "Henry Clay to His Granddaughter on Entering a Convent," American Catholic Historical Researches, XIV (Jan., 1897), 39.

Clemens, Clara. My Father, Mark Twain. New York: Harper, 1934.

Clinchy, Everett R. All in the Name of God. New York: Day, 1934.

Code, Joseph B. "Colored Catholic Educator before the Civil War," Catholic World, CXLVI (1938), 437-43.

Coffey, James Reginald. Pictorial History of the Dominican Province of Saint Joseph, USA. New York: Holy Name Society, 1946.

Condon, Peter, "Constitutional Freedom of Religion and the Revivals of Religious Intolerance," Historical Records & Studies, IV, Part 2 (1906), p. 145-95.

Connors, Francis John, "Samuel Finley Brese Morse and the Anti-Catholic Political Movements in the United States," Illinois Catholic Historical Review, X, No. 2 (Oct., 1927), 83-122.

Cooper, James Fenimore. Correspondence of James Fenimore-Cooper. Edited by his grandson. New Haven: Yale University, 1922.

Courcy-Shea, Henry de and John Gilmary Shea. History of the Catholic Church. New York: Kenedy, 1879.

Crevecoeur, Hector St. John de. Letters to an American Farmer. New York: Doubleday Dolphin, 1782 ed.

Cross, Robert D. "Changing Image of Catholicism in America," Yale Review, XLVIII (June, 1959), 562-75.

_____ The Emergence of Liberal Catholicism in America. Cambridge: Harvard University Press, 1958.

Culver, Elsie Thomas. Women in the World of Religion. Garden City: Doubleday, 1967.

Daly, Mary. The Church and the Second Sex. New York: Harper, 1968.

Deegan, Dorothy Yost. The Stereotype of the Single Woman in American Novels. New York: King's Crown Press, 1951.

Defamers of the Church; Their Character. Huntingdon, Ind.: Our Sunday Visitor, n.d.

Dorchester, Daniel. Romanism versus the Public School System. New York: Phillips & Hunt, 1888.

Drouin, Edmund G. The School Question; a Bibliography on Church-State Relationships in American Education 1940-1960. Washington: Catholic University Press, 1963.

Dubourg, Archbishop William Louis. "Documents," St. Louis Catholic Historical Review, II, 207.

Duratschek, Sister Mary Claudia, OSB. Crusading Along Sioux Trails. Yankton, N.D.: Benedictine Convent, 1947.

Durocher, Aurele, "Mark Twain and the Roman Catholic Church," Journal of the Central Mississippi Valley American Studies Association I, No. 2 (1960), 32-43.

Easterly, Rev. Frederick John. The Life of Rt. Rev. Joseph Rosati, CM. Washington: Catholic University Press, 1942.

Eckel, Mrs. L. St. John /Mrs. Lizzie St. John Harper7. Maria Monk's Daughter; an Autobiography. New York: United States Publishing Co., 1874.

Egan, Maurice Francis, "Chats with Good Listeners," Ave Maria, XXXV (July 23, 1892), 100-101.

_____ "Sunday Nights with Friends. The Convent Graduate," Ave Maria, XXXVIII (June 16, 1894), 660-662.

Elkins, Stanley M. Slavery. New York: Grosset & Dunlap, 1959.

Elliott, Rev. Charles, D.D. Delineation of Roman Catholicism. New York: George Lane, 1841.

Elliott, Charles Winslow. Winfield Scott the Soldier and the Man. New York: Macmillan, 1937.

Ellis, John Tracy. A Guide to American Catholic History. Milwaukee: Bruce, 1959.

Elson, Ruth M. Guardians of Tradition: American Schoolbooks of the Nineteenth Century. Lincoln: University of Nebraska Press, 1964.

"The English Government Prohibits the Religious Orders in Canada from Adding Members, 1786," American Catholic Historical Researches, X (June, 1893), 42.

Farinholt, F. C. et al. "The Public Rights of Women," Catholic World LIX (June, 1894), 301-312.

Fell, Sister Marie Leonore. The Foundations of Nativism in American Textbooks, 1783-1860. Washington: Catholic University, 1941.

Fidell, Estelle A. and Esther V. Flory. Fiction Catalog. 7th Edition. New York: H. H. Wilson, 1961.

Fish, Carl Russell. Guide to Materials for American History in Rome and Other Italian Archives. Washington: Carnegie Institute, 1911.

Fitzmorris, Sister Mary Angela. Four Decades of Catholicism in Texas, 1820-1860. Washington: Catholic University Press, 1926.

Flanigen, Rt. Rev. George J. "Historical Notes; Catholic Chronology in Tennessee" series in The Tennessee Register, Nashville.

Ford, Paul Leicester, (ed.) The Writings of Thomas Jefferson. New York: G. P. Putnam's Sons, 1895.

Fox, Sister Columba. The Life of the Right Reverend John Baptist Mary David, 1761-1841. New York: US Catholic Historical Society, 1925.

Francis, Sister Catherine. Convent Schools of French Origin in the United States, 1717-1843. Philadelphia: University of Pennsylvania Press, 1936.

Gable, Richard J. Public Funds for Church and Private Schools. Washington: Catholic University Press, 1937.

Gale, Robert L. The Caught Image. Chapel Hill: University of North Carolina Press, 1964.

Gannon, Michael V. The Cross in the Sand. Gainesville: University of Florida Press, 1967.

Gillard, John T. The Catholic Church and the American Negro. Baltimore: St. Joseph's Society Press, 1929.

Goffman, Erving. Asylums. New York: Doubleday Anchor, 1961.

Gohmann, Sister Mary de Lourdes. Political Nativism in Tennessee to 1860. Washington: Catholic University Press, 1938.

Gorman, Ashley. "Teachers Wearing Religious Garb," Wayne Law Review, III (Winter, 1956), 57-62.

Gorres, Ida. The Hidden Face. New York: Pantheon, 1959.

Griffin, Martin I. J. "Washington's Masonic Apron and the Ursuline Nuns of Nantes," American Catholic Historical Researches, XXIV (Oct., 1907), 368.

Gross, Neil, et al. Explorations in Role Analysis: Studies of the School Superintendency Role. New York: John Wiley, 1958.

Guilday, Peter. The English Catholic Refugees on the Continent, 1558-1795. New York: Longmans Green, 1914.

_____ A History of the Councils of Baltimore: 1791-1884. New York: Macmillan, 1932.

_____ Life and Times of John Carroll, 1735-1815. New York: Encyclopedia Press, 1922.

_____ Life and Times of John England, First Bishop of Charleston 1786-1842. New York: America Press, 1927.

Harris, Mrs. Julia Collier. Life and Letters of Joel Chandler Harris. Boston: Houghton Mifflin, 1918.

Hart, James D. The Popular Book. New York: Oxford University, 1950.

Hartley, Eugene L. et al. "Attitudes and Opinions," in Wilbur Schramm (ed.) The Process and Effects of Mass Communications. Urbana: University of Illinois Press, 1955.

Hartley, Olga. Woman and the Catholic Church Yesterday and Today. London: Burns, Oates, Washbourne, 1925.

Hassard, John R. Life of . . . John Hughes. New York: Appleton, 1866.

Herbermann, Charles G. The Sulpicians in the United States. New York: Encyclopedia Press, 1916.

Higham, John, "Another Look at Nativism," Catholic Historical Review, XLIV (July, 1958), 147-58.

Holzhauer, Jean, "The Nun in Literature," Commonweal, LXV, No. 21 (Feb. 22, 1957), 527-29.

Hopkins, Vincent, "A Common Protestant Image of the Catholic Church: the Development of a Stereotype," in Robert W. Gleason (ed.) In the Eyes of Others. New York: Macmillan, 1962.

Howlett, William. Life of Rev. Charles Nerinckx. Techny, Ill.: Mission Press, 1915.

_____ Life and Times of the Right Rev. Joseph P. Machebeuf. Pueblo, Col., 1908.

Hudson, Rev. Daniel E. "A Word in Defense of a Dead Author," Ave Maria, LXVIII (May 8, 1909), 591.

Huyghe, Msgr. Gerard, et al. Religious Orders in the Modern World. Westminster, Md.: Newman, 1965.

Hyland, J. S. Progress of the Catholic Church in America and the great Columbian Catholic Congress of 1893. 4th Ed. Chicago: Hyland, 1897.

Hynes, Michael J. History of the Diocese of Cleveland. Cleveland: Chancery Office, 1953.

Index Librorum Prohibitorum. Vatican City: Typis Polyglottis, 1938.

Johnson, Peter Leo. Crosier on the Frontier. Madison: Wisconsin State Historical Society, 1959.

Jones, Howard Mumford. America and French Culture, 1745-1848. Chapel Hill: Universtiy of North Carolina Press, 1927.

Kann, Robert, "Public Opinion Research: A Contribution to Historical Method," Political Science Quarterly, LXXIII (Sept., 1958), 374-96.

Kinzer, Donald L. An Episode in anti-Catholicism: the APA. Seattle: University of Washington, 1964.

Klapper, Joseph. The Effects of Mass Communications. New York: The Free Press of Glencoe, 1960.

_____ "The Effects of Mass Communications," in Bernard Berelson and Morris Janowitz, Reader in Public Opinion and Communication, New York: Free Press, 1966, p. 474-77.

Knox, Ronald. Enthusiasm. New York: Oxford University Press, 1950.

Kunitz, Stanley J. and Howard Haycraft (editors). American Authors 1600-1900. New York: H. H. Wilson Co., 1938.

Lally, Francis J. The Catholic Church in a Changing America. Boston: Little, Brown, 1962.

Lavedan, Henri. *The Heroic Life of Saint Vincent de Paul.* Translated by Helen Younger Chase. New York: Longmans, Green, 1929.

Lawler, Justus George. *The Catholic Dimension in Higher Education.* Westminster, Md.: Newman, 1959.

Lea, Henry Charles. *History of Celibacy.* Boston: Houghton, Mifflin, n.d.

Lenhart, John M. "The State of US Catholic Schools in 1855," *Social Justice Review*, LVI (Nov., 1963 - Feb., 1964), *passim*.

Levin, David. *History as Romantic Art.* Stanford, Cal.: Stanford University Press, 1959.

"London Nun," *Catholic Weekly Instructor; or Miscellany of Religious, Instructive, and Entertaining Knowledge*, I, No. 2 (June 22, 1844), 24.

Lord, Robert H. et al. *History of the Archdiocese of Boston.* New York: Sheed & Ward, 1944.

Lowenthal, Leo. *Literature, Popular Culture, and Society.* Englewood Cliffs, N.J.: Prentice-Hall, 1961.

Loyola, Sister. "Bishop Fenwick and Anti-Catholicism in New England, 1829-1845," *US Catholic Historical Society Records & Studies*, XXVII (1937), 99-256.

Lucey, William Leo. *The Catholic Church in Maine.* Francestown, N.H.: Marshall Jones Co., 1957.

Lyman, Theodore. *The Political State of Italy.* Boston: Wells, 1820.

McAllister, Anna Shannon. *In Winter We Flourish.* New York: Longmans Green, 1939.

McAvoy, Thomas T. *The Great Crisis in American Catholic History 1895-1900.* Chicago: Regnery, 1957.

McCabe, Lida Rose, "The Everyday Life of a Sister of Charity," *Cosmopolitan*, XXIII (1897), 289-96.

McCarthy, Mary Therese. *Memories of a Catholic Girlhood.* New York: Harcourt Brace, 1957.

McConville, Sister Mary St. Patrick. *Political Nativism in the State of Maryland 1830-1860.* Washington: Catholic University, 1928.

McGann, Sister Agnes Geraldine. *Nativism in Kentucky to 1860.* Washington: Catholic University, 1928.

McMaster, John Bach, "The Riotous Career of the Know-Nothings," *Forum*, XVII (1894), 524-36.

Maes, Paul Camillus. Life of Rev. Charles Nerinckx. Cincinnati: Robert Clarke & Co., 1880.

Malone, Dumas. Jefferson and His Times. Boston: Little, Brown, 1951.

Marryat, Frederick. A Diary in America. New York: Colyer, 1839.

Maury, Reuben. Wars of the Godly. New York: R. M. McBride, 1928

Melville, Annabelle M. John Carroll of Baltimore. New York: Scribner's, 1955.

Metzger, Charles. Catholicism and the American Revolution. Chicago: Loyola University Press, 1962.

_____ The Quebec Act: A Primary Cause of the American Revolution. New York: US Catholic Historical Society, 1936.

Mott, Frank Luther. Golden Multitudes. New York: Macmillan, 1947.

Murphy, Mother M. Benedict. Pioneer Roman Catholic Girls' Academies. New York: Columbia University Press, 1958.

Murphy, Robert Joseph, "The Catholic Church in the U.S. during the Civil War Period," Records of the American Catholic Historical Society, XXXIX (1928), 27-346.

Murphy-O'Connor, Jerome, "Religious Life as Witness," Supplement to Doctrine and Life, XVII (1967), 124.

Myers, Gustavus. History of Bigotry in the United States. Edited and Revised by Henry M. Christman. New York: Capricorn, 1960.

Neiman, Lionel J. and James W. Hughes, "The Problem of the Concept of Role--a Re-survey of the Literature," Social Forces, XXX (1951), 141-49.

Newcomb, Theodore M. et al. Social Psychology: The Study of Human Interaction. New York: Holt, Rinehart & Winston, 1965.

Nichols, Thomas Low. Forty Years of American Life, 1821-1861. New York: Stackpole Sons, 1937.

Norman, E. R. Anti-Catholicism in Victorian England. New York: Barnes & Noble, 1968.

O'Connell, William Cardinal. Recollections of Seventy Years. Boston: Houghton Mifflin, 1934.

O'Connor, James F. X. "Anti-Catholic Prejudice," American Catholic Quarterly Review, I (Jan., 1876), 5-21.

O'Daniel, Victor F. The Father of the Church in Tennessee. New York: Pustet, 1926.

O'Daniel, Victor F. "Long Misunderstood Episode in American History," Catholic Historical Review, VI (1920), 15-45; 66-80.

_____ The Right Rev. Edward Dominic Fenwick. Washington: The Dominicana, 1920.

O'Driscoll, Sister M. Felicity, "Political Nativism in Buffalo, 1820-1860," Records of the American Catholic Historical Society, XLVIII (1937), 247-319.

O'Grady, John. Catholic Charities in the United States. Washington: National Catholic Welfare Council, 1930.

Ossoli, Margaret Fuller. At Home and Abroad; or, Things and Thoughts in America and Europe. Edited by Arthur B. Fuller. New and complete edition. Boston: Roberts Brothers, 1874.

Overdyke, W. Darrell, The Know-Nothing Party in the South, Baton Rouge: Louisiana State University Press, 1950.

Parsons, Reuben. Studies in Church History. New York: Pustet, 1901.

Parton, James, "Our Catholic Brothers," Atlantic Monthly, XXI (Apr., 1868), 432-451.

Phelan, Rev. Thomas. Catholics in Colonial Days. New York: Kenedy, 1935.

Philibert, Sister Mary, SL. "Nuns in New Mexico's Public School," America, LXXX (Nov. 27, 1948), 207-8.

Rahill, Peter James. The Catholic in America, from colonial times to the present day. Chicago: Franciscan Herald Press, 1961.

Ray, Sister Mary Augustina. American Opinion of Roman Catholicism in the Eighteenth Century. New York: Columbia University Press, 1936.

Redden, Sister Mary Mauritia. The Gothic Fiction in the American Magazines (1765-1800). Washington: Catholic University, 1939.

Reilly, John T. Collections & Recollections in the Life and Times of Cardinal Gibbons. Martinsburg, W. Va.: the Author, 1890-1904.

"Religious Garb in the Public Schools: a Study in Conflicting Liberties," University of Chicago Law Review, XXII, (Summer, 1955), 888-895.

Riley, Arthur J. Catholicism in New England to 1788. Washington: Catholic University Press, 1936.

Roemer, Theodore, OFMCap. The Catholic Church of the United States. St Louis: Herder, 1951.

Rokeach, Milton, "Attitude Change and Behavioral Change," Public Opinion Quarterly, XXX, No. 4 (Winter, 1966-67), 529-550.

Romig, Walter (ed.) The Guide to Catholic Literature: 1888-1940. Detroit: Walter Romig & Co., 1940.

Rose, Arnold M. Human Behavior and Social Processes. Boston: Houghton Mifflin, 1962.

Rothensteiner, Rev. John, "Father Charles Nerinckx and His Relations to the Diocese of St. Louis," St. Louis Catholic Historical Review, I (1918), 157-75.

Sargent, Daniel. Our Land and Our Lady. New York: Longmans, 1937.

Saveth, Edward N. (ed.) American History and the Social Sciences. New York: Free Press, 1964.

Schauinger, J. Herman. Cathedrals in the Wilderness. Milwaukee: Bruce, 1952.

Schmeckebier, Laurence Frederick, "History of the Know-Nothing Party in Maryland," Johns Hopkins University Studies in History and Political Science. XVII (April-May, 1899), 5-125.

Scisco, Louis Dow. Political Nativism in New York State. New York: Columbia University Press, 1901.

Shea, John Gilmary. History of the Catholic Church in the US. 4 Volumes. New York: J. G. Shea, 1886-92.

_____ "Pioneer of the West--Rev. Charles Nerinckx," American Catholic Quarterly Review, V (1880), 486-508.

Slabey, Robert, "Henry James and 'The Most Impressive Convention in all History,'" American Literature, XXX (March, 1958), 89-96.

Spalding, John L. Life of Archbishop Spalding. New York: Catholic Publication Society, 1873.

Spalding, John L. Life of Archbishop Spalding. New York: Catholic Publication Society, 1873.

Spalding, Martin John. Sketches of Early Catholic Missions of Kentucky from Their Commencement in 1787 to the Jubilee of 1826-7. Louisville, 1844. B. J. Webb.

Stokes, Anson Phelps. Church and State in the United States, 3 volumes. New York: Harper, 1950.

Stritch, Alfred G. "Political Nativism in Cincinnati, 1830-1860," Records of the American Catholic Historical Society of Philadelphia , XLVIII (1937), 227-78.

424

Sullivan, Harry Stack. Conceptions of Modern Psychiatry. Washington: William Alanson White Psychiatric Foundation, 1945.

Tarr, Sister Mary Muriel. Catholicism in Gothic Fiction. Washington:
Catholic University Press, 1946.

Thebaud, Augustus. Three-quarters of a Century. New York: US
Catholic Historical Society, 1904.

Toby, Jackson, "Some Variables in Role Conflict Analysis," Social
Forces, XXX (1952), 323-27.

Tocqueville, Alexis de. Democracy in America. Edited by Phillips
Bradley. New York: Vintage, 1959.

Torpey, William George, "Wearing Distinctive Garb," Judicial Doctrines of Religious Rights in America. Chapel Hill: University
of North Carolina Press, 1948, 258-60.

Traynor, W. J. H. "The Aims and Methods of the APA," North American
Review, CLIX (July, 1894), 69-74.

Trisco, Robert F. The Holy See and the Nascent Church in the Middle
Western States. Rome: Gregorian University, 1962.

Twynham, Leonard /Leo Leonard Twinem/. Maria Monk's Daughter of
Sharon and America. Flushing, New York, 1932.

Tynan, Katherine, "The Higher Education for Catholic Girls," Catholic
World, LI (Aug., 1890), 616-20.

Varma, Devendra P. The Gothic Flame. London: Arthur Barker, 1957.

Vernon, Glenn. Human Interaction. New York: Ronald, 1965.

Vollmar, Edward R., SJ. The Catholic Church in America: An Historical
Bibliography. 2nd edition. New York: Scarecrow Press, 1963.

Wagenknecht, Edward. John Greenleaf Whittier. New York: Oxford
University Press, 1967.

Wakin, Edward and Joseph F. Scheuer. The De-Romanization of the
American Catholic Church. New York: Macmillan, 1966.

Woody, Thomas. A History of Women's Education in the United States.
New York: The Science Press, 1919.

Wright, Richardson. The Forgotten Ladies. Philadelphia: Lippincott, 1928.

Zollmann, Carl. American Church Law. St. Paul, Minn.: West Publishing Co., 1933.

Zurcher, George. Foreign Ideas in the Catholic Church in America. N.p., 1896.

Zwierlein, Frederick J. "Know-Nothingism in Rochester, New York," US Catholic Historical Society Records and Studies,XIV (1920), 20-69.

_____ Life and Letters of Bishop McQuaid. 3 Volumes. Rochester: Art Print Shop, 1925-27.

APPENDIX A

Fiction Books Studied in Connection with Chapter Four

Barker, Benjamin	Cecilia, or the White Nun . . .
Bourne, George	Lorette, the History of Louise . . .
Bunkley, Josephine	Testimony of an Escaped Nun The Escaped Nun
Caldicott, Thomas Ford	Hannah Corcoran
Chaplin, Mrs. Jane	The Convent and the Manse
Ciocci, Rafaele	Iniquities and Barbarities Practiced . . .
Culbertson, Rosamond	Rosamond
Damon, Norwood	Chronicles of Mount Benedict
Frothingham, Charles	Six Hours in a Convent The Convent's Doom The Haunted Convent
Hogan, William	Auricular Confession and Popish Nunneries
Important Facts!! . . .	
Jones, Justin	The Nun of St. Ursula
M'Gavin, William	The Protestant
Mahoney, S.	Six Years in the Monasteries of Italy
Monk, Maria	Awful Disclosures of the Hotel Dieu Further Disclosures . . .
Murray, Nicholas	Romanism at Home . . .
Mysteries of a Convent	
Pope or President?	
Reed, Rebecca	Six Months in a Convent Supplement to Six Months in a Convent
School-Girl in France	
Sister Agnes	
Smith, Samuel B.	Renunciation of Popery
Sparry, Rev. Charles	The Protestant Annual . . .

APPENDIX B

Fiction Books Studied in Connection with Chapter Six

The American Protective Association Magazine

Chiniquy, Charles	Fifty Years in the Church of Rome
Crawford, Francis Marion	Casa Braccio
Fulton, Justin Dewey	Cornelia Harmon
Howells, William Dean	A Chance Acquaintance
	A Hazard of New Fortunes
	Their Wedding Journey
James, Henry	The American
	The Portrait of a Lady
O'Gorman, Edith	Convent Life Exposed
Shepherd, Margaret	My Life in the Convent
Tuttle, Hudson	Secrets of the Convent
Wright, Mrs. Julia McNair	Secrets of Convent and Confessional

THE AMERICAN CATHOLIC TRADITION

An Arno Press Collection

Callahan, Nelson J., editor. **The Diary of Richard L. Burtsell, Priest of New York.** 1978

Curran, Robert Emmett. **Michael Augustine Corrigan and the Shaping of Conservative Catholicism in America, 1878-1902.** 1978

Ewens, Mary. **The Role of the Nun in Nineteenth-Century America** (Doctoral Thesis, The University of Minnesota, 1971). 1978

McNeal, Patricia F. **The American Catholic Peace Movement 1928-1972** (Doctoral Dissertation, Temple University, 1974). 1978

Meiring, Bernard Julius. **Educational Aspects of the Legislation of the Councils of Baltimore, 1829-1884** (Doctoral Dissertation, University of California, Berkeley, 1963). 1978

Murnion, Philip J., **The Catholic Priest and the Changing Structure of Pastoral Ministry, New York, 1920-1970** (Doctoral Dissertation, Columbia University, 1972). 1978

White, James A., **The Era of Good Intentions: A Survey of American Catholics' Writing Between the Years 1880-1915** (Doctoral Thesis, University of Notre Dame, 1957). 1978

Dyrud, Keith P., Michael Novak and Rudolph J. Vecoli, editors. **The Other Catholics.** 1978

Gleason, Philip, editor. **Documentary Reports on Early American Catholicism.** 1978

Bugg, Lelia Hardin, editor. **The People of Our Parish.** 1900

Cadden, John Paul. **The Historiography of the American Catholic Church: 1785-1943.** 1944

Caruso, Joseph. **The Priest.** 1956

Congress of Colored Catholics of the United States. **Three Catholic Afro-American Congresses.** [1893]

Day, Dorothy. **From Union Square to Rome.** 1940

Deshon, George. **Guide for Catholic Young Women.** 1897

Dorsey, Anna H[anson]. **The Flemmings.** [1869]

Egan, Maurice Francis. **The Disappearance of John Longworthy.** 1890

Ellard, Gerald. **Christian Life and Worship.** 1948

England, John. **The Works of the Right Rev. John England, First Bishop of Charleston.** 1849. 5 vols.

Fichter, Joseph H. **Dynamics of a City Church.** 1951

Furfey, Paul Hanly. **Fire on the Earth.** 1936

Garraghan, Gilbert J. **The Jesuits of the Middle United States.** 1938. 3 vols.

Gibbons, James. **The Faith of Our Fathers.** 1877

Hecker, I[saac] T[homas]. **Questions of the Soul.** 1855

Houtart, François. **Aspects Sociologiques Du Catholicisme Américain.** 1957

[Hughes, William H.] **Souvenir Volume. Three Great Events in the History of the Catholic Church in the United States.** 1889

[Huntington, Jedediah Vincent]. **Alban: A Tale of the New World.** 1851

Kelley, Francis C., editor. The First American Catholic Missionary Congress. 1909

Labbé, Dolores Egger. **Jim Crow Comes to Church.** 1971

LaFarge, John. **Interracial Justice.** 1937

Malone, Sylvester L. **Dr. Edward McGlynn.** 1918

The Mission-Book of the Congregation of the Most Holy Redeemer. 1862

O'Hara, Edwin V. **The Church and the Country Community.** 1927

Pise, Charles Constantine. **Father Rowland.** 1829

Ryan, Alvan S., editor. **The Brownson Reader.** 1955

Ryan, John A., **Distributive Justice.** 1916

Sadlier, [Mary Anne]. **Confessions of an Apostate.** 1903

Sermons Preached at the Church of St. Paul the Apostle, New York, During the Year 1863. 1864

Shea, John Gilmary. **A History of the Catholic Church Within the Limits of the United States.** 1886/1888/1890/1892. 4 Vols.

Shuster, George N. **The Catholic Spirit in America.** 1928

Spalding, J[ohn] L[ancaster]. **The Religious Mission of the Irish People and Catholic Colonization.** 1880

Sullivan, Richard. **Summer After Summer.** 1942

[Sullivan, William L.] **The Priest.** 1911

Thorp, Willard. **Catholic Novelists in Defense of Their Faith, 1829-1865.** 1968

Tincker, Mary Agnes. **San Salvador.** 1892

Weninger, Franz Xaver. **Die Heilige Mission** *and* **Praktische Winke Für Missionare.** 1885. 2 Vols. in 1

Wissel, Joseph. **The Redemptorist on the American Missions.** 1920. 3 Vols. in 2

The World's Columbian Catholic Congresses and Educational Exhibit. 1893

Zahm, J[ohn] A[ugustine]. **Evolution and Dogma.** 1896